Although they are integrated into the world economy, most regimes in sub-Saharan Africa have not been very effective agents of capitalist development. Rulers have often used state power in ways that compromise, rather than promote, ecnomic growth. In this book, Catherine Boone examines how the consolidation of a stable ruling alliance in postcolonial Senegal narrowed possibilities for agricultural and industrial development. She shows that this ruling alliance was rooted in forms of economic and social power forged under the hegemony of colonial merchant capital. Senegal's regime shied away from promoting capitalist development because its own bases of power did not lie in capitalist class relations and forms of production. Old trading monopolies, commercial hierarchies, and patterns of wealth accumulation were preserved at the cost of reforms that could have stimulated economic growth.

Boone develops this argument to demonstrate the limits of analyses that identify state institutions or ideologies as independent forces driving the process of economic transformation. State power, she argues, is rooted in the material and social bases of ruling alliances.

T0370711

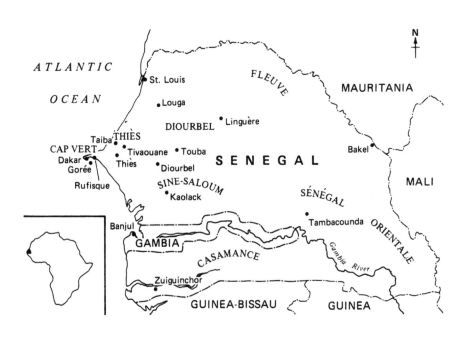

ATLANTIC

OCEAN

St. Louis

FLEUVE

MAURITANIA

•Louga

DIOURBEL   •Linguère

Taiba THIES

CAP VERT

Dakar   •Tivaouane   •Touba

Gorée   Thiès   •Diourbel

Rufisque

SINE-SALOUM

•Kaolack

SENEGAL

SÉNÉGAL

ORIENTALE

Bakel•

MALI

N

Banjul

GAMBIA

CASAMANCE

Tambacounda

Gambia River

Zuiguinchor

GUINEA-BISSAU

GUINEA

MERCHANT CAPITAL AND THE ROOTS
OF STATE POWER IN SENEGAL
1930–1985

CAMBRIDGE STUDIES IN COMPARATIVE POLITICS

General editor

PETER LANGE   Duke University

Associate editors

ELLEN COMISSO   University of California, San Diego
PETER HALL.   Harvard University
JOEL MIGDAL   University of Washington
HELEN MILNER   Columbia University
SIDNEY TARROW   Cornell University

OTHER BOOKS IN THE SERIES

David Laitin,   *Language Repertoires and State Construction in Africa*
Kornberg and Clark,   *Citizens and Community: Political Support in a Representative Democracy*

MERCHANT CAPITAL AND THE ROOTS OF STATE POWER IN SENEGAL 1930–1985

CATHERINE BOONE

CAMBRIDGE
UNIVERSITY PRESS

CAMBRIDGE UNIVERSITY PRESS
Cambridge, New York, Melbourne, Madrid, Cape Town, Singapore, São Paulo

Cambridge University Press
The Edinburgh Building, Cambridge CB2 2RU, UK

Published in the United States of America by Cambridge University Press, New York

www.cambridge.org
Information on this title: www.cambridge.org/9780521410786

© Cambridge University Press 1992

First published 1992
This digitally printed first paperback version 2006

A catalogue record for this publication is available from the British Library

Library of Congress Cataloguing in Publication data
Boone, Catherine.
Merchant capital and the roots of state power in Senegal, 1930–1985 / Catherine Boone.
p. cm.
Includes bibliographical references and index.
ISBN 0-521-41078-9
1. Senegal – Economic conditions. 2. Senegal – Politics and
government – 1960– 3. Industry and state — Senegal. 4. Textile
industry – Senegal. I. Title.
HC1045.B65 1992
338.9663 – dc20

91-46536
CIP

ISBN-13 978-0-521-41078-6 hardback
ISBN-10 0-521-41078-9 hardback

ISBN-13 978-0-521-03039-7 paperback
ISBN-10 0-521-03039-0 paperback

To Peter

En Afrique, . . . les évènements sont . . . difficiles à interpréter. L'époque du nationalisme s'achève, celle des conflits internes commence, mais les forces en présence ne sont pas encore clairement réparties, les problèmes d'hier et ceux d'aujourd'hui se confondent, les facteurs économiques et sociaux les plus décisifs ne sont qu'aperçus, faute d'une évolution économique suffisante.

R. Braudi, *France–Observateur* (7 mai 1964)

[O]r rien n'était encore clairement dessiné, au début des années 70, ni la doctrine concernant l'évolution souhaitée, ni les évolutions du fait, jusqu'ici incertaines.

Régine Nguyen Van Chi Bonnardel, *Vie de Relations au Sénégal* (1978:825)

Une dizaine d'années après, malgré tous les changements intervenus dans chacun des Etats, surtout dans le continent et dans le monde entier, les choses semblent apparemment en être encore au même point . . . .

Abdoulaye Ly, *L'émergence du néocolonialisme au Sénégal* (1981:144)

Contents

Tables and figure

FIGURE

Preface and acknowledgments

In the analysis of economies on the periphery of the world capitalist system, industry studies provide vehicles for testing and generating theories about changing patterns of capital accumulation at the local level, class formation, and the role of the state in shaping economic change. The present study was undertaken in this tradition.

I began studying the Dakar textile industry in 1984. This industry was the core of an "import-substitution" industrial sector implanted during the final decade of direct colonial rule. Like most of light industry in Dakar, it had been heavily protected from foreign competition since its birth in the 1950s. Senegal's foreign creditors were pushing free markets and economic liberalization in the 1980s, policies that would surely spell the demise of the industry. My project, as it was conceived when I set out in 1984, was to study the conflicts, compromises, and bargaining processes that would emerge as the "triple alliance" – the state, foreign capital, and local private capital – maneuvered in the face of external creditors' demands for reform.

I immediately ran up against two major facts about the Dakar textile industry in the 1980s. First, the World Bank's demands for liberalization of the import trade seemed to have had no discernible effect. On paper, the industry was more protected from foreign competition in 1984–6 than it had been in the past. Second, it was soon clear that the textile industry lost the struggle for control of its domestic market long before "structural adjustment" began. The market was swamped with low-cost imports, and the industry was in deep crisis as a result.

Trying to account for this took me far beyond my original project and into an analysis of control over markets in Senegal. I realized that the structure of control over markets was critical to explaining why the process of capitalist development in Senegal had remained so shallow and weak. This led me to study the colonial origins of present economic structures, the postcolonial regime and the agrarian bases of its economic and political power, and the divided character of the ruling class. The results are presented here. This book treats the rise and demise of the Dakar textile industry as the effect, or symptom, of broader changes in the domestic political economy. Ultimately, the industry study provided a point of entrée into an analysis of the relationship between state power, patterns of economic development, and control over markets in Senegal.

At the outset, I can clear ground by situating this study with respect to two major critiques of light industrialization (import-substitution industrialization, or ISI) in sub-Saharan Africa: neoclassical economists' critique, and the critique mounted by the underdevelopment and dependency schools. In the early 1970s, when balance-of-payments disequilibria emerged as a major problem in many African countries, "development economics" began to reverse its original stand on ISI. The view that ISI was one stage in the "take-off to self-sustained growth" gave way to critiques that catalogued the inefficiencies characteristic of ISI: overcapacity, absence of economies of scale, inflated factor costs, limited domestic market competition, dependence on imported inputs, etc. Development economics now argues that this form of industry does not make sense: It is too inefficient.

Critics working within the underdevelopment approach tended to view the issue from a different angle. They emphasized the alignments of foreign and local class interests that sustained the ISI process in the postcolonial period. These analysts faulted ISI less for its inefficiency than for its role in exacerbating external dependency and perpetuating distorted patterns of growth. They stressed the dependency on foreign capital, foreign inputs, and managerial know-how that tended to accompany ISI in sub-Saharan Africa, and pointed to the overseas drain of local wealth that resulted. Underdevelopment theorists showed how foreign monopolies over lucrative industrial opportunities impeded the rise of indigenous industrial classes, and thus the rise of more dynamic forms of industrialization that would be better integrated into national economies at large.

I accept both lines of argument as generally descriptive of import-substitution industry as it developed in Senegal and in much of postcolonial sub-Saharan Africa. The inefficiencies that are often associated with ISI have been striking features of the Dakar textile industry as a whole since its creation in the 1950s. And there is no question that the textile industry was part and parcel of broader economic forces and arrangements that reinforced Senegal's external dependency and the weakness of local capital. Neither critique, however, provided analytic tools to explain the abrupt and "unintended" reversal of the ISI process observed in the case of the Dakar textile industry.

It became clear that important limitations of existing critiques are rooted in narrow conceptions of the domestic political forces that affect the industrialization process in general, and ISI in particular. "Structural features" of ISI, such as limited domestic market competition and production monopolies, are artifacts of ongoing state efforts to control and regulate markets. These economic structures are sensitive to a broad array of domestic-level forces that shape the use of state power. As the analysis presented here suggests, political struggles that can reshape the industrialization process may have little to do with industry per se. In Senegal, markets – "the sphere of exchange" – remained the key locus and site of accumulation within the national economy, not industry. The explanation for why this is so is a critical part of this book. It was state-mediated struggles for control over markets that gave rise to, and then undermined, the Dakar textile industry.

The research for this study was conducted between 1984 and 1986 in Senegal and in France. In Dakar, I relied on the Archives Nationales du Sénégal, the library of the Dakar Chamber of Commerce, and the library and case study data bank of the Ecole Supérieure de Gestion des Entreprises (ESGE), now called the Centre Africain des Etudes Supérieures en Gestion (CESAG). Thanks to the hospitality of the government of Senegal and the extremely favorable research climate that it successfully maintained in spite of all that happened in the 1980s, I was able to conduct extensive interviews in and around Dakar. I spoke with industrialists, firm managers, technicians, firm-level consultants, industry analysts, textile dealers, importers, retailers, and union leaders. Officials in the ministries of development and planning, industry, commerce, and finance were remarkably open and forthcoming with information. I also received help from people working in the state banks, SONEPI, SOFISEDIT, the Dakar Chamber of Commerce, parastatals, and the Inspection du Travail. I returned to Dakar in 1990 and revisited some of these contacts.

Supplementary research was conducted in Paris and Mulhouse. Additional material on the colonial period was collected in the Archives Nationales, Section Outre-Mer and the Chambre de Commerce et d'Industrie de Paris. I was also able to interview representatives of the Syndicat Général de l'Industrie Cotonnière Française, Ets. Schaeffer and Schaeffer Engineering, and the Compagnie Niger-France.

Footnotes in the text refer to the interviewees in general terms to protect them from unwarranted association with conclusions I have drawn. Their interest and patience made this study possible. The interviews were not recorded on tape; I relied on notes.

An excellent secondary literature on Senegal, in French and English, forms the backbone of the study. All the translations from French are my own. Drawing heavily on this literature, I learned that social studies can indeed be "cumulative." I hope I have used this existing work in the spirit in which it was written, without errors of interpretation. As the reader will see, I am particularly indebted to Samir Amin, Donal Cruise O'Brien, Rita Cruise O'Brien, Momar Coumba Diop, Mamadou Diouf, and Edward Schumacher.

Graduate students at the Ecole Supérieure de Gestion des Entreprises in Dakar wrote detailed and exacting case study analyses of firms in Senegal's textile industry. Their work is available in the case study data bank of CESAG. Anonymous analysts in the ministry of industry painstakingly assembled data on a textile industry in crisis in the 1980s. These sources of information were also invaluable.

Many institutions provided support. The project began as a doctoral dissertation in the Department of Political Science at the Massachusetts Institute of Technology (MIT). During the initial phases of research, I received support from MIT's Center for International Studies thanks to the help of Professor Myron Weiner. My first trip to Dakar was funded by the American Association of University Women. Subsequent research was funded by the Social Science Research Council of New York. The Ecole Supérieure de Gestion des Entreprises and its then director M. Tidjane Sylla provided me with an institutional affiliation in Dakar. This affiliation proved to be one of the most pleasant and rewarding aspects of the entire project, thanks to Professor Jean-Claude Nascimento. I received assistance from Professor Moustaffa Kassé of the Centre des Recherches Economiques Appliquée (CREA) at the Université de Dakar. Later, the University of Texas at Austin provided research funding that allowed me to develop some parts of the argument in article form. Finally, the Harvard Academy of International and Area Studies funded the final stage of writing. Dr. Ira Kukin, Professor Henry Rosovsky, Chester K. Haskell, the Academy Scholars, and Harvard's Center for International Affairs deserve much credit for the completion of the manuscript.

Others deserve credit for setting the process in motion. My relatives – James L. Boone, Catherine R. Boone, Francis A. Hennigan, and Joseph J. Bucuzzo – encouraged me to study. David Laitin, Michael Chege, and Jeanne Bergman drew me into the field of African studies. Willard Johnson, my academic advisor at MIT, inspired me to continue and helped to make it possible. Myron Weiner has been a critical and decisive source of moral and professional support. Peter Smith, John Freeman, Suzanne Berger, and John Harris also contributed to my dissertation. So did my friends Kirsten R. Wever, Cathie Jo Martin, Mercedes Hernandez R., and Carol Conaway.

Joel S. Migdal helped me to sharpen and elaborate my arguments by organizing a stimulating research group on state–society relations in 1989 and 1990. I am grateful for his openness and encouragement. Joel Migdal, Peter Lange, and Emily Loose and Herbert Gilbert at Cambridge University Press, were instrumental in bringing this work to fruition as a book.

My most relentless critic has been my friend and colleague Robert Vitalis. Unprepared to accept conventional wisdoms, Bob Vitalis warned me about pitfalls that are easy traps along my path of analysis. Paul Cammack of the University of Manchester was another incisive reader. Naomi Chazan, David Gibbs, Cathie Jo Martin, and Leonardo Villalón (who is now writing on Islam in contemporary state–society relations in Senegal) offered comments that improved the final manuscript.

Thanks to my friends in Dakar, I lived and worked in Senegal without feeling like a complete alien. My warmest and most sincere gratitude goes to Mme. Loty Sow, Loty's husband, Jean-Claude Nascimento, Fara François Brangale, Léon Sarr and Coura Niang, Abdoulaye Fall, Mame Mor Diop, Georges and Yolla Arian, Seydina NDiaye, Justin Diatta, and Amina Boutaleb.

I would also like to express my respect for M. Mohammed Mekouar, M. Bernard Thierry-Mieg, and the Dufours, the businessmen who built a textile manufacturing industry in Senegal. They displayed great business sense and resourcefulness in operating within a broader economic and political context not of their making. The successes of the industry were in large part their achievements; the limits of the industry can be explained in terms of the structure of incentive, choice, and risk that they faced. The same is true for the current owners of the industry.

Peter Trubowitz was involved the most deeply in every phase of this project. He spent months in Senegal, read and reread the manuscript in all its various forms, and pushed me to clarify and explain my arguments. If I had lived up to his standards, this work would be more exacting and refined. Without his patience and support, the book would not exist. Our two other companions, Slim Boone and Rocky Trubowitz, provided constant devotion.

The errors and shortcomings of the manuscript are my own. I trust that over time, they will be brought to my attention by my esteemed colleagues.

Introduction

Analysts of comparative politics share some fundamental assumptions about political economy. One is that states on the periphery of the world economy strive to promote capitalist development. Liberal scholars study the "developing" world, equate economic development with growth, and identify investment of capital in production as the driving force. Underdevelopment and dependency theorists analyzed emergent forms of capitalism. They took the integration of the Third World into the world capitalist economy as their object of study. Marxist scholars have concentrated on the related emergence of capitalist class relations in these societies. In the 1980s political economists turned to the study of entrepreneurial states and dependent development. For better or worse, "the late developing world" is assumed to be on the road of capitalist transformation.

We tend to take for granted that governments are playing a central role in this process. States strive to accelerate economic growth, industrialize, and promote "green revolutions." Their motives seem to be obvious: Governments are either promoting the national interest or the interests of powerful social groups. Because the developmentalist impulse is assumed to be universal, analysts proceed to compare states in terms of their success. Some have argued that the capacity of rulers to promote development is a function of modernizing ideologies and growing institutional capacities of the state. Others look behind changes in the state itself, seeking structural explanations for phenomena observed at the level of institutions and ideology. They often point to the logic of capital that works aggressively to harness land, labor, and natural resources to the world economy. Its dynamics come to dominate peripheral economies and states embedded in them. Indigenous capitalist classes emerge, assert their political power, and accelerate the transformation.

African states born of decolonization in the late 1950s and 1960s have been viewed as one type of peripheral capitalist state. Like their counterparts elsewhere in the Third World, they had far-reaching ambitions for economic growth and development. To achieve growth, most regimes created by the peaceful transfers of power of the early 1960s pursued economic strategies that were decidedly neocolonial: They relied upon international capital to sustain processes of capitalist development set in motion under colonial rule. Production of export crops, an open door to foreign capital, generous subsidies for investors, pro-

tected markets for light industry, and close links to the metropolitan powers –
these were the cornerstones of the neocolonial project in Africa. Some African
regimes appeared to be so devoted to this project that they were viewed as hand-
picked agents of capitalist imperialism. Most analysts expected the neocolonial
form of capitalist development (or exploitation) to continue as long as societal
tensions could be suppressed or defused.

Africa's economic history, however, has not followed the anticipated scenario.
Regimes vigorously pursued the neocolonial project only to find in the 1980s that
capital was retreating, giving up on sub-Saharan Africa. In international flows of
trade and investment, the subcontinent became more and more marginal. Foreign
investors lost confidence, and they began to lose interest. In most cases national
capital has not emerged to take its place. Stagnant rates of economic growth in
the 1970s turned negative toward the end of the decade. Analysts and Africa's
creditors watched with growing unease as changes unfolding in sub-Saharan
Africa no longer seemed to fit into the developmentalist paradigm. In the late
1970s and early 1980s, Africa's current crisis erupted.

The crisis is marked by the decay of neocolonial economic structures that tied
production to the international economy. Across much of the continent, export-
oriented agricultural sectors are shrinking as peasants turn their energies to
cultivating food crops for family consumption. As exports decline, imports fall
because countries can no longer pay for the foreign goods that they consume.
With the decline in national economies, roads, bridges, dams, and railways are
disintegrating. Much of sub-Saharan Africa has been abandoned by private capital, left to international debt collectors who will extract as much as they can and
write off the rest.

Why did open-door policies fail to entice capital to invest and expand in the
ex-colonies? Analysis of African states must figure centrally into the answer.
After thirty years of political independence, it seems that even the continent's
most neocolonial regimes have not served capital very well.

Students of African political economy now speak of the "economic dysfunc-
tionality" of the African state. Bates (1981) has argued that regimes use state
controls over the economy to enhance their ability to remain in power. The
resulting patterns of resource allocation are inefficient and wasteful. They hurt
peasant agriculture, and thus limit possibilities for expanding production, consumption, and investment. Others have described how predatory regimes use
state power to drain resources out of productive sectors and into the hands of
rulers, bleeding economies dry.[1] Sandbrook (1985) goes furthest in showing how
"parasitic" capitalism can degenerate into complete economic collapse, driven
by ruling classes that seem unconstrained in their pursuit of plunder. In the
historical era of developmentalist states, state entrepreneurialism, and dependent
development, in Africa we observe ruling classes that use state power in strikingly unproductive, counterproductive, and even antiproductionist ways.

Growing recognition of these processes has shifted African studies away from

1. See, for example, Ergas 1982; Schatz 1984.

analyses of economic and institutional structures. Scholars now advocate more microscopic and disaggregated approaches to understanding states and societies. This shift comes at a time when most students of comparative politics are moving in precisely the opposite direction: toward the analysis of states and institutions as "actors." If the current crisis has raised new questions for African studies, it then raises even more vexing questions for comparativists who do not focus on this part of the world. What is happening in much of sub-Saharan Africa does not square with near axiomatic assumptions about states, development, and developmentalist states. Doubt creeps into the assumption that all states work to guarantee the existing socioeconomic order. The idea that capitalist development is bound to occur everywhere becomes difficult to sustain. And the assumption that states on the periphery of the world economy are developmentalist states becomes untenable. Analysts are forced back to the drawing board to seek more basic and broadly comparative explanations for the existence of developmentalist states and capitalist development.

This book attempts to explain why the deepening and sustained expansion of capital did not occur in a single African state: Senegal. The analysis will show that explanations of capitalist development or its absence cannot begin with the institutional capacities and ideologies of government, for states and institutions cannot explain their own origins. And the explanation cannot rest on the logic of capital, for just as capitalist states need capital, capital needs a state to create and sustain conditions for its expansion. The postcolonial experience in sub-Saharan Africa shows that the formation of such states is a tenuous and uncertain process. Underdevelopment theory was not discriminating enough to tackle the problem at hand, for it assumed that all states and societies on the periphery of the world economy were "capitalist." Liberal theory missed a large part of the story by thinking that promoting development and social transformation was the *raison d'être* of postcolonial regimes. And state-centered and society-centered theorists of the 1980s neglected a critical factor when they spoke as if all social forces were, a priori, external to the state. They forgot about ruling classes. The explanation of capitalist development (or its absence) in particular national contexts must lie in an analysis of the social origins, material bases, and political underpinnings of states and dominant social strata.

The central task of this book lies in unraveling the paradoxical relationship between the postcolonial state in Africa and capitalist development. The relationship is paradoxical because these states, like others on the periphery of the international economy, are structurally dependent upon deepening integration into the world capitalist system. In spite of this dependence, state power has proved to be a most unreliable instrument for sustaining economic growth, capital accumulation, and on-going integration into worldwide systems of production and exchange. It even appears that postcolonial regimes have forged and exercised state power in ways that circumscribe possibilities for the growth and expansion of capital. As economic stagnation gives way to economic decay, the material bases of the postcolonial order erode along with the political arrangements that were built upon them. Regimes seem to use state prerogatives in ways that erode the bases of their own power.

Understanding this paradox requires an analysis of the political and economic processes that promoted the rise of postcolonial African states and ruling classes. My argument is that these processes compromised possibilities for capitalist development. Through decolonization in the 1960s, what Roger Murray (1967) called "unformed social classes" acceded to state power. They would emerge as new ruling classes whose power was rooted in control over the state itself, rather than in direct control over property or production. Dependent upon interests and forms of power inherent in the established economic order, regimes would try to protect the status quo at the cost of changes that could have cleared the way for the further development of capitalism. The political needs and economic bases of postcolonial ruling strata gave the state its compromised character as an agent of capitalist transformation.

In order to protect the established order, these regimes were forced to consolidate power and to govern. To do so, they were destined "to innovate in their own interests."[2] Regimes ordained to protect the neocolonial order would be forced, because they had no alternative material base, to use it instead as a resource for consolidating their own power. This process inadvertently altered the dynamics of the neocolonial economy in ways that made established forms of production increasingly difficult to sustain. At the same time, using state power to reproduce the political status quo compromised the capacity of regimes to create some alternative economic foundation for their power. For African regimes born of the peaceful decolonizations of the 1960s, consolidating power and promoting economic growth proved to be contradictory imperatives.

This argument is developed through an analysis of Senegal. In this case, the paradoxical outcome of a dependent state that does not sustain the productive activities that tie it into the international economy presents itself clearly. Senegal is the former French colony marked by sub-Saharan Africa's "smoothest transition to neocolonialism."[3] The regime was acutely dependent upon the success of the neocolonial project. Yet in the late 1970s and 1980s, the production of export crops declined along with industrial production. Private foreign capital began to disinvest. Bankrupt, the government cut expenditures, accelerating the downward spiral. Senegal, like much of the continent, found itself in the throes of a profound crisis of state and economy.

What makes this case particularly intriguing is the degree to which political order, stability, and openness accompanied the long process of economic decline. The forces that figure so prominently in Sandbrook's (1985) account of "why capitalism fails" in sub-Saharan Africa – wars, state terror, recurrent military coups, wanton plunder – are not part of Senegal's postcolonial story. Indeed, Senegal produced one of the continent's most stable political systems, along with forms and degrees of democratic practice that are extraordinary in postcolonial

2. This phrase is borrowed from Markovitz 1987:8.
3. See Ly 1981.

Africa. In Senegal, patterns of ruling class and state formation that compromise the process of capitalist development reveal themselves in an unusually clear way: They developed incrementally, systematically, and within the framework of a single, well-consolidated regime.

How the process of ruling class- and state-formation affected possibilities for the development of light industry in Senegal is the specific focus of the study. In the industrial sector, one finds capital in an organized and developed form. Its relationship with the postcolonial state is direct and overt. A study of the rise and demise of the Dakar textile industry provides the vehicle for analysis. This foreign-owned industry included some of Senegal's largest, oldest, and most powerful privately owned firms. As one of the most imposing creations of private capital in the postcolonial period, the Dakar textile industry was long viewed as a structural feature of neocolonialism in Senegal.

Its history is a textbook case of import-substitution industrialization as it was pursued in Senegal and in much of sub-Saharan Africa. By protecting the domestic market and subsidizing foreign capital, Senegal's governments promoted industrial growth and diversification. In the early 1970s the World Bank (1974) viewed the Dakar textile industry as one of the most successful and dynamic branches of local manufacturing. Suddenly, during a period of expansive state spending and relative economic stability, the Dakar textile industry began to collapse. Interfirm linkages disintegrated and many firms closed. In the mid-1980s the few surviving firms teetered on the brink of bankruptcy in the context of a political economy now near total disintegration. All the while, the government's formal commitment to the survival and expansion of the textile industry never waned.

Why did sub-Saharan Africa's most successful transition to neocolonialism not sustain one of the most imposing structures of the neocolonial economy? Although external forces were unpropitious for the expansion of the textile industry in the 1970s and 1980s, they did not ruin it. The intensely competitive nature of the international market for textile goods is a constant in the industry's history. And although the demands of Senegal's external creditors hardened at the end of the 1970s, lenders' pressures for policy reform did not lead to a dismantling of the restrictive trade regime governing textile imports during the period of the industry's precipitous decline: 1975–85. Senegal's droughts of the 1970s also limited possibilities for industrial expansion, but the poverty of the vast majority of Senegal's population is another constant in the industry's history. A captive market of impoverished consumers provided the base for the industry's growth.

The decisive changes were manifest most conspicuously in the uses of state power. Incrementally, with no formal change in policy, the Senegalese government ceased to enforce foreign industrialists' monopoly over the sale of staple textile goods on the local market. Parallel markets developed freely, without state efforts to suppress them. Powerful members of the political and economic elite became importers, circumventing import restrictions and taxes. The formidable system of quotas and tariffs that had protected the industry from the start broke down. Dakar's textile industry, like much of light industry in Senegal, lost its once captive market. The process of light industrialization was reversed. In this case, a regime ordained to protect the neocolonial economic order proved unable to sustain existing industrial structures or to create conditions that would have given rise to new ones.

Like other instances of economic decay that became hallmarks of the continental crisis, the decay of light industry in Dakar raises questions about the administrative capacities of government. And like other cases that expose a persistent contradiction between official development goals and actual patterns of government action, this case raises questions about why state power is used in seemingly counterproductive ways.

The case resonates with previous analyses that have focused on the relationship between state power and Africa's current economic crisis. At the same time, it illustrates their limits. Society-centered analysts (e.g. Hyden 1980; Rothchild and Chazan 1987; Migdal 1988) have described patterns of political practice that erode the organizational coherence of the state and the efficacy of public policy. They show how competing social groups permeate the state, fracture its organizational coherence, and paralyze the state's capacity to sustain programmatic initiatives. At the same time, patterns of grassroots resistance – evident, for example, in the rise of parallel markets – subvert rulers' capacity to control economies, undercutting the hegemonic drives of the state. These processes have been played out in full in Senegal. The problem with what has become known as the society-centered perspective is that it does not tell us enough about the state itself. Ruling coalitions contain powerful and privileged interests vested in sustaining (or undermining) the coherence of state policy. Meanwhile, the interests and political strategies of dominant social strata help to explain why state institutions become so fragmented and permeable in the first place.

By taking the political rationality of rulers as a point of departure, Bates (1981) sheds light on forces at work within the state. Rulers, he argues, use the state coherently and in deliberate ways to promote powerful and privileged interests. They rely on clientelism, policies that produce "divisible gains" rather than economically optimal outcomes, and the particularistic distribution of state resources in order to cement alliances and build political support. These strategies of rule make the state apparatus more permeable and more vulnerable to capture by powerful social elements. By relying in part on resources extracted from agriculture to finance this process, regimes invite the resistance of those most penalized by it. Often the ones most penalized are peasants who turn to parallel markets in order to escape de facto taxation.

Starting from Bates' position, it is possible to see the connections between the political imperatives of rule and the kind of state weakening described by society-centered analysts. It is also possible to see how these processes can lead to the kind of economic and political collapse described by Sandbrook (1985). The connections are logical, but they cannot account for the fundamental contradictions inherent in the processes described. Why would regimes choose and then stick to strategies for remaining in power when these strategies so clearly erode their capacity to rule?

Society-centered and rational choice approaches do not grapple with the issues that one confronts at the structural level, where it becomes possible to see how strategies of rule are shaped by the material and social foundations of postcolonial state power. Analysts drawing upon Marxism have framed the basic issues in these terms. In the 1970s underdevelopment and world-system theorists identified a structural relationship between the postcolonial state and capital: They argued that African regimes were structurally dependent on the "development of underdevelopment" (e.g. Gutkind and Wallerstein 1976:11). State power derived from the economic processes that subordinated African economies to international capital; ruling classes emerged out of patterns of social stratification produced by capitalist development; and state revenues were generated by tapping a share of the wealth extracted by capital. Self-interest and structural imperatives would lead regimes to use state power in ways that perpetuate and intensify the exploitation of African economies by international capital. Others on the left made similar arguments, but they drew no distinction between underdevelopment and capitalist development (e.g. Warren 1973).

Marxist approaches explained why states born of capitalist imperialism would sustain the uneven process of capitalist exploitation, and argued that the inescapable contradictions of this process would shape state structures and class relations. These approaches advanced broadly comparative arguments about the relationship between capital accumulation and the reproduction of state power. Because this is the task at hand, previous arguments about the postcolonial state and capital serve as a point of departure. They do not resolve the paradox of the current period, however, because they do not explain why so many postcolonial African states did not follow the structural imperative of creating conditions required for the expansion of capital.

An analysis of political process is needed to square the long tradition of work aimed at understanding capitalism in Africa with the fact that so many regimes have not served capital very well. The decisive process is regime consolidation; it is the concrete, political corollary of postcolonial ruling class and state formation. Regime consolidation involves on-going efforts to use state power to forge a ruling coalition, to sustain it in the face of challenge, and to secure for its members a larger claim on society's economic surplus. From this vantage point, distinctions between state and society blur. The ruling class can be understood in terms of the disparate social elements it contains, and in terms of the mechanisms for extracting wealth and reproducing power that ground it in society. State power can be analyzed in terms of its organization within the state apparatus and the needs and interests that it serves. Where institutions are conspicuously fragile and where they often fail to contain struggles for power, they no longer appear to be "independent" variables. Institutional structures can be seen for what they are: products of the exercise of state power and objects of political competition.

The notion of power consolidation focuses attention on the insecurities and uncertainties of postcolonial rule, making it possible to see how the contingencies of power came to be expressed in "modes of domination" that ruling classes sought to sustain and elaborate. The structures of postcolonial regimes, their ways of functioning, and their willingness and capacity to promote capitalist development were shaped through the uncertain process of consolidation.

This approach represents a departure from more familiar ways of understanding the relationship between African states and capitalist development. Many political economists have viewed regime consolidation as a narrowly political dimension of Africa's postcolonial situation, one that was overdetermined by circumstances attending the peaceful transfer of power to neocolonial regimes. Processes that worked to consolidate state power in the hands of postcolonial regimes have not been considered determinant in themselves, for many analysts held that the nature of ruling classes was determined by forces outside the political sphere. It is necessary to move beyond this view. This study demonstrates how the process of consolidation – of gathering, institutionalizing, and reproducing political power – shaped class and economic structures. Efforts to gather and maintain power reduced the capacity of regimes to sustain processes of capitalist development set in motion under colonial rule.

The focus on political process is not, however, an alternative to structural logic. I see it as an extension or deepening of structural logic. Structural analysts working in Marxist traditions provided space for such an approach, even when specifically political processes were not a prime concern. Some did so by flagging the "exceptional" autonomy of the African state from local capital.[4] Because local capital was so weak, African capitalists could not ensure that state power would be used on their behalf, much less at their behest. Other analysts stressed the "relative" autonomy of postcolonial states vis-à-vis foreign capital.[5] They created space for an analysis of contradictions inherent in political processes by showing that postcolonial ruling classes had interests and needs that could not be defined solely in terms of serving foreign capital, in spite of the power of foreign capital and regimes' structural dependence upon it.

In identifying forms of autonomy vis-à-vis capital, structural analyses drawing upon Marxism contain the key to explaining the paradox of Africa's current predicament. Decolonization and the weakness of local capital cleared the way for the political ascendancy of social strata that were neither the bearers nor the representatives of indigenous capitalist interests. As Shivji (1976:66–7) writes, decolonization created historically anomalous situations: "power and property were separated." New ruling classes were structurally dependent upon the continuing vitality and functioning of forms of capital established locally, and upon the international capitalist economy. Yet the conditions under which this struc-

4. This position, some of it influenced by Alavi's (1972) notion of an "overdeveloped" postcolonial state, is developed in analyses of Bonapartism in Africa. See, for example, Leys 1975:207–12; and Shivji 1976.
5. For example, Swainson 1980, and Beckman 1982.

tural dependency would be translated into political actions that would guarantee the expansion of capital were by no means assured.[6]

One correlate of the postcolonial state's particular forms of autonomy vis-à-vis capital was a striking lack of autonomy in the face of the disparate and sometimes contradictory interests and political needs of social groups who consolidated their power by capturing the postcolonial state. The coherence of these elements as a ruling stratum rested on forms of political domination and surplus extraction that were rooted in existing economic structures, economic structures that would have been destabilized and transformed by efforts to accelerate the process of capitalist development. To preserve the coalitional structure of the ruling class and its economic bases, regimes shied away from the developmentalist project. Meanwhile, tensions within ruling coalitions came to be expressed in the structures and functioning of the state apparatus, shaping the nature of state power and the mechanisms of social control that underpinned it. As the state moved steadily away from its colonial form, it became increasingly difficult to reproduce economic structures and patterns of economic growth that were, in large part, artifacts of the exercise of colonial and neocolonial state power.

This argument shows how internal political structures, shaped by the needs and interests of rulers, worked to circumscribe possibilities for the growth and expansion of capital. Can this internal focus be justified, given the adverse changes in the international economy (inflation, rising interest rates, declining terms of trade for African commodities) and adverse environmental changes (such as drought) that assaulted sub-Saharan Africa in the late 1970s and 1980s? The premise and implication of this study is that an internal focus is necessary in explaining the outcomes of the present. Actions, interests, and political needs of postcolonial rulers played a critical role in reproducing economic structures that proved so vulnerable to the "exogenous shocks" of the 1970s and 1980s. In Senegal the very success of the regime consolidation process worked to reproduce and exacerbate economic weaknesses and vulnerabilities that were obvious in the 1950s, if not before. Adverse changes in the international economy and drought help to explain the timing of the current crisis in Senegal, and also explain why Senegal's most dramatic period of economic collapse coincided with the emergence of severe economic crises across much of the subcontinent. International forces have made the current crisis more intractable, but a complete answer to why this is so cannot be found at the international level.

THE CONTRADICTIONS OF POWER IN SENEGAL

French colonial rule in Senegal left three legacies that would prove to be critical in shaping the postcolonial political economy: peasant production of an export crop, the primacy of trading networks rather than production itself as a locus of

---

6. See Murray 1967, and Saul 1979. To extend this reasoning to the colonial period, see Phillips 1989.

capital accumulation, and the weakness of the indigenous business class. With the help of the colonial state, merchant capital controlled the commercial circuits that integrated the economy, dominating the pace and rhythm of development.

Colonial merchant capital played no direct role in production. The commercial conglomerates that controlled colonial trade did not seek to establish plantations, agricultural estates, or agro-industries. They did not appropriate land, invest in agriculture, or create a wage labor force. Peasants produced the wealth that drew the European trading houses to trade with the colony. Rural families worked together to plant, cultivate, and harvest Senegal's export crop, groundnuts. Like agricultural producers across most of the continent, their lives as producers were not organized completely around the logic of the capitalist marketplace. Their land was not bought and sold as a commodity, and wage labor was rare. Peasant households produced a large share of their own necessities of life, including foodstuffs. Using revenues they earned from the sale of groundnuts, they purchased imported manufactured goods, especially textile goods, from the commercial houses that exported their crops. Over time, Senegal's peasants bought more and more imported rice.

Merchant capital was confined to what Marx called "the sphere of circulation" (Kay 1975:86–95). Profits were generated through the dual flux of colonial trade: buying groundnuts cheap and selling imports dear. Merchant capital's social agents were the colonial commercial houses, independent traders operating in the import-export circuit, and middlemen of all sorts. Unlike industrialists or farmers, these economic actors did not operate in the "sphere of production" – they did not control land or land use, technologies, laborers, or the labor process. Although merchant capital dominated the colonial economy, it did not master production.

The weakness of the indigenous business class at the time of Senegal's political independence in 1960 was, in part, a reflection of the weaknesses of capital itself in structuring the social relations and forces of production. Peasant households were responsible for producing most of the colony's marketed agricultural surplus. Industry barely existed before World War II. The profitability of the European trading houses rested upon monopolistic forms of control over exchange, and these monopolies worked to circumscribe possibilities for the development of local capital both within and outside of agriculture.

The shallowness of capital's penetration of the productive bases of the economy represented a limit upon the colonizers' ability to remold the colony to serve metropolitan interests. Once the territory was conquered by the French, the colonial administration and the commercial houses sought ways to increase production and expand markets. Their zeal, however, was tempered. A sweeping project aimed at reorganizing agriculture to enhance productivity and enlarge the internal market would involve a restructuring of labor relations and land tenure systems. Such a project promised to disrupt or even undermine the ever tenuous social, economic, and political order established by the French rulers. It would require more violence, and the risk of failure was prohibitively high. Merchant capital, for its part, had no way of controlling the outcome of such a process, no way of ensuring that outcomes would be favorable to its interests. For these reasons, the colonizers' willingness to push forward the process of capitalist transformation was compromised and ambivalent. Merchant capital's interest in expanding the import–export trade was subordinated to its interest in maintaining a dominant position within the existing framework of control over production and markets.

Decolonization brought to power the regime of Léopold Sédar Senghor. With the active backing of France, it would remain in place under the leadership of Senghor and his chosen successor, Abdou Diouf, for the next thirty years (and counting). Senegal's postcolonial rulers used market structures forged under the hegemony of colonial merchant capital to extract surpluses from the peasantry, thereby generating an economic base for the emergent ruling class. These same market structures were the institutions within which a postcolonial mode of domination emerged – a mode of domination grounded in state control over commercial circuits and possibilities for the accumulation of wealth within the national economy. The power, limits, and contradictions of merchant capital were reproduced within the postcolonial state.

Those in power recognized that these arrangements constrained possibilities for increasing total production, enhancing productivity, and expanding markets. But because state power was grounded in the very conditions that constrained economic growth, the ruling class was highly ambivalent with regard to the developmentalist project. In its role as an agent of capitalist transformation, the regime was compromised because the ruling coalition would not have survived the political and economic consequences of such a process. It was threatened by the specter of an independent accumulating class in Senegal; it feared the politically destabilizing consequences of changes in rural social relations; and it depended upon existing market monopolies as the source of its own internal revenue base. The dual imperatives of postcolonial rule – the need to sustain growth and the need to maintain power – proved to be inherently contradictory.

At critical junctures the regime shied away from making changes that were required to deepen the process of capitalist development. State power was used to preserve monopolistic structures of market control and to intensify the transfer of resources from productive to nonproductive spheres of the economy. Possibilities for investment in both agriculture and industry were narrowed in the process. Resting on economic structures created under the hegemony of colonial merchant capital, the regime protected them at the expense of changes that would have promoted the rise of more dynamic and productive forms of capital, both local and foreign. This political process and the conservative logic guiding it account for the persistent shallowness of capital's penetration of productive sectors of the Senegalese economy.

The history of import-substitution industry in Senegal is one part of this larger story. Light industries established in Senegal after World War II proved to be participants in state-mediated struggles for control over the domestic market. With the Dakar textile industry first among them, most of these enterprises were not competitive or efficient by international standards. Monopoly or oligopoly commercial positions on the domestic market were the source of profit. Expansion of the industry rested upon the capacity of the regime to sustain patterns of market control established in the 1950s. Market oligopolies limited manufacturers' interest in deepening their investments and enhancing the productivity of labor. Existing structures of market control also blocked the emergence of new firms. In spite of these constraints on economic development, state power was used to protect the industrialists' commercial oligopolies. This is because these same market structures constituted the regime's own source of political and economic power.

Senegal's strikingly "successful" transition to neocolonialism reflected in large part the regime's success in sustaining the heterogeneous and factionalized ruling coalition that was rooted in these patterns of market control. The arrangements which emerged were not stable or self-reproducing, however. Senegal's ruling coalition came under successive waves of challenge from new contenders for power. It also confronted resistance from below. On-going efforts to sustain and expand the ruling coalition forged in the 1960s produced changes in both the organization and the uses of state power. As pressures to use state-controlled markets to shore up the regime's hold on power became more acute, the regime's ability to protect and sustain the old structure of market control diminished.

Through efforts to consolidate and reconsolidate the regime, power within the state apparatus became more fragmented, reflecting the fragmented character of the ruling coalition. As state power was fragmented and privatized, it was used to manipulate commercial circuits in new ways to intensify the extraction of wealth from existing forms of production and to divert commercial profits into the hands of the regime's domestic backers. These changes made the state apparatus less and less effective as an instrument for sustaining old market monopolies, old patterns of surplus appropriation, and existing forms of rural and industrial production. Collapse of the Dakar textile industry was one consequence. The crisis of state and economy that Senegal has yet to transcend is another.

OUTLINE OF THE STUDY

Chapter 1 expands arguments that have already been introduced, stressing the role of political contingencies in shaping possibilities for capitalist development in postcolonial Africa. The discussion of Senegal follows. It is organized around three time frames: the colonial period, especially from the mid-1920s onward; the immediate postcolonial period of the 1960s; and the period that runs from about 1970 to the mid-1980s.

Chapter 2 analyzes the colonial market for groundnuts and textiles, tracing the forces that gave rise to the Dakar textile industry in the 1950s. Chapters 3 and 4 are devoted to decolonization and the immediate postcolonial period. Chapter 3 examines the rise and consolidation of the Senghor regime in the late 1950s and 1960s. Chapter 4 tracks the Dakar textile industry during its period of expansion: the 1960s and early 1970s. Chapters 5 and 6 deal with the erosion of the neocolonial order. Chapter 5 begins with the political crisis that rocked the

Senghor regime at the end of the first decade of independence. It shows that the regime's responses worked to redefine the locus of control over Senegal's domestic markets. Chapter 6 describes the disintegration of long-established patterns of market control and the resulting collapse of the Dakar textile industry. The postcolonial political order disintegrated in the process. The Conclusion returns to questions of state and capital, and to questions of state and society.

1

Capital and the contingencies
of postcolonial politics

In short, property rights were politicized rather than privatized in many parts of colonial and postcolonial Africa, and strategies of accumulation tended to be directed towards building up power over resources rather than increasing their productivity.

Sara Berry 1984:92

Colonialism bore stark testimony to Europeans' readiness to use state power, through military force if need be, to gain in sub-Saharan Africa what the "invisible hand" of the market had not delivered. The force of armies, tax collectors, and colonial police was used to capture labor, commodities, and markets. Economic access and power so secured were maintained in the same way. The state played a central role in defining terms of exchange and creating discriminatory patterns of access to economic resources, just as it has since independence.[1] Metropolitan and local colonial administrations worked to implant and maintain monopolies, broadly defined as "more or less exclusive control over resources or markets and the prevention of free competition," to shelter colonial interests from international and African competition.[2] They were decidedly nonliberal in both theory and practice. Where they could, colonial regimes imposed or reinforced political controls over factors of production or access to them, over opportunities for private capital accumulation, and over internal markets. These political controls worked to define the forms and dynamics of colonial economies. The list would include land tenure laws, head and "hut" taxes, compulsory labor regimes, forced resettlement, restrictions on migration, import licensing systems, state-regulated access to credit, licensing of merchants, industrial li-

1. A Weberian-type definition of the "state" is sufficient here. Thus, the state is a formally hierarchical and formally centralized system of authority relations within a given territory that depends ultimately for its survival on a monopoly of legal coercion. The term "state power" refers to this form of territorially demarcated, ultimately coercive power. "State apparatus" refers to the formal institutions of government: the army, bureaucracies, courts, parliament, etc. Finally, the group occupying and controlling high echelons of the state apparatus is referred to as "the regime."
2. This is Colin Leys's broad definition of monopoly elements in the relationship between the "metropolis and the periphery" (1975:11).

censing, state-created agricultural "cooperatives," restrictions on cultivation of export crops, compulsory cultivation of export crops, price fixing, crop-purchasing oligopolies, and distribution monopolies. Thanks in large part to such devices, colonial interests cornered the most lucrative economic activities and accumulated a large share of the investable surplus generated in the colonial economy.

In the settler colonies of East and Southern Africa, and in French West Africa, the craft of political management of economic competition reached its highest expression.[3] In the final analysis heavy reliance on the instrumental and routine use of the state's arbitrary, coercive powers reflected the failure of productive capital to establish hegemony within these social formations – hegemony that could be maintained and reproduced primarily through wage-labor relations, the institution of private property, and "the compulsion of the market." From this perspective, the argument that decolonization came when the dominance of European economic interests, or simply the dominance of capital, could be assured through the working of market forces appears to be overstated. To assume that "the bourgeois revolution in the colonies was already accomplished by the imperialist bourgeoisie" is most problematic in this context, for it generates premature conclusions about the character and reproduction requirements of the postcolonial African state and economy.[4]

In most of sub-Saharan Africa, the new regimes of the 1960s did not challenge, and for the most part worked to sustain, established patterns of foreign control over large-scale and lucrative productive activities. This led some analysts of underdevelopment and dependency to argue that political independence in sub-Saharan Africa merely masked the reproduction of patterns of economic growth established under colonialism. They argued that formal political independence was an overrated asset, for its potential for affecting change was extremely limited when compared to the power that interests arrayed behind foreign capital could muster in the struggle to preserve the status quo. In American academic debates of the 1960s and early 1970s, this position had the merit of underscoring continuity in colonial and postcolonial structures of economic domination and control.[5] Framing the problem this way, however, directed attention away from the fact that the locus of instrumental control over state power could be decisive when the structural dominance of capital within African social formations was not assured. Even the reproduction of economic structures established under colonialism would require effective internal control by regimes with an overriding commitment to this end.

Could the commitment be sustained? It is necessary to consider how ruling classes gathered, and how this process would condition their willingness and capacity to sustain existing patterns of economic growth.

---

3. On East Africa, see for example Brett 1973. On Rhodesia, see Arrighi 1973.
4. From Alavi, as quoted by Mahmoud 1983:107.
5. The term "neocolonial" underscored this continuity, and it is in this more restricted and descriptive sense that the term neocolonial is used here.

THE STATE AS A RESOURCE

Newly independent African regimes gained a considerable measure of control over state institutions and regulatory mechanisms designed to create and maintain monopolistic forms of trade and industry.[6] Yet with independence the political influences and pressures that conditioned the use of state power changed in important ways. Ruth Berins Collier (1982:2) states the problem as follows:

Despite the existence of striking continuity, in most cases, between certain aspects of colonial and independent (neocolonial) patterns of rule, one should not lose sight of the problems that arose in the transfer of power to an indigenous political class . . . a new political game was being introduced, and in this context a new political class was created that sought some basis for rule.

Decolonization "opened the floodgates of politics," unleashing internal struggles for political hegemony, the elusive quest for legitimation, and efforts to create internal social bases for regimes.[7] What Bayart (1989) calls "the reappropriation of the state" internalized the social locus of state power. The colonial bureaucratic apparatus became a state-in-the-making.

The turbulent political history of many postcolonial states proves that those who assumed power at the time of independence often failed in their quests to consolidate control, to govern, and to remain in power. Yet in all cases, their efforts began to alter patterns of state intervention in the economy. The domestic social and political pressures generated by political independence extended the scope of direct government involvement in the economy and introduced changes in how state power was used to organize markets, appropriate resources, and distribute wealth to privileged social groups. These changes played a leading role in what Thomas Callaghy (1979:126) identifies as the two major processes of contemporary African sociopolitical life: state formation and the emergence and consolidation of an African ruling class.

Colonialism in most of sub-Saharan Africa did not give rise to well-integrated domestic political coalitions or hegemonic capitalist classes capable of asserting decisive control over the postcolonial state. Instead, the leaders who assumed strategic positions in the "new political game" of the late 1950s and early 1960s constituted a narrow political elite, insecure in their new power and in their ability to reproduce power already achieved. In most cases they faced competition from organized groups excluded from access to the state. From the perspective of new rulers, consolidating regimes while controlling the political participation and economic demands of the unevenly mobilized "masses," especially urban groups, was an immediate imperative. Both as a social stratum capable of reproducing its power and as a dominant class, the postcolonial political class did

6. Even within the boundaries of national economies, postcolonial governments did not always gain complete control over economic policy. For example, France retained control over the monetary policies of the states formed out of the Federation of l'Afrique Occidentale Française (with the exception of Guinea and Mali). This fact provides grounds for the argument that states like Senegal and the Côte d'Ivoire did not achieve full sovereignty at the time of independence.
7. This is Shenton's (1986:115) expression.

not emerge fully formed from the nationalist period.[8] It was constituted largely through the exercise of state power (Sklar, 1979).

Lonsdale (1981:153) underscores the fact that the state was not only the object of internal struggles to consolidate power but also a prime resource.[9] New regimes used the repressive apparatus of the state and their control over heavily regulated economies to stabilize and entrench their positions. Almost everywhere repression and the rise of one-party states played a central role in efforts to consolidate power. In some cases reliance on direct physical repression never abated or intensified over time. Regimes also expanded the public sector of the economy and undertook development programs involving considerable government outlays. The new forms of government intervention in the economy strengthened the internal revenue base of the state, multiplied opportunities for patronage and clientelism, and allowed regimes to channel economic resources to targeted social groups via "development projects." The increasingly strategic role of state resources in structuring power relations within society at large was both a source of strength and of vulnerability for new regimes; it raised the stakes of control over the state apparatus. As Ruth First said, "[N]o wonder the political parties [that gained control of the state apparatus at the time of independence] clung so tightly to power; they had so much to lose."[10]

The corollary of regimes' efforts to broaden their domestic bases of political support was, of course, efforts to exclude nonbeneficiaries from access to political power. Predictably, patterns of state spending and the structure of state-regulated markets penalized the politically marginal. The biases of economic policy became a major force shaping income distribution and the process of social stratification, undercutting or reinforcing social strata formed under colonialism and propelling the rise of what some define as new social classes.

Through the practice of patronage politics, state control over access to resources and economic opportunities was parlayed into political capital. In Senegal and much of postcolonial Africa, patronage and coercion emerged as complementary mechanisms of governance and control. Patronage relations linked those with direct control over state power to those interested in, or in need of, state resources. By infusing these resources into new and existing social hierarchies and organizations, possibilities for gathering and reproducing power in these settings became more contingent on political favor from above. Patronage networks structured like pyramids, linked to state agents and the state apparatus at the top, developed as the flexible, informal political institutions that structured

---

8. One of the earliest and strongest statements of this point is found in Murray 1967.
9. Kasfir (1987:46, 51) highlights the importance of this notion of "the state as resource." "[T]he emphasis that both Marx and Weber placed on the state as a critical organizational resource in the struggle of local interests [is critical]. . . . [N]either would think of the state as merely the arena in which these struggles occur."
10. First 1970:105. In *Power in Africa* Ruth First explains the military coups d'état that swept Africa in the 1960s as the product of fierce intra-elite struggles for control over the postcolonial state. She provides ample evidence that efforts to establish control via co-optation did not always work.

the processes of co-optation and political subordination. Patronage politics played out within and under the shadow of politically repressive states was integral to the postcolonial "mode of political domination."[11]

Like other modes of domination, patronage politics worked to generate acquiescence and enforce the power of a dominant social stratum.[12] What is distinctive about this particular mode of social control is equally significant. Patronage systems are rooted in material conditions structured by politically- or authority-based controls over economic resources. Where markets regulate access to land, labor, and other productive resources in only partial and incomplete ways, there is ample ground for the expansion of patronage-based modes of domination. Through "indirect rule," colonial administrations in Africa readily exploited these opportunities in their attempts to govern peasantries (Berman 1984; Phillips 1989).

It is true that patronage politics can flourish on the margins of systems of resource allocation driven by market forces, as it does, for example, in the corridors of municipal, state, and federal government in the United States. In political economies dominated by private capital, the regulatory and investment powers of the state inevitably draw state agents into preferential dealings with particular business interests. Patronage politics becomes integral to a mode of domination, by contrast, when politically- or authority-based controls govern the allocation of resources critical to the material and social reproduction of dominant and dominated social strata. Patronage systems of political control are more direct, tangible, and instrumental than modes of domination reproduced through the capitalist production process and the compulsion of the market. Analysis of patronage politics becomes most useful in the study of African political economy in the light of this contrast, and in the effort to understand the material conditions underpinning the difference.[13]

As the patronage powers of new rulers expanded, politically mediated access

11. Mouzelis (1989:446–9) introduces and develops the concept of "modes of political domination" to make it possible to move beyond the reductionism or atheoretical treatments of political phenomena that characterize some Marxist analyses. "The aim is to construct a set of conceptual tools [specific to the sphere of politics] that, rather than giving prefabricated answers, help the student to study the economy-polity relationship in a theoretically coherent, albeit *empirically open-ended*, manner. To start with, there is no reason one should not speak of a *mode of political domination* in ways that are pretty similar or isomorphic to those used for the analysis of a *mode of production*. . . . [A] mode of political domination can designate the major political forces or technologies of domination and the main ways in which such political technologies are controlled" [emphasis in original].

12. See Flynn 1974; Sandbrook 1972; Fatton 1987:96, 102–3.

13. There is a large body of literature on African political development that sees patronage politics as a product of political culture or as a mechanism promoting national integration and political participation where state institutions are weak. See, for example, Bienen 1974. This work tends to emphasize the "reciprocity" inherent in patron–client relations. It can be contrasted with the works of Flynn (1974) and Fatton (1987), for example, which emphasize the forms of exploitation and control that are inherent in patronage relations. The contrast between these two approaches emerged explicitly in some of the political development literature on clientelism that sought to present an alternative to class analysis.

to state resources became a main avenue for local accumulation. What Sara Berry (1983:67) called "politicized accumulation" transformed those able to privatize resources appropriated in the name of the state into economically dominant social strata. There is a clear sense in which the beneficiaries of this process emerged as a social "class," for their privilege and cohesion as a social stratum rested ultimately on a shared position in the social relations of surplus appropriation. As Kasfir (1987:50) says, "surpluses flowed from peasants to bureaucrats." They owed this position to their control over the extractive and repressive apparatuses of the state, hence the value of the term "political class." They used the state to impose or inflict their interests and vision of social order upon groups that they had subordinated politically, hence the value of the term "ruling class." I use these terms interchangeably, for both capture defining features of the social strata that coalesced within and around postcolonial states.

The construction of ruling classes was as much a part of the new political game of the 1960s as were strategies aimed at subordinating other social strata. New regimes were divided by competition within their ranks. At the same time they faced rivals not content to sit on the sidelines of power. And like colonial administrations, they needed allies on the local level in order to govern. The state apparatus provided both a site and a means for consolidating power and forging ruling coalitions. If repression set the stage for this process, then co-optation and accommodation were its modus operandi. Strategic allocation of state resources served as a mechanism of co-optation, a means of accommodation and political control within emergent ruling classes.

This means that politicized accumulation was not unstructured, unconstrained, or guided only by corporate or individual interests in material gain. Allocation of state-controlled resources on a patronage basis made economic ascent and privilege contingent on political loyalty or acquiescence to those already, or more firmly, in power. Writers such as Peter Flynn (1974) and Robert Fatton (1987) are right to stress the fact that patronage politics was one means by which dominant social groups worked to subordinate and disorganize subaltern classes. Just as significant for ruling class- and state-formation is the fact that patronage politics also served as a mechanism for gathering and manipulating power *within* ruling coalitions, and for structuring the political class along the lines of fractured, competitive, and clientelisitc hierarchies of power.[14]

Patterns of state control over economic activity, regime consolidation, and ruling-class formation are central concerns of this book. Patronage politics lies at their intersection. Making political machines effective mechanisms of political control required expanding reservoirs of patronage resources and the elaboration of state-mediated avenues of access to them. As Bates has argued, these processes influenced how the economic prerogatives of the state were exercised. Meanwhile, the development of patronage networks within regimes reorganized patterns of control over state power, shaping the institutionalization of power

---

14. Interesting work on clientelism focused on the consolidation of regimes through the construction of ethnic blocs within governments (e.g., Lemarchand and Legg 1972).

within the postcolonial state. Jackson and Rosberg (1982) have been the most systematic and broadly comparative in studying the internal structure of African regimes predicated upon what they call personal rule.[15] Proximity to state power was the sine qua non of politicized accumulation, and within the structures of these "personalized" regimes economically privileged strata emerged. The questions that remain to be explored involve the role of this kind of accumulation in conditioning the ambitions and economic potential of the ruling class.

The "embourgeoisement" of the political class has been analyzed for the most part at the aggregate level of class and economic structures. Those interested in the economic interests and potential of ruling classes have generally not engaged in the micropolitical analysis that characterizes so much of the work on patronage politics in Africa. They tend to take the capacity of regimes to remain in power in the absence of revolutions as given or immaterial, because regimes come and go but ruling classes and states persist. Similarly, those interested in politicized accumulation have not seen the organization of power within the state apparatus as particularly relevant to their inquiries. This is problematic, for as I shall argue below, how power is consolidated and institutionalized within the state apparatus has direct implications for the question that concerns structural analysts: Will politicized accumulation transform the ruling class into an indigenous bourgeoisie, willing and able to further the capitalist transformation of national economies?

INTERESTS OF THE RULING CLASS

There is a long history of research and debate aimed at specifying the class character of dominant social strata in postcolonial Africa. Most of this work takes theories of the state in capitalist society as a point of departure. Within this theoretical framework, what makes most of postcolonial Africa distinctive is the fact that ruling classes were neither a part of, nor did they issue from, indigenous capitalist classes. Ruling classes could not be said to represent a bourgeoisie in the direct sense. Yet fundamental to dependency and underdevelopment studies, as well as to much of the later work on peripheral capitalism, is the notion that there is a structural connection, and thus an intrinsic complementarity, between the actions and interests of the African ruling classes on one hand and the interests of capital on the other.

Early work often viewed the foreign bourgeoisie as sub-Saharan Africa's dominant class, and saw local ruling elites as the opportunistic handmaidens of foreign capital (the "comprador bourgeoisie"). More nuanced formulations emerged as writers sought a firmer analytic grip on the interests and dynamics of this strategic social group. Dominant social strata were defined as auxiliary bourgeoisies, organizational bourgeoisies, state bourgeoisies, or bureaucratic

---

15. Jackson and Rosberg (1982:47) studied clientelistic politics as a system of "personal rule" that emerged in the context of "underlying social conditions of an ethnically divided society."

bourgeoisies.[16] These terms distinguished the ruling stratum from a national capitalist bourgeoisie, underscoring the fact that African ruling classes did not control the means of production. Qualified use of the term "bourgeoisie" was highly significant, however. It implied that the holders of state power were structurally dependent upon and therefore bound to act in the interests of capital.[17] Debates emerged as analysts sought to go beyond this minimalist formulation. The expressions "comprador" and "auxiliary" bourgeoisie implied that African ruling classes were structurally dependent upon a particular faction of capital, that is, foreign or multinational capital. Other qualified uses of the term "bourgeoisie" could imply that members of ruling strata would eventually use state power to acquire control over productive assets, thereby becoming a bourgeoisie proper. Shivji (1976) used the term "bureaucratic bourgeoisie" to argue that the holders of state power were playing the role of a local (dependent) bourgeoisie.

The theoretical debates that ran through this literature concerned the historical potential of Africa's ruling strata. What forms of capitalist development or underdevelopment would they seek to promote? How would relationships between the dominant class and particular factions of capital shape the course of change? The second question was the critical one, for the primary contradiction in the postcolonial situation was identified as the contradiction between local and foreign capital.

For dependency and underdevelopment theorists, this contradiction emerges inevitably as indigenous capitalists find their opportunities limited by the dominant and often monopolistic position of foreign capital. In their confrontation with foreign capital, indigenous business interests will seek to enlist the support of the state, especially in their struggle to move into the industrial sector. Given the state's structural dependence on foreign capital and the already established position of foreign interests, how would those in control of the state mediate these conflicts? Many analysts concluded that the economic position of Africa's ruling classes would determine their interests and actions.

Prior to the mid-1970s, much of the work on Africa political economies demonstrated that intermediary positions in the foreign-dominated economy constituted a prime source of accumulation for Africa's ruling elite. Because of their material stake in the neocolonial order, indigenous ruling classes were expected to do all in their power to encourage foreign investment and guarantee its profitability. The state would assert political control, socialize costs and risks of production, and handle the cumbersome duties of administration, economic regulation, and the provision of public goods. Local business interests would be kept in check so that foreign firms would not be inconvenienced or threatened by competition. In the early postcolonial period this understanding seemed to correspond well with reality. Colin Leys (1975:149), for example, argued in the early

---

16. See Leys 1975; Markovitz 1977; Fauré and Médard 1982; and Shivji 1976.
17. Mouzelis (1989:452) draws out this point and questions its premises.

1970s that Kenya's rulers would promote local capital only to complement, not replace, foreign capital. Around 1970 Leys saw no signs of the emergence of a Kenyan bourgeoisie – within or outside of the state – willing and able to use state power to challenge the dominant position of foreign capital.

As the 1970s progressed, however, analysts became increasingly aware of the willingness and the capacity of African ruling classes to innovate in their own interests. One strand of research was most influential because it claimed to contradict previous arguments about ruling-class interests. The discussion that followed became known as the debate on Kenyan capitalism. On one side of the debate were those who defended the argument that the predominance of foreign capital, and the state's dependence upon it, were overdetermining forces in shaping the postcolonial political economy. No national bourgeoisie could emerge to play a decisive, independent role in shaping the process of local capitalist development.[18] On the other side were those who argued that a national bourgeoisie, with the help of the state, was beginning to crystallize in Kenya. Nicola Swainson (1980) offered evidence of the development of this class stratum and argued that it was struggling to assert dominance within the domestic social coalition controlling state power, redefine the relationship between foreign and local capital, and control capital accumulation and investment directly. Colin Leys (1978:258) revised his earlier position on the basis of new evidence:

[The] older political stratum [is] . . . increasing giving way to a younger generation . . . oriented strongly towards fully capitalist valorization . . . [H]olders of salaried
positions, state, parastatal, and corporate, using their salaries and their privileged access
to credit to create independent bases of accumulation [and] low-profile entrepreneurs, in
the classical mould, with sometimes surprisingly large capitals invested in relatively
advanced fields of production, [constitute] a stratum destined to assume greater importance through the long run growth and deepening of its investments.

The Kenyan case suggests that historical possibilities for evolution of ruling classes interests may be more open than underdevelopment models allowed. In Kenya politicized accumulation itself may be fueling the rise of a class stratum able and willing to use the state to promote an indigenous bourgeois project.

The debate on Kenyan capitalism raised a new set of questions about how politicized accumulation might work over time to change the interests of Africa's ruling classes. Would private wealth acquired through access to the state be transformed through productive investment into private capital?

During the 1970s analysts were more and more inclined to answer in the affirmative. The accumulation of wealth in the hands of local ruling elites pro-gressed in the context of increasingly apparent limits to neocolonial patterns of growth. Fawzy Mansour wrote that "a local bourgeoisie is bound to ap-pear . . . and to present itself more and more insistently as a partner and/or a substitute for foreign capital, thus gradually transforming the regime . . ."[19] Extrapolating from Latin American cases, Timothy Shaw (1982) argued that the

---

18. See Kaplinsky 1980; Langdon 1977, 1980.
19. Mansour 1978:11–12, as cited by Shaw 1982.

limits to sustained local accumulation imposed by neocolonial economic structures would exacerbate tensions between comprador and more nationalistic elements within ruling coalitions. Nationalistic elements would push dependent-development strategies to transcend existing limits to their own accumulation, thereby reinforcing local bourgeois dominance and visibility.[20]

Bill Warren (1973) and Bjorn Beckman (1980; 1982) pushed this line of reasoning further still, arguing that international capital in its current phase of expansion would benefit from the emergence of local bourgeoisies. Denying the existence of any fundamental contradiction between local and foreign capital, these analysts rejected the entire dependency and underdevelopment problematic. Beckman (1982) argued that the Nigerian state was mediating relationships between local and foreign investors in order to promote the interests of capital as a whole. In an analysis of Nigeria, Beckman advanced the purest form of the argument that the African state was structurally dependent upon and therefore bound to promote the expansion and deepening of capital.

Africa's current crisis is marked by economic changes that appear to be quite anomalous in the light of this sophisticated tradition of research. If one of the "functions" of the African state is to promote the internal expansion of capital, then many African states do not seem to be performing this function very well. Stagnant or negative rates of agricultural productivity and industrial growth are indicators of capital's reluctance to intensify the exploitation of Africa's land and labor through productive investment. A large share of the local wealth amassed in the measure and forms necessary for investment is transferred abroad. Meanwhile, international capital has staked its claims on the capacity of the multilateral financial institutions to squeeze resources out of African societies by compressing standards of living, rather than on capital's own capacity to reorganize and intensify the production process.

CONTINGENCIES OF POLITICS

Analysts of Kenya and Nigeria offered what may be more generalizable scenarios, but they remain scenarios of great contingency.[21] They are contingent upon the emergence of indigenous classes or class factions committed to the bourgeois project, the consolidation and effective exercise of their political power, and the existence of states and regimes with the institutional and political capacities required to promote capitalist interests in the face of other interests and political needs. Questions about state capacities, the emergence of a class consciousness, and broader domestic struggles over wealth and power are immediately brought to center stage. These are internal processes and forces that are conditioned, but cannot be determined in any direct sense, by external factors or

20. Kennedy (1988:89–91; 131–4) outlines and discusses this scenario.
21. On Nigeria, see also Iliffe 1983:82–4. Evidence from the Nigerian case is as ambiguous and as debated as that offered in support of the "national capitalism in Kenya" argument. Compare, for example, Biersteker 1987:255 and Forrest 1987. See also Biersteker 1987b:276, inter alia.

the interests of capital. Chances that politicized accumulation will lead to productive investment, therefore, cannot be assessed on the basis of the economic fact that wealth is being amassed in local private hands.

In the postcolonial situation, political and economic forces worked together, sometimes in contradictory ways, to condition the evolution of ruling-class interests. The dynamics of this process can be tracked through analyses of regime consolidation, at the level of struggles for political dominance among factions of the (would-be) ruling class. Conflicts among those close to state power were played out within the broader context of resistance to rulers' claims to hegemony and claims on the economic surplus. Regimes that emerged in the 1960s were the institutional and political expressions of the patterns of co-optation, accommodation, and exclusion that developed. As regimes evolved and regrouped over time, their room for maneuver was constrained by organizational structures and political arrangements devised in response to past challenges, and by deals brokered in response to the long-standing challenges that compounded those of the moment. These organizational and political arrangements conditioned possibilities using state power to promote the expansion of capital, be it foreign or local.

Decolonization in Senegal, as in much of sub-Saharan Africa, brought to power a factious ruling coalition. The political triumph of the Senghor-led Union Progressiste Sénégalaise (UPS) was underwritten by the French and by Senegal's Islamic leaders. The Islamic leaders' power was rooted in noncapitalist ("precapitalist") modes of agricultural production. They allocated land, shaped patterns of production, appropriated part of the agricultural surplus, and commanded the loyalties of peasants in much of Senegal's export crop producing region. UPS party leaders and cadres were drawn largely from the administrative, professional, and political strata created under colonialism, strata that arose as profitable trading opportunities open to Senegalese narrowed and as family wealth was invested in education and municipal politics. The ruling coalition that emerged was organized around these professional strata and the Islamic "rural aristocracy." The colonial economy was dominated by merchant capital, and it was largely through trading structures created by merchant capital that the ruling coalition would extract its share of Senegal's economic surplus.

It is not at all clear that the economic interests and political needs of the ruling coalition as a whole, or of the leading elements within it, were staked on accelerating the emergence of capitalist social relations and forces of production within the society at large, and in the rural sector in particular. This is not to deny that the economy and the ruling class were "dependent" upon forces that linked Senegal's market-oriented agriculture to the international economy, forces that lay in large part beyond the control of the regime. Nor is it to deny that the regime depended upon an inflow of foreign cash and investment capital. It does suggest that when confronted with forces that tended to promote the rise of productive capital at the expense of merchant capital and precapitalist systems of agricultural production, the stance of the ruling coalition would be most ambivalent. If political arrangements forged to sustain the original ruling coalition and to reinforce its hold on rural surpluses succeeded in doing just that, then possibilities for the expansion of capital within this social formation would remain limited.

The evolution of Senegal's political economy over the first thirty-five years of independence appears to support the argument, advanced by Colin Leys (1982:115), that "[i]t would be as mistaken to think that capitalism is in the process of developing all the countries of Africa as it is to suppose that it has not developed, and cannot develop, any of it." In Senegal, state power has not been used in any sustained, coherent, or concerted way to promote the productive investment of politically generated wealth. By the late 1970s, state power was not being used to sustain, much less expand, existing, foreign-controlled forms of capitalist production. This is an essential feature of the current crisis not only in Senegal, but also elsewhere on the continent.

The basic question must be reframed. *Under what conditions* will Africa's ruling classes use state power to promote the expansion and reproduction of capital? As Leys (1978:251) suggested, there is what can be called an "initial condition":

In noting the important role of the [Kenyan] state in facilitating this movement of African capital out of circulation and into production [after 1963], we must avoid the mistake of attributing to it an independent role. Its initiatives reflected the *existing* class power of the indigenous bourgeoisie, based on the accumulation of capital they had *already* achieved.

The robustness of indigenous capitalist strata at the time of decolonization was a critical factor in shaping subsequent possibilities for capitalist expansion. Throughout most of newly independent Africa, indigenous capitalists were too weak to make a bid for power on their own account. Kenya may be an exception that proves the rule, or one extreme on a continuum registering the development of indigenous capital in particular settings at the time of the transfer of power. But was this "initial condition" determinant?

The cases of Ghana and Uganda suggest that in postcolonial Africa, it was not. In Ghana the achieved power of a propertied and trading class, including big cocoa farmer–traders, was not guaranteed because it was not institutionalized in the ruling alliance under Nkrumah.[22] Likewise, in Uganda control over the postcolonial state slipped out of the hands of emergent capitalist class strata rooted in agriculture.[23] The conflicts that emerged in these cases destroyed the political and economic orders established in the 1960s, crippling both political and nascent capitalist classes. Foreign interests vested in these economies were yet another casualty. Ghana and Uganda serve to underscore the impact on capitalist development of political contingencies particular to the postcolonial situation.

In a postmortem analysis of the Nkrumah regime, Roger Murray (1967:31) wrote:

22. For a detailed description of the struggle between cocoa farmers and private traders on the one hand, and the Nkrumah regime on the other, see Beckman 1976.
23. See Mamdani 1976:315, inter alia. Elsewhere, less powerful indigenous planter and merchant classes that had accumulated capital by the 1950s also lost out in political struggles that followed independence. Tanzania is an example.

What we have to recognize is that the ground and perspective of class analysis has to shift away from a simple itemization of the various internal class quantities, qualities and attitudes [of the political class] towards a totalization of the decolonization process, embracing the whole range of determinations exterior to the class "situation" or "interest" (if this could be adequately defined) of the dominant group and its local rivals. This means, above all, seizing the process as an *uncertain historical moment* whose social direction and meaning will be defined and redefined through practice.

The nationalist movements that brought new regimes to power in the 1960s were, as Murray (1976:27) argues, composite formations, "embracing in an externally imposed unity elements which were extremely heterogeneous, both socially and ideologically." Often, these movements were also fragmented along regional cleavages created or deepened by the history of uneven development, giving rise to competing political parties that vied for control over the postcolonial state. The task of those who ascended to the pinnacles of power was to build coalitions while retaining a measure of control sufficient to entrench their own dominance.

"Once coalition building is accepted as a problem, the state ceases to be a thing and becomes a channel of action or a resource" (Lonsdale 1981:153). Forging coalitions required, but did not always give rise to, composite answers at the level of ideology, economic policy, and political organization that could accommodate and contain disparate, sometimes antagonistic elements of the political elite. Underlying and complicating the task of coalition building were even deeper tensions in postcolonial society. The basic conflict of interest was between peasant producers of wealth on the one hand and those who appropriated this wealth on the other. It drove regimes to seek ways to impose a *pax post-colonial* on their rural subjects, one that would win the support or acquiescence needed to sustain or intensify the exploitation of peasantries. The formation of postcolonial states and ruling classes must be understood in the context of these processes. Places where composite answers to the needs and interests of powerful elements within society failed to materialize – Ghana, Uganda, and Nigeria, for example – underscore the contingencies of politics, highlighting the relative indeterminacy of specific forms of state and economy that had emerged in particular countries by the 1970s and 1980s.

SUSTAINING THE RULING COALITION

Zeitlin and Ratcliff (1988:11) write that the internal relations of a ruling class "set limits upon, if indeed they do not actually determine, the ways in which a ruling class recognizes, articulates, organizes and acts upon its own immediate and historical interests." This argument, advanced in the context of a study of Chile, is most relevant to the study of contemporary Africa. The formation of African ruling coalitions crystallized political arrangements that, through their own logic and contradictions, played a role in determining the course of economic change. The idea that the logic of capital would guide this process proves to be unduly restrictive. Politicization rather than privatization of property rights created the material conditions that allowed patronage-based modes of domination to take root and expand. The ways in which ruling classes perceived and acted upon their interests were shaped by the dynamics of this form of rule, the need to sustain ruling coalitions, and the prevailing structure of economic opportunities. As things turned out, patronage politics could cement and enrich ruling coalitions, but it tended to reproduce social and economic structures that constrained economic growth.

Ruling coalitions usually expanded by absorbing rivals, rather than by eliminating them. State power and societally-based forms of power would begin to fuse as possibilities for gathering power in any form became more contingent upon access to the state and state resources. The state apparatus was reshaped in the process. Internal relations within ruling coalitions were institutionalized in clientelistic networks that organized patterns of control over state power and resources. Administrative and distributive prerogatives of the state became increasingly fragmented and localized, allowing the various subunits of state and powerbrokers to respond to particularistic and sometimes contradictory demands. The formation of ruling coalitions thus eroded the institutional coherence of the state, creating opportunities and incentives for the politically powerful to define their ambitions in ways that could be furthered through the instrumental use of state prerogatives and state resources.

Where ruling coalitions embraced elements with different interests and political needs, a lowest-common-denominator solution was found in giving all factions access to a larger share of surpluses generated by *existing* forms of production. Politicized accumulation emerged as a material basis of consensus, otherwise lacking, for the consolidation of a ruling class.

Politicized accumulation took an infinite variety of forms. It could involve the direct appropriation of state resources, securing and defaulting on government loans, or collecting commissions on government contracts. Most widespread, however, was politicized accumulation that took the form of rentier activities in the commercial sector. This form was also the most significant. Rentierism in the commercial sector was the oil that lubricated the political and economic structures of the postcolonial state and spread the logic of coalition building down to regimes' rural foundations. Political and economic conditions that made this form of politicized accumulation possible and widespread worked to inhibit the expansion of capital.

States in sub-Saharan Africa intervened extensively in markets as buyers, sellers, and price-setters. Often they played the role of gatekeepers by authorizing (licensing) private merchants to operate in state regulated markets. These government actions influenced prices, supply, and competition. Where the state created noncompetitive markets or "artificial scarcities," merchants were often able to enlarge their profit margins at the consumer's or producer's expense. Bates (1981) calls these price premiums "noncompetitive rents" or "administratively generated rents." In strategic markets the state itself acted as a trader, and the national treasury could collect the rents created by the state's monopoly position. Rents created by state intervention in markets represented created renewable reservoirs of potential patronage resources that lay under control of state agents at virtually all levels of the political hierarchy. As Bates says, members of regimes could apportion commercial rents to others whose influence they wished to secure. Alternatively, they could use their privileged positions to collect rents themselves.

By regulating or monopolizing major trading circuits, African governments made access to many of the most readily-available opportunities for private accumulation in the domestic economy contingent upon political favors and proximity to the state. The politically powerful usually took advantage of the most lucrative opportunities. The modest trader fell subject to officials exercising the commercial prerogatives of the state. In state regulated markets, traders and rentiers were likely to become clients of some higher-up who regulated access to the market and defined the terms of competition. This made commercial circuits prime sites for building political machines. In sub-Saharan Africa, the best examples of all were found in the markets that linked the state to rural producers.

States nationalized control over the commodity export trade in countries across sub-Saharan Africa. In doing so, governments moved into trading positions controlled formerly by colonial merchant capital. Through commercial channels institutionalized in marketing boards and rural cooperatives, states extracted surpluses from peasants, returning a lesser share to them in the form of agricultural inputs. Chains of innumerable intermediaries handled this two-way resource flow: cooperative officials, weighers, inspectors, transporters, exporters, importers, and bankers were among them. All were authorized to collect a share of the profits and rents generated at various levels of the trading circuit. As these chains of trading relations developed, clientelistic networks battened onto the commercial circuits that integrated the postcolonial economy.

In many cases those who served as marketing intermediaries on local levels were established rural authorities – i.e., authorities who based their claims to privilege and leadership on precolonial traditions and law. Other times these intermediaries were government officials who took over powers that chiefs had exercised during the colonial period. By drawing these authorities into commercial circuits controlled by the state, the chain of patronage relations that extended downward from the state linked up with older hierarchies of authority and patronage in the villages, localities, and regions. The flow of state-controlled resources helped to shore up the powers of local authorities: Peasants who were obliged to submit to their discretion in matters concerning land use rights, communal access to other productive resources, and access to "social services" were now obliged to submit to their discretion in selling, borrowing, and buying transactions as well. These same arrangements extended the reach of the state.

Rural markets controlled by the state provided hierarchical institutional structures and resources that were used to build clientelistic networks of broad geographical scope. Through these networks, the state's power to appropriate and distribute could come to rest upon forms of authority rooted in peasant society and "precapitalist" modes of production. Integrating these two forms of power was the goal of colonial "indirect rulers." Postcolonial regimes sought to govern in analogous ways, often for lack of ready alternatives. Already-powerful elements in rural society were incorporated into the political networks and economic institutions of new regimes, co-opted by the promise of access to rentier activities and by possibilities for enhancing their authority over subordinates. Integration along these lines was not always harmonious or successful. State marketing agencies became major arenas and targets of political competition.

Organizing markets played a critical role in consolidating new regimes. At the same time it set limits upon possibilities for structural economic change. Regimes sank roots in the centralized market structures that allowed colonial merchant capital to extract surpluses from peasant producers, and in rural authority structures that allowed colonial regimes to rule "indirectly." In doing so, postcolonial regimes gained a material and political stake in preserving the old order. Old market structures generated the state's main source of revenue, provided an infrastructure for constructing political machines, and drew rural powerbrokers into the political hierarchy. In the short run, these political and economic arrangements worked to reproduce peasant modes of export crop production. They kept agricultural producers' rates of return low and maintained authority-based or "politicized" controls over productive resources. In the longer run, these economic structures, and the political relations between economic actors that they fostered, tended to stem the rise of local capital within and outside of the agricultural sector.

Within the hierarchical and centralizing structures of markets and regimes, elements within ruling coalitions sized up options for reproducing their power and wealth. State mediated rent-seeking activities existed at all levels of the political/commercial hierarchy, were accessible to those with political influence, and offered something to both patrons and clients. The context within which rent-seeking occurred, however, was not particularly propitious for the productive investment of wealth so accumulated.

Lucrative opportunities for rent collecting expanded steadily throughout the 1960s and 1970s, reducing pressures on the powerful and wealthy to invest in productive activities. Meanwhile, investment opportunities that were lucrative, available, and equally low in risk were not abundant. State action in the rural sector shored up peasant-based modes of production and offered producers low returns. In the industrial sector, government policy systematically favored large-scale investments and foreign investors. Most importantly, those able to amass important sums of wealth were almost invariably clients of some patron; they remained vulnerable to changes in their own political fortunes. Shifts in the alliance-building strategies of their patrons and protectors, or a fall from grace, could mean ruin. Long-term investments in fixed assets were particularly risky when investment funds were accumulated illegally (better to send the funds abroad in this case), or when their profitability depended on markets subject to the discretionary control of potentially hostile, arbitrary, or rapacious state agents. The accumulation of wealth occurred under political conditions that did not encourage productive investment.

In Senegal patterns of state control over rural markets worked to sustain the authority of the Islamic elite in the rural sector and more generally, to shore up precapitalist forces and social relations of production. The ruling coalition and a patronage-based mode of domination were constructed on these bases. Perceived imperatives of rule, the existing balance of powers, and lack of an equally expedient alternative led the postcolonial state to adopt the economic logic of colonial merchant capital as its own. This created the foundations of a system that gave rise to rentierism in the commercial sector as a dominant form of wealth accumulation on the part of the political elite.

These processes constrained the expansion of capitalist forms of production. In even more direct ways, they worked to stifle the emergence of indigenous social strata able to use, or interested in using, state power to promote a bourgeois project. Processes of economic and social transformation likely to threaten the integrity of the ruling coalition, or the viability of the patronage-based mode of domination, were defused. The aim of the ruling class appeared to be "not to advance capitalism, but to . . . prevent it from developing fully."[24]

It is true that creating avenues for local accumulation in rentier activities, rather than promoting the rise of a local bourgeoisie exercising direct control over productive assets, complemented neocolonial interests vested in industry. Foreign monopolies could be preserved. Yet the political logic of postcolonial regime consolidation and the economic logic of neocolonialism were not identical. Analysis of the case of Senegal shows how the logics of these two processes came to diverge. Struggles for control over the market that shaped the economic and political history of Senegal centered around creating, undercutting, maintaining, and gaining access to the state-regulated markets that generated rents. Under these conditions, reproducing the political order established in the 1960s and reproducing the economic order that underpinned it proved to be contradictory processes. These contradictions were revealed in striking ways in economic crisis of the late 1970s and 1980s.

---

24. Lukacs described European petty bourgeoisies and peasantries in these terms. He is cited by Hyden (1980:30), who sees parallels in Africa to the situations that Lukacs described.

2

The colonial market

[I]f it is distressing to watch the constant regression of our exports to foreign countries, it is nonetheless comforting to find that our colonial markets have remained stable. The colonial market, which can never escape us, . . . must be developed for the benefit of French industry and commerce.

M. C. René-Leclerc 1933:4

Merchants do not make their profits by revolutionising production but by controlling markets, and the greater the control they are able to exercise the higher their rate of profit. For this reason merchant capital tends to centralise and concentrate itself into monopolies . . . [M]erchant capital . . . eschewed the principles of laisser-faire and sought state support for monopolistic privileges.

G. B. Kay 1975:96

Senegal's *économie de traite* was an economy structured around and for colonial merchant capital. By buying cheap and selling dear, rather than by imposing direct control over land and labor, capital extracted surpluses from Senegal's rural producers. The colonial state played a central and necessary part in this process. State power was used to promote the extension of export crop production and to sanction and bolster a rural political order that tied producers to colonial trading circuits. The colonial state also underwrote the monopolies that made the operations of French merchant capital profitable. This politically engineered structure of control over trade played a critical role in defining the rate, character, and direction of economic development under colonial rule. Commercial structures and processes constrained the scope of accumulation within the colonial economy, channeled rural surpluses out of agriculture, and narrowed possibilities for profitable investment in activities ancillary to the production of commodities destined for export. Control over trade, then, conditioned possibilities for the expansion and deepening of capital in the economy that took shape under colonial rule.

The social and economic changes that accompanied the spread of export crop production are subjects of an excellent literature on colonial Senegal. This history, however, remains incomplete without a more thorough analysis of control over markets. The main purpose of this chapter is to provide such an analysis, and in doing so to lay groundwork for assessing the significance of patterns of change and continuity in control over markets that marked the first three decades of the postcolonial period. Here, I focus the structure of control over markets from the 1930s onward, tracking the forces that ultimately gave rise to a local textile industry. Interests arrayed behind maintaining the *économie de traite* effectively blocked the development of light industry in Senegal in the pre-World War II period. Interestingly enough, it was these same interests, and these same basic structures of control over trade, that came to dominate and define the structure of the textile-manufacturing industry that emerged in Senegal after the war. By the mid-1950s, the survival and profitability of the industry were predicated upon market structures and political arrangements that had crystallized in the *économie de traite*. In this sense the development of light industry in Dakar was an elaboration of the old, mercantile form of colonial exploitation, rather than a clear break from it.

The dominance of colonial merchant capital is a fact that goes far in explaining the weakness of Senegalese commercial interests at the time of independence. It also helps to account for the political power and character of the Senegalese social groups that competed for control over the postcolonial state. If the state itself was a "resource" in ensuing struggles to consolidate power and to govern, then the powers of the Senegalese state – how it could be used to accommodate interests, extract wealth, and shape economic change – were defined in large part by the mercantile character of the political economy forged under colonial rule.

IMPERIAL PREFERENCE

France's international position deteriorated steadily in the wake of World War I, the Great Depression, and World War II. As this happened, France turned to the vast empire that it had conquered in West Africa in the nineteenth century to bolster the metropolitan economy. Colonial economic policy aimed at creating and maintaining French monopolies over colonial markets – *chasses gardées* – insulated from the competition that France could not withstand. At the time of the Great Depression, the French government adopted a comprehensive set of policies designed to reinforce the autarky of the empire.[1] Within the empire, the colonies were assigned a subordinate position in a division of labor called the *pacte colonial*. The colonies were to provide France with raw materials, agricultural commodities, and protected markets for French industry. Manufacturing was "reserved" for the metropole. For France, the *pacte colonial* would guarantee the cohesion of the empire by promoting complementary, rather than competitive, forms of exchange. To the extent that such cohesion was achieved, it was largely the product of political design backed up with imperial force. An elaborate and well-stocked arsenal of trade restrictions and controls – tariff barriers, quantitative import restrictions, exclusive purchase arrangements, import–export monopolies, and price and currency controls – worked to eliminate

---

1. For a detailed study of debates and political struggles that went on in France over colonial trade and investment policy between 1920 and 1960, see Marseille 1984.

competition from the trading zone and to force the colonies into their assigned role. In West Africa, France came closest to realizing the ideal of an autarkic, noncompetitive imperial economy.

France's vision of a *pacte colonial* did not emerge full-blown from its conquests in West Africa. Once "pacification" was complete, it became obvious that the government had no clear program for exploiting the vast territories acquired in the Sahel. The imperial trade regime remained relatively liberal from the 1880s until the end of World War I. While protectionists and free traders in the government debated, French industry remained largely indifferent to the African colonies.[2] British, Dutch, and Japanese goods dominated French West Africa's import trade. Things changed after the war. French manufacturing interests began to demand formidable measures to restrict the sale of foreign goods in French West Africa. By the mid-1920s the need to secure protected overseas outlets for French products had gained official recognition. The government undertook to capture colonial markets for French industry.

The desire to secure stable markets for metropolitan industry, rather than an interest in guaranteed access to colonial commodities, led to the introduction of sweeping legislation regulating all aspects of Franco-colonial trade in 1928 (Mérat 1937:449–50, 453; Crowder 1978:285–6). France adopted tough measures to reduce foreign competition on colonial markets. It also assumed "responsibility" for absorbing all export commodities produced in the colonies. The latter move ensured that the colonies would not obtain currency that could be used to buy foreign (i.e., non-French) goods. Although the new legislation did stimulate trade between France and its colonies, it was the Great Depression that drove the economic consolidation of the French Empire in the 1930s.

The Depression cast the economic weaknesses of the French economy in sharp relief, highlighting France's vulnerability to increasingly competitive trade on world markets. A consensus in France emerged: Reliance on colonial markets was the way to survive the economic crisis and "to combat international competition" (Monguillot 1944). One French commentator explained the problem clearly in 1933: "Given the increasing difficulty of selling our goods on foreign markets, we find ourselves forced to look more and more toward our colonial markets . . . which have become an outlet that we will never be able to do without" (René-Leclerc 1933:9). Trade policy was revised to make the imperial economy a tighter, more coherent ensemble.

---

2. The 1880s and 1890s debate over colonial trade policy was but one part of a larger discussion of what to do with the West African colonies. Jules Ferry championed the development of West African markets as outlets for French industry. He was voted out of office in 1885. *Guinée* cloth made in India and sold in West Africa by British and French trading firms was the proximate focus of the West Africa trade policy debate in the 1880s. Segments of French textile industry that produced *guinée* cloth pressed for more protection against foreign competition. French commercial firms operating in West Africa lobbied for "free trade." As Newbury writes (1968:337–8), this issue "was at the thin end of a much larger wedge." A general tariff taxing non-French imports to the colonies in West Africa was established in the 1890s to raise revenues for the colonial administration. This tariff was not designed to be a barrier to foreign competition.

Between 1930 and 1940 France adopted a barrage of measures controlling Franco-colonial trade. In French West Africa, two important innovations were introduced. The first was the imposition of quotas to limit the importation of non-French manufactured goods.[3] The quota system dealt a severe blow to British manufacturers exporting to French West Africa, clearing new markets for French industry. The second was a system of price supports for colonial produce sold in the metropole.[4] The two measures served the same end: expanding colonial markets for French goods. Price supports for colonial export commodities were adopted "to deal with the problem of overproduction in metropolitan industry. . . . [T]he collapse of world market prices for colonial agricultural commodities reduces the purchasing power of colonial populations, thereby reducing sales of French manufactured goods in the colonies" (Jacquot 1963:18). Under the new trade regime, the colonies became metropolitan France's best client in the 1930s. In 1929 one-fifth of all France's external trade was conducted with the colonies. By 1933 the figure was one-half. In key product categories (sugar, cotton textiles, clothing, potatoes, shoes, soap) over 85 percent of all French exports were sold on the protected markets of the overseas territories.[5] In the colonies, almost 70 percent of all imports came from France (Moussa 1957:36–7, 56). Any doubts that France's overseas possessions represented an "*intérêt primordial*" for the metropole were laid to rest.[6]

French textile manufacturers: Industrie par excellence de l'Union Française

Of all major branches of French manufacturing, none developed a greater stake in colonial markets than the cotton textile industry. With the rise of British and German textile producers in the early 1800s, the survival and fortunes of the

---

3. In 1934 import quotas were fixed for a wide range of foreign manufactured goods: cotton textile goods, motor cars, tobacco, cement, iron and steel, glassware, rubber goods, perfumery, and pharmaceuticals. In 1936 the Anglo-French Free Trade Convention of 1898, which allowed British goods free access to Dahomey and the Côte d'Ivoire, was put aside and the quota system was extended to these territories. The British government protested the imposition of quotas in 1934 and 1936. See Hopkins 1973:264; Crowder 1968:321.
4. Tariffs were imposed on agricultural commodities imported to France from regions outside the empire. The new tariffs reduced competitive pressures that lowered the prices of colonial commodities sold in France, allowing France to pay more than prevailing world market prices for colonial products. France began paying more than world market prices for Senegalese groundnuts in 1931.
5. See René-Leclerc 1933:3–4. The 85 percent figure pertains to 1936 and 1937 and refers to quantities, not value. For cotton textiles and clothing, 93 percent of all French exports were sold in the colonies. See "Le Commerce franco–colonial en 1937," *Le Bulletin Quotidien de la Société d'Etudes et d'Informations Economiques*, no. 165 (25 juillet 1938).
6. "Les possessions d'outre-mer représentent pour notre économie métropolitain un intérêt primordial. Il appartient aux Pouvoirs Publics d'y protéger les exportations de la France contre la concurrence étrangère" (see ibid.).

French textile industry came to depend upon protectionist measures adopted by the French government.[7] Recurrent, structural crises plagued the industry from the mid-1800s onward. Technical progress stagnated as French textile manufacturers successfully resisted pressures for modernization (Rabeil 1955:119–27; Carponnier 1959; Berrier 1978). High costs, low productivity, antiquated capital stock, and conservative family ownership of a multitude of small firms earned cotton textile manufacturing the distinction of *"le secteur le plus rétrograde"* of all French industry (Marseille 1984). Systematic protection against foreign competition allowed the uncompetitive and fragmented industry to survive.

After World War I the problems of the French cotton textile industry became acute. France's recovery of Alsace, an industrialized region with a high concentration of textile mills, created overcapacity in the textile manufacturing sector. Meanwhile, aggressive new textile exporters such as the United States, India, and Japan appeared, replacing French goods on international markets and underscoring the vulnerability of French industry. Foreign outlets for French goods dried up as industrialization progressed in the Far East and Latin America. Germany imposed heavy import taxes on French textiles in 1926 – yet another blow to the industry. As domestic and world market conditions deteriorated in the 1920s, French textile manufacturers fell back on the protected outlets of the empire.[8]

In this period of great difficulty, the West African market became more attractive to French textile producers. Export crop production in French West Africa grew steadily after World War I, expanding demand for consumer goods. In *Afrique Occidentale Française,* a market long regarded with indifference by French textile manufacturers, textiles were the leading category of imports in both value and volume.[9] Various sources estimated that West African peasants spent 30–40 percent of their monetary revenue on cotton cloth.[10] The French textile industry's producer association, the Syndicat Général de l'Industrie Cotonnière Française (SGICF), began a relentless campaign for privileged access to colonial markets. The association argued that "[i]f the colonial markets are not solidly protected, the French textile industry will be condemned to decay (*déclin*)."[11]

Protectionist measures were reinforced in the early 1930s, and the volume of French textile goods sold in the AOF nearly quadrupled. Within the AOF, Sene-

7. "Le protectionnisme était lié à l'industrie cotonnière française depuis ses origines. . . . L'histoire de cette industrie dépend des mesures de protection" (Carponnier 1959:40–45, 398).
8. See Angliviel de la Beaumelle 1947:2; *Le Journal des Textiles* 1951 (édition supplémentaire): 51; and Rabeil 1955:155–6.
9. Textile goods were to retain this place in the subsequent period. Between 1938 and 1954, textile goods constituted between 21 and 33 percent of all imports to the AOF (by value). See *Marchés Coloniaux,* no. 503 (2 juillet 1955).
10. On the AOF import trade, see Charbonneau 1961:25–5; and Hopkins 1973:177. On West African demand, see Carponnier 1959:285; and *Le Journal des Textiles,* no. 56 (1949): 61.
11. M. de Calan, SGICF, cited in Rabeil 1955:194. See Marseille 1984.

Table 2.1. *Exports of the French cotton textile industry, 1913–55*
(by region, in thousands of tons)

Region	1913	1929	1938	1948	1950	1952	1953	1954	1955
N. Africa[a]	14.2	23.7	19.4	14.9	21.0	23.0	19.7	17.4	18.2
Indochina	8.0	8.6	7.7	3.6	13.2	20.1	15.4	13.8	6.3
AOF	0.9	2.3	8.7	5.0	9.8	12.3[b]	10.0	15.4	10.0
Other TOM[c]	4.9	6.5	5.3	4.5	7.5		6.9	8.8	6.7
TOM, total	28.0	41.1	43.5	28.0	51.5	57.2	52.0	55.4	41.2
Total exports			47.6	31.1	56.0	59.5	55.9		
Exports to TOM as % of all exports			95%	89%		96%	93%		
Exports to TOM as % of total production			33%		25%				25–30%

[a]North Africa: Algeria, Morocco, Tunisia.
[b]1951.
[c]Territoires d'Outre-Mer (TOM) includes the regions listed above plus Madagascar, Cameroun, French Equatorial Africa (Afrique Equatoriale Française, AEF), Syria, and the overseas departments (Départements d'Outre-Mer) such as New Caledonia and the Pacific Islands.
Sources: *Le Journal des Textiles* n. 56, 1949: 46; *Marchés Coloniaux*, n. 298, 28 juillet 1951: 2035–7; Rabeil 1955: 145, 147; Moussa 1957: 57–8; Carponnier 1959: 93, 94, 263.

gal became the largest consumer of French textiles.[12] By the late 1930s about 30 percent of the industry's total output was sold on colonial markets. Sales on all other foreign markets dwindled to less than 10 percent of total exports (see Table 2.1). The decisive turn toward colonial markets in the 1930s made the French cotton textile industry the self-proclaimed *industrie par excellence de l'Union française*.[13]

Manufacturers in the Alsace region, including the Vosges mountains and the city of Mulhouse, were the leading exporters of French textile goods to the colonies.[14] When Alsace was broken off from France (and the French market) in the 1870s, manufacturers had turned to markets for cotton prints in North Africa and Indochina. Once Alsace was reintegrated into France after World War I, the Mulhouse industrialists were poised to exploit the potential of the now-protected French West African market. Quotas restricting the sale of English cotton goods

12. Senegal was the single largest market in the Senegal–Soudan Français–Mauritania customs zone. This customs zone absorbed 60.7 percent of the total tonnage of French textile goods exported to the AOF in 1938, and 57.7 percent of this total in 1954 (*Marchés Coloniaux*, no. 503 (2 juillet 1955): 1,811).
13. Statement of Robert Trocmé, president of the SGICF in 1950 (*Le Journal des Textiles*, 1951 [édition supplémentaire]: 41).
14. *Le Journal des Textiles* (no. 56 [1949]: 60) reported that 58 percent of the French textile goods sold in the colonies in 1948 were supplied by Alsace and the Vosges.

on AOF markets were imposed in the 1930s. Mulhouse textile manufacturers, especially the firm of Ets. Schaeffer et Cie., began to copy English-style prints for export to the AOF.[15] (Ets. Schaeffer reappears later as the first French firm to begin manufacturing textiles in Dakar.) Alsacian manufacturers were alone in adapting production to make specialized goods for West Africa. Their counterparts in other textile-exporting regions of France, most notably in the North, sold surplus stock of traditional, French-style goods in the colonies. Many exported only sporadically. Although most of the French textile industry resisted innovation on the production side and did not specialize in colonial exports, the industry was fully prepared to undertake a political campaign to secure its hold on colonial markets. In the 1930s this meant not only demanding tariff protection against foreign competitors, but also opposing industrial development in the colonies.

Opposition to industrial development in the colonies

The possibility of industrial development in the colonies emerged as a policy debate in France in the mid-1930s, as France leaned ever more heavily on the imperial economy to compensate for the weaknesses of the metropole.[16] The most dynamic factions of French capital began to push for structural reforms of the empire, arguing that it was necessary to move beyond the rudimentary forms of economic integration enshrined in the *pacte colonial*. Financial circles and producer-goods industries insisted that in the medium- to long-run, the economic viability of the empire depended on expanding the colonial economies by raising labor productivity and purchasing power. Support for at least some forms of industrial development in the colonies was the core of the "developmentalist" case: Today's peasant consuming French textiles would be tomorrow's worker, employed in a French-built factory and buying French radios, fans, and stoves. There was a certain urgency to the argument. The French financiers of Indochina, joined by others, warned that "if we do not undertake industrial development in the colonies, the colonies will industrialize against us."[17] The only French interests hurt in the short run, they argued, "were those in the cotton textile industry, but what do they represent in the context of the entire French

---

15. In response to the new quota system, the powerful British colonial trading company, the United Africa Company (UAC), created a Paris-based subsidiary, La Compagnie Niger-France (CNF). The CNF arranged to have the Mulhouse textile manufacturers produce British-style textiles under contract. The CNF supplied print designs, specialized equipment, dyes, and technical experts to teach the French firm to copy fabrics that British manufacturers had developed specifically for sale in West Africa. On the formation of the CNF, see Webster and Boahen 1967:266. On the UAC; see Pedler 1974.

16. The issue of industrial development became the center of controversy at La Conférence Economique de la France Outre-Mer, Paris, 1934–1935. See Coquery-Vidrovitch 1979:77.

17. Comment of M. Edouard Giscard d'Estaing, who was firmly ensconced in the *milieux financiers et industriels d'Indochine*, in heated debates with SGICF representatives, 1937 (Marseille 1982:30).

economy?"[18] Proponents of colonial industrial development ran up against the solid resistance of the weakest sectors of French manufacturing industry and the oldest factions of colonial commercial capital. Exporters of light consumer goods rallied behind the banner of the French cotton textile industry to defend the *pacte colonial* and their direct hold on colonial markets.[19]

For the textile producers' association, the SGICF, and its allies in defending the status quo, industrial production in the colonies was out of the question. It would reduce exports of consumer goods such as textiles to the detriment of traditional exporting industries. It would create unemployment in France during a period of economic hardship. It would add to industrial overcapacity in the empire when France already had trouble selling its manufactured goods. The SGICF argued, in short, that "the industrialization of the colonies will be the ruin of French industry."[20] The defensive reflex was articulated not only in terms of the economic threat of industrialization, but also in terms of a political threat. "We must not create a colonial proletariat . . . which will rapidly become a danger to French sovereignty."[21] This argument found support in the political affairs division of the colonial ministry.

In the 1930s strategies for modernization of the imperial economy were obstructed by the most conservative factions of French industrial and commercial capital, epitomized by the cotton textile industry and the giant colonial trading companies, the *maisons de commerce*. A high-ranking bureaucrat of the French government captured the spirit of the official position in 1937: "There is slight chance that the French government will destroy a branch of the French economy [the textile industry] for some vague economic compensations that would benefit other industrial activities at some undefined point in the future" (Marseille 1982:32–3). During the interwar period the government resigned itself to short-term pressures and a policy of maintaining the status quo, choosing what Jacques Marseille called "the stagnation option" (*la voie d'immobilisme*). By allowing the most backward factions of French capital to have the last word on the colonial industrialization issue, France opted to forgo structural reform and to maintain the essential features of the *pacte colonial*. Once again, France staved off pressures to modernize not only the colonial economies, but the metropolitan economy as well. Observers at the time did not fail to note that this strategy assured the survival of declining French industries such as the cotton textile industry and hindered the emergence of new ones.[22]

18. Cited in Marseille 1982:302-33. The technocratic, neoliberal factions argued that "this industrialization [of the colonies], which is inevitable, will be but a minor problem to metropolitan manufacturers if they seize the initiative themselves." See also Coquery-Vidrovitch 1979:92.
19. Marseille 1982:28. See also idem 1974:409–32. The colonial trading houses also looked quite unfavorably on the possibility of industrial development in West Africa. Coquery-Vidrovitch (1979:72) cites SCOA's 1941–2 company report in this regard.
20. Comment of M. A. Waddington, Secrétaire du SGICF, 1937, cited by Marseille 1982:30.
21. Marseille 1982:33. French business circles talked a great deal about their fear of the rise of communism in Africa. See Chardonnet 1956:41–4.
22. Marseille and Coquery-Vidrovitch stress this point in the works cited above. Marseille shows that technocrats and neoliberals in French government and business circles advanced this argu-

ECONOMIE DE TRAITE OF THE AOF

In the Federation of French West Africa, the AOF, the goals of the *pacte colonial* were realized in their purest form. France pursued a rudimentary and mercantile form of colonial economic development. The *économie de traite*, organized around the principle of buying African commodities cheap and selling French manufactured goods dear, was the defining feature of the AOF economy in the pre-World War II era. Virtually a closed market after 1928, African peasants grew export crops and devoted the largest share of their cash earnings to buying imported French goods, especially textiles. A handful of large French trading houses, the maisons de commerce, monopolized the import–export trade and dominated the colonial economy. Manufacturing activity in the federation was nearly nonexistent before World War II, thanks in large part to concerted metropolitan efforts to stifle even the simplest export-processing industries.

The AOF was run as one vast unit, a single trading zone administered from Dakar.[23] The mandate of the colonial administration was to promote the import–export trade at the lowest possible cost to France. Reluctant to assume "the burden of empire," the French government until 1946 required that all costs of administration and development be financed by the territory itself through local tax revenue.[24] The bulk of local receipts came from tariffs on the import trade. Revenues were spent on administration and invested in infrastructure to promote colonial trade: roads, the port of Dakar, and the railway cutting deep into the interior to evacuate export crops to the coast. On the production side, official encouragement was given to only one economic goal: promoting the production of crops needed by France. In Senegal this meant the expansion of groundnut cultivation.

Patterns of French public and private investment in the AOF reflected the metropole's limited economic goals in West Africa, and the limits of France's interest in enhancing the productivity of land and labor in the AOF. French investment was kept to the minimum required to sustain the colonial trading system. By 1935 France had invested less in the AOF than the British had invested in the Gold Coast (now Ghana), a territory less than one-tenth of the size of the federation.[25] The French colonial administration relied on forced labor

ment at the time. The problem was summarized in a 1946 government publication: "En créant les marchés privilegés, le système favorisa l'inertie des milieux industriels de la métropole" ("Le Régime douanier et l'évolution économique des colonies françaises," *Notes Documentaires et Etudes*, no. 481 [17 décembre 1946]: 6).

23. The AOF, constituted in 1905, was made up of the West African territories of Senegal, the French Soudan (now Mali), Upper Volta (now Burkina Faso), Niger, Mauritania, Dahomey (now Benin) the Côte d'Ivoire, and Guinea. A common tariff structure was applied uniformly throughout the federation.

24. On the principle of "autonomie financière" of the colonies, see Crowder 1978:248; and Gellar 1976:19. The French government made loans to the colonial administration in the 1920s and 1930s that were serviced and repaid out of local receipts.

25. Total invested capital in the AOF in 1935 equaled 30.4 million British pounds. For the Gold Coast alone, the figure was 35.3 million. The total for Britain's West African colonies (Nigeria,

until 1946 to carry out public works projects, a cheap yet primitive way of getting the job done. The largest private investors in the AOF were the maisons de commerce, which built little more than warehouses, trading posts, and offices.[26] Outside Senegal, extractive activities (surface mining, lumber) attracted some French private investment. Low levels of investment in French West Africa were both a cause and a consequence of the persistence of the *économie de traite* that developed in the federation under French colonial rule.

Export crop production in Senegal: Islam and the groundnut

In Senegal French colonialism led to the establishment of a new political and social order – and to the spread of groundnut production. The two processes were intimately intertwined. The internal political order that emerged under direct colonial rule was rooted in a system of export crop production that was expedient and low-cost for both the French administration and the maisons de commerce.

Islamic *jihads* in the Sahel in the mid-1800s weakened the states of West Africa, facilitating French military conquest in the 1870s. French conquest and "pacification" of the territory that became the colony of Senegal was accompanied by rapid Islamization of the defeated Wolof people.[27] In the early part of this century the colonial administration forged an alliance of convenience with up-and-coming Muslim religious leaders, the Mouride and Tidjane *marabouts*. The French supported the marabouts, underwriting the rise of their economic and political power in the rural areas of central Senegal. The marabouts, in turn, counseled their followers to acquiesce to colonial rule.

Groundnut exports from Senegal to France nearly tripled between 1882 and 1913. Production tripled again by the mid-1950s, making Senegal one of the world's leading groundnut producers.[28] The economic contribution of the colonial administration to the initial period of spectacular growth in output was the building of railroads. Production spread rapidly along the lines of rail. This result, so desired by France, the colonial administration, and the maisons de commerce, transformed the economic basis of Wolof society. It would not have been possible without the active promotion of groundnut cultivation by the Mouride and Tidjane religious brotherhoods, or *confréries*.

Gold Coast, Gambia, and Sierra Leone) in 1935 was 116.7 million (Government of the UK, Naval Intelligence Division, n.d. [1942?]: 334).

26. Suret-Canale 1968:30. Thompson and Adloff (1958:271–2) report that of all private investment made in the France's African colonies between 1900 and 1945, 63 percent was in commerce and extractive activities. French private capital invested in sub-Saharan Africa over the course of this period represented only 7 percent of all French overseas private investment (80 percent of French private overseas investment was in areas outside the empire). See also Pfefferman 1968:233.

27. See Klein 1968.

28. Halpern (1972) reports that Senegal's groundnut exports to France totaled 83,000 tons in 1882, and 240,000 tons in 1913. For quantities of groundnuts commercialized in Senegal from 1935 to 1963, see Morgenthau 1964:135. She reports that about 800,000 tons of groundnuts were commercialized in 1957/58.

The modern confréries were established and grew into powerful institutions within the framework of colonial rule.[29] Their power rested on two bases. The first was religious authority. The second was the role of the confréries in institutions controlled by the French: the market economy and the bureaucratic colonial state (D. Cruise O'Brien 1971). Senegalese Islam requires the pious mortal to obey, pay homage, and offer prestations to a marabout – to become the disciple and follower of a spiritual master who has the power to grant ultimate salvation. By cultivating groundnuts on their own land or by working a marabout's groundnut fields, followers produced a cash crop that allowed them to pay their dues to the marabout and to Allah. Religious obligations, new social relations of production, and groundnut cultivation became most closely intertwined within the Mouride order (Copans 1988). Under colonial rule Mouride marabouts promoted the rise of a peasantry in what became known as the "groundnut basin" of Senegal, making the production and sale of groundnuts a spiritual imperative, a saving grace.

With the support of the administration, the Mouride marabouts spearheaded and organized mass movements of agrarian settlement along the railroads. The administration granted the marabouts land, credit, and equipment, which the religious leaders used to establish agricultural estates of their own. These estates were cultivated by disciples who lived austerely at the marabout's expense during seven years of nonremunerated labor. After the period of servitude, the marabout gave the follower land. Through this pioneering process, new agricultural communities (Mouride villages) engaging in groundnut production were born. Members of these communities then paid tithes to their marabout in cash (earned through the sale of groundnuts), in groundnuts, by devoting a share of their time to working the marabout's fields, and/or by providing food crops to feed the disciples devoted to full-time work on the marabout's groundnut estate. Ties that bound followers to their marabouts remained intact over time, for in addition to providing an assured route to salvation, the religious leaders often provided their disciples with credit, seeds, and emergency relief in times of need.

Methods of groundnut production that developed in Senegal's groundnut basin under these arrangements were rudimentary (D. Cruise O'Brien 1971:219–23; Halpern 1972). The hoe was the universal farming tool and fertilizer use was confined for the most part to the marabouts' large estates. A process of extensive cultivation was fueled by the opening of virgin lands for groundnut cultivation, the mobilization of disciples' labor, increases in cultivators' labor time, and the incorporation of (nonwage) migrant labor from regions outside the groundnut zone into the extended household production unit.[30] This process quickly de-

---

29. There are several excellent studies of Senegalese Islam, the marabouts, the confréries, and the marabout–disciple relationship. See Behrman 1970; D. Cruise O'Brien 1971a; Halpern 1972; D. Cruise O'Brien 1975; Coulon 1981; Copans 1988.

30. Migrant laborers called *navetanes* (named after the *navet*, or "rainy season," in Wolof) lived with rural households. During the 6 to 7 months of the agricultural season, heads of households loaned the *navetanes* land and tools, which they used to cultivate their own groundnut crops. The *navetane* kept the cash earnings from this crop. In exchange, these migrants worked an average

pleted fragile Sahelian soils, creating dust bowls as pioneering marabouts and their followers moved on to new land. Established communities in the old parts of the groundnut basin faced declining productivity as they were left to struggle with depleted and degraded land.

The colonial administration defined its goals for agricultural development in Senegal almost exclusively in terms of the extension of lands under groundnut cultivation (Portères 1952). In general, French administrators and the merchant houses sought to accomplish this shared objective either by pressuring and inducing existing rural communities to devote a share of their resources to export crop production, or by supporting the "colonization" of the groundnut basis by the new religious orders. The administration made only marginal efforts to increase the productivity of land and labor, curb the destruction of wooded or pastoral lands, and promote food crops – either in the groundnut basin or in parts of Senegal where soils were more robust and water supplies more secure. French colonizers' limited efforts to play a more direct role in the agricultural production process were undertaken by the colonial state.

In the 1910s the colonial state began to manage groundnut seed stocks in some parts of the colony, in principle to assure an adequate supply at planting time. Sociétés Indigènes de Prévoyance (SIP), French West Africa's early version of agricultural "cooperatives," were the institutions chosen to manage this task.[31] These organizations were placed under the direct control of French *commandants de cercle* in 1923. They were run by Senegalese chosen as local-level agents of the colonial administration (the *chefs de canton* and their subordinates). The near collapse of the groundnut economy during the Depression of the 1930s led the administration to expand the role of the SIP in Senegal, and in the groundnut basin in particular. The fall in groundnut prices of 1931–2 "reduced the Senegalese peasants to misery; their income from groundnuts was not enough to allow them to buy the rice that they needed to eat; they were reduced to eating their groundnut seed stocks" (Suret-Canale 1964:305). To prevent producers from abandoning the groundnut altogether, the colonial administration developed the SIP into a system for stocking and distributing seeds on a widespread basis.

Cultivators were now obliged by law to join, to pay dues, and after 1935, to turn a share of their harvest over to the local SIP. At planting time, SIP officials sold seed on credit, at a rate of interest of 25 percent. Through the SIP the colonial administration gained direct control over a share of the harvest, which it commercialized on its own account. The administration also established an indirect way of trying to enhance productivity in the groundnut economy. SIP be-

of five mornings per week on the groundnut fields of the household head, thus permitting the household head to sustain or increase groundnut production while other family members devoted an important part of their time to food-crop production. Actively encouraged by the colonial administration after 1933, this migrant labor influx reached its peak from 1933–9, averaging about 58,000 *navetanes* per year during this period. *Navetanes* produced an estimated 8 percent of the total value of Senegal's groundnut crop in 1934 (and 6 percent from 1949–58). Figures from Founou-Tchuigoua 1981:59–60.

31. On the SIP, see Thompson and Adloff 1958:311–13, 357–9; Crowder 1968:316–17.

came involved in renting and selling seeding tools to producers and, to a lesser extent, in making loans for groundnut production. Efforts on this front were designed to offset declines in productivity that were occurring as the commercial exploitation of the peasantry intensified.

Thompson and Adloff (1958:357) argue that in Senegal's groundnut basin, SIP were built in part on the "communal solidarities" and social structures of the Islamic confréries. The new institutions enhanced the power and positions of the marabouts. Marabouts and other SIP agents were the main beneficiaries of the SIP: They were able to use their influence to direct inputs and credit distributed by the SIP toward their own landholdings. With more resources at their disposal, these local authorities were also able to reinforce their positions vis-à-vis peasants who depended upon them for access to land, tools, and seeds. For the vast majority of the population, dues and seed stocks turned over to the SIP came to represent an *exploitation supplémentaire*, a tax to be paid in cash and kind to the colonial administration (Suret-Canale 1964:71, 299–310).

The colonial administration divided Senegal into administrative districts, stationed French *commandants* throughout the territory, and controlled the SIP. What was striking about the groundnut basin, however, was the robustness of the system of *indirect* rule that emerged (Copans 1988). French colonizers relied upon the Islamic marabouts to mediate relations between the colonial state and its rural subjects in the groundnut basin. Marabouts sanctioned the colonial order and paid respect to the colonial authorities. They told their followers to submit to the SIP, taxation, and conscription. The confréries, in turn, drew their political power and wealth from their intermediary position in a political economy founded upon the production of export crops destined for sale in France. They accomplished what neither the French nor the colonial merchant houses could do: organize the rapid extension of a peasant-based system of commodity production. In this sense the confréries and the colonial administration served as the political counterparts of French merchant capital.

Grands marabouts, with several thousand followers each, ran the hierarchical confréries. Centralized command lay in the hands of a grand khalif. The colonial administration invested in the prestige of the confréries, contributing to projects such as the building of the Great Mosque at Touba, the religious capital of the Mourides. Colonial authorities deployed their political and economic resources strategically, influencing the succession of grands marabouts to the position of grand khalif and manipulating competition and rivalries between grands marabouts and sects. These political tactics and control over the strings of the colonial purse gave the administration the upper hand in dealing with the marabouts. The French administration and the trading houses got what they needed out of these arrangements: an acquiescent peasantry and mountains of groundnuts. Meanwhile, the Islamic leaders used the colonial system to great advantage. High-ranking marabouts grew wealthy from the earnings of their own estates, the offerings of their followers, and loans and cash subsidies from the colonial authorities. They attracted ever larger personal followings and increased their political power.

Organization of *la* traite

Purchase of groundnuts and sale of French manufactured goods, the nearly closed trading circuit called *la traite,* was the lifeblood of mercantilism and the *pacte colonial* in Senegal.[32] It was carried out by a small group of French trading houses, the colonial maisons de commerce. These trading conglomerates controlled all levels and aspects of the AOF import–export trade, moving merchandise and commodities between the French manufacturer and the African peasant. Uncontested dominance over the commanding heights of the AOF economy from the early 1930s onward made the maisons de commerce the "privileged instruments of French colonialism in Africa." Monopoly control made colonial trade enormously profitable for the largest trading houses and limited the development of commerce and industry in the AOF to the minimum required for effective execution of *la traite.* These firms were the primary beneficiaries of the *pacte coloniale* as it was realized in West Africa.

The three largest maisons de commerce dominated *la traite* in Senegal: the Compagnie Française de l'Afrique de l'Ouest (CFAO), the Société Commerciale Ouest Africaine (SCOA), and the Compagnie Niger–France (CNF).[33] These vertically integrated trading and shipping combines, based in Paris and Marseille, operated extensively throughout the AOF. Working with their affiliates, the large French banks that financed colonial trade, the "big three" handled the bulk of Franco-African commerce. From buying offices in France, they placed yearly orders with French manufacturers for goods to be shipped to the AOF. Commodities they collected from peasant producers were delivered to French processing industries on contract. In the colonies the trading houses conducted *"commerce général,"* distributing the entire array of manufactured goods and imported foodstuffs consumed in the AOF. A second tier of Bordeaux-based maisons de commerce was made up of about ten smaller, older, and more specialized firms.[34] Powerful on the local level in their own right, these companies conducted *la traite* alongside the big three.

The French commercial firms handling the AOF export–import trade coordinated their activities, establishing a cartel form of monopoly control over the French West African market.[35] They fixed groundnut prices, worked out market sharing agreements, and avoided competition among themselves. They also acted in concert in the import trade, coordinating supply and prices to keep retail margins high. To prevent the emergence of competition in the local distribution circuit, the maisons de commerce maintained a common front against indepen-

---

32. See Suret-Canale 1964:11–28.

33. The CNF was an affiliate of Unilever's trading arm, the United Africa Company. See fn. 15.

34. This group includes the import–export houses of Maurel et Prom, Chavanel, Buhan et Teisseire, la Société Parisienne des Comptoirs Africains (SPCA), Peterson, la Compagnie Commerciale Hollando–Africaine (CCHA), Deves et Chaumet, Vezia, and Peyrissac (which became the Senegal branch of the conglomerate OPTORG).

35. See Bauer 1954:77–155; Webster and Boahen 1967:266–8; Amin 1969:19–20; Crowder 1978:244–9.

dent wholesalers. French commercial banks established in West Africa, the colonial administration, and the maisons de commerce joined forces to block independent traders' access to credit.[36] Working hand-in-hand with the colonial administration, the maisons de commerce divided up import quotas among themselves and obtained exclusive rights to import key products, including staple foods such as rice. The profit margins of these firms reflected their success in suppressing competition: the CFAO could earn profits of 90 percent in good years and 25 percent in bad.[37]

The maisons de commerce established a ubiquitous presence in the groundnut basin by wiping out commercial competitors. In the first decades of French colonial rule, Senegalese traders were active in the interior, and commercial circuits were quite competitive (Amin 1969). In the 1920s the French maisons de commerce undertook to eliminate independent groundnut traders by extending their own commercial networks into the most remote corners of the groundnut basin. Hundreds of trading posts, called *comptoirs* or *factoreries* and manned by agents of the French firms, were set up in the groundnut basin. Large numbers of Lebanese immigrants began to arrive in the AOF in the wake of World War I; they supplied most of the required manpower.[38] Lebanese merchants became trading post agents, groundnut collectors, and employees of the maisons de commerce in Senegal. As formidable competitors at the lowest echelon of French-controlled commerce, the Lebanese carved out a stable niche in *la traite* at the expense of Senegalese traders. The onset of the Great Depression was the final blow to independent Senegalese merchants active in the groundnut trade.

By 1930 the maisons de commerce dominated trade in Senegal at all levels of the commercial circuit: importation, exportation, wholesale, and retail. Profits were generated at the point of direct contact between the French trading firm and the peasant producer–consumer. Rural trading posts bought crops from the peasants after the harvest. These same stores sold manufactured goods and food staples (cloth, tools, pots, rice, sugar, oil) to the same peasants all year long, on credit. Farmers, once indebted to the *factorerie*, were trapped. They were bound

36. Senegalese had no access to bank credit until 1956, in spite of Senegalese businessmen's persistent demands that the colonial administration take a stand against the unfair and discriminatory lending policies of the French banks. On how the maisons de commerce used credit to control traders at lower echelons of the trading circuit, see Amin 1969 and Charbonneau 1961:44.

37. These figures are given in Webster and Boahen 1967:267. On the issue of "excessive profits", made possible by the absence of competition on the local market, see also Bauer 1954:77–155; Chafanel et Poncet, "Etude sur la structure de prix et l'organisation commerciale en AOF," République Française, Ministère de la France Outre-Mer, Haut Commissariat de l'AOF, Direction Générale des Services Economiques et du Plan, janvier 1955.

38. With the encouragement of the French government, the Lebanese exodus was redirected toward the AOF during and after World War I. The French occupation of Lebanon was a key factor in this process. The Lebanese in Senegal numbered about 500 in 1914, 2,000 in 1930, 4,000 in 1938, and 8,000 by 1953. See Charbonneau 1961:94–5; Amin 1971:367; and M. Diop 1972:138, 145. For the role of Lebanese in *la traite*, see also *Marchés Coloniaux* (29 septembre 1956): 2,595; Winder 1962.

to produce groundnuts and to sell them to the local *factorerie* agent in order to repay their debts. The colonial trading houses and their local agents exploited their monopoly positions in the rural areas with ruthlessness. Speculative and usurious manipulations of prices and credit terms became the norm – the *scandale permanent* of rural Senegal.[39]

Low levels of productivity in the groundnut economy can be attributed in large part to this structure of control over trade. Peasants' investments in tools and fertilizers were minimal because producer prices were too low to make it profitable and because small-scale farmers were so poor. Lack of competition in the commercial sphere helped to preserve *la traite* in its rudimentary, dual-flux form. As Bernard Founou-Tchuigoua (1981:53) argues, development of the SIP made this system more complex but did not alter it fundamentally. With the extension of the SIP in the 1930s, two intertwined buying and selling circuits emerged in rural Senegal – one that tied peasants to the export trade through the state-controlled SIP, and one that tied peasants to the local outposts of the maisons de commerce. Both trade circuits bound peasants to groundnut production through the debt nexus.

Commercial monopolies and buyers' cartels sustained the profitability of *la traite* in spite of the poverty of peasants and low levels of productivity in the groundnut sector. Monopolies allowed the maisons de commerce to buy cheap and sell dear. They had little interest in, or ability to, undertake costly and complicated strategies for lowering the costs of groundnut production or increasing productivity. Commercial houses like the CFAO, SCOA, and the CNF had no direct role in bringing new land under cultivation, no say in how peasants farmed their land, and no way to force producers to invest. Creation of the SIP signaled the growing seriousness of constraints on productivity, along with merchant capital's inability to address this problem. The colonial state was pressured to intervene with the force of law to sustain the system of agricultural production that allowed the colonial trading houses to buy and sell in Senegal. Colonial merchant capital, confined to commercial circuits, profited from the pioneering drives of the Mouride confréries and from the ways in which state power was used to harness the productive capacities of Senegal's rural societies to the colonial market.

The commercial houses used their monopoly positions to force down the price of groundnuts. French capital purchased "on the cheap" in another sense as well, for it did not pay the full costs of producing Senegal's groundnuts. Metropolitan capital did not bear the full costs of keeping African agricultural laborers alive from one year to the next. These costs were borne in large part by rural households that continued to grow food crops and to meet many of their own subsistence needs. Colonial trading interests also assumed no liability for the "cost" of

39. See Charbonneau 1961:49–50. Usurious credit terms, speculative pricing, and forced purchases of slow-selling merchandise as a precondition for purchasing necessities (*la vente jumelée*) were the norm. See also Chafanel et Poncet, "Etude sur la structure de prix et l'organisation commerciale en AOF," 1955:10.

arable land that was "used up" and, in the case of the marabouts' estates, often abandoned once its potential was exhausted.

Commodities acquired on the cheap were destined for sale in France. In their dealings with French buyers, the colonial trading companies confronted another powerful cartel – the French groundnut-crushing mills. These manufacturers wanted cheap groundnuts. The French government supported their efforts to keep costs low, in part because groundnut oil was a basic wage good in the metropole. This suggests that the purchase and resale of groundnuts was not, in itself, extremely profitable for the maisons de commerce.[40] What made *la traite* profitable for the trading houses was their monopoly command of the dual flux of colonial trade. The purchase of the groundnut crop placed cash in the hands of Senegal's rural population; this cash was recycled back into the coffers of the trading companies when peasants bought cloth, tools, or soap. Lack of competition on both sides of the trading circuit reduced pressures on capital to find new ways to enhance productivity, to raise rural incomes, or to establish a direct hold over production.

The commercial monopolies shaped not only the form and dynamics of rural exploitation, but also possibilities for accumulation on the part of Senegalese social groups not involved in agricultural production. By the 1930s the economic position of the once solid and prosperous Senegalese trading class had been irretrievably weakened (Amin 1969; 1971). Control over the main axes of colonial economy lay squarely in the hands of the French import–export houses. Senegalese commercial families that emerged as an influential force in the local economy in the 1700s and 1800s sought to protect their economic and social positions by other means. Many gained places within colonial administration, in the liberal professions (as lawyers, for example), and in the world of Senegalese municipal politics (see Chapter 3). Most Senegalese who remained active in *la traite* after 1930 became groundnut collectors or *factorerie* employees, working for the Lebanese and the maisons de commerce.

Industry, or lack thereof, before World War II

Interests vested in the *pacte colonial* were barriers to the development of industry in French West Africa. The hostility of French manufacturers toward the idea of industrial development in the colonies was directed full force at the AOF. Before World War II industry in the AOF was confined to activities auxiliary to the import–export trade: repair shops for ships, refrigeration houses, electricity generators, etc. Industry oriented toward the local market was practically nonexistent before the 1940s, thanks in part to the French government's vigorous efforts to discourage its development.

Colonial trade laws stipulated that locally manufactured goods be subject to special taxes in order to ensure that tariffs did not "discriminate" against metropolitan industries exporting to the AOF. There was no tariff-jumping rationale for

---

40. See Kay 1975:101, 120–3.

import substitution industry. Tight monetary union assured free convertibility between the French West African colonial franc and the French franc, and linked the two currencies at a fixed parity. No exchange rate fluctuations or exchange restrictions created incentives for local manufacturing of consumer goods. Colonial policy left all initiative in the hands of private French investors who showed little interest in such projects. Meanwhile, Senegalese entrepreneurs who did show interest in light manufacturing ventures were denied access to bank credit (Amin 1969). Factories in Dakar serving local consumer demand in the 1920s and 1930s were small and produced a narrow range of products: ice, carbonated drinks including beer, biscuits, and bricks. The food products were consumed primarily by Dakar's European population.[41]

Incentives for export processing were also mitigated by a variety of factors. Price collusion and market sharing arrangements among the maisons de commerce, and contract buying and selling between French manufacturers and the trading companies, reduced competition and uncertainty and worked to maintain the established structure of *la traite*.[42] Under these conditions, the development of export processing industry in Senegal was extremely slow, in spite of economies to be gained by local groundnut shelling and crushing. Small independent groundnut refineries producing edible oil for local consumption appeared in the 1920s.[43] These operations posed no threat to dominant interests until the late 1930s. Once imperial price supports for colonial commodities were extended to Senegalese groundnuts, exporting refined groundnut products to France became economically viable (Hopkins 1973:263). The Dakar manufacturers responded to this opportunity (see Table 2.2). In 1936 they exported 5,000 tons of refined groundnut products to France. The rapid development of the Senegal industries alarmed the owners of long-established groundnut oil refineries in Marseille.

This first significant step toward manufacturing in the AOF met with the defensive backlash of metropolitan producers. Although the Dakar firms were small, this case of competition between colonial and metropolitan industries became the *cause célèbre* of those committed to blocking the industrialization of the AOF.[44] In 1937 the French government responded to metropolitan producers'

---

41. See Suret-Canale 1968:49–50. In the Côte d'Ivoire, a French expatriate created a local cotton-spinning factory during World War I (Ets. Gonfreville, in Bouaké). This factory spun local cotton for sale to Ivoirian artisans. Its growth in the 1920s was nearly stagnant due to technical problems, insufficient cotton supplies, and difficulty in finding Ivoirians interested in working in the factory. This installation was written off as insignificant by the colonial authorities.

42. In the British colonies, by contrast, competitive conditions shaping the commodity trade encouraged merchant houses and manufacturers to seek ways to assure stable, low-cost supplies of African products by investing in local export processing. In Kenya export processing was a form of vertical integration that reinforced the position of British trading firms and manufacturers vis-à-vis their competitors (Swainson 1980:69–72). This did not happen in the AOF.

43. Five or six small groundnut refineries existed before 1930.

44. Mérat (1937:457) describes "*les conflits les plus violents*" between metropolitan and colonial industries in the 1930s. The development of cotton textile industries in Indochina, which began to export to Madagascar in 1934, was seen by French manufacturers as an extremely bad omen. They resolved not to let the same thing happen in the AOF. On the conflicts over the exports of the Dakar groundnut-processing firms, see Suret-Canale 1950; Coquery-Vidrovitch 1979:92; Moussa 1957:113–14.

Table 2.2. *AOF groundnut exports to France: Evolution of export processing,*
1905–59 (selected four-year averages in thousands of tons)

Years	Unshelled groundnuts	Shelled groundnuts	Groundnut oil
1905–9	145		
1915–19	177	22	0.07
1925–9	443	1	0.58
1930–4	409	13	1
1935–9	397	150	4
1940–4	20	162	19
1945–9	4	178	41
1955–9	7	314	98

Source: Institut de Science Economique Appliquée (ISEA), "Les Industries de Cap-Vert: Analyse d'un ensemble d'industries légères de l'Afrique Occidentale," Dakar, 1964.

demand for protection. The authorities placed a quota of 5,800 tons on imports to France of refined groundnut products. To prevent the emergence of new groundnut refineries in the AOF, the quota was reserved entirely for firms already established in Dakar.

Restrictions placed on the groundnut refineries in Senegal on the eve of World War II were a dramatic affirmation of France's commitment to the basic principles of the *pacte colonial*. Until the end of the 1930s, the colonial economy of the AOF revolved around *la traite* in its classic form: production of commodities needed by France and the sale of French manufactured goods. The strategic alliance with Senegalese religious leaders made increases in groundnut production possible, even at extremely low cost in terms of investment and effort on the part of the French government and the maisons de commerce. Protectionism within the empire and monopolistic control over AOF commerce were mutually reinforcing barriers to local economic development. The persistence of an *économie de traite* remained the most striking feature of the AOF economy.

WORLD WAR II AND THE UPDATED *PACTE COLONIAL*

In spite of France's best efforts, the empire never recovered from the blow of World War II. During the war, the Franco-African trading ensemble lost the coherence carefully constructed in the earlier period. When the war ended international and internal pressures threatened the very foundations of the Empire. The French reacted defensively in time-tested fashion with *repli sur l'empire*. Rearguard efforts to consolidate control over the colonies in Africa took on new urgency and importance as France lost its hold on territories in Indochina and North Africa. In the fifteen years that followed the war, 1945–60, France worked to expand the AOF economy within the framework of bilateral, Franco-African ties.

These were years of enormous significance for the postcolonial order in French West Africa, an order that the French did not even envision in 1945. They were especially significant years for Senegal. This territory was a primary target of France's major postwar innovation in the domain of economic policy: the attempt to invigorate the AOF economy through the investment of public and private capital. The postcolonial regime that was taking shape in Senegal in the 1950s (see Chapter 3) would inherit both the successes and the limits of France's efforts to stimulate growth in the late 1940s and 1950s.

The wartime economy

The AOF was under British naval blockade from 1940–2, when the federation was under Vichy control. From 1943 to the end of the war, the AOF was part of Free France and integrated in the Allied trading bloc. Wartime conditions affected both production and trade in the French West African colonies. Industry in French West Africa, long discouraged or obstructed by imperial trade policy, finally appeared as a result of the war. And for the first time since the 1920s, commodities produced in the AOF were sold on world markets outside the highly protected French trading zone, mostly to the Americans and the British.

During this period, imports from all sources were reduced drastically. Relative autarky stimulated the creation of import-substitution industries in the AOF to provide necessities in short supply.[45] The French administration was forced to allow and even encourage this process, not only to supply Dakar's population but also to maintain a flow of manufactured goods to the rural areas that would encourage peasants to continue producing export crops. During the war thirty licenses for the establishment of industrial enterprises were granted by the colonial authorities. The small factories set up to manufacture shoes, cigarettes, household goods, food products, construction materials (cement), tin cans, etc., were among the AOF's first import-substitution enterprises.[46] Much of what was manufactured was consumed in the urban areas; both Vichy France and the Allies resorted to crop requisitioning and forced export crop production as output fell and Dakar-centered commercial networks collapsed.[47]

The demands of Vichy France and the Allies for processed agricultural commodities (and the need to economize on scarce shipping space) overrode French manufacturers' traditional opposition to export-processing industry in the AOF. In 1940 the French government removed quotas limiting the export of processed groundnuts to France and French North Africa and encouraged metropolitan groundnut processors to set up refineries in Dakar. The first AOF subsidiaries of French industries were created and the older Senegal refineries stepped up pro-

---

45. For example, imports of petrol fell from 68,000 tons in 1939 to 6,700 tons in 1942. Imports of cotton textiles fell from 12,400 tons in 1939 to 1,200 tons in 1942. Imports recovered slightly after 1943, when the AOF began to receive supplies from the United States. On the effects of the blockade and war shortages on imports to the AOF, see *Notes Documentaires et Etudes*, no. 481 (1949): 13, 21; and République Française, Agence France Outre-Mer, "L'Economie de nos territoires d'outre-mer, 1938–1947," Paris: n.d. (1948?).
46. See Hopkins 1973:263; and Pfefferman 1968:3.
47. Exports of groundnuts from the AOF fell from 419,000 tons in 1940 to 114,000 tons in 1942 (Crowder 1978:276). On crop requisitioning, see ibid.

duction for export.[48] (See Table 2.2.) Saw mills, cotton ginning factories, and palm oil refineries appeared in other parts of the AOF.

Meanwhile, to meet emergency conditions the colonial administration of the AOF was granted sweeping new powers to regulate internal and external trade.[49] The war ushered in a period of strict economic *dirigisme* as AOF authorities assumed responsibility for controlling "the importation, exportation, sale, pricing, circulation, and use of all products and merchandise."[50] Under this regime all imports from France, and later all imports from the Allies, were subject to strict quotas, licensing, and currency controls. The Dakar Chamber of Commerce and newly formed associations of French trading firms worked closely with the colonial administration to divide import licenses and foreign exchange quotas among their members. To support the trading firms "that had contributed so much to building the empire," the main categories of imports were reserved for the largest maisons de commerce.[51] This system ensured that the dominant trading houses monopolized the importation of most consumer goods, including all textiles, during the war years. Internal controls on trade flows thus reinforced the positions that the French maisons de commerce had established in the prewar period, in spite of the fact that the AOF traded on world markets from 1942 until the end of the war. New industries, tight economic *dirigisme*, and the maisons de commerce survived the war to become important facts of economic life in the AOF in the postwar period.

France's efforts to revive the imperial economy

France emerged from the war impoverished, crippled by wartime destruction, and weakened as a European power. At a time when it felt that it needed colonies more than ever, France was besieged by demands for structural changes in the *pacte colonial*, and ultimately, for the dismantling of the imperial system. The anticolonialism of the United States weighed heavily on France.[52] Pressures for open, nondiscriminatory trade forced Europe's first steps toward a European

48. The old Marseille refinery, Lesieur, was the only French groundnut-processing industry to respond to the government's invitation. Additional refineries were set up in Soudan, Haute Volta, and Niger in 1941 and 1942. Exports of groundnut oil increased from less than 6,000 tons in 1938 to 31,000 tons in 1945. See "L'Industrie huilière au Sénégal," *Les Chroniques d'Outre-Mer*, no. 37 (1957).
49. Monguillot 1944; *Notes Documentaires et Etudes*, no. 481 (1946): 24; Guernier 1949:185–8; Jacquot 1963:19.
50. *Le Journal Officiel de l'AOF*, loi n. 379 du 14 mars 1942.
51. See *Le Journal Officiel de l'AOF*, *circulaire n. 566 du 18 août 1948*, for a review of the *période d'économie strictement dirigée*. See also ibid., loi n. 379 du 14 mars 1942; Monguillot 1944; and Guernier 1949:185–8.
52. The Americans pushed the idea of nondiscriminatory international trading relationships. Dismantling the insulated, imperial trading zones was a main target. Proclamations such as the United Nations Charter called for the self-determination of peoples, providing a moral foundation for American anticolonialism. The French saw the Americans' motives as much more instrumental. As one commentator explained: "La démission européenne en Afrique est un crime, vis-à-vis de l'Europe, comme vis-à-vis des Africains, abandonnés dès lors aux imperialismes américain ou moscovite" (Chardonnet 1956:75).

common market. France, clearly on the defensive, vowed to "uphold its commitments" to colonial peoples and to protect them from American imperialism. Yet cracks in the empire began to appear. Vietnam and Algeria mobilized against French domination. A new generation of African political leaders emerged to demand real efforts on the part of France to promote economic development. They demanded a measure of political autonomy as well. In 1944 de Gaulle had acknowledged the West African colonies' contribution to the war effort by promising as much.[53] International political currents and pressures gave the demands of colonized peoples a legitimacy that they had not enjoyed before the war. For France the problem of the postwar order was defined as stimulating forms of economic development that would strengthen, not loosen, the imperial system.

"Tightening economic links within the empire" was seen in France as the path to reconstruction.[54] The country needed raw materials to rebuild and to get industries running again, yet it lacked the foreign exchange to buy commodities on world markets. Importing from the colonies was the obvious solution. And after 1950 French consumer goods industries needed colonial markets even more than they had before the war. World markets overflowed with cheaper manufactured goods, especially textiles, produced by aggressive exporters: India, Japan, Brazil, Hong Kong, and the United States. Uncompetitive French industry, led again by the cotton textile industry, argued that it was doomed unless protected colonial outlets were assured for many decades to come.[55] France's forced withdrawal from Indochina and North Africa – the largest importers of French manufactured goods – was a major blow.[56] Holding onto the AOF, the only "assured" market for metropolitan exports, became all the more important. Given the weakness of the French economy in the immediate postwar years, the United States realized quickly that France's *repli sur l'empire* was in American interests, at least in the short run. If the colonies would help France to recover from the war, then so be it. The Americans moved the issue of decolonization in sub-Saharan Africa to the backburner. France proceeded to reintegrate the Franco-African economy.

Colonial planners understood that the success of their postwar efforts to use the

---

53. Over 100,000 soldiers from France's African colonies fought for the Allies between 1943–5. At the Brazzaville Conference of 1944, the French dismissed the idea of independence for the African colonies as "unthinkable," but advocated economic development and political-administrative reforms in French West Africa. "Development" included some type of industrialization ("avec prudence, sous contrôle des Pouvoirs Publics"). On the Brazzaville conference and its impact, see *Notes Documentaires et Etudes*, no. 481 (1946):14; Morgenthau 1964:37–41; Crowder 1968:498–502; and Crowder 1978:285–6.

54. "Reserrer les liens économiques entre la métropole et les territoires d'outre-mer" was the theme of postwar colonial policy. See Moussa 1957.

55. According to the French cotton textile industry (SGICF) in 1951, "it is necessary to envision a more or less long time period during which the protection of markets will be indispensable" (*Marchés Coloniaux*, no. 298 [1951]: 1,999).

56. Vietnam alone consumed 40 percent of the exports of the French cotton textile industry. Loss of the Algerian market and especially the Indochinese market caused "serious perturbations" in the industry (*Marchés Coloniaux*, no. 503 [2 juillet 1955]: 1,761, 1,765–72).

West African colonies to fuel the recovery of France hinged on their ability to increase the absorptive and productive capacities of the AOF. To fully exploit its hold on West African markets, France would be forced to update and modernize the *pacte colonial*. The basic model was the one defined in the earlier period: West Africa would produce commodities needed by France; French industry would supply manufactured goods consumed in the AOF.

Once again the French cotton textile industry embraced this formula enthusiastically. For textile exporters, the critical and immediate problem was that the capacity of West Africa to absorb French goods was extremely low.[57] The poverty of peasants in the AOF led to anemic demand. Textile producers along with the other exporting industries threw their weight behind the policy of French price supports for colonial export commodities. Price supports could be used to raise producer incomes, encourage the expansion of output, and make African peasants better consumers of French manufactured goods.

During the 1950s, scenarios for breathing new life into the *pacte colonial* were elaborated in detail by the French cotton textile industry.[58] The industry's publications featured glossy photos of well-dressed West African women picking cotton alongside photos of smiling French men working in French cotton mills, producing cloth for the colonies. With this prosperous image of integration in mind, French textile manufacturers mobilized behind one of France's major postwar innovations in agricultural development policy – the development of cotton cultivation to supply textile producers in France.[59]

Planners in France and in the colonies began to envision more complex scenarios to expand the Franco-African ensemble and ensure its coherence in the long run. By the late 1940s the creation of manufacturing subsidiaries of French firms in West Africa was accepted, in theory, as French industry's best defense against competition that would "inevitably" crop up in the colonies. "Competi-

---

57. Yearly per capita consumption of textile goods in France in 1934–8 was 5 kilos. In Morocco it was 2.2 kilos and in Algeria, 1.8 kilos. In the AOF, annual per capita consumption was 1.2 kilos (Carponnier 1959:282; Rabeil 1955:150). Overall, the total value of AOF external trade (exports and imports) was inferior to that of the Gold Coast. See Richard-Molard 1952:211.

58. Pierre de Calan, vice president of the SGICF, argued that "[l]'avenir de L'Union Française depend d'une politique de resserrement des liens qui unissent ses éléments. . . . Une intégration économique de plus en plus poussée est nécessaire. . . . Avant de construire l'Europe (le marché commun), la France doit réaliser une véritable Union Française" (*Marchés Coloniaux*, no. 503 [2 juillet 1955]: 1,758–60, 1,761–3). The industry's plan included "detaxing" French exports to the colonies, tighter restrictions on the use of foreign exchange to purchase of non-French textile goods, special measures against imports from Hong Kong, and price supports for African cotton and groundnut exports.

59. Cotton shortages remained a central problem of the French textile industry throughout the late 1940s and early 1950s. The French government rationed foreign exchange (dollars) to the French textile industry for cotton imports. Dollars for cotton purchases were also loaned to France under the Marshall Plan and through the U.S. Export–Import Bank. The SGICF pointed out that imports of raw materials used by the French textile industry equaled 18 percent of France's balance of trade deficit (*Marchés Coloniaux*, no. 298 [28 juillet 1951]: 2,007; ibid. [17 mai 1952]: 1,233). On French public and private investment in cotton cultivation in the AOF and AEF after World War II, see *Le Journal des Textiles*, 1951 (édition supplémentaire): 39.

tion from colonial industries could be fatal (*funeste*) to metropolitan industry. An equitable solution lies in the progressive transfer of French manufacturing capacity to the colonies."[60] Colonial authorities began to argue that metropolitan industry should take hold of colonial manufacturing branch by branch, driving for "complete symbiosis" of colonial and metropolitan industry. In spite of the logic of this argument, most of French industry continued to view the AOF just as the cotton textile industry did: as a market. They staked their hopes on the expansion of export crop production.[61]

The effort to increase both production and consumption in the AOF led to France's most important economic initiative of late colonial period. The prewar dictum that the colonies "pay their own way" was abandoned, clearing the way for hitherto unprecedented levels of public investment in the colonies. In 1946 major new public spending and investment programs for the AOF, funded mainly through grants from the French treasury, were inaugurated.[62] (See Table 2.3) Postwar French governments saw public spending as a way to accelerate overall rates of economic growth in the AOF, pave the way for French private investment, and reinvigorate Franco-African trade. Public investment was accompanied by a new commitment to economic planning. The state, henceforth, would assume an active role in the development of the colonial economy.

French public investment under the FIDES program (Fonds d'Investissement pour le Développement Economique et Social) was concentrated on communications and transport infrastructure (ports, roads, airports), research to develop new export crops needed by France (especially cotton), and urban public works (electricity, water). Twenty percent of total funds committed under the First Plan (1948–52) went to "social development": public health, higher education, urban housing, etc. Most investment was in Senegal, and most investment in Senegal was in Dakar. The development of infrastructure did facilitate private investment in industry. Yet less than 10 percent of all funds went directly into agriculture, the productive base of the French West African economy.[63]

---

60. Ministère des Colonies, Direction des Affaires Economiques, "Plan de moyens industriels correspondant au Plan Décennal d'Equipement National: Exposé Général," Paris, n.d. (1942?); Ministère des Colonies, Direction des Affaires Economiques, "Etudes sur l'industrialisation de l'AOF," Paris: 1944. By 1955 even the SGICF climbed aboard this bandwagon, arguing that it was "necessary to anticipate in the near future the transfer of some part of French industry to the colonies" (*Marchés Coloniaux*, no. 503 [2 juillet 1955]: 1,758–60).
61. All categories of private investment made up less than 20 percent of all capital inflow to the AOF between 1947 and 1952 (Thompson and Adloff 1958:258).
62. On the sources of the FIDES budget, see ibid., 253. They make the important and often-overlooked point that the colonial territories contributed some 20 percent of total FIDES funds. The metropolitan budget after 1948 also covered the salaries and perquisites of French bureaucrats and administrators in the AOF (costing about 4 billion FF per year). This commitment was extended to other public officials in 1956.
63. On the allocation of FIDES funds during the First Four-year Plan, see Thompson and Adloff 1958:255. Between 1948 and 1952, 64 percent of FIDES funds went into communications and transport infrastructure. On the neglect of agriculture in the first FIDES plan, see the Chambre de Commerce de Marseille 1953:236.

Table 2.3. *French public investment in the AOF*
(in million 1956 £ sterling)

Years	Million 1956 £ sterling
1931 to 1937	4.0
1947 to 1948	4.3
1949 to 1956	25.4

Source: Pfefferman 1968:16.

Herein lay the major limit to the success of the FIDES programs in reinvigorating the Senegalese economy, the economic hub of the federation and its primary market. Price supports for colonial commodities (set at about 15 percent above world prices), rather than investments that would enhance the productivity of land or labor, remained France's policy tool for expanding the output of export crops. In Senegal, export-oriented agriculture continued to draw its dynamism from extensive cultivation (exploiting virgin, rain-fed lands), the confréries that mobilized the labor of Mouride disciples, and increases in the amount of time that peasant households (including the migrant laborers called *navetanes*) devoted to groundnut production.[64]

While the colonial administration invested public funds in AOF infrastructure and tried to encourage French private investment, the French government continued to insist that the empire remain a virtually closed trading circuit. Tight trading ties between France and West Africa were quickly restored through the revival of the preferential trading regime and above all, through the use of monetary and exchange controls.[65] By 1951 82 percent of all AOF imports were supplied by France.[66] Reintegration into the French trading zone led immediately to runaway inflation as high-cost French goods replaced cheaper foreign goods on the AOF market. For African commodities, terms of trade deteriorated sharply. In terms of real purchasing power, a kilo of groundnuts was worth in the early 1950s only about 35 percent of what it was worth before the war.[67]

In part, the high costs of the trading zone reflected the fact that manufactured goods sold in the AOF came from France, and French industry was inefficient

64. The number of *navetanes* fell from an all-time high of almost 70,000 in 1938 to 12,000–21,000 from 1946–8. There was an influx during the 1949–55 period (51,000 and 43,000 for 1949 and 1955, respectively), and a secular fall thereafter, down to 8,000 in 1960. This system of migrant labor was officially abolished in 1963 (Founou-Tchuigoua 1981:59).
65. The creation of the Zone Franc was followed in 1945 by the introduction of the CFA (Colonies Françaises d'Afrique) franc.
66. LeDuc 1954:45. The trade flows went both ways. By the mid-1950s 70 percent of all imported food products consumed in France and 15 percent of France's imported inputs for processing industries came from the colonies (Moussa 1957:33).
67. *Marchés Coloniaux*, no. 550 (26 mai 1956): 1,500. The consumer price index for a basket of mostly imported goods (*consommation européenne*), base 100 in 1945, was 375 by 1954 (ibid. [22 mai 1954]: 1,491). On inflation, see also Thompson and Adloff 1958:446, 449.

Table 2.4. *French f.o.b. prices compared to world market prices:*
Goods imported to the AOF, 1954[a]

Product category	Ratio: French to world price	Part of AOF market supplied by France (in %)
Wheat flour	1.45	92
Sugar	1.88	95
Rice	1.20	88
Concentrated milk	1.72	
Butter	1.92	
Cheese	1.43	
Automobiles/trucks	1.30 (average)	73
Trucks	1.80–2.00	
Tractors	1.50–2.00	
Civil engineering equipment	1.70–2.00	
Electric machines, equipment	1.33	70–88
Enameled cookware	1.39–1.47	
Hardware	1.40–1.50	
Storm lamps	1.50–1.60	
Bicycles	1.20[b]	
Sewing machines	1.50	
Refrigerators	2.30–2.40	
Cotton textiles	1.30 (average)	72
Blankets	1.40–1.75	
Jute sacks	1.47[c]	

[a]free on board (f.o.b.).
[b]French f.o.b. price compared to British f.o.b. price.
[c]French f.o.b. price compared to Indian f.o.b. price.
Sources: Ministère de la France Outre-Mer, Direction des Affaires Economiques et du Plan, "Comparison des prix français et étrangers d'articles de consommation courante et biens d'équipement dans les Territoires d'Outre-Mer," février, 1954; Ministère de la France Outre-Mer, "Intégration actuelle des économies d'Outre-Mer et de la Métropole," mars 1954; and Ministère de la France Outre-Mer, "Intégration des économies de la Métropole et de l'AOF," mars 1954.

and uncompetitive by world standards. The f.o.b. prices of French manufactured goods and foodstuffs sold in the AOF ran 30–70 percent, sometimes more, above world market prices (see Table 2.4). The Zone Franc was closed to foreign competition precisely because high-cost French manufacturers wanted captive markets. AOF import taxes of 15–25 percent on French manufactured goods aggravated the cost problem. Above all, responsibility for the exorbitant retail prices of French consumer goods in the AOF lay in the monopolistic nature of control over the colonial import trade.[68] Freed from the pressures of competition, the maisons de commerce extracted price premiums or rents from the African consumer. On textiles, the leading category of consumer-goods imports, com-

68. Chafanel et Poncet, "Etude sur la structure de prix et l'organisation commerciale en AOF," 1955.

mercial margins at the importation-wholesale stage of distribution made up about 50 percent of final retail prices. Postwar economic policy did nothing to redress this situation; in fact, the trade controls of the 1950s helped the large French import–export firms to retain the dominant positions they established in the prewar period.

Inflation and declining terms of trade for African commodities were symptomatic of structural constraints inherent in metropolitan France's most optimistic scenarios for updating the *pacte colonial*. High costs limited the volume of French manufactured goods that the AOF could consume. High costs also constrained production. French capital goods cost 50–100 percent more in the AOF than they did in France (LeDuc 1954:47). Rural producers lost out on both sides of the dual flux of trade. Inflated prices for consumer goods reduced their capacity to invest in tools and fertilizers. In selling their crops, producers were penalized by the high costs of the export-marketing circuit. Internal transport and shipping between France and the colonies (a business reserved by law for French carriers) were expensive by British West African standards. These costs depressed prices paid to producers by noticeable margins in territories of the AOF that produced groundnuts and cotton.

The AOF's growing trade deficit with France reflected the Zone Franc trade imbalance in an acute and immediate way. Between the time the federation was formed in 1905 and World War II, the value of AOF imports exceeded that of AOF exports by 5–15 percent in all but three years. In the early- to mid-1950s, the value of imports exceeded that of exports by about 35 percent.[69] As AOF administrators and politicians often pointed out, France's willingness to buy West African commodities at a subsidized price about 15 percent above world market levels did not offset the trade imbalance; the colonies were "subsidizing" uncompetitive French industries at a rate of about 30 percent above world market prices. The *surprix* (price premium) of 7 billion French francs that the AOF earned by selling its exports on the protected French market in 1954 did not offset the *surprix* of at least 16 billion francs that the AOF paid that year for expensive French goods.

Colonial authorities argued that the trade restrictions were asphyxiating, strangling, and paralyzing the AOF economy. In 1954 the president of the *Grand Conseil* of the AOF argued that "[w]e must find a way to solve the problem of our commercial ties to lighten the charge that the AOF must bear. Exports cannot cover imports. . . Our contribution to the metropolitan economy puts us in a hopeless situation (*désespérée*)."[70] The message was clear: Imperial trade policies bled the West African colonies dry. Some administrators argued that freeing

---

69. République Française, Ministère de la France Outre-Mer, "L'Intégration des économies de la métropole et de l'AOF," Paris, mars 1954.

70. Ibid (statements of M. Boissier-Palun). See also reports of the Conférence des Gouverneurs de l'AOF (15 mai 1954) reported in *Marchés Coloniaux* (22 mai 1954): 1,490 and ibid. (29 mai 1954): 1,510–11; and Moussa 1957:82–3.

the AOF to trade on world markets was the only solution.[71] The French government did not accept this radical solution.

The makeshift solution consisted of continued reliance on colonial price supports for African commodities. Even if chronic trade deficits could be sustained over time, this solution to the problem of increasing AOF production and consumption could not work in the long run. If agricultural output increased as France hoped, the colonies would produce commodities that France could not absorb.[72] By the mid-1950s the AOF was producing coffee, lumber, cocoa, and bananas in excess of what France could consume, and the French market for groundnuts was nearly saturated (Moussa 1957:188–9). Colonial administrators realized the logical implications of these trends. Ultimately, the colonies would either be forced to limit production (and thus, consumption of imports), or to sell their commodities on world markets. If colonies did earn American dollars and British pounds by selling on the world market, could they still be forced to buy French manufactured goods? In the case of Senegal the dilemmas were most vexing. If Senegal were obliged to sell groundnuts on the world market (at low world market prices), it was unlikely that increases in production could be sustained. What would then happen to the colony that had long been France's best market in the AOF?

Post-World Wart II economic policy initiatives did not redress the fundamental problem of Senegal's economy: low rates of productivity in an export sector that was centered around a low-value crop. Although the FIDES investment programs did not tackle this problem directly, other forces helped to sustain the expansion of groundnut output in Senegal in the 1950s. Imperial price supports for groundnuts were maintained, the colonial regime regulated groundnut-buying prices in order to support producers' incomes, and "groundnut pioneering" continued, opening new lands to export crop production. As output expanded in the 1950s, established social relations of production in the groundnut basin were reproduced, as were the basic mechanisms of surplus extraction that had been forged in the earlier period.

Meanwhile, both commerce and industry evolved in Senegal in the 1950s in ways that worked to sustain old trading circuits organized around the importation and distribution of high-cost manufactured goods.

COMMERCE AND INDUSTRY IN THE POSTWAR AOF

While colonial planners sought to engineer economic growth and policy changes within the framework of established trading relations, the war and the world political economy of the 1950s modified the AOF economy in important ways. Dakar grew dramatically, the pace of the urban economy quickened, and trading

71. This position was outlined in what Thompson and Adloff (1958:256–7) identify as the Poilay report of February 1950, submitted to the Economic Council in October 1950. The report argued that "a lasting improvement [in AOF economic conditions] could be made . . . by freeing commercial exchanges between the overseas territories and the Metropole."
72. See *Notes Documentaires et Etudes*, no. 481 (1949): 26.

circuits became more complex. The postwar surge in Dakar's European and Lebanese population created a new type of demand for imports and urban services.[73] Immigration, government spending, and the Korean War commodities boom of 1950–2 brought new money into Senegal. Understanding the structure of control over the import trade during this period is key to explaining patterns of investment in import-substitution industry that emerged in the 1950s. Market conditions in the last decade of direct colonial rule set the Dakar textile industry on a course of development that was uninterrupted until the 1970s.

Exchange controls and import quotas

A comprehensive system of quantitative restrictions governed wartime imports to the AOF. After the war this system was put to work to reintegrate the AOF into France's trading zone. Quantitative restrictions proved far more effective in protecting French manufacturers against foreign competition on AOF markets than the tariffs of 30–70 percent levied against non-French goods (Moussa 1957:181). This trading regime, however, ran counter to the principles of the newly formed Organisation Européenne de Coopération Economique (OECE), which called for trade liberalization among its members.[74] To comply with OECE rules, France took a reluctant and cautious step toward liberalizing AOF trade in the early 1950s. For a limited range of product categories, quantitative restrictions on imports from OECE countries were removed. Import tariffs were also reduced slightly. The colonial administration hoped that the inflow of foreign goods, limited though it was, would help control inflation in the AOF. For most French exporters, the *libération des échanges* was a bad omen but not, for the moment, a major challenge to their established positions on the AOF market.

To compensate for the measure of trade protection lost through liberalization, France began to rely heavily on tight monetary and foreign exchange controls. These controls proved to be an extremely effective mechanism for insulating the AOF market from foreign competition. Under the monetary control system, all foreign imports required official authorization. The colonial administration drew up an annual *Programme Général des Importations* (bilateral trade accords with foreign countries), a dollar program, and a sterling program. Import licenses and

---

73. Dakar's European population increased from 6,500 in 1936 to 15,000 in 1948, and to 30,000 in 1960. The Lebanese population in Senegal grew from 8,000 in 1953 to 10,000 in 1960.
74. Although the OECE did not insist on immediate extension of the trade liberalization program to metropole–colonial exchange, colonial trade was included in the long-term plan. Liberalization was introduced in metropolitan France in 1950 and extended to cover 25 percent of the AOF import trade at the end of that year. In metropolitan France the program was quickly abandoned. Quantitative restrictions on foreign products imported to France were reimposed in February 1952. The AOF liberalization program, however, was elaborated in 1953 and remained in place until 1957 when it was revoked and replaced by a universal quota system. Of all the OECE countries, France was the most resistant to trade liberalization and the slowest to make moves in this direction. See *Marchés Coloniaux*, no. 298 (28 juillet 1951): ibid., no. 438 (3 avril 1954): 876; ibid., no. 503 (2 juillet 1955): 1,813, 1,821; ibid., no. 550 (26 mai 1956): 1,499; Jacquot 1963:63–4.

foreign exchange quotas were allocated to commercial firms up to the global limits specified under each program. The use of each currency quota was restricted to a product category designated by the administration (for example, $150,000 for American trucks).[75] Quantitative restrictions and currency rationing were effective means of limiting commercial exchange between the AOF and countries outside the Zone Franc. In 1952 about 80 percent of all AOF imports were supplied by France. By 1954 this figure had dropped to about 75 percent. In terms of absolute value, however, French exports to the AOF had increased.[76]

The list of "liberalized" product categories was narrow, constituting only 25 percent of the AOF's total import bill. Quantitative restrictions still governed importation in 350 product categories. The French industry most affected by liberalization was the cotton textile industry. How this industry fared under the *libération des échanges* is a good indicator of how the system worked in practice. By 1949 textile sales in the AOF had regained prewar levels, and French cotton goods reestablished their position as leading the category of imports. West African purchases of textiles grew in the early 1950s when the boom in world commodity prices increased rural incomes.[77] Under the *libération des échanges* program, quantitative restrictions on solid color (unprinted) cotton fabrics were removed in mid-1953. This left tariffs of 15–20 percent as French manufacturers' only defense against West European exporters.[78] Liberalization upset French manufacturers a great deal – it reduced their share of this market from about 80 percent to 50–60 percent. Markets for French textile products not subjected to liberalization remained secure. The French textile industry's market share in these categories increased from 75 percent in 1950 to about 85 percent by 1954. Overall, the French textile industry supplied about 70 percent of all textile goods sold in the AOF in the mid-1950s.[79]

That the French textile industry controlled 70 percent of the AOF market in the 1950s is an important fact. It demonstrates the efficacy of postwar trade and currency restrictions in protecting high-cost French manufacturers from foreign competition. Although the *libération des échanges* did little to open the AOF to non-French manufactured goods, its lesson was not lost on French manufactur-

---

75. There was a loophole in this system. Firms exporting AOF commodities to buyers outside the Zone Franc could use the foreign exchange earned in this way (called Comptes EFAc [Exports, Frais Accessoires]) to finance importation of non-French goods to the AOF. In 1954 the colonial administration placed restrictions on use of EFAc accounts to limit the importation of goods from Japan, Hong Kong, and India. These measures were taken in response to French manufacturers' protests that the use of EFAc accounts was hurting their West African markets.
76. Ministère de la France d'Outre-Mer, "L'Intégration des économies de la métropole et l'AOF," Paris, mars 1954.
77. Consumption of unprinted fabrics increased by 25 percent between 1950 and 1954, while consumption of prints, blankets, and knits more than doubled. This was partially a function of the changing structure of demand. Prints became popular in the AOF after World War II.
78. Meanwhile, quotas still governed imports in this product category from non-European exporters, Japan in particular.
79. See *Marchés Coloniaux*, no. 503 [2 juillet 1955]: 1,811, 1,813, 1,820–1; ibid., no. 550 [26 mai 1956]: 1,499.

Table 2.5. *Senegal: Percentage of all
textile imports supplied by France,
1912–63*[a]

Year	%
1912[b]	16.3
1922	15.3
1929	36.0
1933	37.4
1934	41.8
1935	69.2
1937	69.8
1946	82.4
1948	39.9
1950	78.0
1951	86.0
1952	82.0
1954	73.0
1963	78.0

[a]Figures for 1935–54 refer to Senegal and
Soudan Français.
[b]1912–13.
Sources: Rabeil 1955:1953; *Marchés Coloniaux*, 2 juillet 1955:1813; Carponnier 1959:
260; *Le Moniteur Africain du Commerce et de
l'Industrie*, n. 81, 20 avril 1963:11.

ers. When protectionist trade controls were relaxed, French products quickly lost
ground to foreign competition.[80]

Maisons de commerce confront independent traders

The 1940s and 1950s were a period of rapid change in the role and structure
of the French maisons de commerce. Before the war these horizontally- and
vertically-integrated French trading conglomerates controlled nearly all aspects
of the AOF export–import trade. These arrangements began to give way in the
expansionary and inflationary climate of the 1950s. Changes in the commercial
sector set in motion during this period played a critical role in the rise of the
Dakar textile industry. They were also important in defining the possibilities that

80. The SGICF wrote that "the position of the French cotton textile industry has become difficult
over these last few months because of the development of foreign imports within the framework
of measures connected with the *libération des échanges*. If the 'liberalizing' measures are
maintained, the cotton textile industry will suffer falls in sales that are even more acute than
those that have been connected with the recent deterioration of [the industry's] market position"
(*Marchés Coloniaux*, no. 503 [2 juillet 1955]: 1,767–8). See also Rabeil 1955:152.

were open to Senegal's postcolonial regime as it began to reorganize trading circuits to its own advantage in the 1960s.

In the late 1930s, the maisons de commerce operated hundreds of trading posts in Senegal's groundnut basin. During the war *la traite* was disorganized completely and many of the up-country posts closed down. When the rural economy recovered after the war, *la traite* was a less profitable business than it had been. To encourage production and maintain rural purchasing power, the colonial administration began to regulate groundnut buying prices in favor of producers. This kind of regulation cut into commercial margins.[81] For the large trading houses, operating and overhead costs also increased. Given these new considerations, the maisons de commerce left the postwar reopening of most of the smaller trading posts to independent traders.[82]

The Lebanese, most of them former agents of the French firms, emerged as the dominant independent traders in Senegal's rural areas in the late 1940s and 1950s. Although they now operated on their own account, the Lebanese remained intermediaries in trading circuits controlled by the maisons de commerce. The French firms sold imported merchandise to the Lebanese on credit and collected groundnuts from the independently owned trading posts. Dealings with independent Lebanese traders accounted for over half of the French firms' business by the mid-1950s. Many Lebanese traders did very well for themselves on this basis. For the maisons de commerce, the new system proved to be quite efficient. They cut costs by concentrating rural operations in several large buying and selling points and by cutting back European staff in the rural areas. The costs of collecting groundnuts were also reduced substantially. Risks (and profits) of extending consumer credit to the peasants were passed on to the Lebanese.

In the urban areas, the colonial trading houses faced a kind of competition that they had never before experienced in the AOF. Importation was their exclusive domain in the prewar period. During the war some independent Lebanese and French businessmen in Dakar accumulated large treasuries. When peace came, these small-scale traders began to import European consumer goods to the AOF to meet pent-up demand.[83] Often they worked with upstart exporters in France, creating new currents of trade on the margins of the import–export economy controlled by the maisons de commerce. Rapid growth of the urban economy, increases in Dakar's European population, and the establishment of commercial air links between Europe and the colonies expanded opportunities for these independent merchants. The development of *"importations privées"* was the

81. After the rises in world prices of 1950–2, "the political problem posed by the fall in world groundnut prices [from 1953 on] and the necessity of assuring a certain price stability has led to more and more rigorous regulation [of the groundnut buying circuit], oriented always in favor of the producers and to the detriment of commercial intermediaries" (Charbonneau 1961:47). In the effort to control inflation in the 1950s, the administration also began to regulate the prices of food staples (rice, sugar, tea, cooking oil, etc.). This also cut into commercial margins (idem 1961:28–9).
82. On this change, see Thompson and Adloff 1958:439; and Charbonneau 1961:32, 88.
83. *Marchés Coloniaux* (29 septembre 1956): 2,595.

most dramatic postwar change in the structure of control over AOF trade. The maisons de commerce lost their monopoly over importation.

In some lines of commerce independent traders enjoyed a decisive advantage. As in the case of rural trade, their overhead costs were much lower. Because they operated on a small scale and were extremely flexible, they could import specialty goods in small lots (garments, gourmet foods, books) to supply Dakar's growing white-collar population. Independent traders traveled frequently to Europe, kept abreast of trends in fashion, and turned over stocks quickly. Scouting markets in Europe for good deals, they purchased goods at liquidation prices from manufacturers who did not have established ties to the maisons de commerce. Many opened their own boutiques in Dakar. Freelance French importers in Dakar catered to local European demand and did not represent a real threat to the maisons de commerce.[84] The Lebanese were a different matter.

Independent Lebanese importers represented a challenge to the old colonial trading houses, a challenge that could only become more serious in the medium- to long-run. The Lebanese were competitive traders, they were numerous, and they were interested in underselling the large French trading companies on Senegal's urban markets. Because the maisons de commerce collected such wide commercial margins, they invited – and were vulnerable to – this kind of competition. The *libération des échanges* opened a door for Lebanese traders, and they began to import textile goods in liberalized product categories from both France and other OECE countries. In the 1950s Lebanese importers made major inroads in the urban market for textiles.

The maisons de commerce coped with the rise of independent traders by moving out of activities that they could not control. A new division of labor in the import trade emerged as the old trading companies developed new strategies to retain their dominant positions. The maisons de commerce left retail and competitive segments of the import trade (specialty goods, garments, etc.) to the independent traders and concentrated on the most profitable commercial activities. Independent traders represented no threat in activities requiring bank credit, a great deal of capital or technical expertise, or political access and clout.

Large-scale import, export, and wholesale operations that were the backbone of *la traite* in Senegal remained the stronghold of the European commercial conglomerates. The colonial administration protected their monopoly over exportation by using commercial regulations to eliminate independent exporters.[85]

84. Ibid.
85. The hike in groundnut prices on the world market from 1950–2 encouraged independent French and Lebanese exporters to enter the groundnut trade. The "commercial fever" of 1950–2 allowed some independent exporters to make "scandalous fortunes." When world market prices began to fall, the AOF administration intervened to eliminate the independent exporters and "the market perturbations and abuses they caused." The administration set dates for the opening and closing of *la traite*, fixed buying and selling prices, set up quality-control standards, and enacted new laws regulating exportation. The regulations squeezed independents out of the export business. The maisons de commerce tightened their hold on intermediaries in the rural areas to make sure that independent exporters did not reemerge (Charbonneau 1961:45–6, 105).

The maisons de commerce continued to monopolize the importation and whole-sale distribution of goods imported in huge quantities and destined for the rural areas: food staples and basic consumer goods. Under these conditions the trading conglomerates remained virtually unchallenged as rural wholesalers. They continued to finance the purchase of the groundnut crop and to sell imported manufactured goods to rural merchants on credit.

Meanwhile, these firms expanded aggressively into what was rapidly becoming the most lucrative niche of AOF trade: importation and distribution of big-ticket items. Capital goods, vehicles, large household appliances (e.g. refrigerators), and most imports financed under the FIDES programs were handled exclusively by the largest maisons de commerce. To protect their most profitable markets, these companies established exclusive-buyer contracts with foreign and French manufacturers (General Electric, Renault, etc.) and obtained monopoly rights to import brand-name products.

The maisons de commerce relied on political clout to retain control over lucrative segments of consumer-goods trade that were threatened by competition from independent traders. In the late 1940s all import quotas and foreign-exchange allocations were reserved explicitly for the maisons de commerce.[86] This system was maintained in practice in the 1950s. The Dakar Chamber of Commerce was controlled by the old French commercial houses; it worked hand-in-hand with the authorities in drawing up annual import programs and allocating import quotas. Independent traders, and above all the Lebanese, could not crack this "in-house" system. French trading companies tried to justify their united front against Lebanese importers by branding these upstarts as speculative, un-scrupulous merchants who were disorganizing normal trading patterns in the AOF. French business publications publicized smuggling incidents involving Lebanese and lambasted "unfair Lebanese business practices" (defined, for example, as employing family members and overcrowding shops with merchandise).[87]

Lebanese merchants were thus excluded from the most profitable segments of the textile trade. Printed cotton fabrics called *imprimés* and the staple textile goods produced in the French territories of India (Pondichéry) accounted for the bulk of the AOF textile market.[88] French maisons de commerce continued to

86. From 1942 to 1949, the administration allocated all import licenses, currency quotas, and contracts to import in the name of the administration on the basis of "*antériorité*" (i.e., to the firms that handled the bulk of AOF trade from 1938 to 1941). The administration wanted to do away with this system in 1947 to introduce a degree of competition into the import trade. The Dakar Chamber of Commerce successfully opposed this initiative. In 1948, however, the system of *antériorité* was modified slightly: 75 percent, rather than 100 percent of all quotas were allocated on this basis. For textile goods, a larger share was reserved for the French firms with "*antériorité.*" In July 1949 the system of *antériorité* was replaced by a system of competitive bidding for import quotas and currency rations. The bids were reviewed and contracts awarded by the Chamber of Commerce (*Le Journal Officiel de l'AOF*, Circulaire n. 566 du 18 août 1948: 979; ibid., arrêté n. 3,771 du 21 juillet 1949; Guernier 1949:185–8, 199–200).
87. *Marchés Coloniaux* (29 septembre 1956): 2,592–3; Charbonneau 1961:103.
88. Four French-owned textile mills in Pondichéry (Les Etablissements Français de l'Inde) produced cotton cloth that was exported throughout the empire. Because Pondichéry was part of the Union

monopolize the importation of these goods. Monopoly control ensured that profit margins remained very high. The large French companies were determined not to lose control over this part of the market. Administrative controls over importation ensured that they did not.

The 1950s were enormously profitable years for the largest maisons de commerce. Although costs rose and competition emerged on the fringes of urban trade, the postwar growth of the AOF economy created new commercial opportunities that were far more lucrative than those left to independent traders. At the same time the maisons de commerce consolidated their hold over the mainstays of AOF commerce in the export, import, and wholesale trades. The reorganization they undertook during this period strengthened and modernized their commercial operations in ways that would help them to retain their positions as importers and sellers of manufactured goods in Senegal after independence.

Light industry: Breakthrough of the 1950s

Changes in the postwar AOF – FIDES investment programs, France's acceptance of the idea of industrial development in West Africa, the specter of trade liberalization, growth of Dakar, and creeping competition in AOF trade – are all important in explaining the timing and character of industrial investment in Dakar during the critical decade of the 1950s. Continuities that spanned the historical divide of World War II are equally important in understanding postwar industrialization. The maisons de commerce continued to control the importation of manufactured goods destined for rural markets (including staple textile goods); costs of production throughout the Franco-African trading zone remained high; and constraints on increasing agricultural productivity and rural incomes in Senegal persisted. These continuities go far in explaining the limits of the process of light industrialization that developed during the 1950s and 1960s.

The development of export-processing industry accelerated in the late 1940s and 1950. Groundnut refineries in Senegal expanded dramatically, as did industries in other parts of the AOF processing fruit, lumber, palm oil, and cotton. In general, however, between 1945 and 1953 French manufacturers saw no equally compelling rationale for investment in industry serving the local consumer market.

The small consumer-goods factories established during World War II were created for the most part by independent French and Lebanese entrepreneurs living in the colonies, not by major French companies. These small factories expanded between 1945 and 1949, when postwar scarcities provided a form of

---

Française and the Zone Franc, these products entered the colonies on the same terms as goods produced in metropolitan France. When trading became more competitive after World War II, new rules were drawn up to ensure that the maisons de commerce retained a monopoly over the export of Pondichéry products. From 1942–8, licenses to import Pondichéry goods to the AOF were allocated on the basis of *antériorité*. After 1948 the quotas for the importation of Pondichéry textiles were reserved for importers who could produce an export license granted by the French administration in Pondichéry. This system protected the monopoly of the maisons de commerce over Pondichéry–AOF trade. See *Marchés Coloniaux*, no. 20 (30 mai 1946); *Le Journal Officiel de l'AOF*, Circulaire n. 566 du 18 août 1948: 980, 982.

protection from imports. When normal trading relations between the AOF and France were reestablished at the end of 1949, however, French manufactured goods poured into the AOF. This caused grave and sometimes fatal problems for the small consumer-goods industries in Dakar. Between 1949 and 1953 metro-politan manufacturers launched new campaigns against colonial industry in an effort to retain control over export markets.[89] Price wars closed down some AOF manufacturing firms that had been created in the 1940s. The balance of power lay on the side of the dominant exporters and the colonial maisons de commerce, and until about 1952 very few of them were interested in industrial development in Senegal.

French manufacturers were hard-pressed to find reasons to invest in Dakar under these conditions. As the colonial administration itself had argued, costs of industrial-scale manufacturing were considerably higher in the AOF than they were in France. Conventional wisdom held that the costs of setting up a factory in the AOF were the double of what they were in France. Initial costs of credit, transport, spare parts, and capital goods were compounded by the high cost of operations in Dakar. Most imported capital goods and inputs were taxed at a rate of 15–20 percent.[90] Utilities rates were "infinitely" higher than they were in France. In 1950 the city of Dakar boasted the world's most expensive electricity.

89. The two most celebrated cases are "l'affaire des Grands Moulins de Dakar" and the Melia ruling. The case of the Grands Moulins de Dakar involved a large flour mill in Dakar. Construc-tion of this firm was completed in 1947. It did not begin operations until 1955. Opening was blocked for seven years by metropolitan firms and the maisons de commerce. Traditional exporters were determined not to allow this activity to escape their control (Moussa 1957:117–99). Léopold Senghor denounced the exporters' resistance to the opening of the Dakar flour mill in the French National Assembly: "Dans le cadre du cas des Grands Moulins de Dakar, le pacte colonial s'y montre sous son visage le plus pur et le plus odieux" (*Procès Verbal de l'Assemblée Nationale Française*, 8 avril 1954: 1, 912). The Melia ruling of 1950 was the outcome of a legal case brought by an Algerian cigarette factory (Société Melia) against the AOF administration. In 1943 and 1946 the AOF administration imposed taxes on imported tobacco products of all origins. The Algerian company protested, arguing that these taxes, which in effect protected the AOF tobacco processing industry against competition from goods produced within the Zone Franc, ran counter to the Loi Douanière de 1928 (free trade within the Zone Franc). The 1950 ruling in favor of the Algerian company was a blow to manufacturing industry in the AOF. The Melia ruling meant that the AOF administration could not impose taxes on imports from France or any other part of the Zone Franc to protect nascent AOF industry (Moussa 1957:107, 263–4; Jacquot 1963:110; Suret-Canale 1968:51).
90. Michel Beaulieu ("Les Industries textiles en AOF," *Marchés Coloniaux* [2 juillet 1955]: 1,822) argued that the high costs of local production were aggravated seriously by the AOF tax regime. "Capital goods are subject to heavy surcharges: import taxes of 5–15 percent for French goods and much more for non-French goods. After import taxes are added to the c.i.f. value of the equipment, the total is taxed again at a rate of 8 percent. This last tax is called the *taxe de compensation* [designed to offset any advantage that local manufacturers may have over metro-politan industry]. The locally manufactured product is also burdened by taxes: the *taxe de transaction, taxe locale sur le chiffre d'affaires*, and the *taxe de consommation*. In brief, the tax regime of the AOF is a regime of *fiscalité en cascade*. . . . This tax regime constitutes a handicap (*frein*) on the local industry and is the cause of a *véritable malaise* for industries recently installed in the AOF."

Industrial labor in the AOF was also deemed to be extremely expensive because productivity was so low.[91] Overall, high costs of production made it difficult for most local industry to compete with imports, even imports from France.

The reticence of French manufacturers to invest was a great disappointment to the colonial administration and local political leaders. In the mid-1950s the French government and the colonial administration adopted more direct measures to stimulate French private investment. A colonial "investment code" was announced in December 1953. It represented the government's first effort to use tax and tariff policy to give colonial industry a clearer advantage over French exporters.[92] Colonial authorities, still confident in the future, guaranteed that investors would enjoy these tax and tariff preferences for the next fifteen to twenty-five years. Large industries would be protected against local competition: Production monopolies, granted and enforced by the state, gave first entrants a formidable advantage. To make the offer even more attractive, the Caisse Centrale de la France d'Outre-Mer began to offer state-subsidized loans to French investors.

These innovations in colonial economic policy were not only the cause, but also a consequence, of a gradual change in French manufacturers' attitudes toward colonial industry.[93] Decolonization was not on the agenda in the mid-1950s, and French investors regarded French sovereignty in West Africa as a stable factor. They began to realize, however, that changes in the economic ties between France and the AOF were imminent and inevitable. African political leaders demanded industrialization because they saw it as a way of transcending limits to growth imposed by France's strict mercantilism of the earlier period.[94] OECE plans for more aggressive moves toward trade liberalization also forced French manufacturers to question the security of their West African markets. Direct investment began to look like a way of protecting the AOF market from foreign competition.

91. On high costs of production, see LeDuc 1953; Moussa 1957:109–11; Suret-Canale 1968:35. The labor productivity at the textile factor Ets. Gonfreville in Bouaké, Côte d'Ivoire, was 30 percent of productivity rates in the French textile industry.

92. The investment code of 31 December 1953 offered a "Convention d'Etablissement" or a "Contrat Fiscal de Longue Durée." The code assured private investors "stability in rates and rules of application of taxes of every kind and stability in general juridical, economic, financial conditions affecting local industry." Conditions affecting local industry included free repatriation of capital and free exchange within the Zone Franc, freedom in recruitment of personnel, etc. See Thompson and Adloff 1958:448; Wade 1959:186–92; SONED 1977a:40–3.

93. "A very distinct movement is manifesting itself in *les milieux capitalistes français* that are interested in overseas investment. . . . [They want] to obtain for the Assemblées Territoriales et les Grands Conseils [of the AOF] the power to establish Conventions d'Etablissement [with private French manufacturing firms]" (Moussa 1957:160–1). Meanwhile, the Dakar association of French-owned industries (SPIDS) pushed for the raising of protective tariff barriers to insulate infant industry in Dakar from competition (*Africa* [Dakar], nos. 3–4 [juin–juillet 1958]: 17).

94. At the time, the fact that this industry would be wholly French-owned was not an issue. African political leaders argued for policies that would foster the growth of established French manufacturing firms and encourage new investment on the part of French industry. See Senghor's eloquent defense of the Grands Moulins de Dakar (*Procès Verbal de l'Assemblée Nationale Française*, séance du 8 avril 1954: 1,912).

Table 2.6. *Manufacturing in Senegal circa 1960, production, value-added, and employment (current prices in billion CFA)*

Subsector	Production (1959)	Value-added (1959)	Employment[a] (1965)	Firms with 50–199 workers[b] (1963)	Firms with over 200 workers[b] (1963)
Groundnut-oil production	14.75	3.69	2750	3	4
Foodstuffs (incl. canning)	11.29	4.22	2600	11	3
Textiles and leather	4.09	1.40	3250	6	6
Mechanical/elec. industries[c]	5.45	1.42		12	2
Chemical industries	1.16	0.45		4	1
Tobacco/matches	1.88	1.15			2
Construction materials	1.44	0.63		3	1
Wood industries	1.28	0.41		3[d]	1
Paper and printing	0.85	0.30			
Misc.	0.14	0.08			
Total	42.33	13.75	11,480	42	20
% of GDP	8%				

Notes
[a]i.e., number of workers.
[b]i.e., number of firms.
[c]Mechanical and electrical industries.
[d]Wood and packaging industries only.
Sources: Institut de Science Economique Appliquée (ISEA), "Les Industries de Cap-Vert: Analyse d'un ensemble d'industries légères de l'Afrique Occidentale," Dakar, 1964; Pfefferman 1968:4, 277–8; World Bank 1974:282–3.

The process of "transferring manufacturing capacity from the metropole to the colonies" thus began in earnest in 1954. Existing consumer-goods industries expanded and new firms were created. Most of the new firms were set up in Dakar, the transportation, administrative, trading hub of the AOF and the site of extensive postwar investment in economic infrastructure. Cost-of-production incentives, however, remained very weak. Commercial incentives are what drove the expansion of light industry in the 1950s. French manufacturers invested in Dakar because they saw local production as a way of protecting their access to West African markets in the long run, and not because they hoped to reduce costs of production. Their calculations were predicated on the assumption that the state would continue to restrict competition in the import trade. This is a fact of cardinal importance in explaining the vulnerabilities and interests of the French manufacturers who invested in Senegal during this period. In 1958 the future of the federation, and indeed of French colonialism in West Africa, became uncertain. Investment in industry slowed dramatically.

By the end of the decade, about 150 industrial firms existed in Dakar (see Table 2.6). Of these, all but a handful were created after 1942. Together, they employed about 12,000 people. About two dozen "large firms" in Dakar employed over 200 workers, and about 100 small firms had less than 50 employees. Most of Dakar's industries produced light consumer goods for the AOF market: shoes, textiles, processed foods and beverages, soap and cosmetics, basic pharmaceutical products, tobacco products, etc. French manufacturers with established stakes in the AOF market emerged as the largest investors in consumer-goods industries in the 1950s, when some industrial development began to look inevitable and when advantages were to be had by the first entrant. Some Lebanese entrepreneurs invested capital that they had accumulated in wartime commerce, most notably in foodstuff-processing firms (beverages, biscuits, confectionery goods).

The Dakar textile industry: Difficult start

Forces that shaped the rise of light industry in Dakar after World War II were manifest in the textile-manufacturing sector in particularly stark ways. In general, the French textile industry did not respond to political and economic changes of the 1940s and 1950s by rushing to invest in the AOF. French textile manufacturers were never known for their interest in bold investment strategies that would reinforce their competitive positions on domestic or foreign markets. On the contrary, the industry was notorious for its dependence on political controls that created captive markets for its uncompetitive goods. The conservative French textile industry responded to changes on the international scene and within the AOF with new cries for protectionism, for a stronger and' more insulated Zone Franc, and for a new lease on the *pacte colonial*.

Yet the French textile industry did not wield its political clout to oppose the creation of the first textile factories in Dakar in the 1950s. Why not? First, the local industries were quite small, were not seen by most metropolitan exporters as economically viable firms, and were not expected to survive. Second, the textile producers' association, the SGICF, believed that the existence of a few local firms would reinforce the colonial administration's resolve to keep cheap foreign textile goods off the AOF market.[95] Foreign goods represented the real threat, not the firms in Dakar. This logic may have been short-sighted, but it was not fundamentally incorrect. In spite of the creation of five or six factories producing textile products in Dakar, the AOF remained essentially a market for French exporters throughout the colonial period. In 1960 the local industry covered only 10 percent of Senegal's total demand for textile goods.[96] Yet these five or six small firms survived into the 1960s and 1970s to become the core of postcolonial Senegal's textile industry and some of the largest private employers in the country.

From its origins the textile industry in Dakar was linked inextricably to the

95. From interviews at Ets. Schaeffer, the Syndicat Textile d'Alsace (SGICF local), and the SGICF in Mulhouse and Paris, April 1986.
96. République Française, Ministère de la Coopération, 1965.

structure of control over trade that emerged during the last decade of colonial rule. Investment was motivated primarily by the commercial advantages that could be had by maneuvering within the politically engineered structure of local market control. In many ways the textile-manufacturing firms were probably typical of those established in Dakar before 1954. By and large, the investors in Senegal's textile industry were underdogs in the competition among metropolitan exporters for sales in the AOF. With the notable exception of those who created the largest firm, they were not leading exporters to the AOF. And like other industries established in the early postwar years, they had a particularly hard time.

Although AOF restrictions on imports provided an extraordinary measure of protection against the world's most competitive textile producers, the trade regime did not give local manufacturers much protection against industries exporting from France.[97] By 1950 78 percent of the textile goods sold in the AOF were made in France. French cloth was expensive by international standards, with c.i.f. prices running from 20–60 percent above average world market prices for similar goods (see Table 2.7). And AOF taxes of 15–20 percent were tacked onto the prices of French textiles. In spite of the high cost of these goods, the Dakar textile industry could not compete with French imports in the early 1950s. In 1954 the colonial administration tried to help the Dakar industry by easing its tax burden and providing some tariff breaks on inputs and capital goods. Still, the local textile industry lacked a clear advantage over French exporters. Under these conditions, why did anyone invest in local textile manufacturing?

Those who invested in Dakar textile factories realized that taxes on French imports did not provide a degree of protection sufficient to ensure profitable sales. In the investors' calculations, the advantage of local manufacturing lay in possibilities for undercutting competition at the distribution stage of the textile business. The French maisons de commerce collected commercial margins on textile goods of 30–50 percent. Investors hoped to undersell French goods not because they could produce more efficiently in Dakar, but because the colonial trading houses inflated wholesale and retail prices by such a wide margin. The chance to end-run the maisons de commerce provided the incentive for investment in local production.

The logic of this strategy was clear to all. As a result, the most hostile reaction to the establishment of local textile-manufacturing firms came from the maisons de commerce rather than metropolitan manufacturers. Ultimately these commercial conglomerates, the long-time arbiters of AOF trade, decided the fate and future of Dakar textile manufacturing. In the wake of the installation of several firms making textile goods, the maisons de commerce unleashed devastating price wars that brought the industry to its knees. Once they broke the independence of the local industry, the old trading houses proceeded to reconstitute it on their own terms.

97. Products from Hong Kong, Japan, India, and Eastern Europe – the least expensive goods on the world market – were barred completely from the AOF. About one-fourth of the AOF textile market was supplied by non-French manufacturers: Dutch and British sources, mostly. Import taxes on these goods were set at 60–100 percent of c.i.f. prices.

Table 2.7. *Some textile goods imported to the AOF:*
French versus non-French f.o.b. prices 1954[a]

Supplier	Prints (*imprimés*)		Gray cloth (*écru*)	
	f.o.b. price FF/meter	% under French f.o.b. price	f.o.b. price CFA/meter	% under French f.o.b. price
France	202		393	
Holland	159	27		
Great Britain	157	28	254	36
Belgium	150	35	252	35
W. Germany	162	25	243	39
Hong Kong			222	44
average: non-French	157	23	243	38

[a]free on board (f.o.b.).
Sources: Ministère de la France Outre-Mer, Direction des Affaires Economiques et du Plan, "Comparison des prix français et étrangers d'articles de consommation courante et biens d'équipement dans les Territoires d'Outre-Mer," février, 1954; *Marchés Coloniaux*, n. 503, 2 juillet 1955:1813.

The firms. Ets. Schaeffer et Cie. of Mulhouse, France, was the driving force behind the creation of the first spinning and weaving factory in Dakar.[98] This project was anomalous in the context of Dakar's nascent textile industry because Ets. Schaeffer was a major, well-established producer of textile goods destined for the AOF. Ets. Schaeffer began exporting *imprimés* (cotton prints) to the AOF in the 1930s, filling large contract orders for the maisons de commerce that dominated the AOF textile market. By the 1950s Ets. Schaeffer produced most of the French *imprimés* sold in French West Africa.

After World War II, political troubles in this firm's largest export market – French Indochina – led the company to question the long-term security of its markets in other parts of the French Empire. In the mid- to late-1940s Ets. Schaeffer joined the rush to create French-owned light industries in Morocco that was precipitated by the imminent demise of the preferential Franco-Moroccan trading regime.[99] Ets. Schaeffer was thus in good company when it invested in a cotton spinning and weaving plant in Fédala in 1947–8.[100] Profits from Fédala

98. Information about the postwar overseas investments of Ets. Schaeffer and about the creation of the Icotaf factory was obtained through interviews at Ets. Schaeffer and Schaeffer Engineering in Mulhouse and Pfastatt-Château, April 1986.

99. Many of the new French-owned industries in Morocco exported consumer goods to the AOF during the period of scarcity that followed the war. Morocco lost preferential access to the AOF market in 1952.

100. The Industrie Cotonnière Marocaine (ICOMA) in Fédala was owned by a corporation formed under the leadership of Ets. Schaeffer called the SAIC (Société Anonyme de l'Industrie Cotonnière). SAIC was comprised primarily of French industrialists from Alsace (Ets. Schaeffer, Cosine et Lambert, Caulliez). The ICOMA factory did not export to the AOF.

proved difficult to repatriate to France and were taxed heavily in Morocco. The company decided to create a factory in Dakar modeled after the Morocco plant to provide an outlet for this surplus capital.

Ets. Schaeffer created the Industrie Cotonnière Africaine (Icotaf) in Dakar in 1949.[101] The firm began operations in 1952 with 220 African workers and 18 French managers. It processed AOF cotton. The articles produced by Icotaf in the early 1950s were chosen carefully. Ets. Schaeffer was not interested in cutting into its own export markets and continued to manufacture in France the *imprimés* that it sold in the AOF. The Icotaf factory supplied a different niche of the AOF market: demand for lightweight and heavyweight, unicolor cotton fabrics. The firm concentrated on heavyweight cottons, called *drills*, and became the exclusive supplier of the largest AOF consumer of this fabric, the colonial administration.[102]

The owners of Icotaf planned to reach consumer markets by selling to independent wholesalers.[103] The cost of Icotaf products at the factory door would be about equal to the cost of French goods once they cleared Dakar customs. Ets. Schaeffer planned to carve out a position on the local market by limiting its commercial markup, thus underselling the dominant maisons de commerce. They did not expect a price war because *drills* were not a particularly interesting or profitable item for textile distributors. The production capacity of the Icotaf factory was only two million meters of fabric and one hundred tons of thread per year, not enough to flood any segment of the AOF market. Besides, Ets. Schaeffer had close business relations with maisons de commerce that handled the bulk of the AOF textile trade – the CNF and the CFAO. They worked together in France producing cotton prints destined for West Africa.

Three other textile-manufacturing firms were created in Dakar in the early 1950s. La Cotonnière de Cap Vert (CCV), a small cotton-spinning plant producing thread and yard, was set up in 1951. This firm was an offshoot of a family-

101. Icotaf's *capital social* (paid-up capital) totaled 200 million CFA francs. Ets. Schaeffer held 45 percent outright and was responsible for equipping and managing the firm. The Dollfus Mieg Corporation, through its holding company, TEXUNION, was a minority shareholder. SAIC held the balance of the shares (i.e., Ets. Schaeffer, Cosine et Lambert, and Caulliez, and possibly Riegal Textiles Corporation). M. Pierre Grosse (see note 103 below) owned a 1 percent share in Icotaf and sat with representatives of the firms mentioned above on the Board of Directors. Icotaf's original equipment consisted of 100 automatic looms and 5,000 spindles. Production capacity was 3 million meters of *drills* (various weights) and 125 tons of thread.

102. The colonial administration used *drills* for army, school, and workmen's uniforms. The investors in Icotaf were guaranteed rights to all administrative contracts for this product before the factory was installed in Dakar. *Drills* were also used for clothing in the forest zones of the AOF – Guinea and the Côte d'Ivoire. Icotaf also produced cotton thread that was sold on the local market.

103. Icotaf distributed some of its products through the independent French textile importing and distribution firm, Pierregrosse. Compared with the firms that dominated the West African textile trade (CFAO, CNF, and SCOA), Pierregrosse was a small upstart. It was quite successful in Senegal in the 1950s.

owned spinning industry, Filatures Dufour d'Armentières.[104] The Groupe Dufour did not export regularly to West Africa in the 1940s and was not tied to the maisons de commerce. It became interested in the AOF market after World War II when it modernized its installations in France and looked for a way to break into the West African market.

Groupe Dufour sent some of its used equipment to the AOF and installed it in CCV.[105] The Dakar firm received bulk shipments of thread produced by the parent firm in France, repackaged it, and sold it at the factory gate to artisans and Lebanese wholesalers. The Groupe Dufour created its own market in Dakar, avoiding established commercial circuits altogether. In 1955 used spinning equipment was installed in CCV. The factory began to spin about one hundred tons of thread a year, using cotton produced in French Soudan. Costs of production in Dakar, in spite of the low wages paid to African workers, were about what they were in France. Taxes on competing products allowed for cost overruns of at least 20 percent.

Another spinning and weaving factory was created at about the same time. The leading investor was an Alsace firm, Manufacture Hartmann et Fils, which produced and exported cotton textiles to Dakar in the 1940s. Hartmann et Fils operated outside of the dominant commercial circuits; it exported its products directly to independent Moroccan dealers in Dakar. In 1951 and 1952 these independent distributors – Ets. Ben Amour and Laraki – and Hartmann et Fils invested jointly in the Manufactures de Rufisque.[106]

The Manufactures de Rufisque produced very lightweight cotton fabrics that were widely used in the Sahel. It was a case of classic import substitution – the goods produced in Dakar were similar to those previously exported from France by the Alsacian firm. The factory came on line in 1953 and, like Icotaf, produced about two million meters of cloth a year. Products were distributed through Ben Amour et Laraki's existing commercial network. The owners counted on customs duties on French textile goods and quotas restricting the availability of cheaper non-French fabrics to provide some protection from import competition. They figured that their products would have an advantage over imported goods because their costs of distribution were low.

The Société de Teinture et Blanchissement Africaine (Sotiba) was yet another firm created in the early 1950s. It rose from humble beginnings to become

104. Interviews in Paris, April 1986 and at CCV in Dakar, December 1985.
105. CCV was a low-budget operation. Used equipment was installed in a defunct canning factory on the outskirts of Dakar that was purchased by the Groupe Dufour. The *capital social* (paid-up capital) of CCV totaled only 6 million CFA francs. In the 1950s this firm probably employed about fifty workers.
106. The Manufactures de Rufisque started with paid-up capital of 50 million CFA francs. New equipment was installed: 5,500 spindles and 150 automatic looms. Working below capacity (one shift a day), the firm produced 2.2 million meters of cloth in 1955. Cotton was supplied by the Office de Niger scheme in French Soudan (from interviews with former owners of Sotiba and Icotaf in Dakar, April 1985, and Mulhouse, April 1986).

Senegal's most powerful textile manufacturer after independence. Sotiba began as an artisanal-scale operation owned by two Morrocan textile distributors named MM. Mekouar and Tazi. They worked as distributors for a small-scale textile manufacturer and private exporter in Mulhouse, M. Riebel of Filatures et Tissages Kullman. Riebel built up a trading business in the 1940s by exporting his own products and other textiles that he purchased in Europe.[107] He ran one of the many small, independent firms operating at the margins of a trading system dominated by the maisons de commerce. In 1950 or 1951 Mekouar and Tazi set up a workshop, Sotiba, to dye fabrics received from Riebel.[108] Sotiba produced a local (but inferior) version of the indigo cloth (*guinée*) imported at the time from the French territory of Pondichéry. *Guinée* cloth was prized in the Sahel. Undertaking this activity in Dakar in the early 1950s proved to be a well-timed move.

In the 1940s and 1950s the maisons de commerce monopolized the AOF–Pondichéry trade in *guinée* cloth. In the early 1950s, however, Pondichéry began to look like an unreliable supplier. Uncertainty over the future political status of Pondichéry hung like a dark cloud over the *guinée* trade as France moved toward ceding the territory to the independent government of India. When that happened, Pondichéry textiles, like all Indian textile products, would be barred from the AOF market. Economic problems in Pondichéry compounded the problem of political uncertainty. In the early 1950s Pondichéry manufacturers were cut off from low-cost supplies of cotton and coal.[109] An indirect consequence of this was a series of major labor strikes in the Pondichéry textile mills between 1953 and 1955. Troubles in Pondichéry raised the cost of *guinée* cloth.

Sotiba's European suppliers seized the opportunity to invest an important sum of capital in the Dakar *guinée* dyeing firm. Riebel and a financier from Basel, Switzerland became majority owners. Mekouar became a minority shareholder. With new dyeing and bleaching equipment and indigo experts recruited from Pondichéry, the quality of Sotiba's products improved and production expanded. In 1955 Pondichéry was absorbed into India and the vast AOF market opened up to Sotiba.[110]

---

107. Riebel bought and sold semifinished and finished textile goods on the French market, working as a broker between manufacturers and between manufacturers and exporters. Traders filling this intermediary or brokerage role were called *fabricants-transformateurs*. Riebel also exported products to the AOF himself through his commercial firm in Mulhouse, Ets. Joseph Riebel.
108. From interviews with M. Mekouar in Dakar, April 1985 and with one of the original owners of Icotaf in Mulhouse, April 1986.
109. After 1945, the Pondichéry factories were supplied with cotton and coal by Pakistan. Cotton from Pakistan cost 40 percent more than the Indian cotton used in the Pondichéry mills before 1945. The cost of Pondichéry textiles climbed steadily, leading to the crises of 1953–5 (*Marchés Coloniaux*, no. 298 [28 juillet 1951]: 2,093–4; *Notes Documentaires et Etudes*, no. 481 [1949]: 25).
110. Sotiba's capacity of production in 1955 was 4.5 million meters of *guinée* and 0.9 million meters of bleached cotton fabric. Imports of similar fabrics from Pondichéry dropped from 40,000 tons in 1942 to about 10,000 tons in 1955. Sotiba's total paid-up capital in 1955 was 100 million CFA francs. The firm employed about 200 workers in 1958–9.

The four textile manufacturing firms established in Dakar in the early 1950s were the result of uncoordinated private initiatives. In the mid-1950s the colonial administration supported these efforts by easing the internal tax burden and import duties paid by the manufacturers.[111] Nevertheless, all the Dakar textile firms experienced great difficulties at the onset. First, costs of production in Dakar proved to be higher than anticipated. Second, the *libération des échanges* introduced OECE goods onto the AOF market in 1953–4 that were cheaper than similar goods imported from France. This hurt all the local firms except Sotiba.[112] The third, and greatest, problem for the nascent textile industry in Dakar was the maisons de commerce.

The price wars. The large French trading firms had an important stake in eliminating small-scale, independent exporters and importers from the Franco–AOF textile trade. Competition eroded their commercial margins and could present serious problems if it developed on a sizable scale. For the maisons de commerce, retaining control over wholesale trade was the key to blocking the rise of independent textile traders in the rural areas where their largest and most profitable markets lay. The local industries dealt with independent distributors, creating and strengthening trading circuits operating parallel to the long-established distribution networks of the colonial trading houses. In the early- to mid-1950s, the maisons de commerce unleashed a price war, dumping imported textiles onto the local market to crush the Dakar manufacturers. This strategy was successful.

All the local textile firms sustained consistent losses over the course of the early to mid-1950s. The maisons de commerce sold competing goods on the local market at cost, eliminating the commercial margins of the local firms.[113] The Manufactures de Rufisque went bankrupt around 1955, a casualty of the price war. The local managers of CCV wanted to close the factory doors, and only the parent firm's hopes for the long run kept CCV in business. By the mid-1950s an exhausted Icotaf had entered peace negotiations with the maisons de commerce in an effort to survive. *Force majeure* put Sotiba in the best position: after 1955, the AOF was a sellers' market for *guinée* cloth no longer available from Pondichéry.

By 1956 the maisons de commerce had decided to control rather than destroy the local textile industry. The French government and the colonial administration were actively promoting industrial development in the AOF. French manufactur-

---

111. The Grand Conseil de l'AOF voted certain tax breaks for local textile manufacturers in 1955, including lower duties on imported capital goods. In 1956 taxes on certain non-French textile imports were increased by 15–20 percent to protect the local industry.

112. Sotiba was a finishing operation, not a spinning and weaving plant. It used imported gray (i.e., unfinished) cloth. For Sotiba, the *libération des échanges* was a bonus: lower-cost supplies of unfinished cotton cloth for dyeing became available (*Marchés Coloniaux*, no. 298 [28 juillet 1951]: 2,053). This was an unfortunate development for the Manufactures de Rufisque, which had hoped to supply Sotiba with gray cloth for dyeing.

113. From interviews with M. Mekouar in Dakar, April 1985 and at Ets. Schaeffer, the SGICF, the CNF, and La Cotonnière Française d'Outre-Mer in Paris, April 1986.

ers were investing, and local industrialization looked inevitable. The largest maisons de commerce decided to "play the industrialization game." Icotaf and Sotiba agreed to sign exclusive buyer contracts with SCOA, the CNF, and the CFAO. CCV gave Sotiba rights to buy its thread (for dyeing).[114] Icotaf purchased the Manufactures de Rufisque for one franc, plus debts. As a result of this series of maneuvers, all local output was commercialized by the maisons de commerce by the late 1950s. For the Dakar manufacturers, the strategy of undercutting the dominant trading firms had failed. The entente with the largest importers broke their independence but ensured the survival of the industry.

The entente. By about mid-1956 the commercialization of all staple textile goods – made-in-Senegal products as well as imports – was centralized in the hands of the largest maisons de commerce. These commercial conglomerates were able to coordinate importation and local production; that is, to fix prices, regulate supply, and organize a division of labor between local and French suppliers. This allowed for comfortably high profit margins across the board. Staple textile goods were distributed through a limited number of semi-wholesalers who were financed by the maisons de commerce. Independent importers, mostly Lebanese merchants, continued to import garments and specialty items. These goods were sold primarily in the urban areas and did not compete with the cotton piece goods sold by the old European commercial houses. Oligopoly control over the sale of staple textiles allowed both the maisons de commerce and the local industry to enjoy the profits generated by restriction of competition on the AOF market.

Entente with the maisons de commerce freed the local industry from the pressure of competition. A market was secured for made-in-Senegal textiles, but at considerable cost to the consumers of Senegal and to possibilities for the growth and diversification of local production in the long run. Meanwhile, the largest commercial houses had strengthened their positions vis-à-vis the state. They depended on the state to protect their oligopoly positions in Senegal's import trade, and in dealing with those in control of state power, they now had a hostage. The hostage was the local textile industry, whose fate lay in the hands of the commercial conglomerates.

Once the local textile industry was incorporated into commercial circuits controlled by the AOF's most powerful importers, the Dakar industry represented an asset, not a problem, for dominant commercial interests. Import substitution began in earnest. Sotiba's owners created a factory to print cotton fabrics in 1958. *Imprimés* produced from imported gray cloth were a high value-added item and were well protected from foreign competition. Although the 2.5 million meters of cloth printed at the new Société d'Impression d'Afrique (Simpafric) supplied only a fraction of AOF demand, the creation of Simpafric was enough to assure its owners and their commercial partners all the privileges of first en-

114. Sotiba sold 250 tons of dyed thread (spun at CCV) in about 1956.
115. Simpafric employed about 100 workers in 1959–60. In 1959, Senegalese demand for *imprimés* was about 18 million meters. Total AOF demand would be greater. In France Ets. Schaeffer

trant.[115] On the eve of Senegal's independence, another textile-manufacturing firm was established in Dakar. French textile manufacturers pulling out of Vietnam transferred part of their Indochinese operations to Senegal, taking advantage of tax incentives offered by the AOF administration for precisely this purpose. Installing used equipment, the Société Cotonnière Transocéanique (SCT) began to produce blankets for the AOF. Blanket manufacture was an attractive market niche. In the late 1940s and 1950s French blankets were exceedingly expensive in West Africa and the importation of cheaper, foreign blankets was severely restricted. Senegalese politicians capitalized on widespread bitterness aroused by the high cost of blankets to publicize the exploitative nature of colonial trade regime and to press for a better deal from France. SCT capitalized on the same thing. The high-cost structure of the local market ensured that its sales would be profitable.

By 1960, the Dakar textile industry produced a range of staple textile goods – *guinée, imprimés, drills,* lightweight cotton cloth, and blankets. Protection from competition, coupled with oligopoly control over the internal market, made the industry viable. This structure of market control would remain a defining feature of the industry into the 1970s. State power played a critical and indispensable role in the establishment of a local textile industry, for it was the state that banned less expensive textile goods from the local market. Just as important was the willingness and ability of the colonial state to underwrite the monopoly of the maisons de commerce over the importation of goods that could compete with textile products manufactured in Dakar. State-engineered commercial advantage was thus the critical ingredient driving and sustaining investment in the textile industry.

The economic structures that defined the Senegalese economy in the last decade of colonial rule were not altered fundamentally during the first decade of independence. For Senegal the 1960s were a decade of classic neocolonial arrangements. These neocolonial arrangements are the subject of the next chapter. Chapter 3 shows how the postcolonial regime used the state apparatus and its control over the commanding heights of an economy forged under the hegemony of colonial merchant capital in order to consolidate power. Patterns of market control established under colonial rule remained intact in the 1960s, allowing the state to appropriate a large share of the rural surplus and spurring the expansion of light industry in Dakar. In the rural areas the basic structures of *la traite* persisted in a new, updated form, constraining possibilities for improvements in productivity, rising incomes, and growth of total output in the groundnut basin.

continued to produce West African-style *imprimés* that were exported to the AOF by the CFAO and CNF. Later, when Ets. Schaeffer became interested in transferring this activity to the Icotaf factory in Dakar, it was blocked by Simpafric's local monopoly over this line of production. Allowing control over printing to slip into the hands of the Sotiba group was, for Ets. Schaeffer, "a huge error."

3

Consolidation of a regime:
Neocolonialism in the 1960s

The outcome [of colonialism] was a curious paradox: the establishment of a series of capitalist states with deep roots in non-capitalist societies which they were forced to protect as the foundation of their power.

G. B. Kay 1975:106

The political leaders of newly independent Senegal inherited control over an economy organized by and for merchant capital. In the 1950s the limits to growth inherent in this economy had become increasingly apparent not only to the managers of France's West African Empire, but also to those who emerged after World War II as contenders for postcolonial state power. High-cost, imbalanced trading structures were asphyxiating and strangling French West Africa, limiting both consumption and production. External trade linkages were not the only problem. The organization of production in Senegal's groundnut basin raised equally grave concerns. In the 1950s Senegalese and French analysts voiced serious doubts about the viability and sustainability of established patterns of export-oriented agricultural production. Extensive groundnut cultivation degraded the land as marabouts and peasants worked to extract the maximum product, as rapidly as possible, with the minimum of investment. The productivity of both land and labor showed signs of regression.

In this context a new regime emerged in the late 1950s and sought to consolidate and entrench its power. The dilemma of the time was expressed in this regime's ambivalent position with regard to economic and social changes that would redynamize the economy and spur new forms of growth. Those who gained control of the postcolonial state were beholden to and dependent upon interests and mechanisms of social control that had crystallized around groundnut production and *la traite*. This dependence constrained their willingness and ability to reform the basic structures of the inherited economy.

Yet the old economic and political order was too narrow and exclusionary to provide a basis for postcolonial rule. The growth of commodity production, the colonial state, and the urban economy created new social groups and new interests that could not be contained within the structures of indirect rule – the urban poor, workers, students, independent urban and rural merchants, leftist intellectuals, and a professional class. These social groups, the offspring of the colonial import–export economy, had no clear stake or assured place in it. They therefore represented a challenge to the status quo. Decolonization itself was a partial solution to the problem of containing and controlling these social strata. It created space in an expanding state apparatus for an intellectual and professional elite that demanded a share in the political economy. They would become Senegal's political class.

This solution was partial because it left unaddressed the problems of strengthening the resource base of the state and reinvigorating the economy at large. It also did not resolve the problem of governing or, more specifically, governing in a way that would allow those who assumed control of the postcolonial state to remain in power.

Colonialism gave rise to mechanisms of social control and economic exploitation that were rooted in a precapitalist rural social order and monopolistic trading structures. Building upon this foundation, new networks of patronage and cooptation were built and anchored in the state apparatus. State control over trade proved to be the critical resource in forging a postcolonial order. Markets were managed and manipulated to expand the economy and generate a resource base for the state. By regulating markets and access to them, the regime was able to defend the vested interests and reproduce the mechanisms of social control that guaranteed its political dominance. Strategies for economic growth were defined in terms of more groundnut production within existing rural social structures, and more light manufacturing within the existing structure of control over commerce and industry. Resources tapped from import–export circuits, along with the inflow of foreign aid, were used by the new regime to reinforce the positions of the Islamic leaders – and to bind them to the state. These same resources played another critical role, for they were used strategically to absorb unincorporated social strata into new clienteles linked to and dependent upon the regime itself. At the same time, state control over commercial circuits allowed the regime to guide nascent Senegalese business interests along a path of development that was mediated, structured, and constrained by the state. These processes are the subject of this chapter.

DECOLONIZATION: THE WINNING COALITION

Political independence came to Senegal in "subtle degrees" (Person 1982:170). By the time Senegal became an independent republic in 1960, major internal battles had been fought, coalitions had been forged, and the terrain had been cleared for the decisive showdowns of the early 1960s.[1] The alliances and political structures forged in Senegal in the 1950s were anchored in a long-established urban political elite, in the centralized and powerful Islamic confréries that dominated the groundnut basin, and in an entrenched political

---

1. On Senegalese politics from World War II to independence, see Morgenthau 1964; and Robinson and Mackenzie 1960.

machine of national scope. These political arrangements would structure the Senegalese political scene for the first twenty years of the postcolonial period.

France set the rules of the electoral game that culminated in the establishment of a Senegalese government. The franchise was extended gradually over the course of the 1946–56 period, allowing the elite of colonial society to gather and organize their political power incrementally. Through a series of elections held over the course of this period, local political parties gained control over offices and positions within colonial political and administrative institutions. France defined the character and scope of concrete political prerogatives secured through electoral competition. As far as the French were concerned, independence was not in the cards until after 1958. Until that time, colonial and French authorities retained control over the fundamental economic and political decisions of the day.

Senegalese politics in the 1950s took the form of two distinct yet interrelated struggles. On one level, the stakes of electoral competition were defined in terms of winning control over colonial jobs, offices, and routine administrative and budgetary powers. To the winners went positions in the territorial assembly, the municipal governments, and the councils of the AOF, along with the powers of patronage that these positions conferred. This was the political process that France orchestrated. On another level, the stakes were much larger but less tangible in an immediate political sense. The competition for offices and patronage never overshadowed completely the struggle over Senegal's future. Leftist and nationalist political forces grew and mobilized in the 1950s. In spite of France's efforts to keep local politics focused on narrower questions, these groups forced the issue of national sovereignty and all that this could imply into the political arena. By challenging the powers of France, championing the causes of peasants and workers against old forms of exploitation, and trying to discredit Senegal's long-standing and conservative political elite, these political movements threatened the success of France's effort to give the colonies a "new deal" – as well as the ambitions of those who sought to secure for themselves better places within it. In the final analysis, however, the future would go to those who controlled the levers and resources of government.

That the battle for offices and patronage proved to be the decisive one was for France, and for Léopold Sédar Senghor, the major achievement of the 1950s. The territorial assembly, municipal governments, and rural cooperatives were the building blocks of what emerged as the dominant political party. Patronage resources that circulated through these institutions served as glue for cementing a winning electoral coalition. A political machine dominated by Senghor grew along with the extension of the franchise in the late 1940s and 1950s. After internal self-rule in 1957 and formal independence in 1960, Senegal's machine politicians commanded not only a vastly expanded pool of patronage resources, but also the state's capacity for internal repression.

In retrospect, continuities in Senegalese politics that span the divide of World War II are as striking as ruptures (Johnson 1971). Léopold Senghor's career in

Senegal was launched from the political world of the *Quatre Communes*. The *Quatre Communes* were political relics of an earlier era when France nurtured the ideal of "assimilating" a colonial elite. Africans born in these four coastal cities – St. Louis, Gorée, Dakar, and Rufisque – were considered to be French citizens. They exercised a considerable degree of autonomous control over municipal affairs and budgets, and together, they elected a deputy to France's National Assembly.[2] The Senegalese political elite of the *Quatre Communes* was the product of this long and cosmopolitan political tradition.

In the nineteenth century, politics in four cities was dominated by the Creole trading families of St. Louis and Gorée and by members of the local French community, most of them representatives of the old Bordeaux trading houses. Political (and sometimes commercial) partnerships were forged as the "Creole-French oligarchy" constructed a formidable political machine in the *Quatre Communes*, jockeying among themselves for position, distributing jobs and municipal funds along patronage lines, competing for the deputyship, and buying the support of indigenous Lebou chiefs and communities in Dakar and Rufisque. Politicians of the *Quatre Communes* sought to win the votes of urban Muslims by securing the blessings and financial backing of Islamic leaders in the countryside.

As colonial rule was consolidated and intensified, and as the colonial economy expanded, the economic and political locus of the colony shifted to Dakar and Rufisque. Increasingly politicized African communities began to press grievances against the French and to insist that the colonial state honor their birthright as French citizens. In this context a new breed of urban politicians emerged in Dakar and Rufisque to challenge the hegemony of the old St. Louisienne families. The shift was manifest most dramatically in the successes of Blaise Diagne, an African born on the island of Gorée, who won the deputyship in 1914. Blaise Diagne capitalized on urban resentment toward the arrogant Creole oligarchy and the frustration bred by France's reluctance to make good on promises to assimilate the African elite. In 1914 Diagne won the backing and financial support of the Mourides, a factor that played an important role in his electoral victory. For the next twenty years Diagne commanded the political machine entrenched in the communes, using his influence to defend the colonial administration and to serve it well. At the same time, he pursued "the quest for political assimilation," protecting the political rights of Senegal's coastal populations, even at the ex-

2. Johnson (1971:39) writes that "[t]he Third Republic gave Senegal a seat in the French Chamber of Deputies in 1872 and it soon afterward gave Saint-Louis and Gorée the right to organize municipal institutions according to French metropolitan law. . . . Rufisque became the third *commune de plein exercice* in 1880, and Dakar . . . followed in 1887. [Yet] municipal politics had existed in Senegal for more than a century before the Decree of 1872." He argues that "[t]he permanent establishment of local political institutions in Senegal during the 1870s . . . was chiefly intended to benefit the new French *émigrés* who sought the wealth of empire in Senegal and to insure that their voices would be heard in Paris. The generalized idealism of assimilation and the self-serving pragmatism of commercial empire – these were the two cornerstones of French imperial policy" (idem 1971:60).

pense of new urban immigrants and the politically disenfranchised population of
the interior (Johnson 1971: ch. 10). He forged and maintained close ties with
the Bordeaux trading interests. Johnson writes that "Diagne's [political party]
became the model for the urban elitist parties that flourished in 1920–40 and
1945–48."[3]

Lamine Guèye, a Paris-trained lawyer and player in communal politics since
the 1910s, inherited Blaise Diagne's legacy and political tradition. He made the
quest for political assimilation the leitmotif of his political career. As deputy to
France after World War II, Lamine Guèye along with the rest of the French
Socialist Party (Section Française de l'Internationale Ouvrière, the SFIO) stood
firm in their opposition to independence for the African colonies. In Senegal
Lamine Guèye led the local branch of the SFIO and established for himself an
unassailable position in the patronage-focused political world of the *Quatre
Communes*.

In 1945 France implemented reforms that shifted the terrain of colonial politics. For the first time, France extended the right to vote in municipal and
territorial assembly elections to some inhabitants of Senegal's interior (literates,
chiefs, veterans, agents of the colonial administration, etc.). The enfranchised
population could also elect representatives to the French parliament. Races for
local control over this expanded political space catapulted Léopold Senghor into
colonial politics. Lamine Guèye chose Senghor – a distinguished Senegalese
intellectual and poet – as the SFIO candidate in the elections of 1945 and 1946.
For Lamine Guèye, Senghor was the perfect candidate. Senghor embodied the
assimilationist ideal. Like the old coastal elite, he was committed to "perfect-
ing" rather than challenging French rule. Yet he was not a citizen of the *communes*. Senghor was untainted by the resentment felt toward the coastal elite, and
he could never challenge Lamine Guèye on his home turf. Senghor was charged
with organizing the rural vote and was all too successful in carrying out this
mission.

The legal distinction between "citizens" and the rest of Senegal's population
("subjects") was abolished by the political reforms of 1946. These reforms
dramatically altered the balance of political power within the territory. In the
regional towns and rural areas lay the power of numbers, and it was Senghor,
rather than the old guard of the *Quatre Communes*, who realized the political
potential of this fact (Morgenthau 1964:140–5). Senghor mobilized the support
of ethnic and regional leaders in the municipal and territorial governments,
constructing a political coalition that placed itself in opposition to an old guard
elite bent on defending its political hegemony. With this base of support Senghor
and his closest political associate, Mamadou Dia, broke with the SFIO in 1948
and formed a new party, the Bloc Démocratique Sénégalais (BDS). The BDS
courted, bargained with, and made promises to rural notables and influentials –

3. Johnson 1971:215. The Vichy government of France suspended legal political activity in the
colonies during the war.

above all, the Mouride leaders.[4] Senghor campaigned on a platform calling for respect for Islamic values and traditions, higher prices for the groundnut, a better deal for Senegalese merchants occupying subaltern positions in the groundnut trade, and "democracy" for all Senegalese within the framework of the *Union Française*. The BDS won Senegal's two seats in the National Assembly in 1951. Then the BDS swept the 1952 elections for Senegal's territorial assembly.[5] Senghor was able to use the administrative prerogatives of the assembly and his influence as deputy to distribute concrete benefits to his most important supporters – rural notables, patrons, and the leading Mouride *marabouts*.

With a growing command over the administrative institutions and distributive politics of rural Senegal, success bred success for the BDS. Loans from the cooperatives, jobs in the towns and in the colonial administration, scholarships, public works projects, credits for businessmen, and management positions within the SIP were deployed to strengthen the electoral base of the BDS. A new version of the old strategy of indirect rule allowed the party to construct a mass electoral base in the rural areas by drawing established regional, ethnic, and religious authorities into the BDS. The patronage powers and prestige of rural notables affiliated with the BDS increased, largely at the expense of rural agents of the colonial administration – the *chefs de canton* and village chiefs – who tended to ally with the SFIO.[6] Donal Cruise O'Brien writes that political patronage in the 1950s increased the wealth of the most important marabouts "on a scale hitherto unimaginable."[7] This new wealth, coupled with the enfranchisement of the rural population, multiplied many times over the political influence of Senegal's Islamic leaders. In the 1950s they emerged as the arbiters of Senegalese electoral politics. The most powerful Mouride leaders threw their weight and the votes of their followers behind Senghor.

Political reforms and economic changes that quickened the pace of politics in

---

4. "The leaders of the BDS entered into a series of negotiations with the major ethnic and interest groups. Perhaps the most important of these were Muslim, since at least four-fifths of the population of Senegal was Muslim" (Morgenthau 1964:147).
5. See Schumacher 1975:11. The AOF assemblies were very much a part of the infrastructure of colonial rule. Within the strict limits set on territorial powers by the French Parliament, the Assemblies handled "varied and complex matters ranging from policy decisions in the economic field to a mass of administrative detail" (Thompson and Adloff 1958:65). In practice, assemblymen spent a great deal of time dealing with fairly routine administrative work. About one-half of their time was devoted to budgetary matters – the sale and management of state land, public services, loans, social assistance, scholarships, land concessions, rent regulations, etc. See idem 1958:63–70.
6. See Schumacher 1975:7–8; Thompson and Adloff 1958:313.
7. Donal Cruise O'Brien (1971:262) writes "[t]he marabouts became the political agents of the major parties after the rural areas were enfranchised after World War II. The most effective means employed by the political leaders in the efforts to win the marabouts' favor is direct economic assistance. The flow of money from political sources made it possible for certain marabouts to acquire wealth on a scale hitherto unimaginable. In the 1950s, politics became by far the greatest single source of revenue for the Mouride elite." See also Morgenthau 1964:147–9, 152; and Behrman 1970:85–120.

Senegal's rural areas also transformed the politics of the cities. Urban centers swelled with waves of new immigrants from the countryside, workers in new postwar industries, and a professional population that expanded as students returned from France and as the colonial administration grew. Throughout the AOF, student groups coalesced and were radicalized. A highly developed, AOF-wide trade union organization linked to France's Confédération Générale des Travailleurs (CGT) joined the heated debate over the future of the federation and of French colonial rule in Africa. Long, militant, and increasingly politicized strikes erupted in Senegal and elsewhere in French West Africa. The political spectrum broadened as Marxist intellectuals, university students, teachers, lower-rank and first generation civil servants, trade unionists, and a growing population of urban poor pushed onto the stage of territory-wide (indeed, federation-wide) politics. Lamine Guèye, the SFIO, and the old political machine no longer mastered the cities.

More progressive and militant political currents were represented in both the labor unions and in Senegal's branch of the Rassemblement Démocratique Africain (RDA), a federation-wide movement formed in Bamako in 1946 to challenge the moderate reformism embodied by the Lamine Guèyes and Léopold Senghors of the AOF. This "split between conservatives and progressives" would shape Senegalese politics in dramatic ways (Barry 1988:275). Although the local branch of the RDA and other leftist political parties held minority positions in Senegal's electoral game, they represented a serious challenge to the old urban elite, to the gradualist and reformist political project, and to Senghor's bid for regional leadership. By articulating a nationalist ideology of great power and appeal in the urban areas, the left-leaning and progressive political currents raised the intensity and stakes of electoral competition of the 1950s.

In the territorial and municipal elections of 1952 through 1956, the BDS carved out a position in the contested terrain of the regional towns and coastal urban centers. Senghor presented himself as the representative of the new, postwar Senegalese elite – as a leader untainted by the SFIO's elitism, arrogance, and corruption. Whereas the SFIO maintained an unyielding resistance to reforms that would accord the territories limited autonomy from France, the BDS pushed for administrative and political decentralization of the *Union Française* that would expand the prerogatives and responsibility of the local administrative class. Senghor denounced the unfairness of the *pacte colonial* and the racism inherent in France's assimilationist ideal.[8] BDS-style socialism offered a humanistic and democratic vision of political order, one that would free Africans from the oppressions and insults of old-style colonial rule. This humanistic and reformist stance failed to win over the trade union movement and political parties that called for an end to colonial rule. It did win the BDS the support of much of the administrative salariat. Senghor's control over the territorial assembly also

---

8. Senghor's party had no "separatist ambitions," but wanted a federal structure for the *Union Française* that would increase the power of the territorial assemblies. For a discussion of the BDS electoral coalition, see Martens 1983a; 1983b; and 1983c.

helped. For many civil servants, support for the BDS was a bread-and-butter issue.

By the mid-1950s the appeal of more militant strains of nationalism had grown both within Senegal and in the federation. In an effort to preempt the radicalization of nationalist demands in West Africa and to reinforce the *Union Française*, France passed the Loi Cadre of 1956. This reform created semiautonomous local governments in each territory of the AOF, effectively balkanizing the federation.[9] The 1957 elections for control of this semiautonomous government in Senegal were fiercely contested. "Because of this political effervescence and the radicalization of the debate over independence, the BDS leadership embarked in 1956 on a vast unification campaign designed to maintain itself at the helm and stem the RDA tidal wave sweeping over all the African territories" (Barry 1988:276). Senghor assumed a more nationalist and socialist bent, and the BDS absorbed into its highest ranks several prominent leftist intellectuals and trade unionists. The party renamed itself the Bloc Populaire Sénégalais (BPS) to reflect the broadening of the coalition embraced within the party.

Young radicals and trade unionists were placed in important posts in the BPS executive committee. They played a leading role in drafting the party's new constitution. At this point the Senghor-led party took on an ideological coloring that reflected the aspirations of the mostly younger, more progressive elements. The BPS declared its intention to create "a genuine 'mass party' that would defend the true interests of workers and peasants against those of urban and rural notables" (Schumacher 1975:18–19). To mobilize the masses and invigorate the anticolonial struggle, intellectuals within the BPS began to articulate political strategies aimed at challenging local political bosses through consciousness raising in the countryside.

The irony was that the Senghor-led political machine rested squarely upon the influence of the local political bosses who were attacked in the new party platform. The coalition that had grown since 1952 gave top BDS leaders little control over constituent elements of the machine, and in fact relied upon strengthening local brokers and patrons in order to secure the votes of their clients, subordinates, and followers. Maintaining this split between theory and practice was, in the late 1950s, the genius of Senghor and the strength of the party as an electoral coalition.

The political coalition led by Senghor won a clear victory in the decisive 1957 elections. Senghor assumed "semiautonomous" control of the territorial government and with it, control over allocation of the territorial budget. Lamine Guèye and the old elite of the *communes*, seeing the writing on the wall, led the SFIO into Senghor's party. Fusion of the two "moderate" parties – comprising the old

9. As Senghor argued at the time, an AOF-wide governmental structure would have helped to preserve the economic and political cohesion of the federation. The balkanization of the AOF and the AEF (Afrique Equitoriale Française) increased France's control over its West African colonies by dividing two large federations into twelve small, economically dependent units. See Crowder 1978:298, 305. See also Chapter 4.

elite of the *communes* and the new elite of the BDS – created the Union Progressiste Sénégalaise (UPS).

By winning the backing of the centralized and disciplined Mouride confrérie, Senghor secured the rural influence and the mass of peasant votes that underwrote his rise to political power. By systematically extending party control over municipal and territorial government, Senghor created a political machine that rivaled, eclipsed, and finally absorbed the old political machine of the *communes*. The electoral strength of the ruling party was now at its peak. Tensions contained within this grand coalition, however, would prove to be increasingly difficult to manage. Retaining the support of the younger, educated, and more progressive elements "while conserving the original coalition of elites"[10] that guaranteed his political power would be Senghor's major challenge.

The gradual transfer of power was now underway. In 1958 the semi-autonomous government of Senegal began designing strategies to decolonize, dynamize, and balance the economy. Planning commissions and task forces were commissioned to assess Senegal's current economic problems and potential. University-educated intellectuals and other professional elements assumed leading roles. As a result, the planning process came to reflect the strong progressive current both within the UPS and the country at large. A team of French consultants and Senegalese analysts led by Père Lebret, a Catholic priest and "integrated rural development" specialist, launched a comprehensive study of the rural sector.

Six years before, the French government had undertaken a similar project. The Portères mission of 1952 had produced a scathing indictment of Mouride groundnut production and colonial agricultural policy in a report that produced considerable discussion and debate within the administration and the territorial assembly (Portères 1952). In 1958 the Lebret task force reopened the issue. In doing so, it set in motion a process that would ultimately force the leadership of the UPS to confront not only the contradictions inherent in its grand coalition, but also the fundamental trade-off between political expediency on the one hand and reform of the most basic structures of the colonial economy on the other.

The Portères mission argued that forms of extensive groundnut cultivation practiced for the most part by the Mourides and wholeheartedly encouraged by the colonial administration were turning the groundnut basin into an impoverished dust bowl.[11] "Speculative," "abusive," and "rapacious" cultivation depleted fragile Sahelian soils. Production techniques "were inferior to what they had been 100 years before." Productivity per hectare was no better, and in some cases worse, than what it had been in the early 1930s (ibid.:10–11, 15). The Portères mission argued that the exploitative nature of the commercial circuit and the demands of Mouride lords for cash and groundnuts impoverished both

10. Schumacher 1975:17.
11. The same processes were underway in the Terres Neuves ("New Lands") opened to Mouride groundnut cultivation in the 1930s.

the Mouride peasantry and the soil.[12] On the large estates of the marabouts, laborers had little stake in improving productivity and no means to do so. They raped the land and moved on. Mouride peasants represented one-third of Senegal's population and were concentrated in the most densely peopled region of the territory. They "were the moral and material subjects" of the Mouride marabouts. "It is to him [the marabout] that the peasants deliver the products of their labor . . . A new class of serfs, or perhaps it would be better to say 'slaves,' has emerged before our eyes" (ibid.:105). As far as the Portères mission was concerned, this exploitative "feudal" order put an end to traditional cultivation practices that sustained the fertility of the land (fallowing, etc.), subordinated the need to expand food crop production to the demands of groundnut farming, and made technical progress impossible. With the help of the colonial administration, the confréries and the market had created a "miserable" Mouride peasantry that was dangerously dependent on imported rice.

The 1952 mission concluded Senegalese agriculture "had reached a dead-end" (ibid.:15). "Total submission" to the marabouts stifled peasants' initiative and capacity to improve their lots, adopt better production techniques, nurture the land, save, invest, or stabilize the subsistence economy. For the Portères mission, what was needed was land reform to "free the peasantry" from the feudal Mouride order. The cultivator must "be a participant [in the development of the rural economy], not a slave" (ibid.:109).

The colonial administration had been prodded into action. Sociétés Indigènes de Prévoyance (SIP) were expanded in the early 1950s to disseminate better cultivation techniques, make credit more available, and encourage the cultivation of millet alongside groundnuts. The reform effort of the early 1950s had little of the desired effect on rural production or agricultural practice, in large part because the SIP and the resources channeled through them, remained under the firm control of rural notables, including Mouride elite. The SIP became political footballs in the struggle between the BDS and the SFIO for patronage resources and rural influence.[13]

The task force formed under Père Lebret in 1958 recognized the profound structural problems of the rural economy. Pointing to the SIP experience of the early to mid-1950s, it argued that true development required a complete overhaul

12. "We [the French] have demanded and obtained [nothing but] a growth in total output. . . . It is almost inconceivable that in 1952, agricultural laborers will go to the fields on empty stomachs when it is agricultural production that has permitted [us] to bring about the *équipement général* [development of general administrative infrastructure, urban infrastructure, and the like] that we now observe in this territory" (Portères 1952:15, 13).

13. Thompson and Adloff (1958:313) note that the colonial administration tried to resist the efforts of the BDS-controlled territorial assembly to assume direct control over the SIP after 1952 because the administration feared that by doing so, the SIP would become "political footballs." The colonial authorities' attempts to maintain the status quo, however, were not impartial. Established rural agents of the SIP – the *chefs de canton* and the village chiefs – were tied into the SFIO machine.

of the rural economic *and political* order. Lebret and the Senegalese technocrats and intellectuals comprising his task force laid out a "socialist option" for rural restructuring. Local administration and institutions of rural development would be decentralized and democratized to give peasants a direct role and stake in improving agricultural techniques and productivity. Freed from the clientelism, dependency, and exploitations of the old order, rural masses would be empowered. The state would spearhead this process by sponsoring a grassroot cooperative movement built on "traditional communitarian" values. A complex and integrated structure of rural development institutions would channel resources directly to the peasants, invigorate the grassroots movement, and thus revolutionize the production processes. The strategy of *Animation Rurale* was born.

Animation Rurale resonated deeply with the reformist and socialist elements within the UPS, and with the populist and humanist strain in Senghor's own thinking. Senghor's position was contradictory, however, for *Animation Rurale* promised to attack and undermine the existing rural bases of the ruling party's power. To square the circle (to buy time?), Senghor traveled throughout the groundnut basin arguing that Mouridism and socialism were mutually reinforcing, for both rested on communal values and the primacy of work.[14] Socialism, he argued, would mean better returns for all groundnut producers and that, after all, was the bottom line.

As the Senghor government consolidated its position and its program, political events in the metropole overtook those unfolding in West Africa. In the wake of constitutional crisis in France, de Gaulle called for a popular referendum in French West Africa that would allow each territory to accept or refuse a new constitutional framework for Franco-African relations. De Gaulle proposed a *Communauté Française* which would give each of the West African territories limited political autonomy as self-governing republics within a larger political and economic grouping dominated by France. France would retain control over foreign affairs, defense, monetary and financial affairs, and education. Rejection of the proposal by a "no" vote in the colonies would mean "total and immediate independence."

The 1958 referendum fanned the flames of political debate in West Africa between partisans of immediate independence and "moderate" elements favoring the continuation of close ties with France. In Senegal tensions and contradictions within Senghor's loose and heterogeneous ruling coalition quickly came to the surface. Virtually all the trade unions, along with student groups and the left wing of the UPS, demanded immediate independence. A Marxist party, the Parti Africain de l'Indépendance (PAI), campaigned for a "no" vote and attacked Senghor as an agent of French imperialism. At the other extreme of the political

---

14. As Senghor argued at the occasion of the Mouride Magal in 1963, "[W]hat is Socialism if not essentially the economic-social system which gives primality and priority to work? Who has done this better than Ahmad Bamba [founder of the Mouride confrérie] and his successors" (Behrman 1970:118).

spectrum, the marabouts were united in their opposition to independence, fearing that "communist" or other progressive elements would seize power and undermine their authority.[15] The marabouts were also afraid that a rupture in Senegal's relations with France would mean an end to metropolitan groundnut subsidies. Senghor, who had never called for independence from France anyway, could not afford to bend to nationalist pressures that would result in the defection of the powerful religious leaders from his political camp.[16] He sacrificed the left wing of the party instead.

Senghor and the "moderate" wing of the UPS began to campaign vigorously against independence. The party split. Leftist and nationalist elements walked out to form a new party, the Parti du Regroupement Africain–Sénégal (PRA–Sénégal), to mobilize votes for immediate independence. In the September 1958 election, the vote for immediate independence carried the day in Senegal's urban areas. But the rural areas voted massively against independence and decided the referendum outcome in Senegal. The other territories of the AOF, with the notable exception of Guinea, also rejected independence by voting to accept de Gaulle's proposal of limited autonomy within the *Communauté*.

In 1959 Senegal's opposition parties and factions split, fused, and regrouped either to launch new offensives against the dominant UPS or to ally more closely with it. The moderate "center–left" adopted a strategy of support for the UPS and retained its influence within the executive and planning structures of the government and party. Patronage resources drawn from the territorial budget helped the UPS to consolidate its alliances. The more militant factions of the trade union movement and the two opposition parties, the PRA–Sénégal and the PAI, mobilized against the ruling party's bid for the territorial assembly election of 1959.[17] After winning this election, the UPS-controlled government cracked down on the opposition by arresting its most influential and vocal leaders.[18] Top trade unionists and forty-five PAI leaders, including the PAI secretary general, were jailed. Ruth Morgenthau (1964:165) wrote that as a result, "the young radicals of Senegal [who] were perhaps better organized and tactically better placed to take the succession than their counterparts in any other state [of the AOF]" played no independent role in guiding Senegal's final steps to independence. In the wake of the crack-down the UPS immediately began to reabsorb

---

15. Gellar 1982:20; Crowder 1978:303.
16. Senghor's slogans in 1958 were: "Independence has no positive content; it is not a solution"; and "Independence: that's the groundnut at the [low] world market price – 15 francs a kilo" (Crowder 1978:283; Ly 1981:42).
17. The PRA–Sénégal espoused pan-Africanism of the Nkrumah variety and called for immediate and complete independence from France. The PAI also called for immediate independence and denounced the neocolonial orientation of Senghor and his political coalition. It considered the urban working class to be the key to revolutionary action. The PAI was supported by some leftist factions of Senegal's intelligentsia and had an electoral base among members of the working class in Dakar and Saint-Louis (Foltz 1977:247; Martens 1983c).
18. A variety of other repressive measures were implemented (outlawing political demonstrations and "political agitation," etc.). See Ly 1981:93–4.

elements that it had alienated in 1958. Centrifugal forces continued to pull at the factious ruling coalition.

Once again, the pace of reform outside Senegal overtook events within the territory. The *Communauté* disintegrated as France grudgingly accepted the idea of "association" with fully independent African states. Senghor's last-minute effort to avoid the complete economic and political balkanization of the AOF – the union of Senegal and the Soudan Français within the framework of the Mali Federation – fell apart in 1960 amid signs that alliance with the more "radical" Union Soudanaise party would compromise Senghor's power and threaten the Mouride and Tidjane leaders.[19] Senegal declared itself a fully independent republic linked to France through political, economic, and cultural "accords of association." These accords protected the close trading, monetary, financial, and military ties that structured Franco-Senegalese relations during the colonial era. Independence had been achieved without a rupture of ties with France.

Senghor became the president of the republic. Mamadou Dia became prime minister.

CONSOLIDATION OF POWER

At the time of independence, Senghor dominated a loose political coalition comprised of disparate and in many ways antagonistic political elements. As internal power struggles within the UPS festered, the regime confronted opposition parties demanding a decisive break from French economic and political control. The internal political situation was unstable and contentious. On-going struggles over restructuring the *économie de traite* would place the two most organized and politically powerful elements of the UPS coalition – the urban intellectuals and young elite ensconced in the professions and the administration on the one hand, and the Islamic leaders who brokered the political loyalties of rural Senegal on the other – on a collision course. The groundnut marketing sector, "the key to the national economy,"[20] was the site of conflicts that brought deep tensions within the UPS coalition to a head, provoking the political crisis of 1962.

Senegal's constitution provided for a bicephalous, parliamentary regime. Senghor, as the president and head of state, controlled the UPS and specific domains of government policy, including defense and external relations. As prime minister, Mamadou Dia controlled the government administration and day-to-day policy-making and implementation, as he had since 1958. This institutional division paralleled an important political division within the ruling coalition. The UPS was dominated by rural power brokers, regional notables, and

19. The Fédération du Mali existed from January 1959 to August 1960. As Schumacher (1975:62) writes, "[i]ronically, the termination of colonial rule on June 20, 1960, forced to the surface lingering constitutional and political issues that soon proved fatal to the Mali Federation." Two months later, Senegal declared its separate national independence. On this episode see Morgenthau 1964:164–5; and Foltz 1965:97–118 (esp. 114–18), 166–79.
20. Schumacher 1975:85.

politicians with personal power bases. It was structured along the lines of the UPS political machine and it controlled the national parliament. Central government administration in Dakar, by contrast, was the stronghold of mostly young, well-educated technocrats and reform-minded intellectuals. Both before and after political independence, progressive elements drawn into the ruling coalition had been rewarded with important administrative and planning posts. Progressive currents within the administration became stronger as university graduates and other educated urbanites joined the UPS and filled the rapidly expanding ranks of ministries, bureaucracies, and other agencies of government. Within the administration there was a strong sense of the potential of independence and of the efficacy of reform. Aided by French planners and policy analysts who provided technical and financial resources that would greatly expand the scope of "development" initiatives, Senegal's government administrators set about realizing the socialist option. Mamadou Dia emerged as the leader and symbol of those within the government committed to structural reform. First and foremost, this meant reform of the rural economy.

Independence cleared the way for bold initiatives. One of the first acts of the new government was the nationalization of the groundnut trade. The creation of the Office de Commercialisation Agricole (OCA) gave the government a legal monopoly over the purchase of the crop. In the name of freeing groundnut producers from exploitation of private traders, money lenders, and colonial commercial oligopolies, the government had secured a major new source of internal revenue. It was clear at the time that this move would have far-reaching consequences for the structure of the national economy. What remained to be determined was precisely how the government would use the "key to the national economy," and thus, what the consequences would be.

Officially, the Senegalese government and the UPS embraced the ideals of rural socialism and comprehensive national planning. For those committed to these ideals, the direct extension of the state apparatus into the rural economy was merely the first step toward dismantling the *économie de traite* and transforming the rural social order. Following the recommendations of Lebret's task forces, planners within the administration began to elaborate and implement plans for integrated rural development. The old SIP were to be transformed into genuine rural cooperatives. "Real" cooperatives would become the grassroot component of a complex and hierarchical structure of rural development agencies and institutions (Behrman 1970:133). The entire apparatus would be aimed at empowering the peasantry vis-à-vis rural notables and patrons. By revolutionizing rural social relations, it would be possible to revolutionize agricultural production. Credit, technical assistance, training in better production techniques, and political education of the peasants were the cornerstones of *Animation Rurale*. Young activists – rural "animators" – were sent to the countryside to raise the consciousness of the peasantry and to mobilize the masses in support of comprehensive rural reform.

By 1961 Mamadou Dia was convinced that in order to realize the government's vision of a new political and economic order, even more dramatic reforms of the political economy were necessary. The process of rural restructuring was floundering amid the anarchy of rural marketing circuits that followed the creation of the OCA, continuing corruption and political manipulation of the cooperative movement, and the general unwieldiness of the government apparatus. Pressure for more decisive action mounted daily. Dia was acutely aware of the growing budgetary deficit of the government, a deficit aggravated by the disorganization of rural trade and the slump in rural economic activity that accompanied it. Perhaps he was also aware that time was not on his side, for as the days and months passed, those with a vested stake in the established rural political order consolidated their positions and power.

As Schumacher (1975) argues, three initiatives undertaken in 1961 and 1962 galvanized opposition to Mamadou Dia and to the socialist option that he had come to represent. First, Dia wanted to expand the OCA's marketing functions in the rural areas. The OCA was already mandated to purchase the crop and to sell seeds, tools, and fertilizers (on credit). Dia and the Lebret teams began to formulate plans that would give the OCA a central role in importing consumer goods and distributing these products in the countryside. Under this plan, the state would assure a steady flow of fairly priced consumer goods to peasants. By helping them out of the debt trap, the state would raise producers' standards of living and encourage the cultivation of an expanded range of cash crops, including food crops. This proposal inflamed the opposition of the maisons de commerce and Senegalese private traders.

Second, the administration pushed ahead with plans to expand the political and social functions of the rural cooperatives. The cooperatives were the linchpins of rural reform because they mediated the economic relationship between the state and the peasantry. One of the core objectives of *Animation Rurale* was to use this material link as the basis for establishing direct contact, unmediated by rural brokers and patrons, with the peasantry. This would allow state agents and agencies to respond better to the needs of producers and at the same time, draw peasants directly into the political process. Frustration with the first few years of experience with *Animation Rurale* led the Dia government to move beyond its original, loosely formulated notions of rural empowerment to more detailed, operational, and concrete agendas for freeing peasants from dependence on rural notables and patrons. Schumacher (1975:66) writes that "[t]his entailed a serious consideration of land reform legislation as well as a major administrative reform aimed at curtailing the relative autonomy and politicized character of regional agencies serving not only the cooperative movement but also the patronage interests of local UPS politicians." One proposal that promised to be a major break with the past was the proposal to use strong persuasion, and possibly coercion, to force those who had benefited from the credit facilities of the cooperatives – including Mouride leaders – to repay their loans. The entire thrust of this new phase of reform efforts was viewed "with increasing apprehension" by established rural elites who came to view Mamadou Dia as excessively responsive "to the policy orientation of *Animation* spokesmen identified with the populist 'revolution-from-below' strain in Senegalese development thinking" (ibid.:105). Mouride leaders were particularly antagonized by pressure to repay government loans.

Third, to harness the powers of the Dakar-based administration to the task of development, Mamadou Dia sponsored a move to centralize and coordinate the planning, financing, and policy evaluation functions of government. The creation of a supraordinate planning ministry attached to the prime minister's office would allow for more rigorous policy enforcement by reducing the resources and autonomy of other ministries. Along with this initiative was a more broad-based move, supported by French administrative consultants, to rationalize and professionalize the administration. More systematic, merit-based recruitment standards and training programs would be adopted, discipline would be enhanced, and personnel would be supervised more closely. For Senghor and the UPS, this was the last straw.

Tensions inherent in the ruling coalition could no longer be papered over by the regime's own ideological inconsistency or by glaring contradictions between formal policy objectives and actual patterns of political practice. Those bent on using state power to create what they saw as a new, more viable and dynamic economic order ran up against the defenses of those rooted in the status quo. Party politicians accused government administrators of "insensitivity to local interests" which jeopardized the "collegiality" of the UPS. The administration accused party brokers and patrons of obstructing the government's officially-declared and -endorsed reform program. Conflicts flared and the cohesion of the regime became increasingly precarious. French business interests became nervous; concern mounted over the government's "indecision" between liberalism and socialism. "Although some Frenchmen recognized that this indecision might be due in part to . . . [the attempts of] Senghor to maintain a balance between various factions in the governing party, they obviously could not . . . be certain that the outcome would be favorable to business interests" (R. Cruise O'Brien 1972:129). As *Animation Rurale* progressed, the Islamic leaders began to see it as more and more dangerous, for its reform drive was now explicitly targeted at the economic and political bases of their own power.

The Mouride leaders pressed for removal of Dia from office.[21] They were joined by the old-guard politicians of the UPS and members of parliament with commercial interests. Schumacher (1975:65) notes that it was not the "socialist ideological tone" of official development policy that so antagonized these elements, but rather Dia's "determination to intensify the pace and rigor of policy enforcement."

Mamadou Dia's downfall came in the form of a constitutional crisis in December 1962. A faction of the UPS introduced a censure motion against Dia's government. Dia maintained that this was illegal under the State of Emergency laws then in force, and moved to have the hostile parliamentarians removed from the National Assembly. Senghor countered by sending paratroopers to occupy the Assembly. The next day Mamadou Dia and four ministers loyal to him were

---

21. See Markovitz 1970:91; D. Cruise O'Brien 1971:228; Gellar et al. 1980:72–3.

arrested and imprisoned.[22] Once Dia was deposed, politicians, administrators, and elements within the bureaucracy linked to the "Diaist faction" were purged systematically from the government and party. Supporters of the rural socialism he advocated could not stand up to the established political elite. Left-wing intellectuals left the country or receded into the bureaucracy (Adamolekun 1971:558). The Diaist reform agenda was eviscerated. *Animation Rurale* languished from neglect, inertia, and political obstructionism; the OCA program was scaled back dramatically; and "the autonomy of local party politicians was very much invigorated."[23] French confidence in the regime was restored.

Senghor proceeded to consolidate power in his own hands. The constitution was revised in 1963 to abolish the post of prime minister. Control over the ruling party and the government administration was centralized in the presidency. Amid political violence and outcries of election fraud, Senghor and the UPS won 98 percent of the votes counted in the 1963 national elections.[24] Over the course of the next three years, opposition parties and movements were demobilized through a mix of repression and co-optation. In the wake of the 1963 elections, the strongest opposition parties and movements were outlawed and their leaders arrested. New laws made legal political organization outside the framework of the UPS virtually impossible, creating a de facto one party state.[25] Senghor then succeeded in absorbing influential members of the former opposition into the regime. After militant trade unions were crushed by the government, labor leaders were co-opted into the UPS trade union movement. Leaders of the opposition movements, parties, or factions thereof joined the government in exchange for attractive political and administrative posts. The *coup de grâce* came in 1966, when the PRA–Sénégal joined the UPS and three of its leaders were given ministerial posts.[26] In the words of Ruth First, opposition was "smothered in the bosom of the party" (1970:118). By 1966 all legal political activity had been incorporated into the UPS. What remained of the leftist opposition went underground.

22. Dia was accused of trying to stage a coup d'état. According to Senghor, under Dia "the whole administrative apparatus, instead of being at the service of the State and the Nation, was placed, not even at the service of the dominant party, but of the *clan* of [Mamadou Dia]" (Adamolekun 1971:547). The cabinet ministers imprisoned in the wake of the constitutional crisis were freed in 1969 and 1970. Dia was released and exiled in 1974, partly in response to years of pressure from human rights groups in France.
23. Schumacher 1975:39. See also Barker 1985:63–4.
24. Urban riots were put down by government troops, resulting in a number of deaths of PRA–Sénégal militants at the gates of the Presidential Palace. See D. Cruise O'Brien 1967.
25. "The PAI faced increasingly effective repression from the government. The appointment of an ex-PAI member as director of national security in 1963 enabled the government to round up many of the leading militants of the PAI. By 1967, the leaders of the PAI were either in exile or in prison" (D. Cruise O'Brien 1967). The Bloc des Masses Sénégalaises (BMS), created in 1961 and the strongest opposition party in 1963, was banned in 1963. The Union Générale des Etudiants de l'Afrique de l'Ouest was declared illegal in 1965 (*Marchés Tropicaux*, 13 mars 1965:665). From 1964 to 1975, the UPS held all seats in Senegal's National Assembly.
26. D. Cruise O'Brien 1979:216. On the co-optation of the opposition, see also Gellar 1982:33; and Ly 1981:95–6.

Institutionalization of the regime

Assimilation of opposition parties and leaders into the government expanded the ruling coalition, drawing formerly incorporated elements of the political elite into the UPS political machine. This "coalescing of elites within the matrices of the state" compounded the complexity of factional divisions already existing within the party.[27] After the ouster of Dia and his vanguard force of reformers, party and administrative structures were meshed. Factional alliances and divisions within the party were reproduced within the administration. What Bayart (1989) calls "the reappropriation of the state" progressed rapidly, linking the state apparatus to powerful elements within Senegalese society, giving them a share of the fruits of independence, and thus strengthening their positions as brokers and patrons of clienteles, constituencies, and followers.

The UPS political machine that came to dominate the political life of the country was an amalgam of political factions – a political structure built and rebuilt over the course of the post-1946 period through alliances of convenience between political parties, movements, and powerbrokers. No particular ideological vision or programmatic agenda other than "stability" and Franco-Senegalese "cooperation" was imposed on its members. The overriding goal was "organic unity" within the party and the administration. In practice organic unity meant that patrons and brokers enjoyed considerable political autonomy and considerable discretion over resources they controlled. This had been the modus operandi of the ruling party since its origins. The politicos, marabouts, leaders of interest groups, urban bosses, ethnic leaders, big administrators, and labor leaders who were UPS patrons and brokers used this autonomy to cultivate personal power bases.[28]

Political networks that formed at local levels or within administrative agencies were institutionalized as UPS cells or "committees." These units were aggregated hierarchically and linked to regional and national-level political structures.[29] Electoral politics persisted as a mechanism for regulating access to political office at the national, regional, and local levels. Local big men and notables were thus pressured to consolidate and maintain personal followings, or clienteles, in order to underwrite their claims to office. Appointive posts (e.g. regional governorships), in turn, usually went to powerful politicians. Within the UPS and the administration, political barons jockeyed for influence and favor,

---

27. This is Bayart's (1989) phrase.
28. "Tight party unity was not a goal of the UPS. Diversity was tolerated as long as electoral goals were not compromised. Informally, the party was structured into competing 'clans' and the formal power and independent initiative enjoyed by the local party committees made a monolithic façade impossible to attain. Issues, programs, and party units were deeply personalized" (Foltz 1965:140).
29. A youth organization, a women's movement, student and teacher organizations, a national trade union, and business organizations were also part of the overall UPS structure. See Zuccarelli 1970:138–61; Barker 1973:287–303.

cultivating ever-broader clienteles to enhance their influence and to promote their ascent within the political hierarchy.

Myriads of patron–client relations held together by the distribution of patronage resources formed political factions – or *"clans"* – which competed for the spoils of office.[30] Donal Cruise O'Brien (1975:149–51) described Senegalese *clan* politics in these terms:

Clans are the effective units of political competition in the Senegalese single-party state. The clan is a political faction, operating within the institutions of the state and the governing party. It exists above all to promote the interests of its members . . . and its first unifying principle is the prospect of the material rewards of political success (jobs, material benefits which accrue to the job-holder and his following). . . . Clan politics is the particular Senegalese form of spoils-oriented factionalism.

"Political clientelism and machine politics," writes Schumacher (1975:1–2), "epitomize the style of participation and organization embodied by Senegal's ruling party. . . . [Clientelism and patronage] pervade the functioning of political, administrative, economic, and social structures. . . . Politics is about governmental jobs, sinecures, contracts, licenses, subsidies, loans, scholarships, public works, payoffs and favors." Patrons and brokers formed vertical alliances with those located upstream and downstream in the flow of government resources. Fluid, shifting alignments emerged and disintegrated in response to the changing political fortunes of faction leaders.

The central task of those at the top was to play off factional rivalries, check and balance the growth of powerful factions, and control *clans* by closing off room for maneuver outside the structures of the government and the party. Senghor was particularly astute in maintaining control by playing on local rivalries. His immediate subordinates and appointees enjoyed considerable freedom of action, but their tenure in office was contingent on loyalty to the president (Adamolekun 1971:555). Elites circulated fitfully within the political system, building personal power bases but not solidifying entrenched power blocs.[31] This skillfully manipulated system of patronage-oriented factionalism was credited with performing "integrative functions" in Senegal and maintaining a certain degree of political cohesion at the national level (Foltz 1964; Cottingham 1970; D. Cruise O'Brien 1975). It helped to build and sustain a heterogeneous and fissiparous ruling coalition.

The lifeblood of this system was state control over an expanding reservoir of patronage resources. In the 1960s the regulatory and distributive capacities of the

30. Political *clans* in Senegal are not defined by kinship and therefore are not "clans" in the conventional anthropological sense. *Clans* in Senegal are the personal followings of political influentials, tied to the leader through patron–client relations. Kinship is not necessarily a factor. See Foltz 1977; D. Cruise O'Brien 1975:149; Fatton 1987:91–6. For case studies of local-level *clan* competition, see Barker 1973 (factional competition in an *arrondissement* of the Sine Saloum region); and Cottingham 1970 (factional competition between two UPS party branches in Kebemer). Pfefferman (1968:81–8) discusses *clan* politics in the national trade union movement.

31. See Migdal (1988:214–17) on the politics of "the big shuffle."

state were broadened, giving administrators and politicians discretionary control over an expanding array of resources critical to individuals' survival and advancement: access to jobs, health care, housing, educational opportunities, government subsidies, contracts, credit, building permits, etc. Between 1959 and 1964 general government expenditures, heavily concentrated on administrative and social services, expanded five-fold. During the same period about 80 percent of the government's current budget was allocated to general administration and social services (World Bank 1974:25, 126).

The leading beneficiaries were holders of mid- and high-level offices in the party and the administration. Access to the state, and resources allocated by the state, constituted the economic base of this social stratum and the foundation of its social privilege. In this sense, its members emerged as a political "class." This group expanded rapidly, absorbing social groups that had posed immediate challenges to Senghor and his agenda in the 1950s: university graduates and urban intellectuals. By the mid-1960s, almost half of annual government expenditure was devoted to the salaries of about 35,000 civil servants.[32] The UPS political machine also assured a trickling down of government resources to faithful voters in the politically volatile urban areas. Urban *communes* that provided electoral bases for UPS heavyweights received infrastructure, schools, potable water supplies, health centers, etc.[33] The rural areas, where 70–80 percent of Senegal's population was located at the time, received less than 20 percent of total government investment in the 1960s (see Table 3.1).

This kind of political integration and cohesion was bought at the expense of administrative coherence. The logic of machine politics governed policy implementation and the allocation of government funds. Predictably, then, government programs and expenditures often served to enhance the power and wealth of local patrons rather than to further the formally stated goals of policy.[34] When new policies threatened individual power bases, they were often derailed in administrative circuits or on the local level. There were ways of disciplining bosses and patrons from above: Higher-ups could always divert resources away from one faction leader and into the hands of his rivals. This tactic was more effective in ensuring the smooth functioning of the political machine than it was in enforcing administrative coherence.

In spite of the urban bias in state spending, the core electorate of the UPS lay in the rural areas. Over half of all card-carrying UPS members in 1965 were

32. In 1964–5, 47.2 percent of annual government expenditure went to civil service salaries (D. Cruise O'Brien 1971b:272). By 1974, Senegal had 63,000 civil servants and public sector employees (World Bank 1974:52).

33. Obtaining the post of *commune* mayor is "one of the safest and surest methods of building up an electoral clan in Senegal" (Adamolekun 1971:553).

34. Schumacher (1975:xix) argues that "the patronage and status-oriented political ties on which Senegalese leaders have relied in order to build their party machine and expand its bases of support constitute one of the main factors undermining their efforts to transform the state bureaucracy into a system of development administration requisite for achieving the regime's basic economic goals." Gellar et al. (1980) make the same case.

Merchant capital and state power

Table 3.1. *Central government expenditures, 1961–8*
(in billion CFA, current values)

	1961–4	1964–8
Current budget	25	30
Public investment		
Housing, social services, gov't buildings		
Other (rural development, transport,	5	3.6
etc.)	5	6.3
Total	35	40

Source: World Bank 1974:26, 126.

located in the groundnut basin – in the regions of Thiès, Diourbel, and Sine-Saloum. To draw a distinction made by René Lemarchand (1977:102), these rural constituencies were for the most part "brokered constituencies" rather than clienteles organized into political units created by the state. The power of rural brokers – from marabouts to village heads – rested in part upon claims to authority (such as links to Allah) and upon control over goods and services (such as land and rural labor) and lay beyond the scope of the political machine. By integrating these powerholders into the political machine, the regime secured the political compliance of their subordinates "indirectly," much as the colonial administration had in the earlier period. State resources enhanced the power of these brokers and made the reproduction of their power more contingent upon state largesse. The state did not, however, create relations of dependency and control *de nouveau*. On the contrary, power relations in the rural areas that were rooted in long established social hierarchies and relations of production constituted the regime's most solid and reliable bases of political power. Strengthening the control of these rural brokers over their dependants and subordinates was a political imperative, in spite of the contradictions that this often engendered between the official purposes of state spending on the one hand and actual patterns of resource use on the other.

It follows then that the state paid more to win the compliance of urban populations, and that the regime proved less successful in doing so. The UPS created a women's association, a youth organization, students' and teachers' associations, and a national trade union federation to draw hitherto "uncaptured" social groups into political networks tied to the regime. Direct co-optation through the allocation of government jobs and political posts helped to subdue restive elements of the urban middle class. Such links to the political machine, however, remained tenuous and unstable. Terms of support for the regime were renegotiated continuously, and ties of clientage within these networks had to be renewed on an on-going basis. As political factions coalesced or splintered, demands for co-optation proliferated. Physical mobility, occupational mobility, and the expansion of the urban economy and population meant that the political cards were reshuffled constantly, placing relentless pressure on the regime to expand the political machine. In spite of the disproportionate share of resources distributed in Dakar, support for the regime and the UPS remained weakest in the capital.

The effectiveness of the UPS political machine as a mechanism for gathering political power reflected the degree to which opportunities for mobilizing personal power bases, for individual advancement, and for reproducing earlier gains came to depend upon political favors from above. The system functioned within parameters that were analogous to the parameters that narrowed the scope of politics in the *Quatre Communes* during decades of direct colonial rule. Centralization of power in the hands of President Senghor, like the centralization of power in the colonial state, removed executive and legislative decisions from the arena of political competition. Within these limits, political influentials wielded administrative prerogatives and discretion over policy implementation. The race for office and the spoils of office became the focus of political activity. Both before and after independence, the narrowness of opportunities for economic advancement outside of the "race for preferments" raised the stakes of this form of competition. As long as these parameters could be maintained, those who did not play the game of machine politics were likely to be left out entirely.

Containing the scope of politics within the limits of the political machine allowed those at the commanding heights of the ruling alliance – Senghor and his top advisors – to manage factional competition in a way that preserved the coalitional structure of the regime. A narrow circle of high-ranking bureaucrats and advisors close to Senghor defined public policy in the areas of industry, commerce, and finance. Here, French *assistants techniques* and advisors played a critical role. They were largely insulated from currents of factional competition within the party, and they were committed to maintaining Senghor in power.

The "parallel administration"

French civil servants "provided a kind of parallel administration in the first decade of independence" (R. Cruise O'Brien 1979:119). As the political machine took root in the agencies, bureaucracies, and offices of government, Senghor relied upon this "administration within the administration" to maintain a critical measure of centralized control over administration and economic policy-making. Key policy domains were insulated from factional competition. Unlike his counterparts in many other newly independent African states, Senghor resisted pressure to accelerate the "Africanization" of top administrative posts. Ruth Morgenthau (1964:164) observed that "Africanization proceeded at a much slower place than might have been [the case] as a result of Senegal's comparatively high number of qualified men. UPS leaders were reluctant to replace Frenchmen with Senegalese who were their opponents politically."

About seven hundred French bureaucrats and political advisors held posts in the government administration from 1960 to 1965. Their numbers tapered off thereafter, but as Rita Cruise O'Brien argues, "[t]heir power and effectiveness far outweighed their numerical presence."[35] French advisors and administrators held high-level posts in every ministry throughout the 1960s. Some domains were effectively hived off to expatriates. Frenchmen served as ministers of finance during 1957–70, while the ministry itself was "virtually monopolized" by expatriate bureaucrats. French civil servants also held strategic posts in the ministries of industry, information, planning, rural development, and the interior. In addition to positions in the administration, they held senior advisory positions in the cabinet and the executive offices of the presidency.[36] While professional politicians and most Senegalese administrators were rotated frequently from post to post, their French counterparts enjoyed long tenure in office.

The National Assembly, the stronghold of UPS notables, rubber-stamped laws originating in the Executive branch. Economic decision-making and control over the direction of policy were concentrated in the presidency and in the top ranks of the ministries, underscoring the preeminent legislative role – and political function – of these expatriate civil servants. Decisions affecting industry and large-scale commerce were thus removed from the domain of public debate, and from the crosscurrents of factional competition. In this way Senghor retained administrative control, continuity, and a considerable measure of coherence in pivotal domains of policy-making and implementation.

French business interests operating in Senegal enjoyed a privileged place in the narrow circle that exercised power over economic decision-making. The French owners and managers of Senegal's industries, banks, and large commercial houses not only enjoyed regular contact with Senghor, government ministers, and French *assistants techniques,* but also sat on strategic advisory bodies and planning commissions.[37] Representatives of Senegal's two employers' associations occupied positions on virtually all regulatory boards concerned with economic matters.[38] It is almost an understatement to say that "Senegal's economic policies stressed close collaboration between the French business community and the State in economic planning" (Gellar et al. 1980:27).

---

35. R. Cruise O'Brien 1979:101. From about 1,000 in 1961, the number dropped by about 100–150 a year until the mid-1960s. French administrative personnel in the Senegalese government numbered about 450 in 1965. In 1974 French "technical assistants" constituted about 3 percent of the total civil service. See R. Cruise O'Brien 1979:118–21; Foltz 1964:50–1; and Adamolekun 1971:554–8.

36. The *Présidence* includes the commissioners of special services attached to the presidency and the secretary general of the president's cabinet. These individuals were appointed by Senghor and reported directly to him.

37. In the 1960s French businessmen and corporate executives were highly visible members of commissions charged with writing national development plans. See R. Cruise O'Brien 1972:200, 201.

38. The two main *syndicats patronaux* in Senegal were the Union Intersyndicale d'Entreprises et d'Industries (UNISYNDI) and the Syndicat des Commerçants Importateurs et Exportateurs du Sénégal (SCIMPEX). UNISYNDI was a federation of nine *syndicats patronaux* grouped by industrial subsector. SCIMPEX, created as an AOF-wide association of large French export– import companies in 1943, became an autonomous Senegal-based organization in 1960. In 1964

The most visible channel of private sector influence on policy was the Conseil Economique et Social, created in 1961 to allow "leading figures in the private sector" to advise the President on economic and political matters. Members of the Conseil included French bankers, industrialists, the heads of the largest maisons de commerce, top-level government planners, and Senghor himself.

[B]oth officially and informally, [the *Conseil*] is recognized as an extremely important area of discussion and influence. For economic purposes, the government uses it as a sounding-board for intended policy changes which would affect private investment; and businessmen use it to initiate proposals of their own or defend their own interests on proposed government policy. (R. Cruise O'Brien 1972:207)

Significantly, discussions about the proper limits of state intervention in rural markets dominated Conseil proceedings in the early 1960s. The French private sector used this platform to encourage economic "liberalism" when this served their interests – that is, when proposals were made to use state power to promote Senegalese *commerçants* (traders) at their expense, or when state intervention in markets would encroach on their own oligopolies. In particular, the Conseil consistently opposed moves that would give the state a direct role in the rural distribution of consumer goods. Senghor was most responsive. He hinted in 1967 that he might look to the Conseil as a "new cabinet" because, he argued, it kept distance from party politics and government in-fighting (ibid.).

Underwriting the infrastructure of French influence within the Senghor government in the 1960s was a detachment of French troops stationed permanently near the Presidential Palace. "At moments of greatest internal challenge," Senghor relied upon this praetorian guard.[39] French troops were called out in support of Senghor in 1959–60 at the time of the breakup of the Mali Federation, during the constitutional crisis of December 1962, in violent national elections of 1963, and later, during the 1968–1970 period of widespread urban unrest. Within Senegal's own army, French military personnel served as *assistants techniques*. French troops and "advisors" curbed the ambitions of Senegalese military leaders and their subordinates, reminding all concerned of France's active commitment to the political status quo.

---

53 commercial firms belonged to SCIMPEX, including the most important maisons de commerce active in Senegal. These organizations provided "consultative services" to the government and held posts on the Conseils d'Administration of, for example, the Conseil Consultatif National du Travail et du Sécurité Sociale, the Office de la Main-d'oeuvre, the Régie des Chemins de Fer et du Port du Dakar, and the Office des Habitations de Loyer Modéré (*Africa* [Dakar], no. 32 [1964]:63). As pressure groups, these organizations were especially important in mediating the relationship between the government and the smaller French enterprises. Large French firms (including those in the industrial sector) made use of more direct channels of access.

39. Joseph 1976:12. The number of French troops stationed in Senegal reduced from about 28,000 in 1960 to about 7,000 in 1965. France also maintained air and naval facilities in Senegal. The air base was used as a springboard for French military operations in West Africa throughout the 1960s. See also D. Cruise O'Brien 1979:210.

Alliance with the marabouts

Alliance with the Islamic leaders remained the domestic bedrock, the center of gravity, of Senghor's own power. In rejecting de Gaulle's 1958 offer of immediate independence, Senghor protected this alliance at the cost of dividing the UPS. In withdrawing from the Mali Federation, Senghor protected the alliance while forfeiting the economic promise of a regional union. The sacrifice of Mamadou Dia, Senghor's longest and closest political associate, opened vast new horizons for solidifying the pact between Senghor and the Islamic leaders. With Dia went the political impetus and will to use state-controlled rural markets to drive a wedge between rural powerbrokers and a long-subordinated cash crop producing peasantry. As Barker writes (1985:66), "[i]t was at the point when *animation rurale* showed some potential for challenging local power structures that it was stopped."

The support of the Islamic elite guaranteed the political hegemony of the UPS and Senghor's dominance within the party. The sprawling UPS political coalition rested upon this foundation. Irving Leonard Markovitz (1970:92) summarized the regime's stake in alliance with the marabouts:

In addition to their great spiritual and political power, the religious brotherhoods have tremendous economic power. The Mourides alone are said to control considerably more than half of the groundnut crop, which accounts for over 80 per cent of Senegal's gross national product. . . . Because of the power of the marabouts, many political reasons exist for coalition with them. No rural force is more effective in getting out the voters, in keeping the peace, in ensuring that the peasant pays his taxes and submits to military service. In addition, the power of the marabouts in controlling the peasantry enables the Government to satisfy some of the tremendous demands exerted by civil servants and other powerful organized urban groups at the expense of the rural standard of living. These are some of the reasons the Government is unwilling to alienate the marabouts, in either ideological or political terms.

The Dakar-based political elite relied upon the marabouts and the organizational structure of the confréries to perform the delicate task of harnessing groundnut producers to markets controlled by the state while limiting peasants' access to the political arena. Islamic leaders, in turn, used the postcolonial state as they had used the colonial administration. Extension of the state apparatus into the rural areas and official attempts to develop the groundnut economy increased the prestige, wealth, and political clout of the marabouts.

Leaders of the Mouride and Tidjane confréries became central players within the regime and the party. Islamic leaders influenced the appointment of government officials to posts in the groundnut basin and often selected local candidates for regional and national office (Behrman 1970:111–16). In Dakar their representatives sat in the UPS Executive Bureau and in Senghor's cabinet.[40] Grands marabouts were involved in the making of all policies affecting their interests.

40. Four Mourides with close relations with the Grand Khalif were in Senghor's cabinet and the UPS Executive Bureau. Falilou M'Backé, the Grand Khalif of the Mourides, had a full-time, personal representative in the ministry of foreign affairs.

Senghor visited them regularly in the rural areas (often bringing gifts). Islamic leaders could mediate factional disputes within the party and the administration, making or breaking the careers of many a politician or government official. Lucy Behrman (1970) writes that in political power and influence, the Grand Khalif of the Mourides, Falilou M'Backé, was seen in Senegal as second only to Senghor himself. The Islamic leaders successfully blocked, derailed, or simply ignored administrative initiatives that compromised their interests.

Given what appeared to be enormous government concessions to the marabouts in the 1960s, questions about the balance of power between the party–administrative elite on the one hand and the "traditional" rural elite on the other quickly emerged as a central question in analyses of Senegalese politics.[41] Development theory of the 1960s encouraged analysts to frame their questions in these terms: modernization theory defined tension between modernizing elites and traditional society as the main axis of conflict in African politics. Observers of Senegalese politics argued consistently that the Dakar-based politicians retained the upper hand in this relationship.[42] They pointed to two factors that inhibited the mobilization of a broad Islamic front. First the marabouts were divided as a group. Rivalries within the confréries and competition between the Mouride and Tidjane orders for economic resources and political influence limited possibilities for collective action.[43] Senghor successfully played on these rivalries, just as he fueled and manipulated other forms of factional competition. Second, the rising economic status of the marabouts in the 1960s – a critical ingredient in their ability to attract and retain ever-larger followings, and thus in their ability to command political power – was largely a reflection of the expanded inflow of government resources.[44] In this sense, the marabouts found themselves in a position similar to that of the powerbrokers rooted in the party-bureaucratic apparatus. The 1970s observers of Senegalese politics noted that these factors limited the collective bargaining power of the Islamic leaders, denying them the power of political initiative. The same factors compromised the ability of other factions within the ruling elite to exercise the power of initiative,

41. See, for example, Behrman 1970; Markovitz 1970; D. Cruise O'Brien 1975.
42. The rural elite "appeared as very much the subordinate partner in a governing alliance with urban politicians and bureaucrats" (D. Cruise O'Brien 1971b:272).
43. The marabouts attempted only once to organize a common front to counterbalance the secular political elite and advance their collective interests: in 1957–8. This attempt occurred just after Senegal acceded to "self-government" under the UPS. Lucy Behrman writes that in 1956–7, "Muslim leaders still feared that an African government might seek to alter the pattern of relations set up by the French and might attempt to reform the brotherhoods and injure the position of the [marabouts]" (1970:80–1). Senghor reassured them (idem 1970:82). On the question of the limited capacity for "united action" on the part of the confréries and the marabouts, see also idem 1970:69–79; Foltz 1964:115. On the current period, see M.-C. Diop and M. Diouf 1990:69–78.
44. Foltz 1964:49. Donal Cruise O'Brien (1971b:272) also stresses this point: "While the cooperative movement increased the institutional resources of the rural notables, it should be made clear that these resources were made available by the national government."

and thus helped to preserve the coalitional structure of the regime and Senghor's place within it.

When viewed as core members of a widening and heterogeneous ruling coalition rather than as "rivals" or obstacles in the path of the Dakar-based elite, the question of bargaining power has a different meaning. Once the Diaist threat was defused, the Dakar-based leaders never attacked the rural foundations of the marabouts' power; on the contrary, they reinforced them. Mouride and Tidjane marabouts and confréries thus had no cause to organize as a collective force to defend their positions. The clout of the Islamic elite lay in the dependence of the regime as a whole upon reproducing their power. To use Mouzelis's (1989) language, this was a "reproduction requirement" not only of the Senghor regime, but also of the internal political order that was constructed under colonialism and expanded in the 1950s and 1960s. If the efforts of the Islamic elite were directed at preserving the existing social structure in the rural areas and fortifying their own positions within it, then the rest of the regime was an accomplice in this project, either by design or by default. Government initiatives that were opposed by the marabouts – from *Animation Rurale* to land reform to the rapid extension of public schooling in the rural areas – were dropped.[45]

The central and indispensable place of the Islamic elite within the ruling coalition bound the regime as a whole to a rural order already showing clear signs of economic stagnation and decay, a rural order that constricted possibilities for accumulation and investment in the productive base of Senegal's economy. The Senghor regime sank its roots in a rural political economy forged through the logic of colonial indirect rule and the workings of merchant capital.

MATERIAL BASES OF THE NEOCOLONIAL ORDER

The political class cast its lot with interests vested in the economic status quo. Established forms of control over productive domains of the economy remained intact, giving the Senegalese economy its starkly neocolonial character. Macroeconomic indicators reveal little change in the structure of the economy in the 1960s (Table 3.2). Within this framework, the import–export trade remained the primary locus of accumulation. Rural surpluses were appropriated from peasant producers, much as they had been in the earlier period, through the dual flux of a buy cheap, sell dear trading system. Commercial reforms of the 1960s gave the state a larger share of this process and a larger role in it. Development policy in the 1960s aimed at expanding agricultural and industrial production within existing economic structures through the intensification of policies worked out in the 1950s.[46] This meant that limits to development that had presented themselves clearly in the preceding decade would be reproduced.

---

45. "[C]haque tentative de réforme entreprise par l'Etat était voué à l'échec, si elle visait les intérêts et les privilèges des marabouts" (Halpern 1972:118).
46. Economic development policies in the 1960s "closely resembled those which the French had furthered through FIDES during the last years of the colonial period" (Gellar et al. 1980:27).

Table 3.2. *Senegal: Gross domestic product, 1959–70*
(constant 1970 prices, billion CFA francs)

	1959	1963	1965	1968	1970
Rural sector					
value	60.3	68.5	79.9	70.3	63.9
% of GDP	32%	34%	37%	33%	27%
Industrial sector					
Manufacturing					
value	16.7	20.7	22.9	27.1	28.6
% of GDP	8%	10%	10%	13%	12%
Total ind. sector[a]					
value	19.3	24.9	28.5	34.6	36.3
% of GDP	10%	12%	13%	16%	15%
Tertiary sector					
Commerce					
value	30.0	30.4	33.9	37.7	39.5
% GDP	15%	15%	16%	18%	16%
Total tertiary					
value	57.1	56.9	60.0	65.8	68.3
% GDP	30%	28%	28%	31%	29%
Public Administration					
Senegalese admin.					
value	15.7	21.5	21.4	22.4	23.6
French admin.					
value	17.6	11.3	6.6	4.2	3.7
Assistance technique					
value	8.9	8.0	7.8	8.4	8.4
Total admin.					
value	42.2	40.8	35.8	35.0	35.7
% GDP	22%	20%	16%	16%	16%
Total GDP at factor prices[b]	187.8	198.6	211.8	211.0	233.4

[a]Total industrial sector, including utilities and mining.
[b]Includes handicrafts and construction.
Source: World Bank 1974:270.

Complicating the picture was the Senegalese commercial class that began to re-emerge in the 1950s. At the time of independence, this social stratum was poised to compete for a share of the groundnut trade. For the regime, the specter of competition in this area was threatening politically as well as economically. The regime relied upon state control over major resource flows in the groundnut economy to draw the rural elite into patronage networks linked to the state. Competition in the groundnut trade could create alternative channels for accumulating rural wealth and influence, ones that by-passed channels mediated by government agents and UPS officials. It would also allow a nascent local private sector to tap part of agricultural surplus, reducing the share that the state could appropriate for itself. How the Senghor regime dealt with this challenge is an important part of the history of Senegal in the 1960s.

The agricultural sector: Groundnuts first

The overall prosperity of the Senegalese economy hinged on the fortunes of the groundnut and, as time would tell, on the fortunes of groundnut producers. French colonial rule turned Senegal into a monocrop exporter by harnessing a large share of land and labor, predominantly in the central basin, to the production of groundnuts. Throughout the 1960s groundnuts continued to generate over 70 percent of all Senegal's foreign exchange. Rural production consumed the energies of almost 80 percent of the population and constituted about 35 percent of gross domestic product (see Tables 3.2 and 3.3).

The postcolonial government adopted the agricultural priorities of the colonial administration (the *priorité de l'arachide* or the groundnuts first policy). It also adopted the agricultural development strategies of the late colonial period. With the demise of *Animation Rurale,* quantitative goals replaced the goal of qualitative changes in production techniques and rural social relations. The centerpiece of the Senghor regime's post-1962 agricultural development effort was a groundnut program aimed at increasing overall output for export. There was a modest infusion of technical inputs into the existing system of extensive cultivation, and total production did increase. By the end of the decade, however, the groundnut economy showed clear signs of recession. Declining productivity and falling export prices for groundnuts, soil erosion and depletion, poor climatic conditions, and the progressive immiserization of the peasantry made the limits and risks of the regime's groundnut strategy painfully clear.

The groundnut program had two basic tenets. The first was the extension of land under groundnut cultivation, within the framework of the existing system of land tenure and land use. The second was the sale of fertilizers and agricultural equipment (hoes, seeders, etc.) to producers. This strategy involved minimal state expenditures (about 14 percent of total development outlays in the mid-1960s) and minimal state intervention in the production process. Mouride leaders spearheaded the drive to open new lands to groundnut cultivation, and thus remained not only the most aggressive "pioneers" but also the largest landholders in the groundnut basin. They were the leading rural beneficiaries of the groundnut program.

State presence was projected into the rural areas by extending the governmental apparatus downward, along the lines of commercial circuits now controlled by the state. Fifteen hundred producer cooperatives were established. Institutions that were SIP in their first incarnation, and the building blocks of grassroots socialism in their second, were restructured and expanded a third time to become the rural outposts of the postcolonial regime. The cooperatives collected the crop from peasant producers in the name of the state monopoly, transported groundnuts to central purchasing stations, and sold agricultural inputs (seed, fertilizer, tools). Peasants mortgaged future harvests to obtain inputs by buying on credit

Table 3.3. *Total employment, 1970 estimates*
(thousands)

Sector	Persons (thousands)
Rural sector	1,200
Traditional handicraft	125
"Modern sector"	
Public, incl. civil service	63
Private sector[a]	54
(Industry)	(25)
Self-employed[b]	50
Domestic workers[c]	20
Unemployed	110
Total (estimate)	1,600

[a]Private sector: industry plus "formal sector" trade and services.
[b]i.e., "informal sector" trade, services, urban production.
[c]Wage-earning domestic workers
Sources: World Bank 1974:53–4; Pfefferman 1968:10.

and repaying later either in cash or in kind. The debt trap tied them to the groundnut and to a purchasing monopoly just as it had in earlier days.

Cooperatives fell under the immediate control of already-powerful elements in rural society, most notably the marabouts (D. Cruise O'Brien 1971b; Copans 1988:210–2). This institutionalized rural notables' control over the flow of resources between the postcolonial state and the peasantry, reinforcing peasants' dependency upon rural authorities who also exercised powers over land allocation, claims to family labor, and claims to a share of the harvest. The state's mechanism of rural extraction – cooperatives linked to the groundnut marketing monopoly – was thus embedded in existing relationships that bound peasant producers to rural elites. Two forces that subordinated the peasantry within the economic and political order – the market and authority structures rooted in precapitalist relations of production – remained locked together as one.

Reinforcing these arrangements was the 1964 *loi sur le domaine national*, which placed all land not held under private title under state control. The state, in turn, confirmed the land-use rights of peasant farmers. Analysts tend to read this law as an (unsuccessful) attempt on the part of the regime to curb the speculative land pioneering of the Mouride marabouts.[47] The law failed in this regard because the Mouride leaders continued to push onto virgin land with or without

47. In 1964, "la loi sur le Domaine National a accordé le droit à la propriété de la terre à chaque cultivateur-paysan. Mais jusqu'en 1967, cette loi qui devait restreindre les droits des marabouts n'a pas été mise à exécution, à cause de leur opposition" (Halpern 1972:114).

state authorization. Indeed, the government granted new land use concessions to the marabouts in areas that under the 1964 law were to be spared the ravages of groundnut cultivation. From another perspective, the *loi sur le domaine national* looks like a move to defend authority-based systems of control over land use rights. As Verdier (1971) wrote, "inspired by the principles of 'African socialism'," the land law of 1964 "aimed to restore the communal aspect of customary tenure . . . and provided for the creation of local councils to allocate land to farmers and to oversee the use of the land." The land law worked to shore up the land-use and land-allocation prerogatives of established rural authorities.

Within villages and households, rural cooperatives worked to shore up existing social relations of production. As members of the local cooperative, household heads were in a position to mediate the access of young persons, unmarried men, and adult women to productive resources (tools, seeds, credit, and fertilizer) distributed by the state.[48] These household heads, in turn, depended upon the fairness, goodwill, and favors of the cooperative officials who mediated their access to state-controlled markets and resources. Donal Cruise O'Brien (1971b: 271) argued that these resources became the objects of "differential distribution" and were often allocated on a patron–client basis.[49]

Marabouts used their influence or control over the cooperatives to consolidate and enlarge their personal followings.[50] At the same time the marabouts used the cooperatives for their own economic purposes. Credit, agricultural inputs, and equipment channeled through the cooperatives went in disproportionate shares to develop the marabouts' own holdings. Large concessions of public land allowed them to establish new estates as they moved from the exhausted soils of the traditional groundnut basin to hitherto unexploited terrain. New roads were built at their request, and the size of their estates increased. In 1967 twenty-seven of the twenty-nine largest landholders in Senegal were marabouts. Twenty of them were Mourides (Halpern 1972:113–5). Government trucks, equipment, loans turned into de facto grants, and the labor of their disciples brought the Mouride leaders' land under groundnut cultivation. The religious leaders also collected the obligatory offerings of their followers. Halpern (ibid.) estimated that prestations paid in cash or kind to the marabouts equaled about 10 percent, and in some cases as much as 20 percent, of the harvest. Much of the wealth so accumulated

---

48. See Waterbury (1987) for a general discussion of the social relationships that organize groundnut and food crop production within extended rural households.

49. "Illicit arrangements developed in the cooperatives' transactions, especially in connection with the various government services which were channelled to the peasants through cooperative officials. Agricultural credit, relief food supplies, medical supplies, refunds on the sale of crops, all became objects of either commercial speculation or of differential distribution" (D. Cruise O'Brien 1971b:271).

50. From a purely religious standpoint, about 4,000 persons in Senegal could be counted as marabouts in the early 1970s (D. Cruise O'Brien 1975:76). The more important ones had followings of at least several thousand persons. The size of a marabout's following redounds directly on his wealth because followers are obliged to make yearly offerings in cash or in kind, as well as to provide labor (and food crops) to sustain production on the marabouts' estates.

was reinvested in attracting and retaining followings (in ceremonies, mosques, pilgrimages, gifts, the organizational structures of the confréries, etc). A share was also invested in urban real estate and commerce. As rural incomes and standards of living declined in the 1960s, leading marabouts accumulated some of the largest personal fortunes in Senegal.[51]

In design and intent, the groundnut program represented an effort to infuse productivity-enhancing inputs into a peasant-based system of production. As such, was the groundnut program the driving wedge in a process that was progressively subordinating peasants to capital? Bernard Founou-Tchuigoua's (1981) analysis of Senegal's groundnut economy suggests that this was the case. He shows how peasants' control over seeds, fertilizer, and the flow of credit essential to the production process diminished steadily during the colonial period. Meanwhile, agricultural extension agents intervened by trying to influence training and production techniques. Founou argues that interventions in the rural economy aimed at controlling inputs and farming methods gave agents of international capital growing control over the production process itself, as well as a direct claim to the harvest through the credit nexus. Producers, in Founou's view, assumed a progressively more proletarian character (1981:48–52). Samir Amin (1981) draws the link between this process and the groundnut program by extending Founou's analytic framework to the postcolonial period. Although something along these lines may have been the aim of international capital (represented, for example, by the World Bank in the postcolonial period), the state's actions as well as the actual course of developments in the groundnut sector raise questions about such an interpretation of the groundnut program and its net effects. In the final analysis, it was enduring limits to the penetration of capital, rather than the progressive "intervention" (*ingérence*) of capital in production, that determined the outcome of the processes that so interested international capital.

Peasants, rather than capital, retained control over the land they cultivated within a noncapitalist system of land tenure and land-use rights. This structure of land control and use was bolstered deliberately by the state. In the immediate postcolonial period, these arrangements did help to reproduce the "conditions of *surexploitation*" of the peasantry.[52] Within this system, however, producers retained control over their own labor (subject to the claims of household, village, and religious authorities), and continued to produce a share of their own "means of subsistence" (food). Thus, in spite of peasants' dependence on groundnut revenues, the allocation of land and labor between commodities that interested the state and international capital on one hand, and food and other necessities that producers would consume themselves on the other, lay in the hands of the direct producers. Because land was not mortgaged to obtain productivity-enhancing

---

51. These marabouts would be the most important ones; only they had personal economic and political clout at the national level. D. Cruise O'Brien 1975:76.

52. Founou (1981:144–5) shows how the *économie de traite* was built through the *surexploitation* of land, groundnut producers, and workers in the groundnut refineries.

inputs, the agents of capital had no access to it, and thus could not turn to a process of land alienation to enforce the extractive relationship. As time would tell, peasants could take "independent" action to curtail the processes that Founou describes by backing out of this relationship with capital. Unlike proletarians, they could abandon the use of productivity-enhancing (purchased) inputs, consume the products of their labor themselves, or even turn away from groundnut production.

Total groundnut production increased over the course of the 1960s at an annual rate of 4 percent. Most of this expansion did not come from the growing use of fertilizers, tools, or new agricultural production techniques. "About sixty percent of this gain came from the expansion of cultivated land," rather than from an intensification of the production process.[53] Per hectare productivity stagnated or even declined. For large marabout-landholders, the availability of new land and the unpaid labor of disciples reduced pressure to adopt more intensive farming techniques. Small-holders found that productivity-enhancing inputs sold through the cooperatives were high-priced and subject to commercial speculation on the part of cooperative officials. The cost of these supplies, coupled with declining producer prices for groundnuts, constrained both the capacity and the willingness of peasant producers to adopt more intensive farming practices. The structure of control over commercial circuits and pricing continued to compromise possibilities for rural development.

Peasants became poorer. The groundnut program was based on the theory that by increasing output, peasant incomes would remain stable in spite of the appropriation of an ever larger share of the surplus by the state. As export prices for groundnuts fell in the 1960s and as the "costs" of rural administration and groundnut marketing mounted, the government tried to maintain its net income from groundnuts by pushing losses onto the producers. Peasants absorbed the full impact of the fateful withdrawal of France's groundnut subsidy in 1967–8. That year, they suffered a sharp, 20 percent fall in producer prices.[54] At the same time, government prices for inputs, set in the 1960s to allow the government a profit margin on these transactions, increased. Because the cooperatives deducted the costs of these inputs (plus interest) from the producer's earnings, sums that peasants actually took home after the harvest were even smaller than nominal or real producer prices would suggest. Producer prices in real terms fell again in 1968–9 in spite of improvements in world prices. Donal Cruise O'Brien (1971b:273) cited one official who estimated, based on 1971 prices, that the

53. World Bank (1974:144–5). Total acreage under groundnut cultivation almost doubled between the early 1950s and 1969, from 700,000 hectares to 1,200,000 hectares as production continued to spread beyond the central groundnut basin to Sénégal Orientale and the Casamance. The World Bank (1974) indicated that groundnut production increased from about 830,000 tons in 1959 to what was then an all-time high of 1,170,000 tons in 1965. See Table 5.1; Halpern 1972:110; and Nascimento and Raffinot 1985:786.

54. Before 1968 France bought the total groundnut harvest from Senegal at a preferential price 17 percent above world market prices. See Chapter 2. Application of EEC rules ended this practice. Producer prices in current CFA francs fell from 22 per kilo to 18 per kilo.

state's net profit per kilo exceeded the official purchase price paid to the producer.

Real producer prices for groundnuts declined almost continuously over the course of the 1966–80 period.[55] Nascimento and Raffinot (1985) argue that postcolonial pricing policies were guided by the objective of maximizing state revenues in the short-run, and suggest that this policy was counterproductive in the medium run and long run. In the earlier period, colonial authorities had recognized the counterproductive tendencies inherent in this process. That is why they tried to maintain total production and exports by subsidizing producer prices. After 1953 the colonial authorities had compressed the margins of the maisons de commerce by regulating prices in favor of producers. When the postcolonial state nationalized the groundnut circuit and assumed the position previously occupied by the maisons de commerce, it chose the squeeze-the-peasantry option in order to maintain the state's income level. As Nascimento and Raffinot (ibid.) show, this process of draining wealth out of the rural economy limited total output (export earnings) in the long run. It also short-circuited processes that could have produced gains in productivity.

Declining real producer prices and rising input costs worked in tandem to reverse an early-1960s trend toward more intensive farming practices on small plots under groundnut cultivation. Particularly serious was a decline in the use of fertilizer on small holdings. As the Portères mission of 1952 had shown so dramatically, groundnut cultivation in fragile and sandy Sahelian soil quickly degraded the land. The prime means of combating this process was the ever-intensifying use of fertilizer. Fertilizer use had increased 25 percent annually between 1962 and 1967, reaching 62,000 tons in 1967. In the mid-1960s, fertilizers were used on 28 percent of the land under groundnut cultivation. Total sales of fertilizer began to drop dramatically toward the end of the decade, falling to only 13,000 tons in 1970. "Similarly, in 1970 the purchase of agricultural equipment fell to less than 50 percent of its 1967 peak level" (World Bank 1974:63). The intensity of extractions engineered through agricultural marketing circuits led peasants to reduce the level of their investments in agricultural production. At the same time, however, they remained largely dependent upon the groundnut for cash and for access to tools and other necessities allocated through the cooperatives. In the early 1970s Senegal's rural population derived an estimated 66–90 percent of its monetary income from the groundnut (ibid.: 138; Anson-Meyer 1974:17). The peasants were caught in a bind. Groundnut production worked to impoverish small-scale producers, but they could not afford to abandon this activity. They coped by minimizing their investments of land, labor, and financial resources in groundnut cultivation.

The paramount place of the groundnut in Senegal's *programme agricole* implied only marginal and half-hearted efforts on the part of the government to promote the diversification of commodity production on small holdings. Yet

---

55. The real drop over the 1960–83 period was 30 percent (Nascimento and Raffinot 1985:780). See also Casswell 1984:49.

crops other than groundnuts (i.e., food crops) covered 50–55 percent of all
cultivated land during the first decade of independence. Fertilizers were used on
only 12 percent of this land in the mid-1960s.[56] After 1965 the World Bank
(1974:142–3) and others began to discern a marginal shift away from groundnuts
and toward food crops, mostly millet and sorghum. For the most part, these
crops were devoted to family consumption (to supplement rice, most of which
was imported), not as an income-earning activity. As the decade wore on, however, the total volume of cereal crop output began to fall dramatically, signaling a
deepening of the crisis of productivity and production in the rural sector as a
whole. Cereal crop production fell below 1965 levels by about 24 percent in
1966, 19 percent in 1967, and 28 percent in 1970. "More than three-quarters of
this drop in production was due to a fall in productivity" caused by the deterioration of soils and a 50 percent per annum drop in the use of fertilizers between
1967 and 1970 (ibid.).

During the period of the Second Plan (1965–9), the government tacitly acknowledged the limits of a development strategy centered on peasant cultivation
of groundnuts. Rather than trying to reform the groundnut basin, where much of
the rural population lived, the regime opted to by-pass it. Foreign investors were
invited to spearhead agro-industry projects that would decrease Senegal's dependence on groundnuts as a source of foreign exchange. The most important of
these projects involved the intensification of a process begun in the 1950s: the
development of cotton cultivation in Eastern Senegal on the basis of out-grower
schemes. From the perspective of earning foreign exchange, this project proved
to be quite successful after 1970.[57] Other schemes hatched in the late 1960s
aimed at producing sugar and fresh vegetables for export. These projects did not
reduce Senegal's dependency on the groundnut as a earner of foreign exchange in
the first decade of independence. Only the cotton project would prove to be
successful in this regard in the 1970s.

Agricultural surpluses appropriated from rural producers fueled the growth of
government employment and expenditures on social services. As Markovitz
(1970:92) argued, these expenditures helped the regime to consolidate the party
and to cultivate support where the regime's electoral base was weaker – in the
cities and among the urban educated class. For the regime, enhancing the power
of established rural notables, especially the power of the Islamic marabouts, was

56. On fertilizer use in the mid-1960s, see also IMF 1970:514.
57. The CFDT (La Compagnie Française pour le Développement des Fibres Textiles), a mixed
    private–public French corporation formed in the late 1930s for research and development of
    cotton cultivation in the French colonies, introduced cotton cultivation in eastern Senegal around
    the time of independence. This experiment proved successful and was turned into a large-scale
    project in the mid-1960s. The goal was to supply the local textile industry with cotton fiber (15–
    20 percent of projected total production) and to export the balance to Europe. The CFDT ginned
    and marketed cotton produced by Senegalese producers using CFDT seeds, fertilizers, and
    credit. Between 1965 and 1968, cotton production increased from 300 tons to 9,700 tons. The
    area under cultivation increased from 400 hectares to 6,700 hectares (IMF 1970:502, 516). By
    1971, production reached about 21,000 tons, yielding 3,500 tons of cotton fiber for the local
    textile industry and 4,000 tons of fiber for export (World Bank 1974:148). See Lele et al. 1989.

a low-cost and "indirect" means of controlling the politically and economically strategic rural population.

The industrial sector: Promotion of import–substitution

In his 1969 annual report to the UPS congress, Senghor stated that "[w]e want, by the year 2000, to achieve the status of an industrial society and all our efforts will be aimed at this objective. . . . Our major objective is to supply the Senegalese market to the maximum degree with products that are made-in-Senegal" (Ediafric 1970:468). Rapid industrialization would be achieved by assuring the "profitability and security of investments" (CINAM et SERESA 1960). Established French-owned industries would be expanded, and new subsectors of light manufacturing would attract an inflow of French investment.

At the time of independence, Dakar represented the largest concentration of industrial activity in Francophone Africa. Dakar's oldest and largest factories processed groundnuts for export to France. Most of the newer factories (implanted after World War II) produced basic consumer goods from imported inputs.[58] The largest of these were affiliates or subsidiaries of French firms engaged in the same manufacturing activities in Europe. Industrial surveys undertaken immediately after independence counted about 150 industrial firms in Senegal. Thirty-six "large firms" accounted for more than 50 percent of total output.[59] French capital accounted for 95 percent of all investment (R. Cruise O'Brien 1979:109). Because local industries covered, on average, only about 30 percent of domestic demand for the goods they produced, there was substantial room for further import substitution aimed at the Senegalese market.

Import-substitution industry in Senegal was built upon an elaborate structure of market control that worked to deliver captive markets to local manufacturers. This was as true after independence as it was in the 1950s. Under competitive market conditions, production could not generate profits sufficient to attract foreign capital into industrial-scale manufacturing. In the 1960s and early 1970s, the package of commercial incentives offered to foreign firms was decisive in attracting new investment. Import controls, domestic market monopolies, and guaranteed market shares – all granted and enforced by the state – gave manufacturers a great deal of control over the terms of domestic market competition. Under this system of market control, the profits that attracted investment were what Bates (1981:103) called noncompetitive rents, or "increases in earnings of firms created by the ability of prices in the protected industry to rise above the level that would be sustained if the industry were subject to competition." The profits that induced investment were extracted from consumers in the form of high prices, rather than from wage laborers in the form of surplus value. Manufacturers' constant complaints about excessively high wage rates and "excessively low" labor productivity in Senegal underscored this point.

58. See Chapter 2.
59. "Large firms" were those employing more than 200 workers. ISEA 1964.

Although overall costs of production in Senegal remained higher than those in France, the low degree of competition prevailing on the domestic market allowed for very large commercial markups. The interests of light industries and of the dominant French commercial firms were closely aligned, and even complementary. Market-sharing *ententes* between local industrialists and the leading maisons de commerce meant that the rents generated by import controls could be shared by these two parties. And as the maisons de commerce had discovered in the late 1950s, the existence of import-substitution industry provided a justification for fortifying restrictions on competition that guaranteed their positions. The state played a critical role in protecting the ability of light industries and their commercial partners to appropriate rents generated by import restrictions. Authorizations to import goods in heavily regulated product categories – that is, goods likely to compete with local industry – were allocated to importers named by the government through a system of *autorisations préalables*. Foreign exchange was rationed in a similar way. Throughout the 1960s, French maisons de commerce operating hand-in-hand with local industries continued to monopolize the importation of goods governed by quotas, *autorisations préalables*, and foreign currency rationing.

Foreign industry and commercial interests were also direct beneficiaries of the "accords of association" signed by France and Senegal at the time of independence. These accords renewed the Zone Franc monetary guarantees that assured free convertibility of the CFA franc (at a fixed parity of 50 CFA to one French franc) and guaranteed unrestricted capital flows. Decolonization did impose one particular inconvenience on commercial and industrial interests operating in Dakar. Balkanization of the AOF and the consequent rupture of trading relations with Guinea (in 1958) and Mali (in 1960) fragmented the large regional market that absorbed made-in-Senegal manufactured goods in the 1950s.[60] In 1960 and 1961 the Senegalese government moved quickly to compensate for the loss of regional markets by capturing a larger share of the domestic market for local industry. New tariffs and bans were immediately placed on the importation of key consumer goods.[61] From the start, the postcolonial government demonstrated its willingness to rely upon a battery of market controls inherited from the colonial administration in order to stabilize and underwrite the growth of local industry.

In 1961 the government announced an Investment Code that renewed the favorable tax and customs arrangements that the colonial administration had granted to local manufacturing industries. French businesses did not find this

60. Guinea withdrew from the Zone Franc and switched to a nonconvertible currency. Diplomatic and trading relations between Mali and Senegal were formally broken when the Mali Federation fell part. Mali rerouted its trade through Abidjan. The long-term consequences of the dissolution of the AOF for the Dakar industries became increasingly obvious over the course of the 1960s. Neighboring countries began to tax intraregional trade to bolster state revenues. They also raised barriers to intraregional trade to promote the development of industries to serve their own domestic markets. Three regional agreements governed trade among the CFA Franc countries between 1959 and 1980. Each was more restrictive than the last.
61. The textile industries were the main beneficiaries of these new tariffs and bans. See Chapter 4.

code satisfactory because it failed to declare explicitly that foreign investors would enjoy all rights and advantages that might, in the future, be extended to local investors. In 1962 a new Investment Code appeared. It resolved uncertainties about the regime's commitment to foreign capital.[62] General dispositions of this Investment Code also protected foreign capital from all forms of nationalization, guaranteed free and unrestricted repatriation of invested capital and profits, and granted foreign firms easy and even preferential access to state-subsidized sources of credit.[63]

Tax breaks, import tax exemptions, and utilities subsidies were granted to new investors and to industrialists *sur place* extending their operations. The largest investors were granted the most favorable place under the investment code: *entreprise conventionée* status. This status provided a *"régime fiscal de longue durée"* wherein the government renounced all rights to modify a firm's tax and customs status for a twenty-year period. By 1974 sixty-seven manufacturing firms had been granted this most privileged status. Twenty-four others were registered as *entreprises prioritaires,* which provided similar incentives and tax breaks without the twenty-year guarantee.[64] Privileged status under the Investment Code was granted to "practically all of the more important firms in Senegal." Even the World Bank would raise "serious doubts" about the merits of Investment Code arrangements, arguing that incentives granted for foreign manufacturers were "too automatic" (*peu discrétionnaire*), "too generous," and "too costly" in terms of the national tax base.[65]

Most importantly, the Code stipulated that protection against competing imports would be granted as needed to import-substitution industries. When investment agreements were written, new tariff levels were set according to the manufacturer's estimate of the rate of tariff protection needed to ensure profitable local sales. "When it is decided that import restrictions are in the interest of a factory,

---

62. Title I of the 1962 Code stated that "[l]es investisseurs étrangers bénéficient des mêmes droits et facilités que les nationaux."
63. "In general, bank credit is more easily secured [*plus largement accordé*] and clearly less expensive than in Europe, especially when investments benefit from Investment Code status and when the BCEAO [the central bank] offers to rediscount the loan [*accorde le réescompte*]." The BCEAO could discount loans to private foreign enterprises when these projects "offered an economic benefit, conformed to the objectives laid out in the national development plan, or were approved by the interministerial investment committee" (SONEPI 1973:72–83). Loans for foreign investors could be drawn from foreign aid accounts held in the national development bank (BNDS) and the Union Sénégalaise de Banque (USB) (idem).
64. The Investment Code distinguished between *prioritaire* and *conventionnée* enterprises on the basis of either scale or the desirability of the project in the eyes of the government's Comité Interministériel des Investissements (CII). In principle, *entreprises prioritaires* involved investments over 50 million CFA francs (raised to 100 million in 1972) or created at least fifty permanent jobs for Senegalese. *Entreprises conventionnées* involved investments of 200 million CFA francs (raised to 500 million in 1972) and were accorded the long-term fiscal and customs guarantees. Exemptions to project size criteria were made for projects that were "particularly interesting" given the objectives of the Development Plans, that created factories outside Dakar, or that created an "important number" of jobs. See SONÈPI 1971:53–4; idem 1973:80–3.
65. World Bank 1970; idem 1974:160, 164, 169, 212–13.

the government and the industry concerned agree upon the price at which the product in question should be sold. . . . [T]he price levels that are established obviously tend to assure the industry a substantial profit margin" (World Bank 1970:19–23). Monopolies or guaranteed market shares could also be arranged upon request. Exceptions to this rule were made only when projects threatened the interests of established manufacturers. As the 1962 Code stated, "[n]ew ventures may not compete with industries already established in Senegal in a manner contrary to the general interest."[66] The privileges of first entrant were protected.

The Senegalese government adopted the colonial administration's comprehensive system of discrimination against imports from non-Zone Franc countries. The minimum import tax levied against all consumer goods was about 20 percent. Imports from outside the Zone Franc also carried customs duties that could run in excess of 100 percent. Zone Franc policies singled out a set of so-called cheap labor exporters (such as Japan, India, Eastern Europe, and Portugal) for the heaviest customs duties or outright import bans. Quantitative restrictions (quotas) and currency rationing reinforced the system of tax and tariff barriers.[67] This formidable structure ensured that France remained Senegal's primary supplier of imported goods, protected local industry, and generated 40–4 percent of the government's fiscal receipts in the 1960s.[68]

When quotas, taxes, and customs duties did not offer sufficient protection to local manufacturers, and when outright import bans were inconvenient, the government resorted to *valeurs mercuriales*. *Valeurs mercuriales* were arbitrary tax bases set by the administration and applied to low-cost imports. This system ensured that the absolute tax burden on a given category of imported goods would be high, even when c.i.f. values were low.[69] *Mercuriales* were an often-used, flexible, and powerful tool for artificially inflating the prices of imports in targeted product categories.

Market protection in all its various forms was an advantage "often demanded" and "willingly and easily accorded" to foreign investors (SONED 1977a:53). Revisions were arranged at the initiative of manufacturers as market conditions changed over time.

66. *Le Journal Officiel du Sénégal*, 31 mars 1962, modifiée par la loi 65-34 du 19 mai 1965.
67. Many of the quantitative import restrictions were laid out in the annual Programme Général des Importations (PGI), as they had been in the 1950s. The PGI governed the importation of goods purchased with foreign exchange (i.e., goods purchased outside the Zone Franc). In addition to regulating the balance of payments, the PGI served a protectionist function. Foreign exchange was not allocated for imports that would compete with locally manufactured goods.
68. On fiscal receipts, see IMF 1970:563.
69. For example, say that shirts are imported from Portugal. The c.i.f. value declared by the importer is 100 CFA francs per shirt. The tax rate on this item is 100 percent. After the shirts clear customs, each is worth 200 CFA francs. Now say that the local shirt manufacturer cannot compete with shirts sold for about 200 francs and wants additional tariff protection. The administration can declare a *valeur mercuriale* (tax base) for shirts equal to 300 francs. Then the import tax on each shirt would be 100 percent of 300. After clearing customs, the shirt *mercurialisée* would be worth 400 CFA francs.

Table 3.4. *Rates of domestic market protection by manufacturing activity, 1972*

Activity	Domestic Mkt. protection[a] (observed)	Nominal protection[b] (tariff)	Effective protection[c]
Wheat flour		1.50	2.13–4.59
Canned vegetables	1.44	1.61	4.07
Biscuits		1.49	
Milk products	1.34		1.81
Gray cloth	1.49–1.69[d]	1.50	3.29
Finished cloth	1.48		2.06
Cotton thread			1.52
Garments		1.68	1.06–1.17
Knitwear			1.99
Paint			2.04
Soap			1.96
Matches			8.43
Cement	0.97	1.44	
Animal feed	1.17	1.37	2.33
Beds		1.61	
Mattresses		1.61	
Paper products			1.47

Notes: These figures are estimates.

[a]Rates of domestic market protection (observed). These are price comparisons observed at the level of particular firms: i.e., ratio of domestic ex-factory prices to world (EEC) border prices. As the authors of the reports cited below note, in all cases except gray cloth, these figures are lower than the tariff. This suggests the existence of tariff redundancy.

[b]Nominal rates of protection (tariff). These figures compare the domestic price of an import (c.i.f. plus import duty and the *taxe sur le chiffre d'affaires*, or TCA) to the c.i.f. price of the import, adjusted for the TCA paid by local manufacturers.

[c]Effective protection. These are effective protection coefficients (EPCs), designed to measure real rates of protection to local value-added. Calculations were made at the firm level.

[d]For gray cloth, the observed rate of protection of 1.49 is based on comparisons with EEC prices. The 1.69 figure is based on a comparison of domestic ex-factory price with the c.i.f. price of similar goods imported from China.

Sources: World Bank, "Economic Incentives and Resource Costs in Senegal (a study directed by Bela Balassa)," unpub. ms., June, 1975: 41–4 (restricted circulation); World Bank, "Incentives and the Economic Efficiency of Resource Allocation in Senegalese Industry, 1971–1973," unpub. ms., September 1984: 2.23–2.24 (restricted circulation).

The ad hoc, particularistic decision-making that characterized the writing of Investment Code agreements and revisions in the tariff structure was characteristic of the government's routine relations with the foreign owners and managers of industry in Senegal. Industrialists took their requests for exemptions from import taxes, exemptions from labor code or commercial regulations, additional protection against competing imports, and other special advantages to "the high-

Table 3.5. *Senegal's manufacturing sector, 1962–7[a]*

	Employment (#)		Turnover (in billions CFA)[b]		Value-added (in billions CFA)[c]		Firms (#)[d]
	1962	1967	1962	1967	1962	1967	1967
Subsectors							
Groundnut processing	2,790	2,840	17.0	20.4	4.2	5.1	5
Food and beverages	3,205	4,060	2.5	12.4	3.8	4.1	24
Textiles	2,975	4,030	5.0	8.0	1.8	3.8	13
Metalworking		800	6.5	10.0	2.3	4.1	10
Other Industries:							
Chemicals (soap/fertilizer)			1.3	6.4	0.5	1.7	12
Tobacco and matches			1.8	1.6	1.1	1.1	5
Construction material			1.4	1.3	0.6	0.6	7
Wood and furniture			0.9	1.1	0.6	0.8	6
Paper and printing			1.4	1.3	0.2	0.3	8
Subtotal, other industries	1,760	2,910					
Overall Total	10,730	14,640	37.8	62.5	15.1	21.6	90

[a]All figures are indicative of orders of magnitude only since important inconsistencies and irregularities exist in the data.
[b]Turnover in current prices, CFA francs.
[c]Value-added in constant 1971 prices, CFA francs.
[d]Number of firms. Only firms ranked among Senegal's top 100–120 firms are counted.
Sources: IMF 1970:531; Courtois 1971:10; World Bank 1974:282–3.

est levels of government."[70] When broad government objectives such as those stated in the development plans did not suit firm-level needs, industrialists simply tended to ignore them.[71] In practice this meant that the government granted extensive and unilateral concessions to local industry.

Senegal's industrial development strategy was fairly successful in stimulating investment in import-substitution industry in the 1960s (Table 3.5). The manufacturing sector's contribution to GDP rose from 10 percent in 1959 to 18 percent by the end of the 1960s. Investments in manufacturing increased at the rate of about 14 percent a year between 1962 and 1967 and sped up at the end of the decade, fueling a 5–6 percent annual rate of growth in the context of an

70. From interviews in Dakar with textile industry executives and with agents of the ministries of commerce and finance, the BCEAO, the *Présidence*, and the Inspection du Travail, April 1985 through April 1986.
71. In 1960 these objectives included Africanization of shop-floor supervisory and skilled posts, local reinvestment of profits, and more local purchases of inputs. With regard to these objectives, Pfefferman argues that "[t]he freedom of the government to influence . . . the private sector is very limited indeed. . . . It might be realistic for national planners to exclude industry from their plans and to focus on agricultural development; the government does not have significant influence on decisions to invest, to recruit, and to train" (Pfefferman 1968:252).

Table 3.6. *Economic growth rates, 1959–71*[a]

	1959–60 to 1964–5	1964–5 to 1970–1	1967–8 to 1970–1
Industry[b]	5.8	6.6	8.4
Rest of the economy	1.4	0.6	1.5

[a]Average annual rates of growth in constant prices. Source does not indicate base year for calculating constant prices.
[b]Excluding groundnut processing.
Source: World Bank 1974:152.

otherwise nearly stagnant economy (see Table 3.6).[72] By the early 1970s about 75 percent of this industrial sector consisted of consumer goods manufacturing; groundnut processing made up most of the balance. The textile industry remained the most dynamic subsector of import-substitution industry.

Senegal paid a high price for the industrial growth achieved in the 1960s. Tax concessions granted to French firms reduced industry's direct contribution to government revenues to almost zero. When government subsidies and import tax breaks accorded to manufacturing were taken into account, the industrial sector's direct contribution to the overall tax base was negative.[73] Repatriated profits and earnings helped to make Senegal a net exporter of capital to its ex-colonial ruler. The government, however, did not come away empty-handed. It shared in the benefits of local market protection. Import taxes and duties constituted the government's leading source of fiscal receipts. Consumers bore these costs of taxes and rents generated by "sell dear" policies. Rural producers lost on both sides of the dual flux of trade. They sold groundnuts "cheap" and bought manufactured goods "dear," just as they had during the colonial period.

The practice of according foreign firms monopoly status through the Investment Code condoned large inefficiencies and high profits in manufacturing. In most subsectors, "2 or 3 firms controlled more, sometimes much more, than 50 percent of the domestic market" (World Bank 1974:160). Pfefferman (1968:58) reported that in the mid-late 1960s, 52 percent of Senegal's largest 160 firms enjoyed a monopoly position on the local market. Of the remainder, 22 percent were part of a coordinated oligopoly. Pfefferman comments that, "The expatriate firms' policy is essentially one of profit maximization in the short run; . . . Protection and monopoly situations on the domestic product market ensure high

72. IMF 1970:528; World Bank 1974:80.
73. Senghor, in his annual address to the UPS Congress in 1968, "a fait remarquer qui si les investissements privés ont été particulièrement importants ces derniers temps au Sénégal, ils ne se traduisent pas pour autant par des recettes budgetaires, mais au contraire par une moins value fiscale. . ." (*Marchés Tropicaux* [11 mai 1968]: 1,269). This same point is made by the World Bank: "Les moins values résultant des exonérations accordées aux entreprises en vertu du Code des Investissements sont assez considérables" (World Bank 1970:19–23). See also idem 1974:10, 30, 109.

Table 3.7. *Profit ratios: Net profit/turnover,[a] 1956–67*

	1956	1959	1962	1967
Subsector				
Mines (salt, phosphates)	33.3	12.9	−11.3	
Energy	35.5		33.9	28.0
Food industries	3.3	10.1	8.3	
Textiles	14.9	10.0	13.1	29.1
Metalworking[b]	12.5	10.6	5.4	17.8
Soap, fertilizers, etc.	19.2	13.3	17.7	15.9
Woodworking	4.4	3.1	2.7	
All industry (construction excluded)	9.8	9.2	9.3	

[a]The author of the table (Courtois 1971:122) notes that, from the investor's point of view, returns on capital invested would be a better indicator of profitability than net profit/turnover ratios. Cross-sectional data to calculate this ratio were not available.
[b]There are irregularities in the accounting categories *"industries métallurgique"* and *"industries mécaniques."* The 1956 and 1967 figures are rough estimates of averages for the two subsectors combined. Apparently, in 1959 and 1962, the industries were lumped together in the BCEAO study cited below.
Source: Guy Courtois 1971:120, Table 42 (based in part on BCEAO, *Le Développement Economique du République du Sénégal*, juin, 1963).

rates of profit and fast amortization of capital. There is virtually no competition in Senegalese industry" (1968:63).

Courtois (1971) calculated profit ratios (net profits / turnover) for the main subsectors of manufacturing industry from 1956 to 1967. His results are reported in Table 3.7. Increasing rates of profit in the textile industry after 1959 stand out. The average for all Senegalese manufacturing works out to be 9 percent, three times higher than average rates of profit calculated in the same manner for manufacturing industry in France.[74] As Courtois argued, "high prices and the structure of direct taxation explain the high profit rates. The absence of internal and external competition, in effect, permits enterprises to fix their prices at very remunerative levels, independent of their costs. Protection from imports is the essential cause of high rates of profit."

Meanwhile, consumer goods industries in Senegal remained heavily reliant on imported inputs (see Table 3.8). Reduced taxes on imported intermediate goods, and the duty-free importation of capital goods, fostered the expansion of last-

74. Courtois 1971:120–5. The calculation is based on a sample of the 500 "leading industries" in France. Net profits/turnover ratios averaged 3 percent for this set of firms.
75. Under the terms of the Investment Code, industrialists in Senegal were exempted from many of the import taxes and duties levied against capital goods and inputs used in the local manufacturing process. "Les exonérations de droits et taxes sur les matériels et matériaux non produits au Sénégal et nécessaires à la réalisation du programme [d'investissement] sont très généralement accordées" (SONED 1977a:48). See Amin 1973:18–19; Pfefferman 1968:208.

Table 3.8. *Industrial intermediate goods:*
Domestic inputs as percentage of total 1962–6

	1962	1966
Subsector		
Food products and misc.[a]	18	51
Textiles	37	26
Clothing, shoes	40	39
Soap, fertilizer, etc.	25	21
Beverages	19	36
Paper, wood	17	34
Grain milling	19	15
All manufacturing industry.	62	50

[a] I.e., *industries alimentaires et diverses.*
Source: World Bank 1970:Table 15.

stage processing industries.[75] Incentives to forge links with local suppliers of intermediate goods or to undertake backward integration were limited. Owners of industry, therefore, tended not to invest or otherwise modify production to accommodate such changes. The process of "capital deepening" was restrained and industry itself remained a large-scale consumer of imports. Manufacturers solidified direct links with overseas suppliers or made their foreign purchases through the large maisons de commerce. As a result, the growth of the manufacturing sector did little to stimulate – and in some ways actually constrained – the accumulation of capital in the hands of entrepreneurs who found themselves outside of this privileged circle.

By pursuing the kind of industrial development achieved during the last decade of the colonial period, the Senegalese government left control over the secondary sector in the hands of private French manufacturers. Throughout the 1960s and 1970s, light industry remained overwhelmingly foreign-owned and -managed. Compared to foreign firms operating in other African countries, French-owned firms in Senegal were unusually reticent to absorb Senegalese into supervisory and managerial posts. Most continued to rely on large expatriate staffs, including technicians often hired from parent firms or equipment suppliers in France. Foreign personnel was considerably more expensive than local personnel would have been. The fact that firms continued to rely on expatriates reflected the absence of compelling pressures to reduce costs of production. It also suggests that returns on investment were collected in part in the form of contract fees paid for foreign personnel. Foreign firms in Senegal were also unusually reticent to sell shares to local investors. Because they had easy access to government-subsidized investment funds in Senegal, they had no compelling incentive to do so. Throughout the 1960s and 1970s, the Senghor government resisted pressures to create conditions that would give industrialists strong incentives to behave otherwise.

The maintenance of French control over industry and finance had at least two important implications for the nature and scope of machine politics in Senegal. First, channels of government–private sector intermediation by-passed the centers of authority and decision-making that were most affected by factional maneuvering and competition. Informal and formal channels of French private sector representation and influence by-passed the ruling party, the parliament, and the Byzantine networks of the Senegalese bureaucracy. The French private sector enjoyed direct access to top government administrators. As argued above, this system worked to insulate important sectors of economic activity, policy-making, and policy implementation from the influences and pressures of *clan* politics. Second, the de facto French monopoly over lucrative opportunities in industry, commerce, and banking left open very few avenues of economic advancement in the private sector to Senegalese. The main avenues of economic advancement open to Senegalese were in the public sector, and these avenues were controlled by politicians and bureaucrats.

The commercial sector

Established forms of control over urban and rural production remained intact in the 1960s. To expand the state's internal revenue base and to create "space" for a local private sector, the Senghor regime began to reform the commercial sector.

Nationalization of the groundnut trade in 1960 was the government's major and most dramatic move in the domain of economic policy. The stage had been set in the mid- to late-1950s, as the profitability of the groundnut trade declined and as criticism of *la traite* mounted. Peasants' and Senegalese merchants' frustration with French colonialism was directed in large part at the exploitative trading companies. Both the leftist and "moderate" wings of the nationalist movement also attacked the parasitic foreign trading oligopolies. Although colonial officials did not share in the nationalism of this cause, their concerns over the AOF's balance of trade and high-cost structure, and their fears that squeezing the rural areas would lead to collapse of the groundnut economy, were also articulated in part as a critique of the trading practices of the maisons de commerce. These pressures for reform were mutually reinforcing, and they emerged at a time when the maisons de commerce themselves were beginning to back out of rural trade.

The government of Senegal nationalized the export circuit in 1960 in the name of liberating peasants from the exploitation of the trading companies and usurious trading post agents. The state and state agents were now in a position to appropriate a share of the surpluses that had gone to colonial merchant capital in the earlier period, and also in a position to squeeze the peasants harder as the value (and even volume) of these surpluses declined. Over time it would become increasingly clear that nationalization "socialized" the losses and costs that weighed ever more heavily on this sector of commerce.

The new state marketing board, the OCA, was authorized to regulate and control the commercialization of the entire groundnut crop.[76] Producer prices for groundnuts, set by the OCA, averaged about half of export prices. The difference, minus the costs of shelling and crushing, belonged to the state. Income from the groundnut export tax averaged about 20 percent of the government's fiscal receipts in the 1960s (Anson–Meyer 1974:17). In principle these revenues were earmarked for investment in the urban areas. In practice they were absorbed in the current expenditures of the government and government employees; a growing share of the financing for public investment came from abroad. Much of the state-appropriated groundnut surplus never reached the national treasury. By the mid-1960s the state agencies responsible for handling the groundnut crop constituted some of Senegal's largest and most important reservoirs of patronage funds. Donal Cruise O'Brien (1971b:274) wrote that "one [source] has estimated that 'losses' and acknowledged fraud in the central marketing board . . . in 1965 accounted for more than annual net profit."

Nationalization of the export circuit sped the largest maisons de commerce along a trajectory that they had chosen in the 1950s.[77] Pressures on the European trading houses to cut costs intensified in the wake of poor harvests of the early 1950s, as world groundnut prices fell in the mid-1950s, and as the colonial administration tried to regulate producer prices to maintain output. Meanwhile, productivity in Senegal's most intensively cultivated groundnut zones – those along the railway – showed clear signs of deterioration. Collecting produce from the more productive, outlying regions raised costs and encouraged the European firms to leave this activity to independent Lebanese and Senegalese traders. In the context of this process, the imposition of direct state control over the groundnut circuit in 1960 was not (and was not perceived as) a major blow to the large trading companies. In response to the creation of the OCA, the maisons de commerce abandoned what remained of their rural operations. They continued to restructure in order to concentrate on the most lucrative points of the consumer goods trade – importation and wholesale distribution. They pared down the array of articles they sold on the domestic market, deemphasizing *commerce général* to specialize in equipment, vehicles, consumer durables, construction materials, and the light consumer goods (such as staple textile goods and hardware) that remained very profitable.

76. The Office National de Coopération et d'Assistance au Développement (ONCAD) was created in 1966 as a subordinate agency of the OCA. In 1967/8, ONCAD assumed responsibility for buying the groundnut crop and transporting it to the refineries.
77. On the CFAO, SCOA, NOSOCO–CNF, and Peyrissac–OPTORG, see *Marchés Tropicaux* (23 décembre 1961): 2,990; CINAM and SERESA 1960; and Schumacher 1975:137. For the smaller French trading firms in Senegal (Vezia, Maurel et Prom, etc.), nationalization of the groundnut trade was a hard blow. For the large firms, this process of "pulling back from the interior" predated the 1950s. As one source reported, "from 1939 to 1955, the shrinking (*régression*) of the interior networks of the large [commercial] firms has been constant. In Senegal [as compared to the rest of the AOF], this phenomenon is the most accentuated" (*Industries et Travaux d'Outre-Mer*, no. 27 [février 1956]: 69–70).

In the 1960s and early 1970s economic and political factors worked together to maintain the large European firms' dominant position in the import trade in Senegal. Two factors were particularly significant. First, the dominant *maisons de commerce* commanded the financial and organizational resources needed to carry out importation on a very large scale. This gave them formidable advantages over independent traders. Second, the maisons de commerce continued to receive the licenses and quotas that governed importation in heavily regulated product categories. By selling these imported goods to rural and urban semi-wholesalers on credit, the maisons de commerce also collected interest payments and kept their commercial clients in tow. French trading conglomerates fought vigorously to maintain their control over importation and wholesale distribution in these heavily regulated product categories. For the most part they were successful. Their institutional partner in this task was the Dakar Chamber of Commerce.

The Dakar Chamber of Commerce, a colonial institution dating back to the 1930s, became a Senegalese public body in 1963. It remained a bastion of French commercial interests until the end of the decade. One observer at the time wrote that this institution "offers the *particularité étonnante* of being one of the few official bodies untouched by independence."[78] As a locus of business influence on state policy, its importance declined in the 1960s. Other, more direct channels became choice routes of access to the state. Even so, throughout the 1960s the Dakar Chamber of Commerce retained regulatory and administrative powers in a key domain: It allocated import licenses and quotas. These powers were used to guarantee the French trading firms' monopoly over imports that competed with the products of local industry.

Lebanese merchants were clearly dominant at the semiwholesale and retail levels of trade. As the maisons de commerce concentrated on big-ticket items and staple consumer goods, Lebanese entrepreneurs continued to expand into "specialty goods" imports. By the end of the decade the most important Lebanese firms in Dakar had reached the scale of the smaller, family-run French trading houses. Some were counted among the thirty largest commercial firms operating in Senegal.[79] Most Lebanese merchants gradually withdrew from the rural areas over the course of the 1960s, consolidating their operations in the regional towns or in Dakar. Some invested capital accumulated in the commercial sector in small- to medium-scale urban business (bakeries, movie theaters, real estate firms, hotels, restaurants, laundries, travel agencies, hair salons, etc.) and in urban real estate. Some of the smaller import-substitution industries were also Lebanese-owned (beverages, biscuits, confectionery products).

---

78. *Africa* (Dakar), no. 43 (1968): 15–19. The twenty-nine-member bureau of the Dakar Chamber of Commerce included only five Senegalese in 1968. In spite of its declining influence as a lobbying front, "the leadership of the UPS was not so keen to support Africanization [of this institution], since a capable Senegalese president [of the organization] could have used the Chambre de Commerce as a power base to play *clan* politics with the financial backing of French investors" (R. Cruise O'Brien 1972:204).
79. See La Société Africaine d'Edition 1975.

The political status of this segment of the private sector remained ambiguous and somewhat insecure. They were perceived universally as "foreigners" by Senegalese even through many took dual Senegalese-French or Senegalese-Lebanese citizenship in the 1960s. Because their activities were concentrated at the lower, more competitive levels of the commercial circuit, Lebanese businesses were the first barriers that Senegalese entrepreneurs confronted as they tried to break into these domains. For economic as well as political reasons, the Lebanese were much more vulnerable to nationalist pressures for Africanization of the private sector than the French were. The Lebanese community in Senegal protected itself by investing shrewdly in politics. Important Lebanese businessmen provided financial support to the UPS and its politicians from the late 1950s onward, establishing political connections as they extended their business operations. "The system of payoff [for political protection] operates up to the highest level of public life" (R. Cruise O'Brien 1975:112).

Insecurity of political status was a factor that militated against the productive investment of capital accumulated within the Lebanese business community. "Most of them . . . feeling themselves to be insecure as a group anyway, . . . took the conservative option of remaining in their existing business, even with declining profits" (ibid.:106). Many of those with investment funds chose either to send this wealth abroad, to diversify into a wide range of commercial activities, or to invest in urban real estate.[80] This meant that resources accumulated by the Lebanese, like resources accumulated by the French commercial houses and by the state, were rarely harnessed to the task of expanding the productive base of the national economy. The powerful place of the Lebanese in the commercial sector also had implications for the course of political change. Rita Cruise O'Brien drew the following conclusion: "Following independence, national politicians seemed by design to be more interested in letting the Lebanese operate their system of [political payoffs for] protection rather than support the rise of a local bourgeoisie which might have been politically more outspoken and more of a challenge" (ibid.:112).

The nationalist discourse of late colonial years and widespread criticism of *la traite* created a political climate that appeared to favor the Senegalese merchant class that began to re-emerge in the 1950s.[81] Most Senegalese traders operated in rural areas, and they began to expand their operations (alongside or with the Lebanese) as the maisons de commerce scaled back operations in the countryside. Around the time of independence, the Senegalese merchant stratum was made up of perhaps three hundred "medium-scale" commerçants in semi-wholesale trade and a few thousand small-scale transporters, former trading post

---

80. "[T]hey have turned their vulnerability into an economic success by exploiting persistently every available opportunity for earning short-term profits. . . . [This raises] fundamental questions about . . . the long-term place [of the Lebanese], if any, in the Senegalese economy" (R. Cruise O'Brien 1975:111, 107).

81. Pushed out of rural trade and importation by maisons de commerce in the 1920s and early 1930s, most Senegalese merchants had either withdrawn from commerce completely or taken positions as employees, transporters, or agents of the French merchant houses.

managers and agents, moneylenders, and rural retailers (M. Diop 1972). These traders constituted an important part of the rural electoral coalition that brought Senghor to power.

A postindependence reorganization of commerce promised to open new horizons for Senegalese traders. They were in a position to compete for a larger share of the groundnut surplus. With the backing of the state, leading Senegalese traders could claim a share of the import trade. Leaders of the regime, however, had different scenarios in mind. In the 1960s they tried to rein in and domesticate this merchant stratum in ways that would have weighty implications for development of the Senegalese private sector.

The regime's decision to impose a state monopoly on groundnut collection and purchase was a blow to Senegalese traders. State control over the groundnut circuit would close off an avenue of local private accumulation that began to open in the 1950s. For the state this move was critical. State-controlled groundnut circuits were the veins through which government influence and patronage flowed into the rural areas. Competition in the groundnut purchasing circuit would short-circuit this emerging hierarchy of power and influence, jeopardizing a structure of "indirect rule" in the countryside that was reinforced by credit, groundnut purchasing, and input distribution systems set in place and financed by the state.

After the creation of the OCA, Senegalese commerçants repositioned themselves to deal with the next frontal attack coming from the regime: the proposal to socialize the rural distribution of consumer goods. The rapid consolidation of the European trading companies at the importation and wholesale stages of the commercial circuit had disorganized rural trade. Government spokesmen announced that a commercial "vacuum" now existed in the rural areas. Mamadou Dia proposed to deal with this problem by expanding the functions of existing rural cooperatives or by creating a new network of consumer cooperatives in the interior. Under this plan, the state would be the primary buyer and seller in the rural areas, pushing private traders to the margins of the rural economy. This plan was discarded when Dia fell from power, much to the satisfaction of rural Senegalese traders who had aligned themselves squarely with Senghor in the Senghor–Dia conflict (Schumacher 1975:135–8). Senghor stood behind the principle of a commercial sector "under private control." On this important choice, he was also congratulated by French business interests who feared further nationalizations and excessive *étatisme* in the Senegalese economy (R. Cruise O'Brien 1972:112–13).

For Senegalese business interests, the patterns of state intervention in internal commerce that began to crystallize in the early 1960s would prove to be a mixed blessing. State power was used to protect foreign monopolies over the most lucrative parts of the consumer goods trade, canalizing the ambitions of Senegalese merchants into less profitable niches or into activities directly controlled or mediated by the state. The nascent Senegalese trading class would find itself operating in sectors and on terms defined by the regime.

The Senegalese government elaborated and extended the web of state regulations mediating traders' access to all levels of the commercial circuit. Now, all wholesalers, semiwholesalers, and retailers were required to obtain prior state authorization. The licensing process gave state officials, especially those in the ministry overseeing commerce, broad control over access to the "formal sector" commercial opportunities that opened to Senegalese traders after independence. "Licenses were granted to *bons militants* of the UPS," said one former ministry of commerce official. The Dakar Chamber of Commerce railed against the patronage politics that infused the commercial licensing process. To underscore its indignation, in 1965 it offered the government a list of economic criteria to be employed to ensure that only "professional traders" received licenses.[82] The old guard's first shot in what would be a long war to eliminate UPS-style patronage politics from the commercial sphere scored no success, and commercial licenses at the wholesale and semiwholesale levels of the trade circuit remained a prime patronage resource. Political intermediation of this sort served a gatekeeper function. It also allowed members of the political class a direct means of entry into trading circuits: They could license themselves as traders. Alternatively, state agents could tap trading profits indirectly. *Prête-noms* (front men) earned commissions by obtaining licenses for commerçants without political access. One group of analysts commented in 1974 that "[i]t is difficult to distinguish the real commerçants from intermediaries of all sorts" (IDET–CEGOS 1974:9).

The most dynamic and influential Senegalese businessmen set their sights on importation, where the most interesting commercial margins were to be had. Here they were frustrated by the continuing dominance of the maisons de commerce.[83] To channel the energies of these more prominent traders, the government created "space" for them in the wholesale trade. This process worked to suppress the emergence of direct competition between Senegalese traders and the French maisons de commerce, reinforcing the prevailing structure of foreign control over large-scale private trade.

The centerpiece of the government's efforts to organize and Africanize the commercial sector was the creation of new corporate structures, or trading consortia, that linked several hundred Senegalese traders to the largest maisons de commerce. Senegalese traders selected by the government received state loans to buy into the consortia, making it clear to all that although the state took away with one hand, it could give with the other. According to the government, the new consortia would "promote the rise of a new class of Senegalese commerçants."[84] In effect, the consortia allowed the government to boost traders and other individuals worthy of the regime's support into positions of greater access to goods and credit distributed by the maisons de commerce. For the French

82. From interviews at the ministry of commerce and the Dakar Chamber of Commerce, April and November, 1985. See the *Le Bulletin de la Chambre de Commerce et d'Industrie de Dakar*, no. 1 (mars 1965): 15.

83. Amin (1969:72–4) commented that "l'accès à l'importation directe, qui constitue l'objectif de tous ces grossistes [sénégalais], reste difficile."

84. See *Marchés Tropicaux* (28 avril 1962): 950. See also ibid. (30 septembre 1961): 2,385; and ibid. (4 novembre 1961): 2,625–7.

companies still interested in the distribution of basic consumer goods and most food products, the consortia were new distribution networks (Amin 1969:34–47).

SCOA assumed the directorship and controlling share of a trading consortium with about seven hundred Senegalese stockholder-traders.[85] SCOA continued to import merchandise as it had during the colonial period. With SCOA financing, Senegalese commerçants sold these goods on commission through independently owned retail outlets or through stores leased from SCOA. The CFAO created a trading company along the same lines in association with the government and about three hundred local traders.[86]

These experiments ended in failure in the mid-1960s. SCOA and the CFAO claimed large losses on Senegalese traders' defaults on credit. To the extent that this was true, the consortia worked to transfer resources into the hands of the Senegalese beneficiaries of this government-sponsored initiative. Senegalese traders, meanwhile, claimed that the large European trading firms used their control over credit and importation as a stranglehold over local commerçants. This was certainly true. Neither joint-stock company ever distributed dividends to its Senegalese shareholder-retailers.

The government was not deterred. It remained intent upon organizing the distribution circuit from above. In the mid-1960s the regime devised a new formula for "inserting" local commerçants into trading circuits dominated by the French trading companies. The consortia were restructured into a mixed private–public company, the Société Nationale de Distribution au Sénégal (SONADIS). SCOA originally held about 60 percent of the shares of SONADIS; the government owned 17 percent.[87] The maisons de commerce supplied this new company with imported and locally manufactured goods. SONADIS created a wholesale and retail distribution chain in the primary and secondary urban areas, establishing itself as the country's largest retail distributor of consumer goods by the late 1960s. These arrangements further narrowed the playing field for the Senegalese private sector, and allowed the state and the French trading conglomerates to keep a hand in the semiwholesale and retail trades. Senegalese traders participating in this system became employees and clients of SONADIS.

For Senegalese traders and aspiring businessmen with good political connec-

85. This consortium was called the Société Sénégalaise de Commerce et de la Distribution (SOSECOD). It was supplied through SCOA's *bureau d'achat* in Paris. SCOA contributed 23 percent of total paid up capital (of 50 million CFA francs) and managed the company. Senegalese traders held the rest. Of the 700 Senegalese traders in this group, only 25 were considered "large shareholders" with ten to thirty shares each. Over 500 traders held only three shares. SOSECOD was liquidated in 1964. See Amin 1969:36–41.

86. The CFAO "Africanized" its distribution circuit through the creation of AFRIDEX. The CFAO contributed 25 percent of a total paid-up capital of 20 million CFA francs. AFRIDEX originally had about 300 Senegalese shareholders. This number had dwindled to 104 in 1967, when AFRIDEX was liquidated and the CFAO abandoned *commerce général* (Amin 1969:36–41, 70–6).

87. SCOA's shareholding in SONADIS was reduced to 12 percent in December 1973. On SONADIS, see *Marchés Tropicaux* (17 juillet 1965): 1,755; Amin 1969:38–41.

tions, more attractive trading niches in internal trade opened up in the 1960s. Opportunities in the commodities trade generated feast and substantial profits for the private traders and political bigwigs who obtained contracts to do business in domains controlled directly by the state.

Although the OCA assumed monopoly control over the commercialization of groundnuts in 1960, new commercial structures to execute this trade were not fully in place until 1968. In the interim the OCA licensed about one thousand private Senegalese agents to purchase the crop. Many of these licensed traders were political influentials at local levels of the UPS (Schumacher 1975:136). Commercial margins set by the OCA allowed the largest and most favored traders to accumulate large treasuries during the transition period. After the government took direct control of the collection and purchase of the crop in 1967–8, some of them moved into transport, wholesale distribution, and the rice trade.[88]

In 1961 the OCA established a monopoly over the importation and distribution of rice, a staple food in Senegal. Rather than sell rice through the cooperatives, the government designated Senegalese traders and other individuals with political clout to market this rice in the name of the government.[89] Commissions earned in the rice trade provided a tremendous boost to a wealthy stratum of local commerçants linked to the regime. Samir Amin (1969:72) writes that in the rice trade, many big Senegalese businessmen "made their original fortunes." Rice quotas and rice were sometimes bought and sold on a speculative basis, creating additional rents for those politically secure enough to engage in this illegal activity.[90]

The government's quota system for distributing rice ensured that private profits from this trade were highly concentrated. In the 1960s an annual rice quota of 50,000 tons was divided among the five largest French trading companies (including SONADIS). Another 30,000 tons was allocated each year to the three largest Senegalese trading companies. About 40,000 tons were distributed among 15 leading Dakar commerçants. Finally, 50,000 tons went to 50 large traders and 200 medium-scale traders in the rural areas. In 1968 200 to 300 government-named individuals and companies controlled the distribution of rice throughout the entire country (Amin 1969:66–8, 72; M. Diop 1972:151).

That Senegalese private capital remained confined almost exclusively to the commercial sector persisted as a key fact of the political economy. Without sufficient financial resources of their own and without the backing of the state, indigenous entrepreneurs were effectively barred from industry and the more

88. Amin 1969:60–3. M. Diop (1972:151) reports that of the 1,000 groundnut buyers named by the OCA, 50 made annual gross profits of over 1 million CFA francs. Of the 50, 6 made annual gross profits over 4 million CFA francs.
89. Rice quotas often went to commerçants "qui en réalité sont des intermédiaires souvent sans aucune installation" (Société Africaine d'Edition 1975). These individuals were named by the OCA until 1971, when the Ministère des Finances et Affaires Economiques took over the job.
90. Speculation in the rice trade was a problem denounced by the government almost yearly from 1962 onward. See *Marchés Tropicaux* (31 octobre 1962): 2,157; ibid. (6 avril 1963): 837; Bye and Le Moal, 1965; *Marchés Tropicaux* (18 décembre 1971): 3,887.

lucrative service activities. The vast majority of Senegalese commerçants remained at the lower, less profitable levels of the internal distribution chain, downstream from the French and Lebanese.

Guy Rocheteau (1982:149–50) reported that in 1972, "observers of various origins agree that the local private sector is responsible for 10–15 percent of all business activity, including commercial activity (total *chiffre d'affaires*), in Senegal." Yet over the course of the 1960s an elite group of dynamic and wealthy Senegalese commerçants had emerged. Majhemout Diop estimated in 1968 that about 250 Senegalese traders had achieved *"une certaine importance"* on the national level.[91] A few, particularly those working most closely with the government, amassed fortunes. Commerce and politics were firmly established as the main avenues of local private accumulation.

The government's role in the commercial sector – "the key to the national economy" – clearly expanded the state's revenue base. From this position, the regime built mechanisms of agricultural surplus extraction upon an existing peasant-based mode of production and system of indirect rule in the groundnut basin. State controls over trade also served to preempt the emergence of a Senegalese private sector that could have represented an independent force in domestic politics.

The Senghor regime consolidated a ruling coalition upon this foundation. Government spending, hiring, and the allocation of politically controlled opportunities for private gain enlarged the circle of beneficiaries of the political status quo, and linked these beneficiaries to the regime. How this process was financed tells much of the story of the Senegalese political economy in the early postcolonial period. Internally generated government resources came, for the most part, from taxing the import–export trade. Profits on groundnut exports accounted for about 20 percent of the government's fiscal receipts; taxes on imports accounted for another 40–45 percent. In this sense the government rested squarely upon the economic structures created by merchant capital.

Resources appropriated through commercial circuits, however, could not support the growing weight of state spending. By the end of the decade 67 percent of total government development outlays (for housing, education, other social services, administrative buildings, rural development, and transport) were financed through external aid inflows.[92] Deficit spending covered 10 percent of total development outlays over the course of the decade. The proportion of public investment financed by inflows of capital from abroad would increase over time. Political stability was also dependent on maintaining Senegal's status as a "client state."

91. "Une certaine importance" means yearly turnovers of 100–200 million CFA francs (M. Diop 1972:149–50).
92. External aid came on soft terms: in 1964–6, 85 percent of total gross external aid came in the form of grants. In 1966–7, the proportion was 75 percent (World Bank 1974:xxix–xxxi, 33, 34; Anson-Meyer 1974:60). On deficit spending and the operations of the Central Bank, see Engberg 1973: 537–45; Diarra 1972.

4

Growth of Senegal's textile industry, 1960–1975

In Senegal, "the costly mistake of trying to work against the maisons de commerce was not repeated. After 1960, the industrial–commercial combinations seemed to work the best. . . . Competition had corrosive effects on business."
Reminiscences of a textile manufacturer, 1985

During the colonial period, the largest maisons de commerce imported (mostly) French textile goods to the AOF by way of the port of Dakar.[1] In the early 1950s, this link in the chain of merchant capital's operations was threatened. A few industrialists tried to cut the colonial trading houses out of the distribution chain by jumping the tax and tariff barrier, producing textile goods in Dakar, and selling these goods directly to dozens of local traders. The effort to end-run merchant capital failed.[2] Through dumping and price wars, the trading companies succeeded in breaking the independence of the Dakar textile manufacturers. In the late 1950s, the maisons de commerce began to absorb the local factories into their sphere of commercial control.

This process would continue unabated after independence. By the mid-1960s, local production, importation, and the wholesale distribution of staple textile goods lay in the hands of a few industries and large commercial houses. These firms worked in concert, dividing the market amongst themselves, setting prices, and calibrating the flow of imports and made-in-Senegal goods onto the local market. The use of state power to restrict access to the local market made this possible. State-enforced monopolies and oligopolies insulated the closed, integrated circuit from the pressures of competition.

In this way, capital that was invested in the local textile industry and ex-colonial merchant capital reached an accommodation in Senegal that mitigated conflicts of interest between the two. The terms of this accommodation, however, were set by merchant capital. Subordinated to merchant capital, industry would progressively "internalize" its logic and its local modus operandi. Investments would be reduced to the minimum required to retain and expand monopoly control over markets. They were amortized in short order. In the absence of

---

1. The AOF was a unitary trading zone without internal barriers to trade.
2. See Chapter 2.

competition, there were few compelling incentives to invest in enhancing the productivity of labor or capital stock.

The state controls over trade that underpinned monopoly and oligopoly control in the textile business were also used to promote the expansion and diversification of the industry in the 1960s and 1970s. The government of Senegal pushed established firms to invest in the production of intermediate goods, and the industry achieved a degree of vertical integration that would not have materialized without official pressure. These processes – the growth, diversification, and integration of the Dakar textile industry – are the subject of this chapter. Three central points are developed. First, the observed structure of market control was the product of extensive political intervention in markets. Second, this particular structure of market control gave rise to, and ensured the viability of, new investment in the local textile industry. Third, this structure of control over trade limited the extent to which reinvestment and the progressive deepening of capital would occur in Senegal's industrial sector.

Processes working to limit the expansion of industrial capital throughout Senegal's manufacturing sector can be tracked in a particularly systematic way in the textile industry. In textiles, the process of light industrialization in Senegal reached its pinnacle. Because the industry was organized around several firms, monopoly control was not guaranteed as it was in single-firm branches of light industry. The task of maintaining oligopoly control required explicit bargaining and strong-arm tactics. And because the textile industry was structured around firms operating at different stages of the production process, some firms within the subsector had a vital stake in seeing the process of vertical integration move forward. Limits were imposed on the process of vertical integration through a most contentious and conspicuous process. And although textiles, like the rest of the light manufacturing sector, was heavily protected from import competition, pressures for more efficient production did arise from within the industry itself. Local intermediate-goods suppliers (firms weaving unfinished cloth) sold their output to the finishing industries (printing and dyeing firms). In principle, both of these groups had a stake in lowering the costs of semifinished goods. A critical part of the history of the Dakar textile industry in the 1960s and early 1970s is the story of how a priori pressures for capital deepening, cost cutting, and productivity-enhancing investment were reduced, dodged, or defused. This occurred, for the most part, through manipulation of the state-enforced structures of control over the domestic market.

THE INTERESTS OF FRENCH CAPITAL

In promoting import-substitution industrialization (ISI), Senegal embarked upon a postcolonial industrial policy that resonated with nationalist discourse and nationalist development goals as they were articulated at the time. Leaders in the African colonies had demanded industrialization to raise their economies above the status of mono-crop exporters and "dumping grounds" for metropolitan manufactured goods. But like decolonization itself, ISI was a nationalist strategy that was narrower in scope and conception than the problems it promised to solve. As it happened in much of sub-Saharan Africa, ISI did not compromise, and could even be most conducive to, the interests of established factions of foreign capital. The neocolonial face of ISI was particularly obvious in places like Kenya and Senegal, where the process began during the colonial period.[3]

Senegal's postcolonial ISI policies followed precedents and goals set by a defensive colonial power facing the dual threat of African nationalism and American "internationalism." During the post-World War II years nationalist demands for industrial development in the colonies dovetailed with international capital's demands for the dissolution of the protected colonial trading empires. Both forces were arrayed behind the banner of decolonization. In response to this challenge, France's colonial planners had argued in the early 1950s for policies that would "transfer manufacturing capacity from the metropole to the colonies." That is what happened. Senegal's postcolonial ISI policies furthered a process set in motion by the colonial administration in the late 1950s.

What made ISI in Senegal so conspicuously neocolonial was the extent to which it served the particular interests of factions of French capital that were, at the time of independence, already established in the territory. The most direct beneficiaries of postcolonial ISI were the maisons de commerce and industries implanted in Dakar before 1958. These same interests benefited directly from Zone Franc accords governing trade, monetary policy, and capital flows. But did these policies, both before and after independence, promote the interests of "capital in general" or "capital as a whole"? The answer to this question is ambiguous.

Poulantzas (1973) contributed to Marxist theories of the state and capital by highlighting the distinction between particular capitalists' interests (e.g. the interests of particular firms or narrow subsectors of industry) and the interests of capital in general. The expansion of capitalist economies, he argued, hinges on the ability of the state to maintain conditions conducive to overall economic growth; that is, to promote the interests of capital as a whole. This reasoning would suggest that the French state tried to negotiate the decolonization of West Africa in a manner consistent with the interests of French capital as a whole. Just what those interests were, however, was difficult to assess under the circumstances. Capital's political needs (e.g. political stability) and the economic changes required to break down barriers to the expansion of capital (the dissolution of old commercial monopolies and of precapitalist forms of control over agricultural land and labor) could not be reconciled in one neat bargain. To borrow Anne Phillips's (1989) phrase, decolonization was a "makeshift settlement." It protected factions of French capital operating in West Africa from their worst political fears, at the cost of long-run possibilities in the former AOF for the expansion of these firms and corporations and, it seems, for the expansion of capital as a whole. Nowhere was the compromised and contradictory character of the decolonization process clearer than in the breakup of the AOF.

3. See Leys 1975.

Balkanization of the AOF divided one vast federation into eight independent states.[4] Like the old strategy of "divide and rule," this process created political units that were weaker politically vis-à-vis France and more economically dependent upon it than the whole might have been. The economic and political weakness of these new states helped to ensure that decolonization was achieved on terms defined by France.[5] Monetary, trade, political, and military "accords of association" assured that continuity and close, bilateral ties with the metropole would be maintained. Fragmentation of the federation-wide nationalist movement in the 1950s contributed decisively to this process. It deflated the power of leftist and militantly nationalist leaders within the AOF in favor of moderates like Houphouët-Boigny and Senghor in the most strategic territories of the federation. The emergence of conservative, pro-French regimes neutralized direct political threats to France and to established factions of French capital. Collapse of the short-lived Mali Federation completed the process of balkanization.

The cost to merchant capital operating out of Dakar, and to industrial capital implanted in Dakar, was the fragmentation of the federation-wide market – the object of their ambitions. Balkanization placed new political hurdles in their paths, created barriers to the circulation of goods, and raised the expense of exploiting the markets of the region. For these companies, however, all was not lost. The interest of newly independent governments in import-substitution industrialization led by foreign capital (with textile manufacturing high on the list) offered a solution to the problems created by the breakup of the AOF. The largest maisons de commerce and French textile manufacturers had everything to gain or regain from ISI. Manufacturing within the various countries of the ex-AOF was the surest strategy for maintaining privileged access to national markets. Leading French textile manufacturers with West African interests and the maisons de commerce went to work throughout the ex-AOF, building factories in exchange for politically guaranteed market access.[6] The lesson learned from their experience in Dakar in the 1950s was that "the industrial-commercial combinations seemed to work the best."

Between 1960 and 1970 major French textile manufacturers and trading companies combined forces to create textile industries throughout the ex-AOF.[7] Complex webs of interlocking directorships and financial participations were institutionalized in the form of joint ventures and joint holding companies. By investing together, manufacturers and importers avoided the competition and conflicts of interest that had resulted in costly price wars in Dakar in the 1950s. One of the foremost industrial partners in these new ventures was Ets. Schaeffer,

4. These states were Senegal, the Côte d'Ivoire, Guinea, Mali, Niger, Upper Volta (Burkina Faso), Mauritania, and Dahomey (Benin).
5. On the role of France in the breakup of the AOF, see Foltz 1965:105–12, 154–7. See also Berg 1960.
6. For SCOA's shareholdings in African industries in 1962, see *Marchés Tropicaux* (21 avril 1962): 914. For SCOA's and the CFAO's portfolio investment in industry in the ex-AOF in 1969, see Ediafric 1969:41–2, 58.
7. See *Europe France Outre-Mer*, no. 491 (décembre 1970).

the controlling interest behind Dakar's then-largest textile firm, Icotaf. Its engineering wing, Schaeffer Engineering, built and equipped several turnkey factories in the region, always in partnership with the ex-colonial trading conglomerates – the CFAO, CNF, or SCOA.

The most extensive new ventures in textile manufacturing were in the Côte d'Ivoire. Ivoirian markets were the largest and richest in the ex-federation. After 1960, Abidjan quickly emerged as the region's most attractive site for new investment in light industry.[8] Ets. Schaeffer, CFAO, CNF, and the Ivoirian government invested jointly in what soon became the region's largest manufacturer of printed cotton fabric.[9] New dyeing, spinning, and weaving factories appeared in rapid succession. Through holding corporations or joint ventures, the maisons de commerce and large French textile manufacturers built and controlled the Ivoirian textile industry while retaining and expanding their interests in Senegal.[10] In 1968, the Côte d'Ivoire replaced Senegal as the leading textile manufacturer in Francophone West Africa.

Between 1960 and 1975, new foreign-owned textile industries came on-line in all the African countries of the former Federation. The most prominent beneficiaries of this process were factions of French capital that had staked out their positions in the AOF before the time of independence: the maisons de commerce, large manufacturers with long-time interests in the AOF textile market, and French suppliers of capital goods. Together, they reaped the advantages of "first entrant."

In the long run, however, this strategy of ensuring commercial access to the markets of the ex-AOF compromised possibilities for the expansion and deepening of capital in the West African textile industry as a whole (Amin 1973). Because all the industries of the region produced similar finished goods, possibilities for intraregional trade in textiles diminished as industrialization progressed in each country. Economies of scale were difficult to achieve; manufacturers tended to avoid investment in backward integration and to concentrate on

8. Because industrial investment in the AOF during the colonial period was concentrated in Dakar, opportunities for investment in import-substitution industries in the Côte d'Ivoire were relatively unexploited in 1960. Manufacturers based in the Côte d'Ivoire were at the hub of a regional network of trade and transport infrastructure that provided access to markets in Upper Volta, Mali, and Niger – poor, landlocked countries that would attract only minimal investment in light industry. The Ivoirian government used its relatively extensive financial resources to engage in direct state investment in manufacturing industry through joint ventures with foreign firms. This lowered the costs incurred by private investors. Underpinning these arrangements was the Ivoirian Investment Code, which was as liberal as Senegal's.

9. L'Industrie Cotonnière Ivoirienne (ICODI) was established in 1962. See Campbell 1973.

10. TEXUNION, a high-profile, joint-holding/investment corporation, brought together Ets. Schaeffer & Cie, the CFAO, the Dollfus Mieg Corporation, and a series of smaller French textile manufacturers. TEXUNION took partial ownership of Ets. Gonfreville, which was controlled by OPTORG. Agache-Willot, one of the leading French textile manufacturers involved in trade with West Africa, invested aggressively in the Côte d'Ivoire after 1960. Through CEGEPAR–Industrie, SCOA took shares in the Ivoirian textile firms. For an analysis of the complex web of foreign industrial and commercial interests controlling the Ivoirian textile industry, see Campbell 1973.

the last stages of the finishing process. In the early 1970s, the Ivoirian textile industry was the most striking exception to this rule.[11] By the 1980s, however, growth of the Ivoirian industry would be constrained by high costs and by limits imposed by the size of the national market. On the level of the region as a whole, the shallowness of investment limited the extent to which returns to capital invested in West African manufacturing would derive from real value added through the manufacturing process (i.e., from the exploitation of labor). At the same time, the narrowness of national markets for finished manufactured goods meant that virtually all of these industries would operate with considerable excess capacity, making the problem of high costs difficult to resolve through productivity-enhancing investment.

In Senegal and throughout the ex-federation, these factors conspired to make the profitability of capital invested in textile manufacturing dependent upon the ability of states to restrict competition on the local market. The logic of merchant capital – buying cheap to sell dear, the tendency to monopolize markets in lieu of enhancing productivity, the habit of collecting rents rather than investing capital in order to increase value added – tended to infuse the operations of light industry. If this meant that possibilities for the expansion of capital in general were circumscribed, then it also protected those who staked out their positions in the earlier period, at least in the short run. For factions of merchant and industrial capital that were active in French West Africa during the colonial period, the strategy of dividing and ruling the ex-AOF warded off the threat of radical nationalism. In the process, however, these factions of capital incurred another risk – the risk that in the long run, the new states would prove too weak and too poor to promote and guarantee their interests.

IN SENEGAL THE FUTURE LAY IN THE DOMESTIC MARKET

The newly independent government of Senegal, like its counterparts in the region, hoped to achieve rapid progress in import substitution through the expansion of local textile manufacturing. Staple textile goods made up 20 percent of Senegal's total import bill in the early 1960s. Existing firms in Dakar covered only 10–25 percent of domestic demand. There was ample room for investment in new and existing lines of production to cover a larger share of the local market. Government planners envisioned the development of an integrated chain of textile production, running from the cultivation of cotton in eastern Senegal to the manufacture of finished garments and household textile goods in Dakar. They placed the cotton textile industry at the center of a grand strategy that would open

11. In the early 1970s, liberal access to EEC markets granted under the Lomé I convention led interests controlling the Ivoirian textile industry to invest in more technologically sophisticated equipment, upstream factories, specialized large-scale production, and "export-platform" assembly plants. At the same time, they sought more stringent import controls in order to protect their Ivoirian markets. For a discussion of this strategy and the limits of its successes, see Mytelka 1983:258–62; Duruflé 1988:104–5.

new zones of agricultural production, attract new investment in processing local raw materials, push the forward and backward integration of the manufacturing sector, and stimulate the rapid growth of urban wage employment.[12] The Investment Code and import controls would be used to attract foreign capital. Established manufacturing interests and the expansion of existing factories would lead the way.

In the early 1960s the Senegalese government and planners from France's Ministère de la Coopération began to identify intermediate and finished textile goods that could be produced in Senegal.[13] The French analysts estimated in 1960 and 1961 that the costs of textile production in Senegal exceeded those in France by at least 30 percent. To offset this disincentive to local investment, the planners recommended higher tariff barriers, import bans that would channel demand toward locally produced goods, and import quotas to assure local manufacturers an adequate share of the market. Their investment feasibility studies were based upon the following economic parameters: estimates of the total absorptive capacity of the internal market in a given product line (the sensitivity of demand to changes in price was not taken into account), an average rate of protection of 60–70 percent on similar textile goods imported from France, and returns that would allow for the amortization of investments within five to seven years.[14]

Given these parameters, the planners concluded Senegal's highest priority should be the local production of gray cloth (*écru*), woven from Senegalese cotton.[15] If locally woven *écru* supplied the printing and dyeing factories, nearly 100 percent of the value-added in Senegal's most widely consumed fabrics would be domestic. The importation of intermediate goods could be cut drastically. For the planners, expanding local spinning and weaving capacity was the single most important step toward vertical integration of the industry. Local printing and dyeing factories, in turn, could increase capacity to cover all of Senegal's demand for staple cotton prints (*imprimés*).[16] These goals were deemed technically feasible and inscribed as priorities in the official development plans. The First Plan (1960–5) reflected the ambition and optimism of the times. It called for a 300 percent increase in local spinning output, a 400 percent increase in local weaving output, and a 500 percent increase in the production of prints.[17]

12. See *Europe France Outre-Mer*, nos. 380–1 (octobre 1961).
13. CINAM et SERESA 1960: II-7-54; CINAM 1961; République Française. Ministère de la Coopération 1965.
14. See République Française, Ministère de la Coopération 1965.
15. In weaving, planners also identified the creation of local capacity to weave cotton fabric with colored threads (*tissés fils couleurs*) and percales as priority projects.
16. By about 1963 the Dakar industry was producing 3–4 million meters of cotton prints (*imprimés*) a year. The government estimated the total absorptive capacity of the local market at 20 million meters.
17. The projected increases during the period of the First Plan (1959 to 1964) were: spinning – from about 1,000 tons to 4,000 tons; weaving – from 650 tons to 3,500 tons; printing – from 300 tons to 2,000 tons. See *Marchés Tropicaux* (22 avril 1961): 1,091; Ediafric 1965; and the *Bulletin de l'Afrique Noire*, no. 354 (1965): 305.

Established manufacturers in the local textile industry defined their immediate priorities for the 1959–62 period in somewhat different terms. They needed to create internal markets for existing productive capacity and output.[18] Dakar's textile industry, conceived with the goal of supplying the entire federation, was hard hit by the loss of the Guinéean and Malian markets in 1958 and 1961. Loss of these two markets resulted in a drop in demand of as much as 50 percent for some made-in-Senegal textile goods.[19] Ivoirian textiles soon began to displace made-in-Senegal goods on markets in the Côte d'Ivoire, Haute Volta, and Niger.[20] Between 1958 and 1964, the regional sales of the Dakar textile industries dropped from about 45 percent to about 20 percent of total production (with fairly stable output).

Fragmentation of the regional market led to recession in the Senegalese textile industry that would last until 1965. Existing factories turned inward, toward the domestic market, where import restrictions could be used to capture local demand. In the early 1960s the government complied by imposing import bans on textile goods similar to those already produced by local industry.[21] At the same time import restrictions were extended to cover a broader range of goods, allowing manufacturers to diversify output targeted at the Senegalese market. As the 1960s progressed the expansion of the Dakar textile firms would require even more restrictive controls on importation and the local commercialization of textile goods.

Control over the Senegalese textile market would belong to interests controlling the local textile industry. Ready to play the industrialization game, the trading companies solidified their links to established manufacturers.

OLIGOPOLY CONTROL

Partnerships between the dominant trading companies and the local textile manufacturers – upstream in the production process, downstream in the commercial

18. Precise data concerning "exports" of made-in-Senegal textile products to regional markets before 1960 were not available. For planners working in the early 1960s, this problem complicated the task of estimating the size and composition of Senegal's domestic market for textile goods. Estimates of the absorptive capacity of the local market that planners generated at the time seem to have incorporated margins of error of 500–1,000 tons and 0.5–1.0 billion CFA francs for each product category (i.e., margins of error of 10–20 percent). Pfefferman (1968:61) estimated regional exports at 46 percent of local production in 1958 and 23 percent of all sales in 1964. These figures approximate those cited elsewhere.
19. Most affected were sales of *drills* (heavy, unicolor cotton cloth woven by Icotaf, sold in part to the colonial administration for uniforms and in forest zones like Guinea where people preferred *drills* for making clothing), *filés teints* (dyed yarns used in the Sahelian zone, including Mali, for hand-loom weaving of fabrics and blankets), and *guinée* cloth (light, indigo-dyed fabric, also consumed throughout the Sahel).
20. Between 1963–9, Ivoirian production displaced Senegal's *tissus teints* and *fils teints* (dyed thread) on the markets of Upper Volta, Niger, and Côte d'Ivoire.
21. The importation of products that had been sold in Mali and Guinea (thread, yarns, *drills*, cotton blankets) was banned indefinitely by *décret* #60-348 (17 oct. 1960 and 8 jan. 1961), *décret* #61-194 (9 mai 1961), and *le décret du 9 juin 1962*. An exception was made for imports from the Côte d'Ivoire of cotton thread packaged for retail sale.

circuit, and horizontally across firms engaged in the same activities – were forged and institutionalized in the early 1960s. These alliances, designed to *eviter la concurrence sauvage*, protected and promoted the industrial and commercial interests that dominated the textile business in Senegal in the 1960s and early 1970s.

The leading maisons de commerce consolidated their positions "downstream" from the local textile industry by coordinating and tightening their hold on distribution. Under "designated buyer" or "exclusive buyer" contracts with the local firms, five to seven French trading companies purchased virtually all of the finished textile goods produced in Senegal.[22] These companies divided the market among themselves. The three largest textile-trading companies (CNF, CFAO, and CITEC) each purchased 20–25 percent of Sotiba–Simpafric's yearly output. CITEC bought 60 percent of Icotaf's annual output by the late 1960s. Designated buyers coordinated prices among themselves to avoid competition at the wholesale stage of the distribution circuit. They purchased from the local factories at fixed prices. Through their depots in Dakar, the maisons de commerce resold these goods to Lebanese semiwholesalers and retailers – at fixed prices.[23] This distribution chain insulated wholesalers' profit margins from the erosive effects of competition.

In the 1960s this chain of local distribution generated attractive margins for manufacturers and wholesalers alike. Manufacturers sold finished goods at 10–20 percent above costs of production. Wholesalers also collected profit margins of 10–20 percent. For some product categories such as *imprimés*, overall markups could be as much as 45–50 percent. Of this, only 3–5 percent went to the independent Lebanese merchants at the bottom of the distribution circuit. The average "cost of distribution" for made-in-Senegal textile goods was 40 percent of final retail price. By contrast, distribution costs for all basic consumer goods sold during this period averaged 20–23 percent.[24]

22. The largest maisons de commerce engaged in the local textile trade were the CFAO (through its textile division, QUALITEX) and the CNF (through its Senegal division, NOSOCO). I have included CITEC in this category, although technically speaking this firm was rather different in character. (CITEC was a trading arm of Boussac, a large French manufacturer of textile goods. See Campbell 1973:105, 155.) Pierregrosse, the French trading company that specialized in textile imports to Senegal in the 1950s, was also a member of the exclusive group that purchased from the local industries. In the 1960s Maurel et Prom, the CCHA, and (to a lesser extent) SCOA also purchased directly from the Dakar factories. The only exceptions to the "designated buyer" rule were cases in which *fin de série* (discontinued lines) or *deuxième choix* (imperfect articles) were sold to independent traders, unsold goods were exported to parent firms in France, or intermediate goods were sold "as is" on the local market.

23. SCOA's distribution system for textile goods and part of CITEC's commercial network constituted the primary exceptions to this rule. In these circuits, distribution was handled by the maisons de commerce through the retail stage. SCOA used the sixty stores of its retail chain, Chaine-Avion (which became SONADIS) for retail distribution, and CITEC maintained retail outlets in Dakar and Zuiguinchor. Direct distribution allowed these firms to collect margins of 20–25 percent on locally produced goods. See République Française, Ministère de la Coopération 1965:68; and SONED 1974: vol. 3, pp. 17–20.

24. These estimates come from marketing studies presented in République Française, Ministère de la Coopération (1965); Société Africaine d'Edition (1975); SONED (1979); and from interviews

Meanwhile, the maisons de commerce consolidated "upstream" positions in the textile circuit, gaining the upper hand in decisions over what, when, and how the local textile industries would produce. From the early 1960s onward, the largest manufacturers of finished goods – Icotaf and Sotiba–Simpafric – worked *sur commande* (on a contract order basis) for their largest clients.[25] This gave the trading companies a direct hand in planning the expansion and diversification of local production. Engaging quite literally in the process of import substitution, CITEC arranged for the local production of its staple product lines at the Icotaf factory. In exchange, Icotaf granted CITEC exclusive rights to purchase these goods. The CFAO and CNF followed the same strategy, supplying Sotiba–Simpafric with designs for *imprimés* that they had imported to the AOF during the colonial period. Print designs remained the property of the trading companies, preventing Sotiba–Simpafric from selling the finished products to third parties. The maisons de commerce placed massive yearly orders with Icotaf and Sotiba–Simpafric, in effect organizing and financing the factories' yearly production.

In a few cases the commercial firms' interest in the production side of the local textile business was institutionalized through minority share participation and/or representation of the boards of directors of local textile industries. The CFAO, for example, took a 15 percent ownership share in Icotaf in the early 1960s. This move reflected CFAO's growing interest in Icotaf's parent firm, Ets. Schaeffer. By the late 1960s the CFAO owned 40 percent of it as well.[26]

Within the industry, collusion, muscle, and outside pressures drove manufacturers to work out a division of labor among themselves. The period between 1960 and 1968 was marked by mergers, new ownership links, and the rise of a new set of interlocking directorships, which would assure what the government called "the harmonious and coordinated development of the textile industry."[27] Final-stage manufacturers succeeded in establishing control over intermediate goods producers early on in this process. It took a few more years for the finishing factories to agree to specialize in noncompeting product lines.

Firms producing intermediate goods lost their independence to the final-stage producers in the late 1950s and early 1960s. Icotaf absorbed the Manufactures de Rufisque, eliminating a potential source of competition in the weaving and finishing business and giving Icotaf complete control over local supplies of *écru*. Some of the output of what was now the "Icotaf–Rufisque" plant was channeled to the Icotaf factory at Pikine (also located in the greater Dakar metropolitan area) for dyeing and finishing. The rest was sold either to Sotiba–Simpafric or "as is" on the local market. CCV, the spinning factory, threw its lot in with

with independent textile importers-retailers and the commercial directors of the CNF and CFAO textile divisions in Dakar, April 1985 through January 1986.
25. SOTIBA and SIMPAFRIC fused to become Sotiba–Simpafric in 1966.
26. From interviews at Ets. Schaeffer, the SGICF, and CNF in Mulhouse and Paris, April 1986. For the Ivoirian case, see Campbell 1973.
27. See *Marchés Tropicaux* (3 février 1968): 229.

Sotiba–Simpafric. Sotiba–Simpafric remained the primary outlet for CCV's cotton yarn through the 1970s.

The major showdown occurred between Dakar's two largest textile firms, Icotaf and Sotiba–Simpafric. In the early 1960s, the most lucrative investment opportunity in the textile sector lay in the expansion of local capacity to print *imprimés*. Interests controlling Icotaf, like some of the interests vested in Sotiba–Simpafric, specialized in printing cotton fabric in France. Both groups were interested in expanding the production of *imprimés* in Senegal. At the same time, a British textile group entered the scene and expressed interest in building an integrated weaving and printing factory in Senegal.[28]

As Icotaf and the British group eyed the local market for prints, Sotiba–Simpafric remained determined to maintain its monopoly over this line of production. Sotiba–Simpafric was also determined to continue importing *écru*, the gray cloth used as the base for printing, from low-cost overseas suppliers. On this front, Sotiba–Simpafric was vulnerable, for its practice of importing *écru* stood in the way of the government's well-elaborated plans for a vertically integrated textile industry. In 1964 Icotaf tried to outmaneuver its rival by seeking government authorization to build a new, integrated weaving and printing factory.[29] Icotaf figured that the government's commitment to vertical integration would outweigh Sotiba–Simpafric's claims to monopoly control over *imprimé* production. Sotiba–Simpafric used its political influence to block both the Icotaf project and the British investors,[30] but not without making some concessions to government planners pushing for vertical integration.

In 1966 Icotaf, Sotiba–Simpafric, and the government reached a compromise over the vertical integration issue. Schaeffer Engineering, a subsidiary of Icotaf's parent firm, would participate in the construction and equipment of a new weaving factory. This new factory, the Société Textile Sénégalaise (STS), would be constituted as a juridically independent entity, jointly owned by Icotaf, Sotiba–Simpafric, and CCV.[31] STS would supply 30–50 percent of Sotiba–Simpafric's

---

28. Platt Brothers, the British group, became interested in textile manufacturing in Senegal as early as 1962. See *Marchés Tropicaux* (28 avril 1962): 950; and ibid. (30 octobre 1965): 279.
29. The Icotaf proposal was called the "ICOSIM project" (ibid. [30 octobre 1965]: 279).
30. Sotiba–Simpafric's relations with the government were so close, and so profitable for the firm, that many people in Dakar came to believe that Senghor himself was a major shareholder in Sotiba–Simpafric. He probably was not.
31. The ownership structure was 40–40–20, with CCV holding the 20 percent share. This structure was intended to ensure that neither Icotaf nor Sotiba–Simpafric gained majority control over the new weaving firm. However, interviewees in Dakar argued that CCV's dependence on Sotiba assured Sotiba–Simpafric de facto majority control. STS was located in Thiès and granted *régime conventionné* status under the Investment Code in 1968. Initial investments amounted to 1.2 billion CFA francs, one-third of which was financed through a special long-term loan from the CCCE (guaranteed by the government of Senegal through the BNDS), one-third through suppliers' credits from Schaeffer Engineering, and one-third through investment of *fonds propres* by the owners (i.e., 200 million CFA francs for the principal partners, 100 million for CCV). Production capacity was 9 million meters of gray cloth (*Le Fichier Industriel*, 15 janvier 1975; *Le Fichier Industriel*, 3 mars 1976).

demand for *écru*. Tariff protection for *imprimés* would be increased to compensate Sotiba–Simpafric for "surcharges" incurred in the purchase of more costly, locally produced *écru*. The high dividends that STS would pay to its three parent firms were calculated as part of these inflated costs. To seal the deal, Sotiba–Simpafric was assured monopoly rights to all further extension of local textile printing capacity.[32]

The creation of STS established a financial partnership between Icotaf and Sotiba–Simpafric. In the late 1960s and early 1970s the interests behind the two companies proceeded to set up additional direct and indirect ties. Both firms participated directly in STS's Conseil d'Administration and a few individuals took positions on the boards of both Sotiba–Simpafric and Icotaf.[33] Sotiba–Simpafric backers took ownership shares in Icotaf's parent firm, Ets. Schaeffer, and in Schaeffer's holdings in Morocco.[34]

Détente between Senegal's two major producers of staple textile goods paved the way for the "harmonious" diversification of production. Icotaf and Sotiba–Simpafric expanded into noncompeting product lines. Together, they produced all finished fabrics that were made in Senegal in the 1960s and 1970s. During that period, no third-party proposals for investment in the local production of finished piece goods were approved by the Senegalese government. And as the STS case illustrates, Sotiba–Simpafric and Icotaf – the major industrial buyers of intermediate textile goods – retained control over the development of critical backward linkages in the textile industry. In the words of their owners, Icotaf and Sotiba–Simpafric were "very profitable" in the 1960s.[35]

The closed production-marketing circuit gave rise to a system of oligopoly control over the production and sale of made-in-Senegal textiles. Underwriting this restrictive, collusive system was an elaborate structure of tariff barriers and quantitative import restrictions.

RESTRICTIONS GOVERNING TEXTILE IMPORTS

During the 1960s textile goods became the most heavily regulated category of imports and the Dakar textile industry became one of the most protected subsectors of local manufacturing.[36] Import controls that Senegal inherited from the

---

32. In 1966, when SOTIBA and SIMPAFRIC formally merged, the firm was granted *régime conventionné* status under the Investment Code for planned extensions of printing capacity.
33. For example, Gilbert Gross, the *fondé de pouvoir* at Sotiba–Simpafric, sat on Icotaf's Board of Directors.
34. Mr. Mekouar took 60 percent ownership of ICOMA, Icotaf's sister factory in Morocco, by buying out Ets. Schaeffer's original partners. This made Ets. Schaeffer and Mr. Mekouar partners. Mr. Riebel of the Sotiba group took 15 percent ownership of Ets. Schaeffer.
35. From interviews in Mulhouse and Dakar, 1985 and 1986. Data on net earnings, dividends paid, and fast amortizations that are presented below confirm that the finishing factories did very well indeed, from a financial point of view, in the 1960s and early 1970s.
36. Only local industries producing matches and flour were more protected (complete bans on imports).

Table 4.1. *Taxes on import shipment of French cotton cloth, circa 1965*[a]

	% f.o.b.	Cumulative %
Value ex-factory	98.6	98.6
Transport, factory to port	0.8	99.4
Loading	0.6	100.0[b]
Freight	1.2	101.2
Insurance	0.5	101.7
Commission de siège: 3% of c.i.f.	3.0	104.7[c]
Droit Fiscale d'entrée and Droit de Statistique (on c.i.f.)	17.8[d]	122.5
Droit de Douane	—	122.5
Taxe Forfaitaire: 20% of total	24.5	147.0
Turnover tax (TCA): 10% of total	14.7	161.7
Disembarkation charges: 1% of total	1.6	163.3[e]

[a]Import shipment valued at about 2.5 million CFA francs.
[b]f.o.b. price, exporting country.
[c]Value c.i.f.
[d]The *droits fiscale d'entrée* were higher for *filés* and *tissés de fibre artificielle ou synthétique* (20%) and for clothing (*vêtements de confection et de la bonneterie*) (20–25%).
[e]Cost upon delivery to wholesaler (*rendu magasin*).
Source: République Française, Ministère de la Coopération 1965:65.

colonial period ensured that France, a high-cost supplier by international standards, supplied 70–90 percent (varying according to product category) of all imported textile goods available on the local market. In the early 1960s, only 3–4 percent of Senegal's registered textile imports came from *pays à concurrence anormale* – low-cost suppliers such as India, Japan, Hong Kong, and Rumania. Across-the-board import taxes also ensured that no finished textile goods, including French goods, were taxed at a rate lower than 50 percent. Table 4.1 illustrates the typical *cascade des prix* in the mid-1960s for an import shipment of French cotton cloth.

When the government approved proposals for new investment in textile production, nominal rates of protection were set according to the manufacturer's estimates of price disparities between the locally manufactured product and similar, imported goods. As the local textile industry expanded and diversified between 1962 and 1975, tariffs on textiles were revised upward and extended to cover a wider range of products. Table 4.2 shows how general import taxes affected prices of textile goods imported from EEC and non-EEC countries in 1965.

Textile manufacturers quickly found that taxes and tariffs offered them insufficient control over the flow of imports onto the local market. They began to rely upon trade restrictions that they could manipulate and control more closely – licensing and *valeurs mercuriales*.

Import bans imposed between 1960 and 1962 to cushion the shock of the break-up of the AOF were gradually lifted and replaced by import licensing. The

Table 4.2. *Price increases: From f.o.b. to value after clearing
Senegalese customs, circa 1965*[a]

Article	Origin	Augmentation (in %)
Percales	France	64–65
Percales	Netherlands	72 (on *valeur mercuriale*)
Bazin	France, EEC	65–70
Divers teints[b]	France, EEC	66–68
Fancy prints	France	64
Fancy prints	EEC	68
Fancy prints	Hong Kong, China	97
Fancy prints	Japan	155
Wax prints	Netherlands	68
Wax prints	U.K.	93
Wax prints	Japan	155
Tissés, fils couleurs[c]	France	66–68
Clothing	France	73–90 (on *valeur mercuriale*)

[a]f.o.b. (free on board). This table does not take into account the impact of nontariff import restrictions (quotas, licensing). It is not clear how or if the authors of the table took the difference between f.o.b. prices and c.i.f. prices (about 6% to cover shipping, insurance, and freight) into account.
[b]*Popelines*, etc.
[c]Cloth woven with colored threads (yarn).
Source: République Française, Ministère de la Coopération 1965:66.

licensing regime was extended incrementally as local production diversified. By 1970 licensing governed the importation of nearly all textile goods deemed to compete directly with made-in-Senegal products. A *Commission de la Protection Industrielle* placed categories of imported textile products under the licensing regime at the request of local manufacturers. Import licenses were then allocated on a case-by-case basis by a Chamber of Commerce committee that met regularly to review textile importers' requests for licenses. Meeting behind closed doors, the committee assembled the industrialists concerned, representatives of the French trading companies, and spokesmen from the ministries overseeing commerce and industrial development.[37] Requests for import authorization were rejected when they received manufacturers' *avis défavorable* on the grounds that the import shipment could "perturb" a domestic market for locally produced goods. Manufacturers could veto any particular importers' request. They were thus in a position to decide which commercial companies would be granted licenses to import textile goods.

37. Only members of SCIMPEX, the association of French trading companies operating in Senegal, represented commercial interests on this committee. Lebanese and most other independent traders thus were excluded from the license-allocation process. Requests for *autorisation d'importation* specified the quantity, quality, origin, supplier, f.o.b. price, and anticipated Dakar retail price of the shipment of textile goods in question.

In practice, licensing worked as an informal quota system that allowed local manufacturers and the maisons de commerce to balance supplies of domestic and imported textile goods on the Senegalese market. Manufacturers and their commercial partners could decide what fraction of the local market would be "reserved" for imports with the understanding that these informal import "quotas" would be allocated to the maisons de commerce.[38] A few large French trading companies could control the entire local market for certain product categories (such as *imprimés*), adjusting the balance between made-in-Senegal goods and imported goods as local market conditions fluctuated. As local production expanded, these informal import quotas diminished and the maisons de commerce supplied more and more of the Senegalese market with domestically produced goods. Yet through the early 1970s licenses for tightly restricted imports continued to generate rents for the maisons de commerce. These rents bolstered the overall profitability of their textile operations in Senegal.[39]

Valeurs mercuriales were another important device for raising effective levels of tariff protection for local textile manufacturers. *Valeurs mercuriales* are artificially inflated tax bases, assigned to products in specific product categories by weight or on a per unit basis. The system was originally developed by the colonial administration to combat the under-invoicing of imports. Over time, it became a mechanism for ensuring that import tax burdens would be heavy in absolute terms, even for low-cost goods. By 1966 textile manufacturers in Dakar participated directly in the *mercuriale*-setting process.[40]

Mercuriales were set and revised on a yearly basis by a commission that operated under the jurisdiction of the ministry of finance. Upward revisions were initiated by local industrialists and calculated on the basis of manufacturers' estimates of what was needed to provide the local industry adequate protection against "cheap imports." By all accounts, the government was most responsive to industrialists' demands to keep *valeurs mercuriales* at levels close to the retail prices of locally manufactured goods. *Valeurs mercuriales* for textile imports climbed steadily every year after 1966. By the end of the 1960s textile imports

38. For example: Icotaf and the main distributor of its products, CITEC, would set a ratio that divided the market for a given product category between local goods and imports. The ratio would be based on estimates of Icotaf's production capacity and of domestic demand for the product line in question. The licensing system would govern the importation of goods in this category since they would be similar to those produced at Icotaf. When CITEC's request for an *autorisation d'importation* was presented to the *Commission Textile*, Icotaf would give its *avis favorable* (from interview at CITEC, Dakar, December 1985).

39. Profit margins were higher on imported goods, partially because the licensing system was used as the primary import-control mechanism, rather than import taxes. If taxation had been the primary mechanism, the state treasury, rather than the trading companies, would have collected more of the difference between local-market and import prices.

40. From 1959–65, only jute sacks and *friperie et chiffrons* (used clothes, rags, and cloth scraps) were mercurialized. At the end of 1966 and then rapidly thereafter, almost all categories of textile goods imported to Senegal were subjected to mercurialization. *Arrêté ministeriel du Ministère des Finances et Affaires Economiques no. 17165 du 9 décembre 1966* published in *Le Journal Officiel du Sénégal*, was the turning point.

were subject to the most complex and comprehensive system of *mercurialisation* in effect in Senegal.[41]

In 1972 analysts working for the World Bank estimated coefficients for effective rates of protection (EPCs) in Senegal's textile industry. EPCs are ratios that compare local value-added in domestic prices to local value-added in "world prices." Because this measure of market protection takes taxes and tariffs on industrial inputs into account, it is a better indicator of net protection than nominal tariff rates. An EPC of 1.0 is an indicator of "perfect competition." The World Bank study assigned EPCs of 3.29 to locally produced gray cloth and 2.06 to cotton yarn, thread, and finished cloth (including *imprimés*).[42] These rates are striking. They were among the highest EPCs calculated for all major subsectors of Senegalese import-substitution industry (see Table 3.5). High EPCs attest to the efficacy of trade controls restricting the volume and raising the prices of imported textile goods.

Restrictions governing textile imports also allowed the maisons de commerce to retain control over the importation of *produits de choix* – especially *imprimés*. Of all the textile products sold on the Senegalese market, *imprimés* generated the widest profit margins. This fabric was the staple in the rural areas; it was also consumed widely in the cities. High rates of effective protection and price collusion kept prices high for both imported and locally produced *imprimés*. These arrangements imposed heavy costs on consumers of staple textile goods. Noncompetitive rents collected by the maisons de commerce and the local manufacturers were paid by groundnut producers, other rural consumers, and urban wage earners and salary earners.

The link between the groundnut marketing circuit and the textile trade was obvious at harvest time. Most textile goods sold in rural Senegal were purchased immediately after the cooperatives paid peasants for their groundnut crops. Groundnut revenues were recycled through the commercial circuit to the maisons de commerce and manufacturers, much as they had been in the old days of *la traite*. Hierarchical, Dakar-centered trading circuits underpinned this system.

Meanwhile, Lebanese traders became unbeatable importers of products that were not governed by import licensing. They specialized in garments, *nouveautés* (specialty goods), synthetic fabrics, and household textile goods (e.g. sheets, rugs). These goods were sold mostly on urban markets, where higher incomes and attention to rapidly changing fashions diversified demand. Textile markets controlled by the Lebanese were competitive, riskier, and less profitable than the tightly controlled market for staple goods.

Lebanese merchants were obviously not satisfied with this de facto division of the market. At the margins, they pushed for more space, skillfully manipulating

41. Even product categories controlled by licensing were mercurialized in the late 1960s.
42. World Bank, "Economic Incentives and Resource Costs in Senegal (a project directed by Bela Balassa)," unpub. ms., June 1975 (restricted circulation). This study was based on 1972 data. Its results were incorporated into World Bank, *The Economic Trends and Prospects of Senegal*, vol. 3: *The Industrial Sector*, unpub. ms., December 1979 (restricted circulation).

customs code classifications to expand their import operations and, when they could, cutting deals with French importers or government agents. The maisons de commerce and manufacturers were relentless in pressuring state officials to ride herd on fraud in the import trade, registering complaints in response to the slightest perturbations of their markets.

The government's willingness to enforce restrictive trade policies and to underwrite exclusionary trade practices sustained the high profit margins of the maisons de commerce and the local manufacturers. This structure of market control led to new investment in the expansion and diversification of the local textile industry.

EXPANSION OF THE TEXTILE INDUSTRY

Senegal's textile industry grew faster than any other subsector of light manufacturing between 1965 and 1975, recording significant increases in investment, production, and employment. During this expansionary period, however, structural weaknesses in the industry – feeble vertical integration, low present value of firms and poor capital stock, excess capacity, and inflated production costs – persisted and were aggravated. With commercial guarantees, new investment could generate attractive returns in spite of the high costs of manufacturing textile goods in Senegal. High production costs were passed on to the Senegalese consumer.

Investment in the textile industry was guided by the goal of diversifying production in order to cover the Senegalese market more broadly. Firms that specialized in the production of a few articles for sale on AOF markets in the 1950s restructured to produce a variety of articles for the smaller, domestic market. This usually required some investment in new production capacity. The result, for the 1960–75 period, was growth of Senegal's textile industry. Output and total employment doubled between 1960 and 1975 (Table 4.3). Exports declined steadily over the course of this period (Table 4.4) and the local market absorbed most of the increase in output.[43] By 1975 the local textile industry covered 46 percent of Senegal's total officially estimated demand for textile goods.

Investment on a firm-by-firm basis

New investment and new import barriers appeared in lockstep coordination. In the basic textile industry firms established a decade earlier expanded their spinning, weaving, and dyeing capacity. Import restrictions shifted demand away from cheaper imports, creating markets for locally made yarn, thread, and cloth.

---

43. Senegal continued to export intermediate goods (*écrus* and *filés écrus*) to the Côte d'Ivoire in the 1960s and early 1970s when the demand of the Ivoirian finishing industries exceeded Ivoirian spinning and weaving capacity. Until the mid-1960s, Mauritania and Niger absorbed most of Senegal's declining production of *guinée* cloth.

Table 4.3. *Some rough and aggregate indicators of growth in Senegal's textile industry, 1960–76*

Year	Index of industrial production[a]	Total turnover[b]	Employment[c]			% all industry	Value-added[d]
			Basic	Other tex.	Total		
1959	100.0						
1960	113.2						
1961	124.8						
1962	122.3	3.5	1,439	550	2,000	18	1.0
1963	134.6						
1964	134.0		1,800	560	2,400	14	
1965	151.2						
1966	188.0						
1967	210.6	6.5	2,500	700	3,000		
1968	199.3		2,468				
1969	212.2				3,214		3.52
1970	230.2	7.5					
1971	230.1						
1972	257.8				3,815		
1973	231.6	9.8	2,500				
1974	226.8	10.0	3,200	800			6.4
1975	231.9	12.0	3,400	800	4,230	16	
1976	244.0						

[a] Index of industrial production: No 1960–80 time-series exists. For given years, different sources report different changes in the index. In these cases (1967, 1968, 1977), I averaged. In some years, the index for textiles included leather industries (i.e., shoes).
[b] Total turnover (*chiffre d'affaires*): Current values in billion CFA francs. A time-series is difficult to compile because sources rarely specify which firms or segments of the industry are included in the "overall" *chiffre d'affaires* of the textile industry.
[c] Employment: Data are broken down into *industrie textile de base* and "all other segments of the industry" including garments and knitting (*bonneterie* and *confection*) and sack-making firms.
[d] Value-added. Basic textile industry only. In billion CFA francs, current value.
Sources: Le Bulletin de l'Afrique Noire (various issues 1959–1977); GOS, Direction de la Statistique, *Indice de la Production Industrielle* (yearly); République Française, Ministère de la Coopération, 1965; *Le Sénégal d'aujourd'hui*, 30 nov. 1973; World Bank 1974; Ediafric, *Le Sénégal en Chiffres*, 1978; SONED 1979.

The secondary segment of the textile industry (manufacturing garments and knits) also grew in the 1960s, largely through the creation of new firms. Increased production in both the segments of the textile industry was accompanied by a corresponding fall in registered textile imports.

Table 4.6 is a statistical profile of the textile industry. It provides summary data for 1965 and 1975 on a firm-by-firm basis. A few cautionary notes are in order. Because no time-series data exist for the entire period, the data were drawn from numerous sources. This reduces the reliability of the table as a

Table 4.4. *Exports of textile goods manufactured in Senegal,^{a} 1958–80*

Year	Value in CFA billion (current prices)	Volume (tons)	% of total production
1958			49
1961	1.1		41
1962	1.0		38
1964	0.8	1,800	23
1967	1.2		18
1968	1.0		
1969	0.9	1,185	
1970	1.8	1,755	20
1971	1.0	1,141	
1972	1.2	1,121	
1974	0.9	956	9
1975	1.8	1,004	15
1976	1.6	1,223	
1977	2.0	1,424	
1978	1.6	795	
1979	0.9	404	
1980	0.8	454	

^{a}Goods wholly made in Senegal and goods processed (dyed, printed, bleached, sewn into finished garments) in Senegal. The data presented here are indicative of orders of magnitude only. Inconsistent accounting procedures, definitions of product categories, definitions of "exports," etc., make the figures imprecise.
Sources: United Nations, *UN Commodity Trade Statistics* (yearly); République Française, Ministère de la Coopération 1965; World Bank 1974:297.

whole. Moreover, important inconsistencies exist in the accounting procedures of the Senegalese government, in the accounting procedures and reports of firms that supply the raw data to the government (the government does not check these data for accuracy), and in the reporting procedures of the business periodicals, international organizations, etc., that track developments in Senegalese manufacturing. Table 4.6 and other, similar tables should therefore be read to gain a rough sense of what was going on at the time; data presented seem to fall within the correct range, even if they are not very precise. Figure 4.1, by contrast, was drawn with broad brush strokes. It offers a general picture of the structure of the Senegalese textile industry in the early 1970s.

Icotaf, Dakar's first manufacturer of finished textile goods, doubled its weaving capacity over the course of the 1960s and early 1970s.[44] Jacquard looms were installed in Icotaf's factory at Pikine in 1963. In 1968 a new unit was added to weave cloth destined for use as *pagnes* in the rural areas (*tissés fils couleurs*).

44. By the mid-1970s weaving capacity at the Icotaf–Pikine factory was 4 million meters a year, up from 2 million meters in 1959–62.

Table 4.5. *Recorded imports of textile goods to Senegal, by product category, 1959–75*[a]

Year	All textiles[b] (v)	Prints[c] (v)	Synthetics[d] (v)	Blankets[e] (v)	(t)	Clothing[f] (v)	Knits[g] (v)	(t)
1959	6,716			39	266		228	227
1960	6,887		511	76	520		243	261
1961	6,030		617	4	27	605	192	216
1962	6,017	1,784	477	1	1	661	148	194
1963	5,580	1,334	564	1	1	471	149	179
1964	6,548	1,527	784	1	1	461	115	178
1965		1,095	713			310		
1966	4,028	741	629			252		
1967	5,222	526	369			230		
1968	4,787	662	258			226	226	191
1969	3,874	629	228			246		
1970	3,312	885	237					
1973[g]		514					245	147
1974–5		276					330	134

Notes: (v) = value in million CFA francs in current prices; (t) = tons.
[a]Data for 1971 and 1972 not available.
[b]Including all cloth (including synthetics) and thread, yarn, and household textile goods.
[c]*Imprimés de coton.*
[d]*Tissus synthétiques et artificielles.*
[e]*Couvertures de coton.*
[f]*Vêtements de confection.*
[g]*Bonneterie.*
Sources: République Française, Ministère de la Coopération 1965; *Marchés Tropicaux*, 1967–78 (various issues); *Le Bulletin de l'Afrique Noire*, 1969–75 (various issues); Commission des Communautés Européennes 1974.

Competing imports were subjected to licensing in 1970.[45] Another new unit was added in 1973, this one to weave synthetics from imported yarn. Imports of synthetic cloth were restricted by licensing the same year.[46] By the mid-1970s, Icotaf manufactured seventy different product lines including *gabardines, popelines, cretonnes, damassés,* blankets (until 1974), *drills,* and yarn. Although most production units worked at 40–60 percent of capacity, Icotaf was very profitable during this period.

Icotaf's increases in output were achieved with minimal investment. It seems

45. *Décret du 6 mai 1970 soumettant tissés fils couleurs à autorisation préalable (Le Journal Officiel du Sénégal* 1970). Analysts working for the World Bank estimated that the Effective Protection Coefficient (EPC) for weaving at Icotaf in the mid-1970s was 1.97. Data from: World Bank, *The Economic Trends and Prospects of Senegal,* December 1979.
46. *Décret du 25 janvier 1970 soumettant tissus synthétiques et artificielles à autorisation préalable (Le Journal Officiel du Sénégal* 1970). These imports were also taxed at a rate of over 60 percent.

Table 4.6. *Profile of the Senegalese textile industry, 1965–75*

Firm	Year[a]	Activity[b] 1975	Employees (number) 1965	Employees (number) 1975	Total sales (m. CFA)[c] 1965	Total sales (m. CFA)[c] 1975	Exports (% sales) 1965	Exports (% sales) 1975	Production (volume)[d] 1965	Production (volume)[d] 1975	Capacity utilization (in %) 1972	Ownership (% local) 1974
SOTIBA[e]	1951	f	411	1,000	1,000	7,500	30	15	3.5 mm	19 mm	50	0
Icotaf[f]	1949	s,w,f	750	1,063		2,200	50	0.4	4 mm	8.5 mm	40–60	0
CCV	1952	s	160	140		370		13	400 T.	660 T.	67	0
SCT	1957	b	220	207		413			450 ar.	626 ar.	60	0
SOSEFIL	1966	f	85[g]	145	328[g]	700		50	100 T.[g]	185 T.	90	0
STS	1970	s,w		460	480[g]	1,323		0		9.3 mm	90	0
La SIV	1961	g	180	300	300	505	15	38	200 ar.	500 ar.	50	25
TMS	1961	k		110	95[g]	220	20[g]		275 ar.	1,250 ar.		0
Mabose	1965	k		90						850 ar.	57	0[h]
Soboco	1960	k		65	160	226	20		770 ar.	850 ar.	60	0[h]

[a]First year of operations.
[b]Activity: s (spinning), w (weaving), f (finishing)), g (garments of woven cloth), k (knitting, knit garments), b (blankets).
[c]Million CFA francs, current prices.
[d]Volume per year. T. (tons), mm. (million meters), ar. (thousands of articles).
[e]Sotiba–Simpafric.
[f]Icotaf–Pikine and Icotaf-Rusfique.
[g]Figure pertains to 1969, 1970, 1971, or 1972.
[h]Lebanese owners who may have had Senegalese citizenship.

Selected Sources: *Le Bulletin de l'Afrique Noire* (1964–79, various issues); République Française, Ministère de la Coopération 1965; *Le Fichier Industriel* (1966–79); Ediafric, *Le Sénégal en Chiffres*, 1975, 1982–3; Ediafric, *Les 500 Premières Entreprises de l'Afrique Noire*, 1975; GOS, Ministère du Développement Industriel 1976; *Marchés Tropicaux*, 17 février 1978; SONED 1979; GOS, Chambre de Commerce et de l'Industrie 1980; *Afrique Industrie*, nov. 1984.

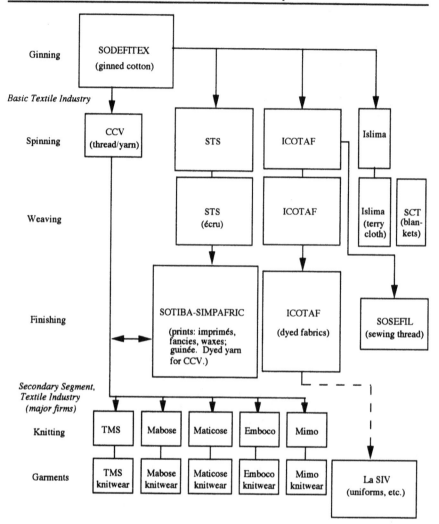

Figure 4.1. Structure of the Senegalese textile industry, circa 1974–6. Horizontal levels of the chart indicate stages of the textile production process (e.g. spinning, weaving). Arrows represent interfirm linkages. All firms in the sector are also supplied to varying degrees with imported inputs.

that 60–100 million CFA francs were invested in the 1960s. All new capital went into the factory at Pikine; the weaving factory at Rufisque was not expanded or modernized. The Rufisque plant ran at about 80 percent of capacity in the early 1960s, producing up to 5–7 million meters of *cretonnes* and light *écru* per year for Sotiba's bleaching and indigo dyeing units. As Sotiba's production of *guinée* cloth fell after the loss of the Malian market, the Rufisque factory was marginalized. Output at Icotaf–Rufisque declined along an erratic course after 1965.

Sotiba–Simpafric, Dakar's second producer of finished cloth, redefined its *métier* in the early 1960s, turning away from the dyeing of *guinée* cloth to concentrate on printing cloth for the Senegalese market.[47] Output of *imprimés* (called *fancies* or *lagos*) grew cautiously in the 1960s when taxes on similar goods imported from France ran about 60 percent. Cheaper prints from the Far East were restricted by yearly quotas and subjected to taxes of 90–150 percent. Between 1965 and 1975, Sotiba–Simpafric invested 500 million CFA francs to achieve a ten-fold increase its printing capacity. The firm's goal was to supply 100 percent of local demand. Sotiba–Simpafric's *imprimés* were durable and beautiful – in general very much appreciated on the Senegalese market. Production and local sales jumped dramatically in the early 1970s, from 7.2 million meters in 1970 to 17 million meters in 1976.[48] This increase was accompanied by 1970 and 1972 laws that reinforced licensing restrictions and imposed *valeurs mercuriales* on this category of imports.[49] The new laws reduced registered imports of competing goods by about 80 percent (see Table 4.5).

Nearly all the *écru* used as the base for printing was imported until 1970, when STS – the new weaving factory owned jointly by Icotaf, CCV, and Sotiba–Simpafric – came on line. STS produced 9 million meters of *écru*, supplying about one-half of Sotiba–Simpafric's yearly demand.

Sotiba–Simpafric added a new production unit in 1966.[50] The new unit produced wax prints (*waxes, or javas*), a *tissu de luxe* that had been imported to West Africa since the midcolonial period. When the wax factory opened, competing imports were taxed at rates of about 60–150 percent. *Mercuriales* were imposed on this product line in 1972.[51] The market in Senegal for these luxurious fabrics, however, was limited. Wax prints were too expensive for most rural buyers, and members of the urban salariat tended to prefer the English and Dutch varieties imported by the CNF and the CFAO. Sotiba–Simpafric produced 4 million meters of wax prints a year; the CNF and the CFAO exported a large share of this to Togo and Benin (where some presumably found its way onto the Nigerian market) and to the Côte d'Ivoire, where a population of generally wealthier consumers could afford the brilliant colors and stylish designs of Senegalese wax prints. Installation of the wax print factory raised Sotiba–Simpafric's total investment for the 1960–73 period to around 800–900 million CFA francs, dwarfing the investments made by Icotaf during the same period.

47. Sotiba–Simpafric's production of *guinée* dropped from 8 to 3.7 million meters between 1963 and 1974.
48. Sotiba–Simpafric's printing capacity grew from about 3 million meters a year in the early 1960s to 35 million meters in 1975. A rough time series for actual production (output) of *imprimés* runs as follows: 4.5 million meters (mm) in 1965; 7.2 mm in 1970; 7.6 mm in 1971; 8.5 mm in 1972; 12 mm in 1975; 17 mm in 1976; and 16 mm in 1977.
49. *Décret du 6 mai 1970 soumettant à autorisation préalable les importations des tissus de coton imprimés ou similaires présentant les motifs obtenus par peinture, application de tonisses ou autrement. Arrêté du 27 juillet 1972 portant modifications des valeurs mercuriales des Fancies et Javas (Le Journal Officiel du Sénégal 1970, 1972).*
50. Capacity of Sotiba–Simpafric's wax production unit was officially stated at 5 million meters. Investments amounted to 450 million CFA francs.
51. *Décret du 27 juillet 1972 modifiant les valeurs mercuriales des fancies et javas.*

CCV, the spinning firm, survived the breakup of the AOF by linking its fate to Sotiba–Simpafric's. Import bans in the early 1960s created new internal markets for locally made cotton yarn.[52] CCV diversified its market by sending about half of its yearly output to be dyed in Sotiba's factories. The rest was sold either to the Dakar knitting firms or "as is" on the local market. Total output was stable between 1959 and 1969: 400 tons a year. Prospects for growth brightened in the early 1970s as the Dakar knitting firms expanded. CCV's production increased by about 60 percent. In 1975 the modest sum of 60 million CFA francs was spent on modernization.

A new firm was added to Senegal's basic textile industry in 1964, when the Icotaf group and one of its European industrial partners, the Dollfus Mieg Corporation (DMC), mounted another import-substitution operation in Dakar.[53] DMC exported sewing thread to its own sales office in Dakar in the earlier period. The DMC–Icotaf factory manufactured the same product locally. Icotaf supplied the new dyeing plant, the Société Sénégalaise de Filature (SOSEFIL), with gray thread. Imported sewing thread was eliminated from the local market in 1966, when SOSEFIL came on line, allowing the firm to double production by 1974.[54] Through the DMC connection, SOSEFIL exported about 40 percent of its output to the Côte d'Ivoire in the 1960s. Export sales dropped off considerably in the 1970s and SOSEFIL concentrated on the domestic market.

After 1961 bans on competing imports allowed Dakar's two blanket producing firms, SCT and Icotaf, to redirect their production toward Senegal's rural markets. In 1961 SCT increased its output by about 30 percent and diversified its product line. Icotaf increased its output of cotton blankets in the same year. In 1965 Icotaf covered about 30 percent of the internal market for cotton blankets, just enough to check the expansion of SCT.[55] Icotaf finally withdrew from this line of production in 1974 and sold its blanket-making equipment to SCT. With its new monopoly on production, SCT expanded its output by about 40 percent.[56]

---

52. Exports to the region constituted only 25 percent of CCV's sales in 1965. Exports fell even further, to 10 percent of total sales, by the early 1970s (*Le Fichier Industriel* 1974). The effective protection coefficient for CCV was estimated by the World Bank in 1979 as 1.52–1.63 (World Bank, *The Economic Trends and Prospects of Senegal*, December 1979:66).
53. SOSEFIL was owned by Icotaf and the Dollfus Mieg Corporation (DMC) in a 34–66 percent split, with DMC in majority control. The Icotaf group and DMC were linked through the holding company TEXUNION.
54. Original production capacity of 200 tons per year was increased to 400 tons per year in 1974, when investments of 130 million CFA francs were added to the original investment of 90 million. The 1974 investments were carried out in part with a loan of 50 million CFA francs from the Caisse Centrale de la Coopération Economique (CCCE), France's public lending institution subsidizing private French investment in industry in the former colonies. See *Afrique Industrie*, no. 128 (1 décembre 1976).
55. Blocking the expansion of SCT was Icotaf's goal. Icotaf feared that if SCT were too prosperous, it might expand into more sophisticated weaving activities and pose a competitive threat to Icotaf. During this period, most of SCT's inputs seem to have been imported in the form of *déchets* (cloth scraps) from Europe.

In 1974, near the end of the time period covered in this chapter, a terry-cloth weaving factory was set up in Dakar by Belgian textile interests. The Industrie Sénégalaise de Linge de Maison (ISLIMA) was designed to cover 50 percent of domestic demand for towels and to export towels woven from Senegalese cotton to Europe. In timing and conception, the ISLIMA project was part and parcel of a mid-1970s vision of export-led growth targeted at EEC markets.[57] This vision never resonated deeply in Senegal, and certainly not in the Dakar textile industry as a whole. Unfortunately for the investors, ISLIMA's story would not be part of the Dakar textile industry's history of expansion.

For Senegal's basic textile industry (producing blankets, thread and yarn, prints, gray cloth, and wovens), new import bans and restrictions performed a stabilizing function in the early 1960s. These firms began to diversify production as new import controls created internal markets to replace regional markets that were increasingly difficult to penetrate. The total volume of output increased after 1966, once positions on the internal market were firmly established.

The development of the secondary segment of the textile industry (producing garments and knits) followed a somewhat different course. This segment of the industry was less developed than the basic textile industry at the time of independence. Opportunities for the creation of new firms were wide open in 1960. Unlike the manufacture of basic textile goods on an industrial scale, garment production can be carried out on a small scale. Initial investments can be quite modest. This is precisely what happened. Between 1960 and 1965 independent French and Lebanese importers created several new garment-making firms in Dakar to supply their own boutiques and other retailers. Overall output in the secondary segment of the industry increased rapidly in the initial postindependence period and grew steadily through the early 1970s.

CITEX and DITEX, two Dakar garment-making firms that existed in the 1950s, were downstream subsidiaries of French textile manufacturers exporting cloth to West Africa.[58] The parent firms exported cloth to Dakar, where it was

---

56. Overall blanket production remained relatively stable over the course of the 1965–77 period:

Production of Cotton Blankets, 1965–77
(in thousands of articles)

	SCT	Icotaf	Total
1965	450	175	625
1973	400	150	550
1975	625	0	625
1977	750	0	750

Sources: Ediafric, *L'Industrie africaine en 1969*, 740; idem, *L'Industrie africaine en 1975*, 13; Commission des Communautés Européennes, 1974: 23; and *Le Fichier Industriel*.

57. The Lomé trade conventions promised to open the EEC market to manufacturers in West Africa.
58. The CITEX garment-assembly factory was part of the large commercial network of CITEC, the subsidiary of Boussac.

sewn into garments. In 1961 independent French textile importers created a similar type of operation, La Société Industrielle de Vêtement, or La SIV.[59] Like the two older firms, La SIV specialized in the assembly of pants and shirts. To protect the garment-making firms, the importation of inexpensive shirts and pants was banned in 1960. Competing imports were taxed at a rate of 70–80 percent on a *mercuriale*-inflated tax base.[60] These measures cut registered clothing imports by half by 1966 (see Table 4.5).

In spite of the import restrictions designed to promote industrial-scale garment making, CITEX and DITEX suffered negative effective rates of protection on the internal market. In order to protect Icotaf, the government imposed heavy taxes on the imported cloth they used to make garments. Penalized by the overall structure of protection, these firms closed down in the early 1960s. La SIV found new marketing strategies and survived, expanding by 400 percent over the course of the 1960s.[61]

In 1962 the BNDS, Senegal's national development bank, purchased a 25 percent ownership share in La SIV. Two years later, SCOA, one of West Africa's most powerful maisons de commerce, also took partial ownership of La SIV. Through SCOA, La SIV imported low-cost cloth (under an *admission temporaire* scheme), sewed this cloth into garments, and reexported to other countries in the region. Cloth processed in Senegal for reexport was not subject to import taxation. For the 60 percent of its output that was sold in Senegal, La SIV used costlier cloth that was woven by Icotaf. Tariff barriers allowed La SIV to sell some of its production on the domestic market. The firm also obtained contracts to supply uniforms to the Senegalese government, no doubt through the BNDS connection. This probably explains most of the growth in LA SIV's local sales.[62]

The external trade regime was one enduring constraint on the expansion of industrial-scale firms making garments of woven cloth in Senegal. Perhaps even more important, however, was the competition that firms like CITEX, DITEX, and La SIV faced from the artisanal tailors who made garments *sur commande* for most of Dakar's population. In 1962 the formal sector firms targeted their attacks at these Senegalese tailors, raising the battle cry of "unfair competition." The competition they objected to was "unfair," they said, because the artisanal tailors did not pay business taxes, minimum wages, social security charges, etc.

---

59. La SIV was created by three French expatriates living in Dakar and specializing in the importation of textile goods in the 1950s. The third member of the group sold out to his partners almost immediately. Second-hand equipment purchased in France was installed in the factory.
60. In the early 1960s the importation of shirts with a declared value of less than 1,700 CFA francs c.i.f. and of pants below 1,900 francs was banned, along with a list of similar articles. In 1965 new *mercuriales* were placed on clothing imports. The importation of some types of garments was restricted by quotas (*Le Bulletin de la Chambre de Commerce et de l'Industrie – Région Cap Vert*, no. 434-v (juin 1965); République Française, Ministère de la Coopération 1965).
61. La SIV's output increased from 200,000 articles per year in 1962 to 800,000 articles per year in 1970.
62. By turning debt into equity, the BNDS share increased to 62 percent in 1975.

The Senegalese government obliged by passing a law outlawing *travail noir* and *travail clandestin*.[63] *Travail noir* was defined as the production of goods for retail sale by unregistered operators. That the Senegalese government had no interest in enforcing this law was clear by 1965, when the French government planners assigned to Senegal's textile sector pressured the local authorities to adopt a firm stand against artisanal production. This initiative went nowhere. Interests arrayed in defense of artisanal production included not only the tailors and the vast majority of Dakar's consumers, but also the importers and manufacturers who supplied tailors and consumers with locally made and imported *imprimés* and wax prints.

Rapid growth of Dakar's market for knits in the 1950s and 1960s is what drove the expansion of the secondary segment of the textile industry. To jump tariff barriers, independent importers invested in the local manufacture of knitted garments. By 1962 three firms were active in this line of production. Two were created by French textile importers residing in Dakar (Ets. René Tardy and Les Tricotages Mécaniques du Sénégal, or TMS). One was created by a local Lebanese importer: the Société de Bonneterie et de Confection Dakaroise (SOBOCO).[64] The knitting firms were designed to supply the preexisting distribution networks of their owners. TMS ran into trouble almost immediately and was taken over in 1962 by CCV and SCOA.[65] CCV supplied TMS with cotton yarn and was interested in controlling a stable outlet for this product. SCOA was interested in commercializing the firm's output.

By 1964 it was clear that tariff barriers of 60 percent did not provide sufficient import protection for the knitting firms. In response to pressure from the manufacturers, the government created a *Commission de la Bonneterie* at the end of 1964 to coordinate the implementation of a licensing system. Local manufacturers sitting on this commission reviewed applications for authorization to import knits on a case-by-case basis, rejecting those that could "perturb" the market for locally manufactured knits. Import controls allowed for commercial markups of 55 percent on knit garments made in Senegal.[66]

Shortly after the formation of the *Commission de la Bonneterie*, SOBOCO absorbed Ets. René Tardy and expanded operations.[67] TMS began to grow rapidly and diversified into the production of higher-quality, synthetic knits. A new firm, MABOSE, was created by Lebanese commerçants. All three were of

---

63. *Loi du 6 juin 1962 portant interdiction du "travail noir" et "travail clandestin."*
64. Ets. René Tardy was a knitting firm created in 1956. TMS was created in 1961, when used knitting equipment purchased in France was brought to Dakar.
65. CCV and SCOA took 30 percent and 60 percent ownership shares, respectively.
66. République Française, Ministère de la Coopération 1965:68. Except for the firms linked to SCOA (La SIV and TMS), knitting and garment-making firms in Dakar distributed through the manufacturers' own commercial networks (boutiques, factory-door sales to retailers, etc.).
67. Ets. René Tardy was renamed "MATICOSE." SOBOCO and MATICOSE operations were centralized in a new factory in 1967.

roughly equal size by 1970.[68] Together they supplied about half of Senegal's officially estimated demand for knitted garments.

High profits for local manufacturers, despite high costs

Wide profit margins and high production costs were two defining (and related) characteristics of the Dakar textile industry in the 1960s and early 1970s. In part the problem of production costs reflected charges that were levied against manufacturers for water, electricity, and some intermediate goods. Textile manufacturers paid state-owned utilities companies up to four times more for water and electricity in Senegal than they would have in France.[69] In the 1960s and early 1970s Dakar textile manufacturers also paid import duties of 45 percent on chemical inputs (dyes, etc.). The fact that cotton was produced in Senegal gave local manufacturers no competitive edge – they paid world market prices for Senegalese cotton.[70]

At the same time, serious firm-level inefficiencies and excessive "overhead costs" played an important role in inflating costs of production. These inefficiencies and costs often reflected the production and investment strategies of manufacturers who enjoyed oligopoly or monopoly positions on the local market. Manufacturers' tendency not to renew and modernize existing capital stock, coupled with extensive product diversification, made the Senegalese textile industry extremely inefficient. Much of the equipment installed in Senegal's textile factories was purchased secondhand in France in the 1950s.[71] This machinery was being replaced in France precisely because it was antiquated. Throughout the Senegalese textile industry, investment in the renovation of capital stock between 1960 and 1980 was marginal.[72]

In the 1960s and early 1970s the sorry state of capital stock accounted for low labor productivity in most firms in the industry. Potential cost advantages inherent in Senegal's low minimum wage rates were thus offset by the low productivi-

---

68. Production of SOBOCO–MATICOSE increased from about 600,000 articles per year in 1966 to 1 million articles per year in 1967. TMS production figures (in thousands of articles): 270 (for 1966); 850 (for 1968); 1,200 (for 1971). MABOSE produced 1 million articles in 1967.
69. SONED 1979. Electricity alone accounted for 10 percent of the costs of producing a kilo of cotton yarn in Senegal.
70. Under the terms of the agreement between the CFDT (which monopolized the commercialization of Senegalese cotton) and the government, local manufacturers paid world-market prices for Senegalese cotton. These arrangements were modified in the late 1970s and 1980s. See Chapter 6.
71. World War II–vintage equipment was installed in Icotaf–Pikine, in the 1950s, and in Icotaf–Rufisque, La SIV, TMS, SCT, and CCV.
72. See *Le Fichier Industriel;* SONED 1979; 1980. Other sources: World Bank, "Economic Incentives and Resource Costs in Senegal," June 1975; World Bank, *The Economic Trends and Prospects of Senegal,* December 1979; Gouvernement du Sénégal, Ministère du Développement Industriel et de l'Artisanat, "Rapport du Groupe de Travail Textile," 25 septembre 1981; Gouvernement du Sénégal, Ministère du Plan et de la Coopération, Commission Nationale de Planification n. B-6, Sous-Commission: Textiles, "Rapport provisoire," 1982.

ty of wage labor. As one group of French analysts wrote, "one factor cancels out the other."[73] The problem of labor costs was compounded by the high cost of staffing managerial and technical posts with expatriates. Expatriate salaries in the Dakar textile industry were two to three times greater than salaries for equivalent posts in European firms. In addition to these salaries the Dakar firms provided expatriates with extensive perquisites (usually including housing, cars, children's school fees, yearly trips to France for the whole family, etc.). In 1972, more than a decade after the end of colonial rule, 35 percent of total wages and salaries paid in the Senegalese textile industry went to Europeans.[74]

When investments were made in production, they were limited to expanding capacity in a few especially lucrative product lines (such as *imprimés*) or to diversifying the production of finished goods. The Icotaf–Pikine factory was notorious for fragmenting its production capacity. Sotiba–Simpafric made a specialty of short production runs. The knitting and garment-making operations adopted a similar strategy, placing a premium on producing a wide variety of articles, rather than on trying to cover local demand for one type of garment. Opting for extensive diversification enhanced market control, for the government would impose "extraordinary" import restrictions (licensing, *valeurs mercuriales*) only on goods that would compete directly with made-in-Senegal products. This pattern of diversification eliminated the advantages of economies of scale. Capacity utilization was low for most firms in the industry. Because import controls were broad and formidable, producing a wide range of articles in limited quantities was an attractive strategy, in spite of higher per unit costs.

Local manufacturing firms' "costs of production" often included charges that are more accurately categorized as profits to parent firms and shareholders. Amortization payments, scheduled to pay off investments in five to six years, apparently continued far beyond the five to six year period.[75] Local textile firms transferred profits to parent companies via fees and other charges associated with management contracts, technical assistance, interest on suppliers' credits, and

73. "If in Senegal the level of wages and benefits [*charges sociales*] can often be a third of what it is in the metropole, it is necessary to note that, in general, labor productivity . . . is only a third of what it is in France. . . . [O]ne factor cancels out the other and 'labor cost' does not represent an advantage in calculating costs of production [*le poste 'main-d'oeuvre' ne constitue pas un élément favorable dans la formation du coût de production*]" (CINAM et SERESA 1960:II-7-3). See also Ferrandi 1962; World Bank 1974; and SONED 1979.
   See also Ferrandi 1962; World Bank 1974; and SONED 1979.
74. World Bank, "Incentives and the Economic Efficiency of Resource Allocation in Senegalese Industry, 1971–1973," unpub. ms., September 1984: 3.6 (restricted circulation). In the manufacturing sector as a whole, salaries paid to expatriates averaged 56 percent of total wages paid to all Senegalese workers in 1962 and 40 percent of total wages to all Senegalese workers in 1974 (SONED 1977a:iii).
75. Gouvernement du Sénégal, Ministère du Développement Industriel et de l'Artisanat, "Etat de l'outil de travail de l'industrie textile," 9 janvier 1985. Using data on amortization schedules and payments reported by textile manufacturers, the MDIA estimated that most of the equipment in the textile industry was only six years old!

wide commercial markups on inputs purchased directly from parent firms.[76]
STS, Senegal's costly producer of *écrus*, sold its output to one of its owners,
Sotiba–Simpafric, at a markup of as much as 20 percent in the mid-1970s.[77]
Sotiba's costs were high, but so were the dividends that it collected from STS.

Even with high factor costs, firm-level inefficiencies, and extra charges paid to
parent firms, the gross profits of the firms in the textile industry were strikingly
high. Guy Courtois reported gross profits for Senegal's textile industry of 13
percent in 1962 and 29.1 percent in 1967. By the same calculation, the average
for Senegal's industrial sector as a whole was 9 percent.[78] This made textile
manufacturing one of the most profitable industrial activities in Senegal in 1967.
Other studies arrived at similar conclusions. Dividends paid to shareholders in
Senegal's textile firms were deemed "excessive" by World Bank analysts eval-
uating industry in Senegal in the mid-1970s.[79] The Bank defined a "normal rate
of foreign profit" as 19.5 percent of paid-up capital plus revenues. The largest
"excess rates of foreign profit" identified in its cross-sectional study were in the
textile industry and in Senegal's monopoly producer of wooden matches. Rates
of return on investment of up to 30 percent a year were estimated for Dakar's
largest textile firms. "The presence of rents" in the industry was attributed to
"local market structure and/or excessive protection." The analysts concluded
that "there is a very strong case for reduction of the protection accorded to this
industry" in order to oblige firms to reduce the markups they take on locally
produced goods.[80]

Obstacles to vertical integration

Between 1960 and 1975 only limited progress was made toward the government's goal of vertically integrating the textile industry. For the manufacturers,
the logic of market protection reached its limit when tariffs raised the prices of
the intermediate goods that they had to purchase. Although powerful textile
producers in Senegal consistently pushed for higher tariff barriers against
finished goods, they opposed the imposition of high tariffs on imported intermediate goods. This opposition shaped and limited progress toward vertical
integration.

76. Ets. Schaeffer took *assistance technique* fees from Icotaf that were calculated as a fixed percentage of total sales "to balance dividends, which are dependent upon profits" (Ets. Schaeffer et
Cie, *Procès Verbal des Réunions du Comité International*, 1975–77).

77. Inquiries into losses generated by STS in the late 1970s also revealed what analysts deemed to be
inflated amortization payments and dividends (World Bank, *The Economic Trends and Prospects
of Senegal*, December 1979; SONED 1979).

78. Courtois (1971:120–6) defined "gross profits" as net profits plus amortization payments divided
by total sales revenues. See Chapter 3, Table 3.7.

79. World Bank, *The Economic Trends and Prospects of Senegal*, December 1979:47, 61–6. See
also SONED 1979; 1980. Similar arguments about firms in the textile sector were made by
interviewees working in the ministries of finance and industrial development, April 1985
through January 1986.

80. World Bank, *The Economic Trends and Prospects of Senegal*, December 1979:63, inter alia.

The government's ideal of a tight production circuit, running from local cotton production to the manufacture of finished goods, was never fully realized. Between 1964 and 1974 the consumption of cotton fiber by the local spinning and weaving industries increased by only 35 percent. Total output doubled over the course of the same period.[81] The industry remained heavily dependent upon imported inputs. The basic textile industry imported 63 percent of its intermediate goods (*consommations intermédiaires*) in 1962 and 49 percent of its intermediate goods in 1974. In the garment-making and knitting segment of the industry, imports accounted for 63 percent of all inputs in 1974.[82]

The largest, most powerful, and most profitable firms in the industry were final-stage producers. As monopsonistic buyers of locally produced intermediate goods, they exercised considerable control over the development of upstream industries. The growth of upstream firms created in the 1950s (CCV and Icotaf–Rufisque) and of the weaving factory created in 1966 (STS) was restricted because the final-stage producers preferred to import intermediate goods. Another look at the case of STS and *écru* production illustrates the problem.

By the mid-1960s, Sotiba–Simpafric, Senegal's monopoly producer of printed fabric, had drastically reduced its purchases of locally made *écru*. As a result, much of the *écru* produced in Dakar at the time did not undergo further processing. The Icotaf–Rufisque weaving factory languished. Between 1965 and 1972, Senegal's imports of unfinished gray cloth grew from about 600 to 2400 tons a year, mostly to supply Sotiba–Simpafric. This *écru* was imported from some of the world's cheapest suppliers: Eastern Europe and China.[83] As noted earlier, the Senegalese government was committed to reducing *écru* imports. The integration of weaving and printing would establish the critical link between cotton production and the manufacture of the most widely consumed fabric in Senegal – *imprimés*.

In the mid-1960s, government pressure and the presence of British investors willing to undertake the weaving project convinced the Dakar manufacturers that the expansion of local *écru* production was inevitable. At that point they invested in a new weaving factory themselves in order to control the terms of production and sale of this product. Financing the STS factory constituted a relatively light burden for Icotaf, Sotiba–Simpafric, and CCV. And the size of the STS project was restricted to cover only 30–50 percent of Sotiba–Simpafric's demand for *écru*.

As STS's sole client, Sotiba–Simpafric retained control over the new firm by setting the purchase price of its output. The cost *écru* produced by STS ran about

---

81. Consumption of cotton fiber by the local industry increased from 3,000 tons in 1964 to 4,100 tons in 1974 (SONED 1974; 1977a:iv).
82. SONED 1974; 1977a:iv.
83. *UN Commodity Trade Statistics*, 1962, 1967, 1972 (for Senegal's imports of *écru*: SITC 652.1). As early as 1965, 75 percent of the *écru* imported to Senegal came from Eastern Europe and China. As imports from these areas were strictly controlled, this fact suggests that the Sotiba group had some type of special arrangement with the government.

45 percent above the c.i.f. prices of similar imported goods.[84] After STS came on line in 1970, Sotiba–Simpafric used the costlier, locally manufactured *écru* for the production of *imprimés* destined for domestic consumption. Because the Senegalese government raised tariffs on imported *imprimés* to compensate Sotiba–Simpafric for the "surcharge" involved in using locally made *écru*, Sotiba was able to pass these costs on to the consumers. Exports of *imprimés* declined to only 15 percent of Sotiba–Simpafric's production in 1974, when 50 percent of Sotiba–Simpafric's *imprimés* were printed on inexpensive, imported *écru*. Ultimately, then, the arrangements that led to the creation of STS proved to be very profitable for Sotiba–Simpafric.[85]

Heavy protection of final-stage producers in Senegal's basic textile industry also limited forward linkages to the garment-making firms. High taxes on imported cloth, and the high cost of similar goods manufactured by Icotaf, clearly discouraged the industrial-scale production of garments made of woven fabric. Garments made of Icotaf cloth by La SIV were sold mostly to the Senegalese government. The local knitting firms purchased cotton yarn from CCV, but the increases in output they achieved between 1965 and 1975 did not generate corresponding increases in CCV's sales.[86] The knitting firms preferred to use imported synthetic thread.

The government's strategy for developing textile production reinforced manufacturers' inclination to rely on imported inputs. By granting production monopolies to last-stage producers early on in the process, the government gave these firms considerable control over the process of vertical integration. They concentrated on increasing their output of finished goods. STS was the only intermediate goods supplier created after independence. Restricted in size and controlled completely by its sole client, STS came to symbolize the limits of the vertical integration strategy rather than its success.

Senegal's ISI strategy did encourage new investment in expanding and diversifying local textile production between 1960 and 1975. At the time, the government succeeded in guaranteeing the profitability of these investments. In this sense the ISI strategy was successful in the 1960s and early 1970s. Yet new investment was accompanied by new barriers to competition on both the production side and the commercial side of the business. These barriers reinforced the hold of established manufacturers and allied commercial firms over the local market, and over the lion's share of the profits made in the textile trade. Oligopoly control constrained both the expansion of the industry itself and possibilities for the ac-

84. World Bank, *The Economic Trends and Prospects of Senegal,* December 1979:63.
85. Exports of *imprimés (fancies)* declined from 35 percent of Sotiba–Simpafric's output in 1968 to 15 percent of output in 1974 (Centre de Commerce International [UNCTAD/GATT] 1975). Exports of *imprimés* increased again after 1977.
86. CCV sold 150 tons of yarn to the local knitting firms in 1964. These sales had almost doubled by 1974, reaching over 240 tons, while the production of knitted garments increased by a much larger factor (probably about fourfold).

cumulation and investment of capital on the part of entrepreneurs who operated in competitive segments of the market.

Throughout the industry, manufacturers allowed capital stock to deteriorate and opted for production, financial, and managerial strategies that inflated local production costs. The horizontally segmented structure of the industry, weak linkages between firms, production inefficiencies, and manufacturers' high profit margins made the firms in the textile industry extremely vulnerable to price competition. The industry's fortunes depended upon politically engineered market controls (licensing, import bans, *mercurialisation*, and tariff barriers) that restricted competition. This meant that the industry's greatest vulnerabilities lay at the political level, where decisions about import control were made and implemented.

Fifteen years of ISI in the textile sector produced what was, in the final analysis, a weak and rather shallow industry. In many ways the outcome was an artifact of government policy. Yet from the perspective of the government of Senegal, the outcome was unintended. Forces that militated against the deepening of capital in the textile industry were by-products of the broader strategies that guided state intervention in markets.

The postcolonial regime used state controls over internal markets to structure and regulate access to possibilities for accumulation. Market controls were used to promote ISI in the textile sector by making it possible for final-stage producers to profit by collecting rents. The result was patterns of control over internal trade that reduced pressure on the industry to reinvest in production. Market controls were also used by the regime to generate patronage resources (in the form of commercial rents) and to canalize the emerging Senegalese business class into state-mediated rentier activities. The regime retained control over the most dynamic indigenous business interests by drawing them into party-bureaucratic patronage networks. This strategy, however, impeded the rise of an indigenous business class willing and able to compete against established foreign interests in ways that could have led to new investment in domestic industry.

The size of Senegal's internal market was itself a political artifact, one that was fashioned by political leaders who sacrificed long-term possibilities for growth in order to deal with immediate political needs. Efforts to maintain neocolonial links with France – through the Franco-Senegalese trade and monetary accords and through extensive concessions to established French business interests – constrained, by default, possibilities for the emergence of more dynamic forms of capital. The decision to forego the Mali Federation course of "regional integration" protected the Senghor regime's prerogatives and shored up the ruling coalition, but it exacerbated the problem of market fragmentation that had been imposed on Senegal by the breakup of the AOF. Maintaining hierarchical and centralized control over the internal groundnut circuit also helped to consolidate the Senghor regime, but it aggravated problems of rural stagnation and impoverishment that limited the capacity of Senegal's own market to absorb the products of local industry.

In spite of limitations and weaknesses in the textile industry that were clear at the end of the 1960s, government planners and foreign analysts were optimistic about its growth prospects in the early 1970s. The textile industry covered only 50 percent of consumer demand for textile goods, and basic producer goods like thread, yarn, and *écru* were still imported. The "easy phase of import substitution" was not exhausted.[87] If the government could continue to deliver captive local markets, then the industry could continue to expand its output of finished goods as it had before 1975.

87. See Hirschman 1979:69–70.

5

Reappropriation of the state: The 1970s

[T]he state, born of the colonial occupation, has been the object of multiple processes of reappropriation which move it steadily away from its original form.

Jean-François Bayart 1989:258

The neocolonial state assumed a dual task. Sustaining processes of economic growth set in motion under colonial rule was the first. The second was creating and maintaining a form of political order that would make this possible. Ann Phillips (1989) argued that its predecessor, the colonial state, had failed to reconcile these dual imperatives, for economic growth tended to destabilize mechanisms of social control (such as indirect rule) that underpinned colonial state power. This contradiction was manifest starkly in the postwar crises of the colonial political economy. Wartime exploitation of the colonies, followed by public investment to break the deadlock of economic stagnation, unleashed social forces that the colonial state could not contain – including new working classes, ambitions indigenous merchant strata, and the postwar nationalist elite.

Independence and the political arrangements of the 1960s worked to incorporate these social strata into the sphere of state control. Coalitions forged within the structures of postcolonial states allowed disparate but powerful elements within African societies to share in the benefits of maintaining the economic status quo. These arrangements, however, were not self-equilibrating and self-reproducing, for they were predicated upon continuous expansion of the state's capacity to extract and distribute resources. Shoring up peasant forms of agricultural production allowed postcolonial states to assume the extractive role played by colonial merchant capital in the earlier period. Dictated by political expediency and by the power of vested interests, this solution tended to exhaust itself in short order. The postcolonial state, like merchant capital, would find that the willingness and capacity of peasants to produce ever-larger surpluses under these conditions was limited.

In Senegal, limits to economic growth inherent in the logic and functioning of merchant capital were reproduced after independence. The regime built upon these economic foundations protected vested interests, but the sluggish and monopolistic economy would prove to be too narrow and rigid to contain social forces that had no real place within it. As the 1960s wore on, the political disorder that confronted colonial administrations across sub-Saharan Africa a decade before would rear its head again in Senegal. Efforts to reestablish order accelerated and deepened political changes set in motion by decolonization.

Constrained on one side by economic structures already in place, by the interests vested in them, and by the regime's dependence on continuity and close ties with France, and on the other side by threats to the survival of the regime and the specter of political disorder, the regime fell back on the political formula of the 1960s. Social groups and individuals powerful enough to press demands on the state were absorbed into the clientelistic networks of the regime. The ruling coalition forged in the preceding decade was broadened and restabilized as its constituent elements appropriated larger shares in the state apparatus, and thus gained a larger stake in the established political order. The locus of instrumental control over state power was internalized.

As this ruling class reappropriated the state, the state apparatus was remade in its likeness. Yet as a "class," the ruling stratum was weak. It was composed of disparate elements, driven by contradictory political needs. Not sited in the production process, its internal economic base lay in the appropriation of agricultural surpluses produced by the peasantry, a social group that it had subordinated but could not control directly. And it had been emptied of any transformative project by the repression and political compromises of the 1960s. As a ruling stratum, it was united by a lowest common-denominator interest in reaping the benefits of the status quo. The state that was controlled by this ruling class could be no more than the sum of its parts.

A form of political stability was achieved in the 1970s and the ruling coalition retained its hold on power. As the next chapter will show, what was lost was the capacity of the state to guarantee the market monopolies that sustained neo-colonial patterns of growth in the 1960s. As neocolonial economic and political arrangements gave way, the usefulness of the state apparatus as a tool for promoting some alternative economic project also diminished. The postcolonial state, like the colonial state, failed to reconcile the imperatives of economic growth and political control.

THE POLITICAL CRISIS OF 1968–70

By the end of 1963, opposition to Senghor, to the ruling party, and to the conservative orientation of the regime had been disorganized and driven underground. Nationalist and reformist political currents lost institutional bases when opposition parties were dismantled and when the Diaists were purged from high- and middle-level government posts. In the late 1960s, frustration and defiance of the political status quo exploded in a broad-based attack on the Senghor–UPS political monopoly and on the economic strategy of "continuity" and close ties with France. Agendas for structuring the Senegalese political economy that had been suppressed and marginalized over the course of the decade resurfaced with a vengeance and were articulated with a force that shook the foundations of the Senghor regime. The temporary but generalized dislocation of state authority of 1968–70 constituted a watershed period for the Senegalese political economy.

The protest was launched in the urban areas in the spring of 1968 (Martens 1983c; Martens 1983d). At the vanguard were two movements that the regime had failed to absorb or control completely: student groups and labor unions. University and secondary school students staged strikes in March and May to protest Senghor's educational policy, continuing French control over the state and the economy, and more fundamentally, repressive and conservative Senghorian rule. In May the army closed down the university. Scores of students were beaten and a few were killed.

To protest the brutality of the regime's tactics and to force the government to respond to workers' grievances, the National Federation of Trade Unions (UNTS) called an illegal general strike. Thousands of workers, students, and unemployed Dakarois marched in the streets calling for the return of democratic liberties. "National control" over the economy and the government was their demand – real independence first; and then economic policies that would create jobs and arrest the post-1960 decline in Senegalese standards of living.

Senghor proclaimed a state of emergency and called out the police and the army. The general strike exploded in violence with street barricades, store lootings, car burnings, and attacks on the homes of some UPS leaders. The government accused the students and unions of revolutionary insurrection. Dakar and secondary urban centers were paralyzed. Almost 1,000 people were arrested, including 31 labor leaders and 900 people massed in anger at the gates of the Presidential Palace. At the government's request, the marabouts issued a call for order.

The climate of crisis and emergency persisted throughout 1969, with illegal labor strikes in February, and multiple, recurrent strikes of postal workers, teachers, bank employees, and students throughout the spring.[1] In June another general strike was called. Senghor reimposed the national state of emergency. Censorship suppressed "propaganda" hostile to the regime. "Agitators" were jailed. Striking government workers were fired.

Political attacks on the Senghor regime became more direct, aggressive, and widespread. Senegalese businessmen joined in, escalating the attack on the neo-colonial orientation of the regime. During the first wave of urban unrest, the Fédération des Groupements Economiques Africains (FGEA), created in 1960, fused with the Chambre Syndicale du Patronat Sénégalais, created in 1965. The FGEA had a record of trying to advance the interests of Senegalese businessmen: it had called for government policies that would promote Senegalese ownership of industry, Senegalese participation in existing industries, Senegalese representation in the Chamber of Commerce, access to bank credit, and access to the import trade. Significantly, the FGEA had called for deregulation of the rice

---

1. The postal workers and petrol company employees went on strike in May and again in June 1969. Bank employees walked off the job for ten days in June to protest two years of inconclusive labor-contract negotiations with the government. These illegal strikes culminated in the June 1969, 48-hour general strike. The government fired striking employees and hired new workers to fill their posts. See *Marchés Tropicaux* (14 juin 1969): 1,771–2; ibid. (28 juin 1969): 1,880; and Martens 1983c; 1983d.

trade – apparently most of its members were not among the beneficiaries of government control of this activity. It had also questioned the extent to which nationalization of the export circuit "served the interests of the Senegalese people."[2]

Fusion of the two existing organizations in June of 1968 created the Union des Groupements Economiques Sénégalais (UNIGES). The vast majority of the 2,600 members of UNIGES were small-scale traders and transporters (*commerçants-transporteurs*) and artisans. In visible positions at the top were businessmen like Abdoulaye Diop who was a *maître imprimeur* (printer), the heads of the leading Senegalese-owned distribution companies and the owner of a pharmacy.[3] A militant tone dominated the opening congress of UNIGES, echoing the protests of the times:

[T]he present economic system of Senegal works like this: Foreigners are rich and getting richer while the Senegalese are poor and getting poorer . . . Senegalese workers [cannot save] and consume everything they earn (13 billion CFA francs in total). What is worse, they are forced to go into debt. The foreigners, who represent only 5% of the workforce, earn 57 billion CFA francs. Living very comfortable lifestyles, they can still save and send their profits outside Senegal to invest abroad. They repatriate 43 billion CFA francs each year, ¾ of what they earn in Senegal. Every year, foreigners repatriate sums that exceed the national budget of this country.

UNIGES also raised the banner of a frustrated business class:

[Commerce, industry and banking in Senegal] are the *chasses gardées* of foreigners [resting upon] their colonial privileges while Senegalese vegetate in marginal sectors of the economy. . . . Nationals control only 5–10% of the economic activity in this country. After 10 years of independence, this situation is not acceptable." (UNIGES, "Rapport Général du Premier Congrès," Dakar, 1 juin 1968)

The organization called for the renunciation of the Franco-Senegalese *accords de coopération* signed at the time of independence ("any semblance of reciprocity in these accords is purely fictive") and declared that the Senghor regime was "incapable of implementing a coherent policy of promoting the national interest."[4]

UNIGES called for the "Senegalization" of the private and public sectors. It pressed the government to dismantle the French monopoly over the Dakar Chamber of Commerce, ban foreign capital from thirty branches of economic activity, and promote Senegalese participation in the industrial sector. And it was time to get rid of French *assistants techniques* in the administration – they protected foreign interests by thwarting Senegalese access to economic opportunities.[5] The

2. See *Marchés Tropicaux* (16 novembre 1963): 2,706. On the Chambre Syndicale du Patronat Sénégalais, see ibid. (16 octobre 1965): 7,540.
3. Ibid. (13 juillet 1968): 1,779; Ediafric 1970:273; M. Diop 1972:167–74; Schumacher 1975: 180–1; Bonnardel 1978:823–6.
4. UNIGES, "Rapport Général du Premier Congrès," Dakar, 1 juin 1968. See also *Jeune Afrique*, "Les Affaires au Sénégal: Sénégalais s'abstenir," no. 494 (23 juin 1970): 50; and ibid., "Le monde des affaires Sénégalais," no. 446 (15–21 juillet 1969): 47.
5. The list of thirty activities to be "reserved" for nationals was made up of commercial, service, and small-scale industrial activities, including retail and semiwholesale trade, real estate, insurance, private pharmacies, metal working, construction, fishing, the sale of gasoline and petroleum products, transport, butcheries, laundries, cinemas, boat repair and service, garment-making enterprises, bakeries, printing and publishing, and packing and packaging.

local French banks' refusal to extend credit to indigenous traders and entrepreneurs was singled out as a glaring symbol of neocolonial control. "In 1967, the commercial banks [i.e. French private banks in Senegal] lent almost nothing to Senegalese businessmen. . . . It is necessary to ask why banks located in Senegal, and earning profits here, accord credit easily to French and Lebanese borrowers while denying Senegalese enterprise the same facilities."[6] The organization demanded a national credit policy that would permit Senegalese enterprise to develop.

In the domain of commercial policy, UNIGES voiced its most concrete and specific demands. The organization pressed the government to reserve all retail and semiwholesale commerce for national businessmen. It demanded that the government force local manufacturing industries to sell to Senegalese wholesalers. Government-backed foreign monopolies in the import trade were attacked bitterly: Senegalese traders had a right to import licenses and quotas allocated by the government. UNIGES spokesmen blamed the government's agricultural marketing system for economic stagnation in the rural areas. The solution, they said, was the immediate reinstatement of private Senegalese traders in the groundnut sector.

UNIGES' attack on the fundamental economic options pursued by the Senghor government was an attack on the regime itself. The confrontation between the Senegalese private sector and the government signaled the exhaustion of the co-optation strategies that the regime devised in the early 1960s to canalize indigenous business interests, deepening and compounding the political crisis of 1968–9.

As political instability and a cycle of confrontation and repression gripped the cities, the regime faced the first clear signs of the weakening of its hold in the rural areas. In 1968 peasants refused to pay debts owed to the cooperatives for seed and fertilizer. State agents such as agricultural extension workers became open targets of peasants' anger. While the police and army were busy managing political disturbances in the urban areas, state agents in some parts of the groundnut basin began to use force against peasants to extract debts owed to the state.[7] What the government euphemistically termed the *malaise paysan* was peasant resistance to state exploitation.

At the end of the 1960s, the political and economic arrangements of the first decade of independence seemed to unravel in both the urban and rural areas. Senghor's hold weakened. At this uncertain moment, a critique of Senghorian

---

6. "In 1967, out of 22 billion CFA francs in credit disbursed to private parties in Senegal, the portion accorded to Senegalese totaled only 700 million CFA, which equals 3 percent. Out of this 700 million CFA, ¼ went to persons not engaged in business activity. . . . ⅔ of the 700 million was disbursed by the BNDS [the public development bank]. The conclusion, then, is that the commercial banks lent almost nothing to Senegalese businessmen" (UNIGES, "Rapport Général du Premier Congrès," Dakar, 1 juin 1968, p. 12). On Senegalese entrepreneurs' lack of access to bank credit, see also World Bank 1974:42, 105; Rocheteau 1982:90–1; R. Cruise O'Brien 1979:28, 143–4.
7. Schumacher 1975:184. On the *malaise paysan*, its roots and symptoms, see also Gellar et al. 1980:89–90; and Casswell 1984.

rule rose from within the regime itself. Intellectuals, high-ranking civil servants, and party leaders challenged the overcentralization of power in the hands of the President and the extensive influence of French advisors and French *assistants techniques* within the administration.[8] In this context, the tug-of-war between Senghor and powerful figures within his party found expression in terms of a broader, more legitimate critique of the presidential monopoly on power. Within the ruling party and the regime there were calls for constitutional reform to increase the responsibility of cabinet members, decentralize authority at top levels of government, and promote a more participatory form of government.

The crisis which gained momentum over the course of 1968 and 1969 was rooted in structural strains and limits of the Senegalese political economy. After independence, Senghor eliminated avenues of legal and routine dissent and steadily increased the scope of his personal power. The Senghorian program for postcolonial Senegal – close economic, social and political ties with France and reliance on foreign capital – had never enjoyed broad support among workers, students, the local private sector, and the urban middle class. The regime counted on the UPS political machine and rural votes to offset the weight of its critics in the cities.

By the late 1960s it was quite clear that the government's economic program was not delivering what it promised. Economic growth stagnated and standards of living for all but a privileged minority declined. Unemployment grew in the urban areas. By 1967 the government's low wage policy had forced real wages 25 percent below their 1960 level. As the national trade union federation, the UNTS, said: "[S]even years of cooperation with the government have gotten us nowhere."[9] Over this same time period, rural incomes fell and terms of trade in the agricultural sector worsened. Sales of groundnuts to the state marketing board began to decline in 1967, reducing state revenues and raising questions about the long-term future of the groundnut economy. And as the macro-economic savings rate neared zero, France scaled down its foreign aid commitment to Senegal.[10]

France stopped buying Senegalese groundnuts at subsidized prices after the 1967 harvest. Producers bore the brunt of the sharp 20 percent drop in export prices, but the shortfall shook all economic activity linked to rural trade and

---

8. See Adamolekun 1971; Schumacher 1975:81; Gellar 1982:35–6; and Barry 1985:18–20.
9. UNTS 1967 executive report (cited in Martens 1983c:67) and UNTS Declaration of 3 May 1968 (cited in Martens 1983d:63–4). See also Gellar 1982:63. The World Bank (1974:27) had this to say about Senegal's low wage policy: [t]he government succeeded in keeping wages low. In the long run, this achievement was probably one of the government's most important. It had, however, little impact on Senegal's international competitive position." Pfefferman (1968:248–9) explains that the "government justifies a general 'wage freeze' for wage earners based on the belief that wage earners constitute an 'over-privileged' group compared with peasants."
10. Senegal's average rate of national saving (percentage of GNP) in 1960 was 9.6. In 1970 this figure was 0.8 (IMF 1977). On falling levels of (French) foreign aid, see Rocheteau 1982:109–10. Anson-Meyer (1974:102) reports that aid on concessionary terms as a percentage of total foreign aid fell from 100 percent in 1960 and 1961 to 36 percent in 1971.

production.[11] ONCAD, the state marketing board, assumed full responsibility for commercializing the groundnut crop in the same year, pulling the rug out from under private Senegalese traders who were licensed to handle the crop between 1961 and 1967. The general economic recession set the stage for the simultaneous emergence of several mutually reinforcing currents of opposition. The regime ignited the fires of protest by adopting austerity measures affecting students, government employees, and the unions.

The state of emergency and the government's use of force to crush the urban strikes of 1968 and 1969 restored a fragile semblance of political order. Yet the crisis was an ominous sign of how narrow, shallow, and prone to collapse this political order really was. Destabilization of the system from below created an opportunity for the open expression of discord and tensions at the top, threatening the cohesion of the administration and party. The regime was forced to embark upon serious political and economic reforms in order to retain its hold on power. *Africa Confidential* editorialized about Senghor's post-1970 initiatives, writing that "[n]othing helps a man realize how to stay in power like almost losing it."[12]

Senghor moved swiftly on several fronts to demobilize, divide, and co-opt the opposition. The regime offered concessions to disaffected groups and then created new corporatist structures to domesticate and absorb restive groups.[13] Peasant debts to the cooperatives were forgiven and the government raised groundnut producer prices. After granting nearly all student demands for educational policy reform, Senghor gave student leaders attractive government posts. He then outlawed all student political activity outside the framework of a newly created student organization linked to the ruling party. Minimum wage increases in 1968 and 1969 helped to tame the workers' movement.[14] The regime undercut the UNTS by forming a parallel ("moderate and progovernment") trade union federation that was then integrated into the ruling party.[15] Top UNTS unionists who defected to assume leadership posts in the new federation, the CNTS (Confédération Nationale des Travailleurs Sénégalais), were given high-ranking positions in the UPS. In late 1969 the UNTS was dissolved. Proceeding in the same

---

11. Amin 1973:4. The drop in peasant revenues and export earnings reduced the monetary mass in Senegal by almost 4 billion CFA francs, depressed rural demand, cut state revenues in spite of government efforts to push the loss onto the producers, and led to recession in the groundnut-refining industry (*Le Bulletin de l'Afrique Noire*, no. 585 [4 février 1970]).

12. *Africa Confidential* 14, no. 1 (5 January 1973): 1.

13. See Cottingham 1970:112–14; Gellar 1982:25, 35–6; and Barry 1985:18–20.

14. On June 18, 1968, just after the first general strike, the government raised the minimum wage (SMIG) by 15 percent. Inflation ate up this increase and the raise was not enough to preempt the 1969 wave of strikes. The SMIG was raised again in 1969 (Martens 1983c:65–8).

15. The UNTS split on June 11, 1969, in the middle of the 48-hour general strike of June 10–12. The break-away wing of the UNTS, led by Alioun Cissé, issued a "no strike" order that went unheeded but created confusion in the union movement. On August 17, 1969 the CNTS was created under the leadership of Alioun Cissé and the ruling party. More UNTS leaders were then co-opted into the CNTS before the UNTS was dissolved. See *Marchés Tropicaux* (12 juillet 1969): 1,992; *Europe France Outre-Mer*, no. 482 (mars 1970); and Martens, 1983d.

way, the largest Senegalese trading firms split with UNIGES (because it was "excessively politicized and hostile to the regime") and formed an alternative business association linked to the ruling party. State resources began to flow into the hands of "moderate" and "responsible" elements within the Senegalese private sector who were willing to work "within the framework of options defined by the government."[16] Meanwhile, sweeping programs for the "Senegalization" of the public sector made room within the administration for many young technocrats and members of the postindependence generation of intellectuals. Administrative and constitutional reforms created new ministerial posts, devolved power, and reinstated the position of prime minister. The regime "redynamized" the party.

The second decade of independence ushered in renewed, intensified efforts to maintain the ruling coalition and to consolidate a domestic base of political support for the regime. Particularistic demands were accommodated in order to undercut broad-based and destabilizing political attacks on the status quo. Growth of the state apparatus would provide the institutional infrastructure for drawing new social groups into the regime's political orbit; increased state spending would be the magnet. The steady decentralization of control over government ministries, agencies, bureaucracies, banks, and parastatals gave an ever more diverse array of politically influential and strategic individuals greater access to the state and state resources, and the means they needed to broaden and hold onto their clienteles. The political machine became more deeply rooted in the structures and processes of the state. Barriers that insulated key domains of economic activity from the pressures of patronage politics in the 1960s began to give way.

GROWTH OF THE STATE APPARATUS: THE *IMPULSION EXTERNE*

The onset of recession and the 1968–70 political crisis lent new urgency to the regime's efforts to stimulate economic growth and buy political support. Yet the macroeconomic strategies of the 1960s provided no basis for increased state spending. Industry's direct contribution to government revenues was zero or less. State enterprises operated at a deficit. Revenues from the groundnut sector were declining along with sales to the state marketing board. The onset of Sahelian drought in the early 1970s worsened matters. Senegal's external accounts began to deteriorate, underscoring the gravity of the situation. The trade deficit grew steadily after 1967, and the balance of payments showed that Senegal was a net exporter of capital to Europe. The government could not cover its own expenses in the late 1960s, much less finance new spending or investment. In January 1969 Minister of Finance Jean Collin announced that "[w]e carried out the First Plan by exhausting our reserves, and since 1965 we have been carrying out the

16. See *Jeune Afrique*, no. 494 (23 juin 1970): 50; *Marchés Tropicaux* (7 février 1970): 306.

Second Plan by exhausting our treasury. As a result, we can no longer rely on the treasury for carrying out the Third." [17]

Foreign borrowing – the *impulsion externe* – would provide the material base for expanding the state and reconsolidating the Senghor regime during the second decade of independence. The 1970s were years of major new spending initiatives, driven on the domestic level by two related pressures. These pressures would prove most difficult to reconcile. The first was the need to jump start the economy, to propel Senegal into a new phase of growth, and to expand the internal bases of state accumulation at a time when the productive core of the economy – the groundnut sector – was slipping into unmitigated decline. The second was the urgent political need to strengthen the political machine and marshal new patronage resources to fuel this process. New bureaucracies, agencies, and parastatals flush with resources secured through foreign borrowing would provide both institutional infrastructure and the material bases for broadening and enriching the political class.

Senegal's Third and Fourth Development Plans, covering the 1969–77 period, were expansive and ambitious. Outlays for the Third Plan exceeded those of the previous two development plans by 50 percent (World Bank 1974:27–8). The government undertook bold new investments programs designed, like the FIDES program of the 1950s, to entice reluctant private capital (i.e., foreign capital) into new sectors of the economy. State initiatives of the 1970s went beyond the FIDES model, however, for now the state would take an "entrepreneurial role" and with it, a claim on the profits the regime hoped to generate. At a minimum, state investment would subsidize private foreign capital in order to coax it into new activities that would earn foreign exchange.

In 1970 external creditors judged Senegal's "capacity for indebtedness" to be quite high. [18] This provided the opening for multilateral lending institutions, bilateral public lending institutions, and commercial banks to assume more and more of the role that French foreign aid had played in the first decade of independence. Loans to Senegal from the World Bank group increased dramatically in the early- to mid-1970s, tripling between 1970 and 1975 and placing the World Bank ahead of the French government as a financier of Senegalese public investment. [19] At the same time, loans from the African Development Bank, multi-

---

17. Amin 1973:162. The World Bank (1974:109) reports the same problem: "Senegal's foreign exchange reserves are virtually exhausted. . . . By the end of 1971, treasury reserves were nearly depleted [because they were used] to supplement insufficient public savings in the 1960s. . . . Future deficit spending must be financed through borrowing."

18. Senegal's debt service ratio was 3.5 percent in 1969 and 5 percent in 1971–2 (World Bank 1974; Anson-Meyer 1974:57–63).

19. World Bank loans constituted 20 percent of all public financial assistance to Senegal in the early 1970s. When all forms of aid are taken into account (including technical assistance, military assistance, etc.), France remained the number one supplier of aid to Senegal in the mid-1970s (World Bank 1974:130). See Lewis 1987:286–7.

lateral and bilateral European lending institutions,[20] and the United States Agency for International Development provided an ever larger share of the resources mobilized by the regime. When public lending institutions would not finance the government's projects, Senegal turned to the commercial market. Kuwaiti, Iranian, American, and European commercial banks and the Eurodollar market would supply the capital for the most ambitious, high-risk investment projects of the 1970s. Foreign financial aid of about $55 million, mostly in the form of loans on concessional terms, provided almost 85 percent of all capital invested by the state in projects laid out in the Fourth Plan (1973–7). Between 1969 and 1975, the government also borrowed over $90 million from foreign commercial banks.[21]

Foreign loan capital covered not only a share of the government's current expenditures, but also direct state investments in *grands projets* that were conceived on a scale without precedent in Senegal. The government pumped foreign loan capital into a new tourism "industry," developing resort sites, constructing roads, and installing public utilities to lure companies like Club Méditerranée to Senegal's beaches. With foreign partners, the regime invested in two phosphate mining and exporting projects, the Société Sénégalaise de Phosphates de Taiba and Société Sénégalaise de Phosphates de Thiès, and in iron ore mining projects in Eastern Senegal (the Mines de Fer du Sénégal Oriental, or MIFERSO). These "extractive enclaves" would earn foreign exchange. With luck, there would also be profits for the government. Huge and costly agro-industry projects were also financed by the state. Bypassing the groundnut peasantry, the government tried to harness Senegal's land and labor to the task of generating foreign exchange by creating "farming enclaves" under the direct control of capital. The Richard Toll sugar project and the BUD–Sénégal "market gardening" project turned out to be two of the biggest economic fiascoes of the 1970s.[22]

The list of *grands projets* goes on. A consortium of international private banks and the World Bank financed the construction of a naval tanker repair center (Dakar-Marine) at the port of Dakar. The governments of Senegal and Iran developed a petrochemical complex at Cayar. In the domain of light industry, the major initiative of the decade was the creation of an "export platform" in Dakar. Dakar's Zone Franche Industrielle (ZFI) was designed to attract export-oriented assembly firms to Senegal. The government stressed that it was not turning its

20. These lenders included the Banque Européenne d'Investissement (BEI), Le Fonds Européenne de Développement (FED), France's Caisse Centrale de Coopération Economique (CCCE), and the German Kreditanstalt für Wiederaufbau (KFW).
21. See World Bank 1974:128–35, Rocheteau 1982:110.
22. The Richard Toll project was financed in part through a Kuwaiti loan of $10 million, contracted on supplier's credit conditions. BUD–Sénégal, a joint project between the government (68 percent) and "European-American" investors (32 percent) was financed in part by the CCCE. BUD–Sénégal was designed to produce vegetables for export to Europe. The government also sponsored, financed, and took share participation in a large tomato growing and canning project (SOCAS). For an overview of government moves to take a direct stake in commodity export enterprises, see Rocheteau 1982. For an analysis of BUD–Sénégal, see Mackintosh 1989.

back on import-substitution industry. On the contrary, under the statutes of the ZFI, export firms would have no access to the local market. As Senegal's minister of industrial development, Louis Alexandrienne, explained in 1974: The ZFI has "nothing to do with the development of industry tied to the Senegalese economy. Factories [in the ZFI] . . . are completely outside the national economy. The only thing they will take from Senegal is the labor of its workers."[23]

New *sociétés d'études et de promotion* sprang up to provide investors with feasibility studies, project infrastructure, and access to financing. Through Senegal's public and semipublic banks, foreign loan capital contracted (and guaranteed) by the government was placed at the disposal of private investors.[24] The rush to attract new foreign capital into the *grands projets* was accompanied by rear-guard actions to subsidize foreign capital's retreat from old activities that had become increasingly costly, risky, and burdensome. France's cotton parastatal, the CFDT, took advantage of this opportune moment of exuberant state spending to sell an 80 percent share of its local operations to the government of Senegal. Senegal's new cotton parastatal, Société de Développement des Fibres Textiles (SODEFITEX), paid the CFDT to continue to run the company for an annual fixed fee and a share of the export revenues. Under these arrangements the CFDT retained control over the sale and pricing of Senegalese cotton while freeing itself from the risks of this business. In 1975 the Société Nationale de Commercialisation des Oléaginaux de Sénégal (SONACOS) was born when the government nationalized the groundnut oil-processing sector, "leaving the plant and equipment in the hands of the previous owners" (R. Cruise O'Brien 1979:27). The government thus assumed an even larger share of the costs, risks, and hoped-for profits of the groundnut business as well. Senegal's public utilities companies were finally nationalized in the 1970s, removing a glaring symbol of neocolonial domination from the local scene while shouldering the state with the costs of modernizing the water and electricity plants and the cost of providing these public goods.[25]

Foreign borrowing also allowed the state to "take control of the banking sector" (Rocheteau 1982:76–104). Loans contracted by the state bolstered the reserves and lending capacities of the Banque Nationale du Développement du Sénégal (BNDS). The government purchased controlling shares in Senegal's commercial banks, expanding their reserves and their mandates in the process.[26]

---

23. *Le Moniteur Africain*, no. 650 (14 mars 1974): 18. These provisions were designed to protect established import-substitution industries. See Rocheteau 1982:371–2; Anson-Meyer 1974:97.
24. See Rocheteau 1982:120–3, 238–9, 249.
25. The labor unions demanded nationalization of Senegal's foreign-owned electricity and water utility company, the Eau et Electricité de l'Ouest Africain (EEOA), in 1968. The utilities happened to be in need of modernization, a project that the foreign owners would not undertake. The government borrowed on the international market in 1973 to buy the EEOA and again in 1976 (9.2 billion CFA francs) to modernize the installation. See Gellar 1982:54–5; and Rocheteau 1982:110–11.
26. The BNDS was wholly owned by the government. It concentrated on financing the purchase, processing, and export of the groundnut crop and on development projects undertaken by the

At the same time, banking reforms redefined the objectives of central bank intervention in the economy (making "development" a priority) and ushered in a less restrictive national credit policy. The 1974 central banking reforms made more capital available through the rediscount mechanism to the government itself and to state-controlled banks.[27] Within the Agence-Sénégal of the central bank, the Banque Centrale des Etats de l'Afrique de l'Ouest (BCEAO), a "national credit committee" was granted the authority to use the rediscount mechanism to provide loan capital to private parties via the public banks. Reforms of Senegal's credit policy also increased the lending prerogatives of government officials managing these banks. Domestic credit expanded at the impressive rate of 25 percent a year over the course of the 1970s. New liquidity, coupled with new prerogatives, gave the state a degree of control over both credit policy and the allocation of credit that it did not possess in the 1960s.

Inflows of international loan capital, coupled with credit policy reforms, permitted an extension and diversification of the modes of state intervention in the Senegalese economy. The creation of new parastatals and state-owned companies not only placed state agents in control of important domains of economic activity, but also generated a vast new pool of government-controlled jobs for Senegalese. Investing by itself or jointly with foreign partners, the government created seventy new state-owned enterprises and parastatals over the course of the decade. In 1975 parastatal agencies and companies "controlled more than 40 percent of the value added in the modern sector and employed about one third of the workers in the modern wage sector" (Gellar 1982:56).

Guy Rocheteau (1982) was right when he argued that financial power gave Senegal a kind of "economic independence" that it could not have claimed in the first decade of independence. The availability of funds from a multitude of competing public and private foreign sources increased the government's room for maneuver. And it is true that with capital borrowed from abroad, the regime would take responsibility for the *grands projets,* using these projects and the banking system to "respond to national needs." Yet as would become clear over time, Rocheteau was mistaken when he assumed that the state would function as a capitalist entrepreneur, and when he assumed that these "national needs" would be defined solely in terms of creating a balanced and robust economy that would generate profits for the state treasury and private capital.

government. The BNDS handled multilateral public loans and bilateral economic assistance. In 1969 the government began to contract commercial loans to bolster BNDS reserves and lending capacity, when it borrowed $6 billion for the BNDS "development fund." The Union Sénégalaise de Banque (USB), with the government as a major shareholder, was the "instrument of state policy in the industrial sector." The World Bank, the CCCE, the BAD, and the KFW put loans backed by the government of Senegal at the disposal of the USB for relending to local private and foreign investors. The USB also channeled commercial loan capital guaranteed by the state to private foreign investors. The Senegalese government also took 50 percent control of the Banque de l'Industrie et du Commerce du Sénégal (BICIS) in the mid-1970s. See Rocheteau 1982:83–110.

27. On the 1974 Union Monétaire de l'Ouest Africain (UMOA) and BCEAO reforms, see Robson 1983:91, 154–5.

Pushed by the *impulsion externe*, the economic stagnation of the late 1960s gave way to an expansionist and inflationary period that affected various sectors of the economy in highly uneven ways. The secular decline of the groundnut economy continued unabated while the public sector in all its various manifestations grew dramatically. Senegal's debts to public lending institutions and commercial banks grew just as dramatically – from about $100 million in 1970 to over $1 billion in 1982.[28] This money financed a decade of state spending and lending targeted at resuscitating the economy and the regime's political base.

Foreign borrowing and the new "entrepreneurial" role of the state did not produce hoped-for benefits in the form of more private sector employment, increased state revenues, or improvements in the balance of trade. Funds contracted from commercial banks were too expensive. Expected returns on the *grands projets* were uncertain, and many of the projects were ill-conceived. Because they were making state-guaranteed loans, international lenders were less inhibited by the cost–benefit equation than they would otherwise have been. The unbridled quest to earn foreign exchange led the government to invest in export commodities doomed to decline in price on the world market. Dakar's ZFI failed to attract more than a few transient firms. Compounding problems and making them more intractable were changes in the structure of control over the state itself, changes that would undercut efforts to strengthen the entrepreneurial capacities of the government of Senegal.

What World Bank analysts called the "pervasive negative impact of the public investment policies of the 1970s" was not felt until the end of the decade.[29] During the 1970s the government pushed ahead, borrowing, spending, and re-lending in the effort to spur economic growth and rebuild domestic political support for the regime.

SHIFTING LINES OF POWER WITHIN THE REGIME

Looking back at the 1960s from the perspective of the 1970s and 1980s, it is possible to characterize state power in the first decade of independence as institutionalized in a centrally controlled administrative structure. Strategic domains of economic and social policy were in the hands of a tight administrative–political elite. A large corps of French *assistants techniques* formed what Rita Cruise O'Brien called an "administration within an administration," insulated to a large extent from the currents of domestic political competition and patronage politics. State-controlled resources, allocated from above, were channeled into a burgeoning party-bureaucratic political machine structured by clientelistic networks, or *clans*, centered around powerful political figures. The top political leadership

28. In 1980 Senegal's debt service consumed 25 percent of the state budget and 30 percent of export earnings (*Africa Confidential* [7 May 1980]; *Jeune Afrique*, no. 1,022 [6 août 1980]). For growth of the public debt after 1970, see World Bank 1981a.
29. World Bank, "Report and Recommendations of the President of the IBRD and the IDA [re: Senegal]," unpub. ms., November 26, 1980:13 (restricted circulation).

retained political control by manipulating *clan* rivalries and the flow of patronage resources. Important aspects of this system changed in the 1970s.

The *crise économique et sociale* of the late 1960s signaled a near total breakdown of the UPS political machine. Patron–client networks and the trickle down of state-controlled resources had failed to prevent the mobilization of broad-based demands on the state. At the regime's most vulnerable moment, the executive (presidential) monopoly emerged as the symbol of the concentration and exclusiveness of power at the top. Senghor's hold on the reins of the one-party state frustrated the ambitions of elements within the ruling coalition and opened the regime to the charge of authoritarianism. French advisors within the government were a lightning rod for criticism. They not only personified the reality of neocolonial rule, but also represented an obstacle to the upward mobility and influence of Senegal's own political class. Decentralization of power within the growing state apparatus in the 1970s provided a means for rebuilding and reinvigorating clientelistic networks that tied politically strategic social groups to the regime.

Senegalization of the administrative structures of the state was the first step. In 1970 Senghor announced sweeping plans for the "rapid Senegalization of the public sector."[30] French *assistants techniques* were removed from many positions within the ministries. Most of Senghor's French advisors retreated to less visible posts lacking formal legislative or statutory authority. This process opened powerful and lucrative government posts for party barons, other restive elements within the UPS and the administration, and a new generation of professionals.

Senegalization was pursued in the context of administrative and constitutional reforms that gave politically powerful elements within the regime more discretion, autonomy, and room for maneuver. Throughout most of the 1960s, professional party politicians (i.e., deputies to the National Assembly) were barred from holding cabinet posts. The politicians fought this law, and by the end of 1968 it was off the books. Just when party barons were gaining access to the highest ranks of the administration, the administrative and constitutional reforms of 1970 decentralized executive power. These reforms reinstated the post of prime minister and created a series of new government ministries (the number grew from about ten in the 1960s to twenty-seven in 1981). They also widened the scope of authority and control over government funds that was exercised within the ministries.[31] As Schumacher (1975:82) put it, the "reforms aimed at deconcentrating presidential power increased the authority and responsibility of cabinet ministers. [Among other things,] . . . government ministers gained the power to sign executive orders and decrees, enhancing their power of decision and their responsibility for governmental affairs." Appointed by Senghor, party

---

30. *Marchés Tropicaux* (12 décembre 1970): 3,605; ibid. (24 octobre 1970): 3,109; ibid. (7 novembre 1970): 3,227. The second major "Senegalization" push came in 1973, when the government began to ask private firms to hire Senegalese into management positions (ibid. [27 juillet 1973]: 2,338). See also ibid (26 mai 1978): 1,383.
31. See Adamolekun 1971; Schumacher 1975:82–3; Gellar 1982:35–6.

barons as well as young technocrats and seasoned administrators moved into these new, improved ministerial positions.

Personnel changes at the top levels of the administration and in the state-run banking sector allowed Senghor to promote many members of his regime, including erstwhile critics, to important and interesting government posts. New state-owned enterprises, parastatals, and ministries also generated patronage posts and high-powered government jobs for Senegal's most skilled and ambitious professionals. These processes drew a generation of university graduates into the state apparatus at all levels, helping to absorb and defuse the attack on the regime that this critical and volatile social group had mounted at the end of the 1960s. Abdou Diouf, the new prime minister, epitomized the "young technocrat" generation. Like the other *jeunes cadres,* he had no political (electoral) base of his own; Abdou Diouf ascended through the ranks of the administration under the tutelage of Senghor himself. The entry of a new stratum of skilled professionals into the administration and the parastatals did strengthen the technocratic edge of the government. The technocratic influence, however, would be dampened by broader political processes at work in the 1970s.

Several changes unfolded simultaneously. Government institutions such as the ministries, banks, and parastatals grew more powerful. These institutions multiplied in size and number; the scope of their prerogatives and oversight broadened; and they were awash in resources borrowed from abroad. Powerful politicos and other allies of the regime were placed in control of these institutions precisely at the time when the regime most desperately needed to reconsolidate its alliances and expand the political machine. Shifts in the locus of state power set in motion by Senegalization and decentralization thus occurred against the backdrop of intense jockeying to establish and entrench positions on this enlarged playing field. Those at the top were under pressure to orchestrate this process in a way that would allow the various elements within the ruling coalition to see that they too would reap the rewards of the new-found powers and resources of the state. Leaders were also under pressure to show those outside of this privileged circle that cooperation with the regime was not a dead-end proposition. This political process unfolded in the context of an expanding economy that remained under the control of the state and foreign capital. The persistent narrowness of opportunities for jobs, for accumulating wealth, and for accumulating political influence outside the limits of the political game heightened the intensity of the struggle for access to the state. All these forces conspired to reproduce the clientelistic and spoils-oriented logic of the political system.

State power was used as it was in the earlier period: to build and expand the personal power bases of individuals in control of government resources. The strength and scope of clientelistic factions and *clans* grew along with the prerogatives of top government personnel. Adamolekun (1971:556, 558) argued at the time that "administrators," once in high-ranking governmental office, are transformed into "politicians," a development that "drastically reduces their efficiency . . . Invariably, some of the bureaucrats who become ministers are among the most competent members of the civil service. To survive in their new posts, they inevitably find themselves engaged in other activities – especially the search for a political base – which sometimes may have the effect of making them less effective than they were before." Writing twenty years later, Momar Coumba Diop and Mamdou Diouf (1990:89) would matter-of-factly observe that "several personalities in the government were Ministers first, and then important politicians [*responsables politiques*]" with their own electoral constituencies.

Political and administrative reforms at lower levels of government deepened this process. The deconcentration of executive power expanded the responsibilities and prerogatives of party chiefs, regional governors, prefects, and UPS brokers on the local level, providing these individuals with the resources they needed to "redynamize" the party and "respond to local demands." In 1968, when the *malaise paysan* first emerged as a political issue at the national level, "local prefects were instructed by government circulaire to respond to requests from local *clan* leaders for administrative patronage" (Cottingham 1970:114). This initiative was institutionalized in 1972, when each rural *arrondissement* in the groundnut basin was divided into four *communes*, and each *commune* was granted direct control over an annual budget of $40,000–$50,000. Funds allocated by the central government were to be spent as party officials in the *commune* saw fit. To make this possible, the government was forced to overturn a set of administrative procedures established in 1963, when control over local spending was centralized in the ministry of the interior in an effort to "depoliticize" rural government (Gellar 1982:40–1). The purpose of the 1972 reforms was to repoliticize rural government by increasing the resource bases and discretionary powers of local authorities.

Analogous processes were underway at the highest levels of government. The economically strategic ministries of rural development, finance and economic affairs, and commerce became increasingly autonomous as responsibilities previously centralized in the president's office were transferred to these institutions. The ministry of rural development was reorganized in 1968 and given a larger role in planning and executing the government's programs in the groundnut basin. It developed closer links with ONCAD, the state groundnut marketing board, itself a richer and more powerful institution after it gained monopoly control over crop commercialization in 1967. The marketing agencies formed what Casswell called a vast "patronage combine" serving the interests of the ruling party and the rural elite, including the Mouride marabouts. By 1977 ONCAD had an estimated 2,100 full-time employees; one source cited by Casswell as "surely an exaggeration" estimated ONCAD's total number of employees and agents at 7,200 (Casswell 1984:65, 72). No one knew for sure, for ONCAD managers could not furnish the government with precise figures. As ONCAD grew, financial control within it deteriorated, "creating almost infinite possibilities for the diversion of funds . . . by its agents and third parties" (ibid:69).

The ministry of finance also had great potential as an instrument for building and expanding the political machine. It was located at the strategic intersection of inflows of externally borrowed funds and outflows of funds to finance the new entrepreneurial activities of the state. In February 1970 Minister of Finance Jean

Collin was replaced by a Senegalese, Babacar Ba.[32] Babacar Ba was in a position to sponsor the government's efforts to promote a Senegalese business class in the 1970s, developing a political base among rice traders and other big Senegalese businessmen, including notables in the groundnut basin. *Africa Confidential* of December 1, 1987 wrote that "after nine years at the Ministry of Finance and Economic Affairs, [Babacar Ba] had cultivated a power base in the important electoral region of Sine-Saloum. One foreign diplomat commented that 'to say that Babacar Ba enjoyed a position of patronage would be a considerable understatement.' "

When the Chamber of Commerce was "Senegalized" in 1968, its key functions in the domain of commercial regulation were transferred to the ministry of commerce. The allocation of import licenses, quotas, and *autorisations préalables* were now the responsibility of this increasingly powerful ministry. By 1980 the ministry of commerce controlled the implementation of virtually all government policies and administrative procedures governing trade, with the notable exception of business linked to the state-controlled commodities trade. Over the course of the 1970s the ministry became a political fiefdom run by powerful party barons serving a vast clientele made up of what became known as the Senegalese private sector. New ways of implementing commercial regulations created what the ministry's own agents would call "anarchy" in domestic trading circuits. This change would have consequences of the first order for French capital vested in commercial monopolies.

As the 1970s progressed it became increasingly clear that many of the ministries, parastatals, state-owned enterprises, and government banks had gravitated outside the scope of central political control. Some were captured by their own agents. Increasingly, the political machine was fueled by patronage resources that those at the top echelons of the regime could not manage or control directly. These resources were generated within the parastatal sector, ONCAD, the ministries of commerce and finance, and in the state banks and lending institutions. As subunits of the state gained more financial autonomy vis-à-vis the center, constituent parts of the political machine gained more autonomy vis-à-vis the center as well. Control at the top deteriorated. The party-bureaucratic machine became increasingly fragmented.

ONCAD and the BNDS were notorious for what the external public creditors defined as widespread mismanagement and the quasi-total absence of internal auditing, financial control, and government oversight.[33] ONCAD became the symbol of the government's unwillingness to impose financial discipline on increasingly autonomous and self-reproducing patronage networks that colonized subunits of the state. The privatization of state monies distributed by the public and para-public banks (written off as waste or "funds lost and unaccounted for") would contribute to the collapse of the banking sector a decade later. Overstaff-

---

32. Jean Collin became the minister of the interior. See *Marchés Tropicaux* (17 avril 1971): 1,101.
33. In 1980 an independent auditing agency, the Italian firm ITALCONSULT, reported widespread waste and financial "losses" generated within ONCAD. In 1978 a World Bank audit disclosed far-reaching corruption in ONCAD. See *Africa Confidential* (7 May 1980). The definitive work on ONCAD is Casswell 1984.

ing and corruption in the parastatals drained the state treasury, undercutting the effort to use these institutions as mechanisms for the accumulation of capital.

Such changes were the unintended but logical corollary of efforts to extend the party-bureaucratic machine into new domains, to strengthen the patronage powers of many high- and middle-ranking government officials, and to infuse new resources into political factions, *clans,* and clientelistic networks. Institutional and administrative changes of the early 1970s made the state apparatus a more effective instrument for fragmenting, particularizing, and canalizing the wave of new demands pressed on the state. Social groups able to pose a direct challenge to the political status quo – the students who became the young generation of professionals, the union leaders, restive elements within the party, the frustrated Senegalese business class – were demobilized and fragmented as their members were absorbed into the expanding, reinvigorated political machine.

This was a process of reappropriation of the state. The organization of power within the state came to reflect the patterns of control and influence that organized, structured, and animated the political class. Similarly, the use of state power came to reflect the ambitions of members of this class – ambitions that were shaped by the ways in which these individuals perceived the risks and possibilities of different strategies of advancement within the political and economic context of Senegal in the 1970s. Within this context, spoils-oriented factionalism remained the dominant arena of wealth accumulation and political advancement.

The regime's success in reconsolidating power after the political crises of 1968–70 can be measured against this standard. The ruling coalition was sustained by enhancing the power of its constituent elements, and by expanding possibilities for the accumulation of wealth and personal power within the framework of the Senghor regime. New social strata were incorporated into the circle of beneficiaries of the status quo, making the government more unwieldy as the political machine absorbed a larger share of resources appropriated or otherwise mobilized by the regime in the name of development. This makeshift arrangement allowed the regime to remain in power, for struggles between and within groups were channeled away from competition for control over the state itself and into competition for control over constituent parts of the state apparatus.

Patterns of state intervention in the economy bore the imprint of these changes. Barriers that had insulated sensitive domains of economic policy implementation from machine politics in the 1960s eroded. As time would tell, the reappropriation of the state would pave the way for reappropriation of the economy. Through these processes, both state and economy "moved steadily away from their original forms."

AN ACCUMULATING CLASS LINKED TO THE STATE

Economic strategies charted at the time of independence designated no clear role for the Senegalese private sector. The same can be said of the economic strategies of the 1970s. In the 1970s, however, the government adopted a very clear *political* strategy for absorbing and narrowing the ambitions of Senegal's restless and stymied business class. The movement of Senegalese private interests into state-mediated business opportunities was accelerated, financed, and broadened by the regime. This process provided a composite solution to two distinct problems. The problem of canalizing and accommodating the interests of a restive business class was resolved in ways that also multiplied and expanded opportunities for wealth accumulation open to members of the ruling stratum.

UNIGES, formed in 1968, provided a forum that was used to articulate Senegalese businessmen's indictment of the most fundamental economic strategies of the 1960s – reliance on foreign capital and nationalization of the groundnut sector. This was a grave turn of events for the regime, for small businessmen constituted one of Senghor's most reliable bases of political support in the 1950s and early 1960s. The anger of small- and medium-scale Senegalese businessmen threatened to degenerate into a more direct attack on the Lebanese who manned the trenches in the retail trade and in competitive segments of the import trade, a development that could have damaging consequences for Senegal's carefully nurtured investment climate. The simultaneous emergence of the *malaise paysan* added force and credibility to UNIGES' indictment of the state's groundnut program and marketing monopoly, the pillars of state power in rural Senegal.

The regime responded immediately. A rival, pro-Senghor businessmen's organization formed under the wing of the ruling party to represent "moderate" private sector interests. The Confédération des Groupements Economiques du Sénégal (COFEGES) was inaugurated with much fanfare in August 1968, just two months after UNIGES' first congress, when its two hundred members gathered in the company of political dignitaries including Senghor himself, then Minister of Finance Jean Collin, and assorted ministers and ambassadors. COFEGES' leading members were the heads of the largest Senegalese commercial firms, those with close ties to the government.

One of COFEGES' two presidents was Ousmane Seydi, a member of the National Assembly. Ousmane Seydi was also head of the Compagnie Sénégalaise du Sud-Est (CSSE), created in 1959. The CSSE had been one of the largest OCA-authorized rice importers since the early 1960s; it had participated in the distribution consortium formed by the CFAO in 1960 (AFRIDEX); and it held shares in SONADIS, the distribution chain created by the state and SCOA (M. Diop 1972:151, 156). The other president of COFEGES was Ousmane Diagne of the Société Sénégalaise pour le Commerce et l'Industrie (SOSECI). Created in 1965, SOSECI's rapid ascent in the Senegalese business world was "a sensation," propelled by "very favorable political patronage," bank credits, and the "remarkable business sense of its director" (Amin 1969:53). Access to credit from the French banks in Dakar put the SOSECI in a select group; in 1970 only three Senegalese-owned private enterprises could claim this distinction. Like the CSSE, SOSECI was a distribution firm operating mostly in the rural areas and a big rice importer. SOSECI also owned the only Senegalese enterprise licensed by the customs service, presumably to carry out import–export operations.[34]

34. Amin 1969:56. On these two firms, see also Bonnardel 1978:792, 795–7, 819.

In the opening statements of its constitutive assembly, COFEGES confirmed its full support for Senghor and its loyalty to the UPS. The organization's spokesmen expressed their favorable view of the role of French capital in the Senegalese economy. Ousmane Seydi explained that Senegalese entrepreneurs wanted to join with, not eliminate or supplant, foreign investors in Senegal. A "policy of participation" with foreign capital was needed.[35] In what it called a "moderate and progovernment fashion," COFEGES picked up many of the issues that had been raised earlier by UNIGES, especially those related to credit and the promotion of Senegalese businessmen in the retail trade, semiwholesale trade, transport, and service sector activities. The French private sector in Dakar was relieved that a "responsible and moderate group" had emerged to eclipse the "unrealistic and irresponsible" UNIGES.[36]

The government rapidly made several concessions. UNIGES demanded the Senegalization of the Dakar Chamber of Commerce; the regime complied. French expatriates were removed from controlling positions and the bureau of the Chamber of Commerce was renewed for the first time since 1954. Top posts were given to COFEGES President Ousmane Diagne and to Amadou Dème of CHAIDIS, another one of the four largest Senegalese trading firms (Amin 1969:41–4). Other prominent Senegalese businessmen were placed in visible positions in this one-time symbol of French commercial hegemony. The new president of the Chamber of Commerce, Amadou Sow, worked for the petroleum company Shell–Dakar and in the ministry of commerce. After 1964 he would become the director general of the USB, the second government bank in Senegal. Another member of the new bureau was Issa Diop, an engineer and a manager for Dakar's electric power company, the EEOA.[37]

More concrete moves were also made by the regime. In 1968 and 1969 new public financial institutions were created to channel credit into Senegalese business, and the government laid out a plan for promoting the local private sector. Central to this plan was the fusion of UNIGES and COFEGES. At the request of Senghor, the two organizations merged, incorporated representatives of the ruling party, and became the Groupements Economiques du Sénégal (GES). The GES affirmed its solidarity with the ruling party and vowed "to work within the framework of options defined by the government."[38] Thus, within one year of its creation, UNIGES had been co-opted into the corporatist structure of the regime.

Elimination of UNIGES as an independent political force put an end to attacks

35. Discours par M. Ousmane Seydi à la première conférence de la COFEGES, 18 août 1968; *Jeune Afrique*, "Entretien avec M. Ousmane Diagne," no. 494 (1970): 51
36. See *Africa* (Dakar), no. 45 (1968). For the Bordeaux Chamber of Commerce reaction ("The place of Senegalese businessmen is in the retail trade"), see *Marchés Tropicaux* (14 novembre 1970): 3,289.
37. See Ediafric 1970a:274; *Marchés Tropicaux* (16 août 1969): 2,270.
38. The directorship of GES was composed of fifteen ex-members of UNIGES, fifteen ex-members of COFEGES, and five members of the UPS. See *Marchés Tropicaux* (12 octobre 1968): 2,465; *Jeune Afrique*, no. 494 (23 juin 1970): 50; *Marchés Tropicaux* (7 février 1970): 306; and M. Diop 1972:171.

on foreign capital and on the regime. Yet the GES was pushed by the ambitions of its members and the momentum of the times. In 1970 it called for a restructuring of the agricultural cooperatives to allow the Senegalese traders to participate in the marketing of groundnuts. Ousmane Diagne, President of GES, said:

> [E]veryone recognizes the *malaise paysan*. The GES has studied the agricultural institutions of this country and has concluded that setting up the system of cooperatives was a fundamental error. We have discussed the inadequacies of the two state agencies, ONCAD and the OCA, in this area. . . . Today, 90 percent of the peasantry favors the reinsertion of Senegalese businessmen into the agricultural marketing system. . . . Free trade in this area would benefit both the peasants and the Senegalese business sector.[39]

The regime, defending Senegal's socialist option, proved inflexible on this front. In May 1971 Ousmane Diagne was relieved of the presidency of GES and the GES executive bureau was dissolved by the government. An official communiqué explained that Diagne "made declarations that were likely to give the wrong impression of Senegal."[40] In November 1971 a new GES Comité National Provisoire reported that after two years of experience, "it was necessary to free the GES from *clan* struggles which had paralyzed the organization."[41] As the political massaging of the GES continued, the regime came forward with material concessions. The militancy of private sector demands evaporated. Soon the GES was thoroughly domesticated by the government.

This entire episode constituted an important moment in the history of the Senegalese business sector. Majhemout Diop (1972:167–74) offers a nuanced analysis of this period, arguing that the ambivalent nature of the political project advanced by the business stratum, as well as conflicts of interest inherent in it, came to the fore in 1968–70. He was struck by the fact that elements calling for free enterprise had found common cause with the leftist and decidedly socialist current of student and worker opposition. Meanwhile, Senegalese businessmen denounced the regime while demanding that it intervene more actively in the economy on their behalf. Both UNIGES and COFEGES zeroed in on the state groundnut monopoly, but what many wanted was the reinstatement of state-licensed private traders, rather than free trade per se. And attacks on foreign capital that were voiced in the language of nationalism were accompanied by demands that the government pressure foreign enterprises to take on Senegalese shareholders, suppliers, and managers.

The local private sector as such had no economic base from which to advance a specific vision of its role in productive sectors of the economy. Robert Fatton put the matter starkly when he wrote (1987:60) that "after a decade of independence, [the Senegalese private sector] had not developed beyond the artisanal stage." The insecurity and shallowness of this economic base helps to explain

39. *Jeune Afrique*, no. 494 (1970): 51. On the official response, see *Marchés Tropicaux* (7 février 1970): 305; ibid. (19 septembre 1970): 2,736; M. Diop 1972:174.
40. The content of these declarations was not specified. See *Marchés Tropicaux* (29 mai 1971): 1,690.
41. GES, Comité National Provisoire, "Rapport sur l'organisation du GES," Dakar, 27 novembre 1971.

why the essential demands of UNIGES and COFEGES were so basic, focusing on gaining government assistance to secure access to credit and markets. It also helps to explain why the pronouncements of the two groups differed more in tone than in substance. The episode cannot be read as the birth of "national capital" or of a "comprador bourgeoisie" (a *bourgeoisie liée*), or as a struggle between these two "factions of capital."[42] Senegalese private capital had not developed to the point at which two discrete "factions," with different economic bases, different needs, and different visions of the future could be discerned. Senegalese business wanted a better deal. What that deal would be was not determined by the needs of a national capitalist class.

The primary division within this business stratum was not programmatic. Rather, it was the division between the relatively large-scale and politically well-connected businessmen on the one hand, and marginal entrepreneurs confined to competitive activities that offered virtually no prospects for capital accumulation on the other. COFEGES, breaking with UNIGES which it deemed to be excessively political, represented Senegalese interests which had in fact been most systematically favored by the regime in the 1960s. In the final analysis, neither COFEGES nor the rank-and-file members of UNIGES were able to push for a fundamental and programmatic reorientation of the regime's economic options.

The government's success in co-opting, fragmenting, and demobilizing this social stratum attests to the relatively malleable nature of its economic bases and interests. The speed and relative smoothness of this process of co-optation also attests to the readiness of Senegalese businessmen to refocus their ambitions on opportunities for wealth accumulation that existed within the clientelistic structures of the party and the political class. Frustrated by its own weakness vis-à-vis the regime and foreign capital, the Senegalese private sector followed the agenda set by the regime.

Promotion of Senegalese businessmen "in domains that did not encroach upon legitimate vested interests" became one of the government's most prominent policy goals of the 1970s.[43] Given this objective, it is not surprising that the

---

42. Thus, Fatton's reading ("The Senegalese bourgeoisie was calling for the necessary conditions conducive to its crystallization as a national and independent bourgeoisie") seems overdrawn (1987:60). Anson-Meyer (1974:92–5) sees the 1968–71 period as marking the creation of a bourgeoisie tied to foreign capital (*une bourgeoisie liée*). From the perspective of the 1980s, this conclusion also seems to have been premature.

43. Senghor's "Message to the Nation" of 3 April 1970 stated that "a vigorous policy of promoting Senegalese businessmen will be pursued in the sectors of commerce, industry, and services. Our Senegalization policy is not incompatible with our policy of opening the Senegalese economy to international capital. On the contrary foreign capital is indispensable to the development of Senegal." (*Le Bulletin de l'Afrique Noire*, no. 595 [15 avril 1970]: 12,002). In his June 1970 address to the National Assembly, the new prime minister, Abdou Diouf, named "the Senegalization of the private sector" as one of the five "leading problems" facing the country. The other leading problems were unemployment, the *malaise paysan*, dependence upon French *assistance technique*, and costly imports of petroleum products. For the prime minister, the propositions of GES provided a good "basis for discussion" (*Marchés Tropicaux* [20 juin 1970]: 2,010).

regime did not offer a clear agenda for the development of local private capital in productive activities. What it did instead was create "space" for Senegalese business interests outside of the existing structures of control over productive spheres of the economy, just as it had in the 1960s.

Control over the commercial sector and its own vastly expanded capacities for distributing cash provided the regime with the means to promote the rise of a rentier class rooted in ad hoc, speculative, and state-mediated business opportunities. In the 1970s the state apparatus became a more accessible, flexible, and powerful instrument for organizing such a process. The scope of state involvement in banking, services, hotels, and construction, and in handling export commodities, was much wider than it had been in the 1960s. State-contracted and -guaranteed loan capital was now being disbursed liberally to finance the parastatal sector, *grands projets,* and other joint ventures with foreign capital. These changes gave Senegalese state agents and politicians control over a vastly expanded array of opportunities for private gain.

State agents and clients of the regime, now including a wider and more diverse stratum of Senegalese traders and businessmen, would avail themselves of these opportunities. Businessmen moved into the state apparatus. Politicians moved into new, politically mediated business activities. As a distinctive force in national politics, the most dynamic stratum of "local private sector" dissolved and was absorbed into the regime. Looking back at the events of 1968–70, Régine Van Chi Bonnardel (1978:824, 846) and Rita Cruise O'Brien (1979:108) concluded that the Senghor regime feared a "true national bourgeoisie" that could have constituted itself as an alternative force in politics, likely to align with the nationalist undercurrent of opposition and the ever problematic intelligentsia.

To promote Senegalese businessmen, the regime moved on three fronts in the 1970s. First, it officially encouraged small- and medium-scale Senegalese enterprise (*petites et moyennes entreprises*). On the rhetorical level, this goal served as the rationale for government initiatives on the second front. This second front consisted of measures to increase the access of Senegalese nationals to bank credit. Credit helped to finance activities on the third front, where the government accelerated the process of inserting Senegalese into commercial circuits. Borrowing from the World Bank Group, other multilateral and bilateral public donors, and the BCEAO financed these initiatives.

The Société Nationale des Etudes et de Promotion Industrielle (SONEPI) was created with great publicity in 1969. It was the government's first move to defuse the UNIGES challenge. SONEPI's original mandate was to "train local entrepreneurs in the techniques of modern business management." This corresponded nicely with the official response to the frustrations articulated by UNIGES, which was that the behavioral inadequacies of Senegalese businessmen constituted the main obstacle confronting the local private sector. As the World Bank (1974:161) reported:

SONEPI realized immediately that the single most important obstacle to the promotion of Senegalese entrepreneurship was the lack of training in the fields of management, accounting, and marketing. . . . SONEPI began working on an individual basis, making small Senegalese entrepreneurs aware of their deficiencies in these areas. It then established a 'Business Preparation Center' in Dakar, which trains entrepreneurs after business hours.

SONEPI became a financial institution in 1971, when it began making six-year loans to "rigorously selected" Senegalese businessmen who were interested in investing in a range of activities delimited by the government.[44] SONEPI would support rural cottage industries (pottery, weaving, millet processing), artisanal tailoring, market gardening, small hotels, bakeries, woodworking, mechanical workshops, fish drying, and brick making. It also tried to organize artisans into voluntary cooperatives to produce handicrafts for export. In 1972 SONEPI's efforts in these domains were complemented by the addition of a special statute to Senegal's Investment Code. The new *régime de faveur* exempted small-scale Senegalese businesses from registration fees and business taxes during their first five years of operation.[45]

Investments supported by SONEPI, "the major tool in the government's efforts to promote local private enterprise," were for the most part artisanal in scale, decidedly nonthreatening to established business interests, and either politically innocuous or politically useful from the perspective of the regime. After almost a decade of work, SONEPI's concrete achievements were very limited. About 50 local enterprises had received financial assistance. Many newly created enterprises absorbed SONEPI loans for "working funds" rather than for investment, suggesting that the institution's lending practices were considerably more flexible than its formal policy. Several of the largest enterprises that benefited from SONEPI's lending facilities were created to fill government service and supply contracts. With the state as their creditor as well as their client, most of these firms would not survive the government austerity of the 1980s. SONEPI and the Investment Code revisions allowed the government to claim that it was supporting private, Senegalese-owned productive enterprises, even though "[o]fficial support [was] too weak and too artificial to counter the constraints created by a foreign-dominated private sector."[46]

44. SONEPI offered sums of up to 100 million CFA francs. This money came from international public lenders, credits from local banks, and the government of Senegal. UNIDO provided technical assistance. SONEPI's lending facilities consisted of a Guaranty Fund and a Participation Fund. The Participation Fund advanced loans to Senegalese entrepreneurs in exchange for equity in the new enterprises. The entrepreneur was obliged to buy back the SONEPI loan within a period of six years. In 1977 SONEPI began to create "industrial estates" for cottage-type industries in Senegal's major cities.

45. Enterprises involving investments of at least 5 million CFA francs in two years were eligible for the dispositions of the 1972 *régime de faveur*. These dispositions were not very significant – they already existed on the books in the form of the Statutory Investment Incentive. Anyway, the 5 million CFA francs minimum investment level was still high by local standards. Major tax and import duties exemptions were still reserved for large (i.e., foreign) ventures. In 1977 the *régime de faveur* was extended to offer breaks on import taxes and more generous fiscal incentives to enterprises involving investments of 5 million CFA francs and/or more than fifty employees (SONEPI 1973:78–84; World Bank 1974:159; *Le Point Economique*, no. 13 [1978]: 6–9).

46. R. Cruise O'Brien 1979:108–9. On SONEPI, see *Le Point Economique*, no. 13 (1978): 7–8. Interviews with SONEPI agents and borrowers provided information in November and December 1984.

Government efforts to promote Senegalese enterprise did channel loans into local private hands. SONEPI's sister institutions, the Société Nationale de Garantie (SONAGA, created in 1971) and the Société Financière Sénégalaise pour le Développement de l'Industrie et le Tourisme (SOFISEDIT, created in 1974), played the leading roles on this front. SONAGA guaranteed commercial bank loans to Senegalese businessmen. In principle, these loans were made to finance investments in transport (such as the purchase of trucks) and in new commercial installations. SONAGA also offered commercial credit lines of up to 1 billion CFA francs per month at subsidized interest rates. In practice, SONAGA provided liquidity for many individuals engaged not only in commerce, but also in house building and consumption. One economic analyst, apparently better informed about some of SONAGA's actual activities than about the institution's formal mandate, said that "SONAGA finances the purchase of goods like cars and refrigerators."[47]

The largest loans were made by SOFISEDIT. This institution offered medium- and long-term credit for ventures in the tourism business and in "medium-scale" industry. It also bought shares in new Senegalese-owned firms and in ventures mounted by the state and foreign partners. In its first seven years of operations, SOFISEDIT distributed $15 million provided by the World Bank Group. France's CCCE and other European lending agencies contributed additional sums during this period, helping to capitalize the institution and finance its credit lines.[48] In addition, credit was available to SOFISEDIT through the central bank, the BCEAO. By 1977 SOFISEDIT had financed nineteen ventures "controlled by Senegalese" (i.e. joint ventures with the state, local private parties, and foreign capital) and nine wholly Senegalese-owned projects.[49] For its private borrowers, SOFISEDIT also opened the door to short-term loans from government banks. Reforms of central bank rediscount operations and the new commitment of the BNDS and the other government-controlled banks to the local private sector provided additional sources of capital to Senegalese private parties.

While the government made loans to individuals, it also created opportunities for the deployment of these resources – mostly in commerce, but also in new companies that were created by the state in the 1970s. When the state (through SOFISEDIT) financed the purchase of shares in its own enterprises by local businessmen, these individuals could expect a share of anticipated profits. They were also first in line to receive the interesting supply and service contracts let by the state enterprises. Outside this type of arrangement, Senegalese businessmen had strong incentives to place investment capital contracted through the state in

47. From an interview at USAID–Dakar, November 1985. On SONAGA, see *Marchés Tropicaux* (16 janvier 1971): 143; idem (18 mai 1973): 1,379.
48. The IFC funded SOFISEDIT almost single-handedly at the start with a $7.5 million loan in 1974. The World Bank provided another $7.4 million (2.6 billion CFA francs) in 1981. New lines of credit opened in 1978, including a 700 million CFA francs line from the Banque Ouest Africaine de Développement (BOAD). Public lenders that owned shares in SOFISEDIT included the KFW, DEG, CCCE, IFC, and BOAD. See *Le Point Economique*, no. 13 (1978): 10–12; *Marchés Tropicaux* (7 août 1981): 2,049; and Rocheteau 1982:127,130.
49. *Le Point Economique*, no. 13 (1978): 10–12.

quick-yielding, no risk, and lucrative commercial deals arranged by state agents. The alternative was immobilizing capital in risky, fixed investments. It became clear over time that the regime was not committed to seeing that government-sponsored loans were serviced or repaid in full. This reduced pressure on borrowers to place loan capital in activities that would generate any returns at all.

By the end of the decade, even outsiders noticed that the new lending facilities were being run according to political, rather than economic or "developmental" criteria. Many of the loans drawn from these institutions were never serviced or reimbursed. Some were not even recorded. At the BNDS, billions of CFA francs "disappeared." Freewheeling BNDS lending to politicos, marabouts, and other local bigwigs in the 1970s did a great deal to discredit this institution in the eyes of Senegal's commercial banks and foreign donors. At SOFISEDIT, one administrator reported that until 1983, sums up to 20 million CFA francs could be placed "at the sole discretion of the general director." SOFISEDIT lost its original capital of $7.5 million – not through the incompetence of its managers, according to SOFISEDIT defenders, but because politicians higher up in the government commandeered the institution to channel money to themselves and their business partners. One observer in the ministry of industry said "SOFISEDIT has a portfolio full of the worst run enterprises in Senegal. They are all in bankruptcy." Most of the enterprises financed by SONEPI folded after six years when their loans came due. Case studies of loans in SONEPI's and SOFISEDIT's portfolios concluded that "extra-professional considerations" influenced lending decisions.[50] By the mid-1980s SOFISEDIT and SONAGA were near the point of collapse, along with virtually all of the other government banks. The BCEAO observed in 1985 that:

[Senegal's credit reforms of the 1970s] seem to have given rise to a marked increase in lending to private parties without consideration of how this credit is to be used or the creditworthiness of borrowers. The portfolios of the government banks have deteriorated considerably. . . . The new discretion of the banks has led to an ill-considered distribution of credit to the detriment of the rules of banking orthodoxy.[51]

One concrete result of government's liberal lending practices was a construction boom in downtown Dakar and in the exclusive suburbs. From investors' perspective, real estate was good business – investments could yield returns of 25–50 percent a year in the mid-1970s.[52] In some cases civil servants and politicians obtained state loans to build villas and apartment buildings, and then

---

50. From interviews with SOFISEDIT agents and ministry of industry representatives in Dakar, November and December 1984. The Banque Centrale des Etats de l'Afrique de l'Ouest complained about nonreported and falsely BNDS reported loans in BCEAO, "Séminaire sur les règles d'intervention et de distribution du crédit dans l'UMOA," Dakar, 11–15 mars 1985 (restricted circulation). A textbook case of "extra-professional" lending decisions is reported in Ahounou et al. 1983.

51. BCEAO, "Séminaire sur les règles d'intervention et de distribution du crédit dans l'UMOA," Dakar, 11–15 mars 1985.

52. Lucie Gallistel Colvin, "Private Initiatives in the Senegalese Economy," consultant report to USAID–Dakar, mission of June 9–July 25, 1980 (restricted circulation).

rented these buildings to the government itself. Government loans also financed the purchase of luxury cars, Swiss bank accounts, and probably investments in overseas business ventures. They also financed commercial activities, including large-scale importation. Flooding political networks with government-backed loans probably did as much to insert Senegalese entrepreneurs into commercial circuits as policies designed for this specific purpose.

Access to trade (coupled with access to credit) remained the number one preoccupation of the Senegalese private sector in the 1970s. At the Second National GES Congress in 1973 (held at the UPS Maison du Parti and chaired by Minister of Finance Babacar Ba), the GES called for suppression of monopolies in the import trade. It also called for laws that would prevent the same commercial company from engaging in wholesale, semiwholesale, and retail trade.[53] Such measures would break up the vertically integrated commercial conglomerates. Over the course of the decade, the GES forum was used (in a "moderate and progovernment fashion") to call into question virtually every aspect of Senegalese commercial law and regulation that protected the monopolies of French merchant capital. The struggle for control over the commercial sector had clearly entered a new phase.

The regime remained committed to protecting the privileges of foreign capital vested in the integrated and collusive worlds of importation and light industry. Yet political pressure to create opportunities for Senegalese business interests, either within or outside of this rigid structure, was intense. The regime's urgent desire to deflect this pressure away from itself and from the maisons de commerce, combined with its need to generate and distribute patronage resources, set in motion a process of change. Space was created for Senegalese businessmen in the commercial circuit by modifying the implementation of existing policies, rather than by renouncing and reforming policies of the past.

Import licensing, import quotas, de facto foreign exchange rationing, and the licensing of individual importers were state controls over trade that were used in the 1960s to defend foreign monopolies in the wholesale and import trades. These devices generated a reservoir of potential patronage resources, largely in the form of commercial rents, that went largely untapped in the first decade of independence. In the 1970s the regime began to exploit the patronage potential of these regulatory devices. The political class and its allies, awash in cash borrowed from the state banks, lined up to take advantage of these new opportunities. Commercial regulations were modified and manipulated to insert Senegalese into lucrative niches in the trading sector.

State lending and state-regulated commerce promoted the rise of a new class of *hommes d'affaires sénégalais*. Over the course of the 1970s this phrase came to mean more than simply "Senegalese businessmen." It came to refer to politico-businessmen, marabout-businessmen, friends of the regime interested in cultivating commercial activities on the side, and an array of individuals who were able

---

53. *Marchés Tropicaux* (23 mai 1970):1,636–7; GES, "Resolution de politique générale du Deuxième Congrès National," Dakar, 15 juillet 1973.

to use their political positions or connections to tap into profits made in the commercial world. Patronage and clientelism in government-controlled commerce were traditions established in the earlier period. In the 1970s, however, the process involved more traders, more bureaucrats, more politicians, more money, and more spheres of trade. The rise of the *hommes d'affaires sénégalais* would have an enormous impact on the organization of trade.

In the wake of the 1968–70 political crisis, the government promised Senegalese businessmen more access to the consumer goods trade. As it turned out, this access would be controlled on a selective and discretionary basis by state agents, as it had been in the earlier period. In 1971 the system of licensing commercial operators was revamped and extended to cover transporters, real estate agencies, laundries, and car rental agencies, as well as more discrete subcategories of the retail, semiwholesale and wholesale trades. The government announced the new licensing system with the following remarks:

In the effort to systematically insert *hommes d'affaires sénégalais* into the circuits of production and exchange, the government will control the exercise of certain professions through the *autorisations préalables* [licensing] process. This will allow us to avoid the creation of a plethora of commerçants and small enterprises while assuring a legitimate place for capable individuals.[54]

By controlling access, members of the government could retain their gatekeeper role by "inserting" particular individuals into particular business niches. Restricting access (and competition) would help to ensure that these niches would be lucrative.

The ministry of commerce, now in control of regulatory prerogatives formerly lodged in the Chamber of Commerce, abandoned the policy of restricting the distribution of *cartes d'importateur-exportateur* to "formal sector" trading firms. These cards, or licenses, authorized a firm or individual to import goods in a specified product category such as textiles, foodstuffs, or automobiles. In the 1960s restrictive allocation had played a role in maintaining tight control over importation, and over the textile trade in particular. Breaking with this precedent in 1970, the ministry of commerce began to distribute *cartes d'importateur* in large numbers to *hommes d'affaires sénégalais*. The old practice of restricting importers to a few product categories was also abandoned. Importers were now allowed to "specialize" in an unlimited number of trading activities. By 1978 the number of *cartes d'importateur* allocated each year reached about 3,000 – three times the number in circulation in 1965.[55] Licenses designating *spécialisation textile* increased in number from about 200 to about 2,000. The allocation of *cartes d'importateur* was a highly visible sign of the regime's interest in rapidly

54. *Marchés Tropicaux* (31 juillet 1971): 2,268; ibid. (4 décembre 1971): 3,741.
55. République Française, Ministère de la Coopération 1965:ix, 4; SONED 1979; and interviews with ministry of commerce officials and representatives of the Conseil National des Entrepreneurs Sénégalais, Dakar, April 1985. In December 1970, in a gesture consistent with the new policy that carried high symbolic value, a number of small-scale and/or occasional French importers were denied *cartes d'importateur-exportateur*. See *Marchés Tropicaux* (12 décembre 1970): 3,605.

inserting Senegalese businessmen into the commercial sector, but the proliferation of these cards worked to undercut the gatekeeper function that they served in the past. The onus of selectivity shifted to other regulatory mechanisms.

In 1973 the government responded to bitter attacks on exclusive buyer arrangements between local manufacturing industries and the European maisons de commerce. Exclusive buyer deals structured the wholesale distribution of made-in-Senegal goods. They boosted profits for manufacturers and French wholesalers, and also barred Senegalese (and Lebanese) traders from the most lucrative stages of the distribution circuit. Senegalese traders' challenge to this unfair and, technically speaking, illegal business practice (*refus de vente*) zeroed in on the Dakar textile industry.

Local manufacturers were advised in 1973 by a ministry of finance *circulaire* that henceforth, 55–90 percent of the wholesale market for certain locally-made consumer goods would be "reserved exclusively" for Senegalese businessmen. In effect, the government was now prepared to oblige local manufacturers to sell a percentage of their output to licensed *hommes d'affaires sénégalais*. "These individuals and firms will act as wholesalers – that is, they will buy directly from the factories at prices and on conditions (credit, terms of payment) normally granted to wholesalers."[56] The list of reserved products and reserved market shares covered fifteen product categories, including cement (60 percent of the market), shoes (55 percent of the market), cigarettes (60 percent), sugar (80 percent), carbonated drinks (80 percent), concentrated milk (80 percent), and household soap (60 percent). Textiles were "on the list"; after all, the textile wholesale trade was the prime bone of contention. Wholesale margins in textiles were the largest in the business. The ministry of finance, however, was not prepared to confront the textile industry head-on. As the *circulaire* stated, "the textile market should be the subject of specific arrangements. The part reserved for Senegalese will be fixed at a future date." This future date did not come until 1980.

Reserved shares in the wholesale trade were not a collective benefit bestowed on Senegalese traders as a group. The material benefits associated with this initiative, like those associated with other forms of licensing, were divisible and particularistic. According to the 1973 *circulaire*, the minister of finance would name one hundred *hommes d'affaires sénégalais* ("priority individuals") eligible to buy directly from local industries. Their success would be "followed and encouraged" by the government. A number of means were employed to this end. Individuals on the list would "benefit from large market shares, eased access to bank credit, and special access to the lending facilities and credit guarantees of SONAGA."[57]

56. Gouvernement du Sénégal, Ministère des Finances et Affairs Economiques, Direction du Commerce Intérieur et des Prix, *Circulaire n. 0079 du 30 mars 1973 concernant l'insertion des hommes d'affaires sénégalais dans le commerce de gros*, Dakar. This circulaire was addressed to the Chamber of Commerce, UNISYNDI, the Association Professionelle des Banques du Sénégal, GES, and SONAGA. See *Marchés Tropicaux* (18 mai 1973): 1,379.

57. Gouvernement du Sénégal, Ministère des Finances et Affairs Economiques, Direction du Commerce Intérieur et des Prix, *Circulaire n. 0079 du 30 mars 1973*.

The one hundred *hommes d'affaires sénégalais* designated for special encouragement received other benefits as well. They were granted permission to import certain food staples controlled by the government (tea, tomatoes), and they obtained special credit facilities to finance these operations.[58] Efforts to promote *hommes d'affaires sénégalais* also affected the rice trade. Rice importation was privatized and turned over to a handful of firms licensed on a yearly basis by the minister of finance. Six or seven Senegalese trading companies imported and handled the wholesale distribution of all of Senegal's rice in 1971–2.[59]

Of all the measures designed to insert Senegalese *hommes d'affaires* into trading circuits, none were more significant than those affecting the importation of consumer goods governed by quotas or licensing. In the 1960s quantitative import restrictions and import licensing (the system of *autorisations préalables*) served two functions. First, they protected local industries from foreign competition. Second, they allowed the European maisons de commerce to control key segments of the import trade, such as the market for staple textile goods. In the 1970s the import control system was harnessed to a third purpose: the promotion of *hommes d'affaires sénégalais*.

By 1970 the ministry of commerce exercised full discretion over the allocation of import quotas and licenses. It undertook the official task of "selectively insert[ing] Senegalese *hommes d'affaires* into the import trade."[60] The ministry of finance instructed that individuals on its "list of 100" receive priority in the allocation of licenses and quotas. The ministry of commerce selected "priority" *hommes d'affaires* of its own. Several large Senegalese traders moved into the importation of consumer goods on a regular basis. Government officials inside and outside the ministry of commerce became ad hoc importers, along with other well-connected individuals. The maisons de commerce watched as this process chipped away at their monopolies.

The government's effort to insert Senegalese *hommes d'affaires* into trading circuits touched virtually every aspect of state-regulated commerce. In 1978 Prime Minister Abdou Diouf announced dramatically that the problem of Senegalization of the economy had been solved (*"C'est un problème dépassé"*).[61] Yet by the end of the decade, little had been done to respond to many of the concerns voiced by Senegalese businessmen in 1968–70. Industry remained the stronghold of foreign capital, and calls to facilitate the participation of nationals in this sector of the economy had produced few concrete results. The *grands projets* which consumed the lion's share of government investment capital in the 1970s subsidized foreign capital, not local capital. And the legal monopoly over

58. *Marchés Tropicaux* (6 avril 1973): 997–8.
59. *Arrêté du 8 nov. 1971 fixant les conditions d'importation du riz, modifié par la décision ministérielle* du Ministère des *Finances et Affaires Economiques (MFAE) du 23 nov 1971.* See *Marchés Tropicaux* (18 décembre 1971); idem (7 janvier 1972): 85; ibid. (27 juillet 1973): 2,338. For another aspect, see Bonnardel 1978:847 n. 383.
60. *Lien Economique* (Dakar) mars 1979.
61. *Le Soleil,* interview with Abdou Diouf, 28 mars 1978 (reported in *Marchés Tropicaux* [7 avril 1978]: 961).

groundnut marketing, the key to the national economy, remained in the hands of the state.

Official promotion of the local private sector created a stratum of Senegalese businessmen, including many very wealthy individuals, planted firmly in real estate and commerce. The fortunes of this group depended on the discretionary exercise of state power, and on access to state-controlled resources: government credit, licenses, quotas, "reserved shares," and the like. The promotion of *hommes d'affaires sénégalais* co-opted the most dynamic and most vociferous members of Senegal's nascent private sector into the party-bureaucratic political machine. New alliances between members of the political class and the local private sector structured the business world along the lines of political networks rooted in the state apparatus.[62]

As this happened organizations that potentially or nominally represented interest-based political groupings were absorbed into the party-administrative political machine. The Dakar Chamber of Commerce was "just another government bureaucracy."[63] The GES, with no budget or secretariat (neither GES members nor the government contributed financially to the organization), lapsed into passivity. GES leaders argued that the organization was too cumbersome (*lourde*) to accomplish anything.[64] Its grass roots base was inert and inactive. The institutional bases of Senegalese business interests lay elsewhere, closer to the centers of power.

The ministry of commerce became the political fiefdom of powerful UPS barons. State banks, including the BNDS, were run according to their own political logic. Babacar Ba, minister of finance from 1971 to 1978, used his tenure in office to build a personal political base – what *Africa Confidential* called "a state within a state" – by promoting *hommes d'affaires sénégalais*.[65] By the late 1970s this political base was wide and deep enough to place the minister of finance in the top ranks of contenders for presidential power. As Momar Coumba Diop and Mamadou Diouf wrote (1990:90), Babacar Ba had "very solid political alliances [in the Sine–Saloum region] and a relatively important urban clientele. Such alliances were clenched thanks to what seems to be a constant in the political evolution of independent Senegal: nepotism and corruption. Loans distributed with ease to his urban and rural clientele assured him the support of economic, political, and religious notables."

Over the course of the 1970s, the regime had succeeded in stifling the development of a local private sector capable of presenting an alternative force in politics. One clear sign of this was the dramatic fall of Babacar Ba. Babacar Ba's

---

62. "Les hommes d'affaires se constituent en groupe de pression et s'implantent dans le parti. Réciproquement, certaines personnalités politiques, usant de leur influence et des facilités que leur offre l'Etat, s'insèrent dans les secteurs économiques que le plan [de développement] s'efforce de promouvoir" (M.-C. Diop 1981:92, citing a 1974 paper by Guy Rocheteau).
63. From interviews with Chamber of Commerce officials and members of SCIMPEX, Dakar, November 1985 and January 1986.
64. *Lien Economique* (Dakar) mars 1979.
65. *Africa Confidential* (6 June 1979).

personal power dissipated when he lost his ministry, and then his place in the regime, in 1978. The ex-minister of finance disappeared into political oblivion as his one-time allies and clients scattered in search of new alliances with state agents – the prerequisite for maintaining access to resources controlled by the state. Sheldon Gellar wrote in 1982 (p. 34) that "[b]ecause of their heavy dependence upon the government for contracts and credit, Senegalese businessmen have not yet been able to act as an autonomous power center strong enough to force the government to make major shifts in favor of the Senegalese private sector."

Goals that had guided state control over commerce in the earlier period were subordinated to the demands of patronage politics in the 1970s. The restrictiveness of the import control system eroded as more and more *hommes d'affaires sénégalais* gained access to increasingly lucrative opportunities for importation. This process, however, was marked by its own contradictions. Over time, it created a kind of downward pressure on the value of rents to be had in state-regulated commerce. It also eroded the political credibility of the government's commitment to the local private sector. By the late 1970s and early 1980s there were pressures for reform.

Calls for the promotion of "real" Senegalese businessmen (who would come to be called *opérateurs économiques* to distinguish them from *hommes d'affaires*) were heard both within and outside of the state. Small- and medium-scale traders and businessmen, many of whom formed the subaltern ranks of GES and were largely excluded from the benefits distributed by the state in the 1970s, complained that government promotion of the local private sector had been derailed by political manipulation and the corruption of state agents. Meanwhile, officials within the Chamber of Commerce and the ministry of commerce, some well-placed themselves to take advantage of government efforts to promote *hommes d'affaires sénégalais,* called for reforms that would restrict access to state-controlled credit, licenses, etc., to a more select and "deserving" group. It was necessary, they argued, to eliminate *faux commerçants* and intermediaries of all sorts from "anarchic" trading circuits that had been encumbered and disorganized by a plethora of speculators and rentiers. Reformers within the bureaucracies who were committed to the formal aims of government policy argued that administrative discretion was exercised with great arbitrariness at all levels without respect for commercial regulations. This problem, "all too well known within the government and by the public because it is so often deplored," undermined efforts to promote "legitimate traders and real entrepreneurs." In the same vein, the Chamber of Commerce lamented that SONEPI and SOFISEDIT served ends that have "not always conformed to objectives stipulated at the onset."[66]

The most interesting dimension of this critique of standard operating pro-

---

66. Chambre de Commerce de Dakar (CCI-RCV), "Note sur l'élaboration d'un plan de promotion des opérateurs économiques nationaux," mai 1963. Also on this subject: Gouvernement du Sénégal, Ministère du Commerce, Direction du Commerce Intérieur et des Prix, "Note sur les mesures à prendre pour l'amélioration des circuits de distribution," 5 avril 1982.

cedures lay in the position of those who benefited from the status quo and, at the same time, called for moves to restrict access to state-controlled resources. It seems that by the end of the 1970s, competition within the "accumulating class" for resources generated in the commercial and financial sectors became more acute. Even for the privileged, the state's reservoir of patronage was not infinite. As a result, the regime's strategies for accommodating and co-opting powerful Senegalese interests would come under strain in the 1980s.

THE RURALIZATION OF TRADE

Contradictions between the regime's interest in accumulation and its need to shore up the existing political order presented themselves most starkly in the groundnut basin. As the *malaise paysan* gained force over the 1970s, preserving the political alliance between the Dakar political elite and the Islamic marabouts of the countryside – the alliance that served originally as a means of "indirect rule" and state exploitation of the peasantry – became an end in itself. This pact was the center of gravity of the ruling coalition; it provided the internal guarantee for Senghor's political hegemony. It was maintained in the 1970s and early 1980s through processes analogous to those underway within the state apparatus itself.

The fragmentation of the political machine and the dispersion of power within the state apparatus, Senghor's attempt to maintain power by sharing it, cast a huge and exaggerated shadow across wind-swept rural Senegal. In the face of the threat from below that was expressed in the *malaise paysan*, the regime shored up the authority of the rural elite at the cost of its own monopoly claim to the rural surplus. As rural markets slipped out of the state's reach, the Islamic confréries emerged as a parallel authority structure in the groundnut basin, increasingly able to compete with the state institutions that had served them so well in the preceding decade. The Islamic leaders remained an integral part of a regime that needed them as much as they needed it, but the marabouts grew more distant and more autonomous from Dakar's political manipulations. The alliance between the state and the marabouts, born of the colonial occupation, moved further and further away from its original form.

The *malaise paysan* that exploded in the rural areas in 1968–70 coincided with the onset of a disastrous Sahelian drought, "the most severe drought in the last 50–60 years" (World Bank 1974:140). Drought, a rise of 23 percent in the cost of fertilizers between 1965–7, and a fall in real producer prices of 20 percent between 1966–7 and 1969–70 conspired to produce a dramatic fall in producers' incomes.[67] Peasants' responses signaled a quickening of processes that were eroding state power in rural Senegal. Their malaise was manifest in three particular ways. First, a tendency to disinvest from groundnut production was evident in the old groundnut basin. Although there was no massive "flight into subsistence," households prioritized the need to protect their own consumption (es-

---

67. Farmers' cash incomes from groundnuts fell by over half from 22 billion CFA francs in 1965 to 10 billion in 1970 (World Bank 1974:144–5).

pecially by cultivating cereals) at the cost of expanding groundnut output.[68] Second, peasants refused to reimburse their debts to the state, or to contract new ones. In effect, they boycotted the *programme agricole* and the purchase of groundnut seeds, fertilizers, and farming implements sold through rural cooperatives.[69] Third, producers turned away from the state-controlled marketing system, resorting on an ever-larger scale to groundnut trading circuits that escaped state control. These tendencies were accompanied by a general resentment toward the Dakar political elite and toward state agents in the rural areas such as agricultural extension agents (Bonnardel 1978:64–72; Casswell 1984; D. Cruise O'Brien 1984).

The regime first responded with concessions designed to stem the rising tide of peasant protest. That the regime offered what Donal Cruise O'Brien called "too little, too late" was a sign of the compromised position of the state vis-à-vis rural producers. The goal of maximizing groundnut output could not be pursued

68. Production of groundnuts fell from an all-time high of 1,170,000 tons in 1965 to below 600,000 tons in 1970. Thirty percent of this decline came from a decline in area cultivated (World Bank 1974:144–5). Production would recover to about 1 million tons in 1975, 1976, and 1978, with falls to near 1970 levels in 1972, 1973, 1977, 1979, and 1980. (See Table 5.1.) Meanwhile, Senegal's total population grew at an average rate of 2.5 percent a year between 1960–80, doubling over the course of the 1960–80 period. Casswell (1984) and Bonnardel (1978:64–72) argue that a "marked disaffection" with groundnut production (a turn away from groundnut production) was the hallmark of the *malaise paysan*. Waterbury (1987:53) uses his aggregate data to advance what appears to be a strong critique of this position: "The Senegalese peasant of the groundnut basin appears as strongly wedded to his cash crop as ever." To support this argument, Waterbury compares total acreage planted in groundnuts to total acreage planted in millet per year, from 1960 to 1981 (ibid). In 1961–2, 55.2 percent of the total land under groundnut and millet cultivation was devoted to groundnuts. The figure was 53 percent in 1968–9; 48.2 percent in 1969–70; 57.5 percent in 1975–76; and 49.2 percent in 1980–81. Bellot (1985:43–4) shows the same thing: the nation-wide ratio of groundnut to millet output remained fairly stable over this same period. These data do show that producers did not "abandon" the groundnut. However, the aggregate, nation-wide figures that provide the basis for Waterbury's argument may conceal or underestimate what Casswell and Bonnardel identify as a shift toward food-crop production in the groundnut basin. There are two reasons to suspect that this is the case. First, Senegalese farmers' food crops were, in order of importance, millet, sorghum, cassava, rice, maize, neibes, sweet potatoes, beref, and fonio. Cassava, sweet potatoes, fonio, beref, and potatoes represented 27–37 percent of total foodstuff production in 1966–7 (World Bank 1974:139, 144). Total acreage under millet alone is thus not an adequate indicator of food crop production. Second, the years 1960–80 were marked by the opening of new lands to groundnut cultivation in eastern and southeastern Senegal. Waterbury's figures show that *total* land under groundnut cultivation did not increase over the course of this period. So what was happening on the regional level, and in the groundnut basin in particular? The aggregate data suggest that in the traditional groundnut basin, farmers were indeed cutting back on acreage devoted to the groundnut. See also Nascimento and Raffinot 1985:788–9.

69. "The use of fertilizer for groundnut, millet, sorghum, and rice, which had increased at an annual rate of 25 percent between 1962 and 1967, dropped dramatically from 62,000 tons in 1967 to 13,000 tons in 1970. . . . In 1970 the use of fertilizers for groundnut production reached only 13 percent of its 1967 level" (World Bank 1974:141, 145). "Similarly, the purchase of agricultural equipment in 1970 came to less than 50% of its 1967 level" (idem 1974:141). See also Bonnardel 1978:64–5.

consistently when the state sought, at the same time, to maximize its share of the rural surplus in the short run. In 1971 the government cancelled or suspended peasant debts to the cooperatives and passed a modest increase in groundnut producer prices. With the exception of the 1974–5 commercial season, however, real producer prices would remain lower in the early 1970s than they had been in the mid-1960s (Casswell 1984:49). The withdrawal of France's groundnut subsidy in 1968 coincided with a near doubling of world market prices for groundnuts between 1968–73. ONCAD, not the producers, reaped the windfall profits generated by the world price rise.[70] ONCAD retained its legal monopoly on the purchase of the crop over the course of the 1970s. The resources mobilized and consumed by this "obese parasite" continued to sustain the regime's networks of rural clients.[71] Sheldon Gellar (1982:64) reported that real producer prices for groundnuts were 30 percent lower in 1980–1 than they were at the time of independence. Stagnant productivity meant that yields had not improved. As misery spread throughout the groundnut basin, the *malaise paysan* intensified.

Peasants' survival strategies defied the state. The growing tendency of households in the groundnut basin to shift productive resources into food crop production, the rural exodus of young adults into income-earning activities in the urban areas, and the rural population's steady recourse to parallel markets ate away at the state's prime internal source of revenue – the groundnut monopoly. Production and sales to ONCAD fluctuated erratically as rainfall improved in 1975–6 and 1976–7 and then worsened, and as real producer prices, pulled in opposite directions by inflation and stepwise increases in official producers prices, fluctuated unpredictably. At the end of the decade, the state marketing system collapsed. In 1980–1, a year of adequate rainfall, Senegal recorded its smallest groundnut harvest since World War II. Less than half of this disastrous yield was commercialized through the state marketing board. (See Table 5.1.) Reimbursement of peasant debts in 1980–1 totaled more than 2.2 percent of sums due (Casswell 1984:50).

Early on in this process, Donal Cruise O'Brien (1971b:276) observed that it was ominous for the government that peasant resentment was directed more at the Dakar political elite than at the marabouts who had used the rural cooperatives and the state's groundnut program to serve their particular ends. This observation carried even more weight at the end of the decade. It is less paradoxical than it might appear, for the marabouts responded to the *malaise paysan* in a way that shifted and restabilized the material and political bases of their own power.

As the *malaise paysan* gained momentum, the grands marabouts distanced themselves from the regime and disassociated themselves from processes of rural exploitation engineered by the Dakar-based political elite. Falilou M'Backé, the grand khalif of the Mourides and one of Senghor's closest political associates, died in 1968 shortly after the initial wave of urban unrest. His successor to what

70. See Bonnardel 1978:65; and D. Cruise O'Brien 1979:218.
71. *Le Soleil,* 25 août 1985, cited by Casswell 1984:65.

Table 5.1. *Groundnut production and sales, 1960–80*

Year	Area planted[a] ('000 hectares)	Total production[b] ('000 tons)	Purchase price[c] (current CFA)	Purchase price[d] 1971 CFA	Sales to OCA/ ONCAD[e]
1929	604	494			
1938	702	646			
1951	690	571			
1956–7	885	925 (1957)			[677]
1959		907	17.5		
1960–1	977	977 (1960)			809
1961–2	1,025				872
1962–3	1,031				749
1963–4	1,084				782
1964–5	1,055				839
1965–6	1,112	1,168	20.6	23.5	985–1,089
1966–7	1,114	923	21.7	24.1	736–859
1967–8	1,164	1,038	17.6	19.4	842–949
1968–9	1,191	830	18.0	19.3	599–707
1969–70	963	789	18.4	19.1	581–706
1970–1	1,050	583	21.2	21.2	511
1971–2	1,060	989	23.1	21.8	887
1972–3	1,071	570	23.1	19.4	530
1973–4	1,025	675	25.5	18.4	587
1974–5	1,052	981	41.5	25.1	903
1975–6	1,312	1,412	41.5	22.3	1,328
1976–7	1,295	1,182	41.5	20.4	1,090
1977–8	1,161	508	41.5	19.6	467
1978–9	1,154	1,051	41.5	17.6	802
1979–80	1,097	787	45.5		421
1980–1	1,050	530	50.0		190

[a]Estimate of area planted in groundnuts, in hectares. Data for 1929–51 from Founou-Tchuigoua 1981:130; for 1956–7 from Bonnardel 1978:56, 134–5; for 1960–81 from Waterbury, 1987:53.

[b]Estimate. For 1929–60, Founou-Tchuigoua 1981:130. For 1965–6 to 1980–1, Casswell 1984:45.

[c]All data in current CFA francs, from Casswell 1984:49; except 1959.

[d]Price paid to producer per kilo in constant 1971 CFA francs, from Casswell 1984:49.

[e]In thousands of tons. The figure for 1956–7: Volume of groundnuts commercialized, as reported by the Service du Conditionnement (Bonnardel 1978:135). From 1960–6, the state purchasing agency was the OCA. From 1967–80, purchases by ONCAD. Data for 1960 through 1964–5 as reported by Bonnardel, ibid. For 1965–6, the low figures are Bonnardel's; the high figures are from Casswell 1984:45. For 1970–1 through 1980–1, from Casswell (ibid).

Sources: See Notes.

is arguably Senegal's second most powerful post, Abdou Lahatte M'Backé, redefined the character of the relationship between the confrérie and the ruling party. Under the leadership of the new khalif général, the Mourides adopted a stance of greater political neutrality, offering only conditional political support for the Dakar politicians.[72]

The strategy of Abdou Lahatte M'Backé was to ensure that the religious leaders were perceived as defenders of peasant interests, not as collaborators with the state. This option was consistent, as Donal Cruise O'Brien (1984) argued, with the marabouts' role as consummate politicians. Their leverage in dealings with the government rested on their command over the population of the groundnut basin. This authority and legitimacy hinged on the freely accorded devotion of the faithful, and on the marabouts' ability to offer both spiritual and material sustenance to their followers. If the *malaise paysan* was a protest movement initiated and propelled forward at the grassroots level, then the Mouride leaders would have disowned this movement at great risk to their own legitimacy and the very basis of their political power. As it turned out, Mouride leaders were not prepared to mortgage their own legitimacy in attempts to bolster that of the Dakar political elite.

Dakar, for its part, settled for half a loaf, realizing that a split of this magnitude within the ruling coalition, or a divorce between the marabouts and the peasants, could cost it everything. Senghor adopted a nonconfrontational stance and the sorry episodes of 1968, when intimidation had been used to pressure peasants to repay some of the cooperatives, were not repeated.[73] The Dakar-based political class would continue to rely upon the marabouts as arbitrators, *interlocuteurs,* vote gatherers, and pillars of rural order; it was in their interests to ensure that the marabouts could play this role effectively. In the 1970s the power and autonomy of the Mouride confrérie grew as the rural institutions of the state weakened.

Mouride leaders demonstrated this autonomy by legitimizing and in some ways facilitating peasant resistance to state exploitation. In the early 1970s Abdou Lahatte M'Backé called upon peasants to continue to cultivate food crops in order to feed their families and to free themselves from chronic indebtedness. When followers were cautioned to view authority that lay outside of Islam as illegitimate (unholy), the Dakar-based politicians were put on notice. Islam was a force that could be used against the state as well as in its service. Grands marabouts publicly used the threat of the total collapse of the groundnut economy to wrest concessions on producer prices and peasant debts from the government: "Do not lower the producer price because if you abuse your monopoly, we will abandon the groundnut in favor of millet and our survival."[74] In this sense, the Islamic confréries did provide a vehicle for the organized expression of the peasant protest (D. Cruise O'Brien, 1984).

72. *Africa Confidential* 14, no. 1 (5 January 1973): 2; ibid., 17, no. 11 (28 May 1976): 5; Gellar 1982:34–5; Coulon 1981:275–9, 286.
73. See Schumacher 1975:184.
74. Cited by D. Cruise O'Brien 1984.

Meanwhile, the Mouride confrérie provided organizational and financial support, as well as political protection, for the development of marketing circuits that lay outside the scope of state control. Parallel markets for groundnuts were nothing new; in 1963–4, an estimated 10,000 tons of Senegalese groundnuts were sold on the Senegal-to-Gambia parallel market. The following year, about 20,000 tons escaped the state marketing monopoly via this route.[75] What changed dramatically in the 1970s was the scope and volume of this trade. The _malaise paysan_ had reached crisis proportions in 1970 when 40–50,000 tons of groundnuts, still less than 10 percent of the harvest, slipped illegally into the Gambia. Over the course of the decade, massive evasions of ONCAD became the producers' most damning indictment of the state monopoly. In 1980 an estimated 70 percent of the dwindling groundnut harvest was sold on the parallel market. The largest share of this was exported through the Gambia (Casswell 1984:50, 72).

The development of unregulated export circuits on this scale would not have been possible without the tacit _laissez-passer_ of the government. De facto tolerance of the parallel market was one of Dakar's greatest concessions to peasant producers and to the marabouts who played a role in organizing this trade and who profited from it. The Mouride religious capital of Touba, located about one hundred miles east of Dakar, was the nerve center of rural smuggling and contraband.[76] Fleets of trucks based in Touba transported groundnuts across the Gambian border. Corresponding shipments of inexpensive consumer goods purchased in the Gambia entered Senegal through this contraband circuit and were sold on Touba's flourishing market.[77] The Mouride confrérie not only provided logistical and financial infrastructure, but also political protection for the two-way contraband trade.

In the words of Christian Coulon (1981:242–3), "[t]he marabouts enjoy a sort of privilege of immunity vis-à-vis the law. . . . The protection of the marabouts covers illegal [business] activities, in particular the contraband trade across the Senegalese–Gambian border." Most conspicuously, the Mouride leaders secured the government's pledge to keep police, army, and customs agents out of the holy city. Touba was a free-trade zone in the heart of the groundnut basin. That the Mouride elite had financial stakes in this contraband trade was in no way inconsistent with their followers' interests: rural producers and consumers obtained higher groundnut prices and cheaper consumer goods. The parallel market developed at the direct expense of the state treasury and of those who had profited

75. The 10,000 tons a year is an estimate for the decade preceding, and including, 1963–4. Sales of groundnuts in the Gambia increased to 20,000–25,000 tons in 1964–5, when the government deducted especially high sums in payment for fertilizer and materiel from producer earnings (République Française, Ministère de la Coopération 1965:23).
76. See, for example, _Promotion_ (Dakar), "Fraude: du scandale de Touba à l'incompétence des ministres," no. 21 (7 mars 1985); M.-C. Diop 1981:91.
77. Gambia imported consumer goods from some of the world's cheapest suppliers (especially the countries of the Far East), and Gambian import taxes were levied at an average rate of about 30 percent.

from the state trading monopolies. Yet the government obviously lacked the political will to use force to suppress large-scale contraband.[78] After negotiations with the Mouride leaders in 1977 about the importance of limiting the scope of the contraband trade, the government constructed a new marketplace at Touba.

As M.-C. Diop (1981:91) says, the government itself, "because of its commitment to maintain at any price the overall stability of the national political system, bears a large part of the responsibility for the development of contraband traffic at Touba." By backing off in the rural areas, the regime avoided a direct confrontation with the groundnut-producing peasantry. And by continuing to invest heavily in the old political alliance with the Mouride elite, the government helped these leaders retain their hold in the rural areas even as their traditional economic base, the groundnut, sped along its course of decline. The peasantry may have disengaged from the state, but the Islamic leaders certainly did not.

The Islamic leaders continued to profit from their connections to ONCAD and the ministry of rural development, and Abdou Lahatte M'Backé "did not refuse the gift from the state of 2,500 acres of 'declassified' forest land in 1972 and 1974" (D. Cruise O'Brien 1979:224). But increasingly, the economic base of the Mouride confrérie lay elsewhere. Part of the wealth accumulated in the 1960s had been transferred out of the declining groundnut economy and into urban real estate, urban trade, transport, taxi companies, construction, and import–export operations.[79] In the 1970s the grands marabouts and the leading businessmen of the confrérie were among the first clients of the state-controlled lending institutions; they remained in the lucrative rice trade; and they took advantage of new, state-regulated opportunities in the import trade. They also invested in developing the Senegal–Gambia (contraband) circuit. Close associates of Abdou Lahatte, including the general secretary of the Mouride confrérie, were among the richest and most prominent *hommes d'affaires sénégalais* (M.-C. Diop 1981:98). The confréries controlled Senegal's cement monopoly; they owned groundnut-shelling plants; and in the 1970s, leading marabouts held interests in hotels and in the fishing industry, two sectors targeted by the regime for special support and rapid development.

Business successes of leading marabouts and businessmen linked to the confréries, like those of powerful state agents and their relatives, reflected political influence. M.-C. Diop (1981:99) writes that "[i]n practice, at the heart of the Senegalese political and economic system, these two groups – marabouts and Mouride *hommes d'affaires* – are very close to the centers of power [*très liés au pouvoir*]." The shift in the economic bases of the confréries was accompanied by qualitative changes in the nature of their political influence and power. Forces that pulled the economic bases of the confréries toward the urban areas pushed disciples in the same direction. Decline of the groundnut economy, rural exodus,

---

78. *Promotion* (Dakar), no. 21 (7 mars 1985).
79. For an analysis of maraboutique business interests (especially in commerce) in the 1960s, see Amin 1969:48–51, 182–183. For more recent commentaries, see Halpern 1972:115–20; Bonnardel 1978:800–1; *Africa Confidential*, 6 June 1979; and M.-C. Diop 1981:93–4.

and urbanization were accompanied by the consolidation of Mouride social structures and economic hierarchies, and the mobilization of Mouride ideologies and identities, in the cities. Jean Copans summed up these processes most bluntly when he declared in 1981 that "the marabouts of the groundnut" no longer exist.[80] Less dependent upon the groundnut economy for revenue and for followers than they had been in the past, the grands marabouts were freer to condone and support peasants' efforts to protect their subsistence needs at the expense of groundnut production. And although the confréries remained thoroughly ensconced in the state-mediated business world, they were less dependent upon handouts and discrete policy decisions (such as decisions about producer prices, land grants, etc.) made from the president's office. Dispersion of power within the regime in the 1970s multiplied their points of access to the state, and the growing autonomy of subunits of the state (including the ministries, banks, and parastatals) increased their room for maneuver within the structures of the regime. Networks of maraboutique influence, and of Mouride influence in particular, diversified and deepened.

The *malaise paysan* itself contributed to the growing power of the marabouts, for it underscored the regime's dependence on the confréries as agents of rural political order. Using their positions shrewdly, the rural leaders were able to force the Dakar politicians to accommodate not only their political needs, but also their private interests.

The regime continued to respond to the erosion of its control over rural trade with concessions to groundnut producers. In 1973, peasant debts to the cooperatives were written off again. In 1974–5, producer prices increased by 63 percent in current prices, or by about 35 percent in constant 1971 prices. This increase was accompanied in 1975–6 and 1976–7 with favorable weather conditions. Production and sales to ONCAD regained 1965–6 levels. The reprise was short-lived, however, for in 1977–8 production and sales to the state fell by almost 60 percent.[81] At the end of the decade, the last vestiges of *la traite* crumbled. The groundnut economy and the marketing monopoly had served in the earlier period to mobilize resources that could be transferred out of the rural economy. After 1974 the flow was reversed, and the groundnut sector became a net drain on the state's finances (Casswell 1984:63–4).

In 1980 ONCAD collapsed under the weight of its own inefficiency, corruption, and heavy-handed exploitation of the peasants. As Casswell wrote, ONCAD was dissolved by the government at the point when "it threatened the political stability that it had originally helped to create." The government-controlled daily, *Le Soleil*, announced that ONCAD had become uncontrollable, "an obese parasite serving the interests of its own agents at the expense of the state and the peasantry."[82]

80. Copans, "A livre ouvert," *Politique Africaine*, no. 4 (1981): 121; reprinted in Copans 1988:272.
81. D. Cruise O'Brien 1984.
82. Casswell 1984:39; *Le Soleil*'s commentary on the dissolution of ONCAD (25 août 1980), cited in Casswell 1984:65. See also *Africa Confidential*, 7 May 1980.

The ONCAD legacy was a debt totaling CFA 94 billion, or 15 percent of Senegal's gross national product in 1980. Many of ONCAD's employees were moved to a new state agency, called the Société Nationale d'Approvisionnement Rurale (SONAR), which "looked suspiciously like [its predecessor]."[83] SONAR was commissioned with the task of reconstituting rural credit and supply networks (Lewis 1987:309–11; Bellot 1985). Regional development agencies assumed many of ONCAD's other functions, and the rural cooperatives were authorized to sell the groundnut crop directly to the refineries. In January 1981 the producer price was raised again. And peasant debts to the state were annulled, again.[84] These moves would prove to be milestones marking the secular decline of state control over the rural economy.

Over the course of the decade, the government gradually lost the struggle for control over the rural surplus, a battle played out in large part as a struggle for control over rural commercial circuits. In taking the place occupied by colonial merchant capital in the earlier period, the regime took on the political alliances that the colonial state had forged with the rural elite, merchant capital's capacity for exploitation of the peasantry, and also merchant capital's limitations. Donal Cruise O'Brien (1979:223) pinpointed the source of these limitations: "[The regime's] capitulation to organized peasant protest may perhaps with hindsight be seen as a logical outcome of a situation in which the government had no means to *force* recalcitrant peasants to grow peanuts . . . " The state, like merchant capital, could not intensify the exploitation of the groundnut sector by enhancing productivity, for it had no direct control over the production process itself. Ultimately, it could increase its share of rural production only by impoverishing the peasantry. In Senegal as in much of sub-Saharan Africa, producers found a survival strategy in opting to "exit" from this system.

Nationalization of the groundnut trade in 1960 played a specific role in this process by breaking up the integrated trading circuit established by merchant capital in the 1930s. Nationalization broke the link between the purchase of export crops and the sale of consumer goods, the link that bound peasants to a single, monopolistic trading circuit during the old days of *la traite* in Senegal. Although the state and French capital vested in Senegalese commerce and industry continued to depend upon hierarchical, Dakar-centered trading circuits, rural markets became more complex. Competition crept in, expanding possibilities for producers of both groundnuts and food crops to buy and sell where they found the terms most favorable – on the parallel market.

In a process that Régine Van Chi Bonnardel calls the "ruralization of trade," Senegal's rural areas were delinked from Dakar-centered markets that were controlled and regulated by the state. The effects of the demise and then the dramatic collapse of neocolonial trading networks were felt throughout the economy. The regime, weakened by challenge, hostage to the demands of disparate elements

---

83. Lewis 1987:309–11. See also Bellot 1985.
84. The producer price was raised from 50 CFA francs per kilo to 70 CFA francs per kilo. Peasant debts written off in 1981 totaled 31.9 billion CFA francs.

embraced within the ruling coalition, and increasingly fragmented and compromised as a result, could not arrest this process. Nor could it successfully pursue
the project of establishing some alternative productive base for the state and
foreign capital. Its interest in using the state in some "entrepreneurial" fashion
was pitted against its need to reconsolidate old political alliances, the patronage
machine, and its hold on power.

6

Demise of the Dakar textile industry

State authorities face a political choice between certain Senegalese commercial interests and the local textile industry.

"Interview with M. Paul Warnier, director of Icotaf," *Africa*, no. 103, août–septembre 1978

The truth of the matter is that the French industrialists in the textile industry, greedy for super profits, refuse to leave any space in this business for Senegalese in order to preserve their monopoly power and to force the government to subsidize profits which they repatriate to Europe. . . . In whose name, and on the basis of what justification, should we sacrifice [the Senegalese-controlled textile trade] for the benefit of *les industriels français du textile?*

"*Textile:* Halte aux manoeuvres contre les hommes d'affaires sénégalais," *Taxaw*, no. 12, août 1978

President Senghor, in a March 1970 speech in Paris, cited the rising index of industrial production to show that the Senegalese textile industry was in *plein essor* (full takeoff).[1] Employment, production, and local value-added were on the rise, making the textile industry Senegal's "most dynamic sector in import-substitution" (World Bank 1974:222). The drought of 1973 affected the entire Senegalese economy, but the general view at the time was that the industrial sector would recover from this setback. High rates of tariff protection gave textile producers a priori claim to a share of the domestic market in goods times and in bad. State spending, hiring, and lending created an inflationary climate in the mid-1970s, bolstering middle- and upper-bracket incomes in the cities and fueling demand for consumer goods. Good harvests of 1976 and 1977 and nominal increases in producer prices after 1974 contributed to the *conjoncture favorable* of 1974–7 which promised to stimulate rural demand.[2]

Optimistic scenarios for the growth of the textile industry in the 1970s would be rewritten by changes underway in the political domain. Over the course of the decade, patterns of control over Senegal's domestic markets came to reflect the increasingly fragmented and compromised character of state power. Direct access to commercial rents and profits permitted state institutions embedded in

1. *Marchés Tropicaux* (11 avril 1970): 1,175.
2. See Duruflé 1988:26–7.

commercial circuits – such as ONCAD, the ministry of commerce, and parts of the ministry of finance (including the customs service) – to gravitate out of the reach of central administrative authority. Spoils-oriented political factions sited in these institutions grew as Senegalese businessmen and other clients and allies of the politically powerful were invited to take advantage of commercial opportunities mediated by state agents. Similar forces worked to enhance the autonomy of Mouride leaders vis-à-vis other elements within the ruling coalition. Mouride marabouts and businessmen linked to the confrérie not only profited from efforts to promote a class of *hommes d'affaires* rooted in state-controlled commerce, but also tapped the economic potential of rural markets that gravitated outside the scope of state control. Growing financial autonomy from those in highest political office increased the marabouts' room for maneuver, and they used this power to protect commercial circuits that by-passed the regulatory and tax-collecting mechanisms of government.

Between 1975 and 1985 the monopolistic structure of market control forged under the hegemony of colonial merchant capital collapsed. The state's ability to extract a large share of the rural surplus via a monopolistic export circuit was one casualty. The ability of French capital to extract rents generated by monopolistic import circuits – through either importation or import-substitution industry – was another.

Neocolonial commercial and industrial interests lost the struggle for control over Senegal's markets in the 1970s. State power was used to divert the rents they had collected in the earlier period – as well as the commercial revenues that the state treasury had collected in the form of taxes – to the political class, their businessmen allies, and Mouride commercial interests. Captive markets disintegrated. Import controls were manipulated or circumvented to create "space" in the import trade for powerful Senegalese; customs fraud assumed proportions never before seen in Dakar; and rural markets were delinked from Dakar-centered commercial circuits.

Erosion of the old commercial monopolies sent the local textile industry into a free fall. Interfirm linkages in the textile industry unravelled; losses mounted. The industry's downward spiral was marked by waves of bankruptcies and firm closures. French interests would cut their losses and finally pull out altogether. By the late 1980s Senegal's neocolonial textile industry was gone, closing the book on an era of Senegal's economic history that began in the early 1950s.

As the economic base of the state narrowed, so too did the political structures that had enabled the regime to govern. The Senghor regime had mortgaged its future by borrowing abroad in the 1970s to bolster state spending as the traditional export sector weakened. Spending reinvigorated the political machine and financed public investment in ventures that promised to create alternative sources of state revenue. By the end of the decade, however, it was clear that this attempt to reconcile the need to sustain economic growth with the need to generate political support had run its course. The decay of neocolonial structures that marked the 1975–80 period was not offset by the emergence of other sources of dynamism and growth in the Senegalese economy. Meanwhile, Senegal had contracted a foreign debt of over $1 billion.[3]

Much of the money had been dissipated, diverted, spent on importing consumer goods, and invested in ventures that did not pay off. Extractive industries, the great hope of the 1970s, produced commodities worth less and less on international markets. The parastatal sector consumed much more than it produced.[4] These forces conspired to defeat the regime's attempt to restabilize and expand its own revenue base. Yet the debt had to be serviced and eventually repaid. Debt service payments consumed 25 percent of Senegal's (declining) export earnings in 1980. Meanwhile, world inflation and oil price hikes had increased the import bill. In 1980 the government's current account deficit reached almost 16 percent of GNP.[5]

These gaps, as Duruflé (1988:28–9) argues, grew out of "a logic of creation and distribution of revenues that was disconnected from the sphere of production. . . . [This] constituted in Senegal a structural characteristic of the economy linked to the mode of socio-political regulation." The Senghor regime had relied on spending and consumption financed by resources appropriated or otherwise mobilized by the state to build a clientelistic mode of domination within existing, neocolonial economic structures. Profound structural disequilibria of the economy that had been apparent since the early 1950s had been reproduced and aggravated over the course of the postcolonial period. At the end of the 1970s Senegal finally arrived at the end of this impasse.

The World Bank swept in with a "structural adjustment" program. The International Monetary Fund (IMF) was not far behind with a plan for consolidating and restructuring the Senegalese debt. A five-year Plan de Redressement Economique et Financier was announced in December 1979. The government would have to cut spending, stop hiring, sell off parastatals, and compress domestic standards of living.

An economic crisis of "unprecedented proportions" had developed by the end of the decade. It was accompanied by what Momar Coumba Diop and Mamadou Diouf (1990:69–93) called "a dramatic deterioration of the social situation." The social climate in the late 1970s was marked by the growing dynamism and politicization of social movements that coalesced outside the corporatist structures, political networks, and ideologies of the state. Declining living standards for the vast majority intensified disaffection toward a regime and ruling class widely perceived as corrupt and guilty of gross economic mismanagement. Senegal's urban areas were the site of a renewal (*reprise*) of Islamic identities and

---

3. World Bank 1981a; *Jeune Afrique* (6 août 1980); *Africa Confidential*, 7 May 1980. See also Lewis 1987:296–301.

4. In 1981–2, the parastatal sector operated at a net loss of 19.7 billion CFA francs (Elliot Berg Associates 1990:27).

5. In 1981 it reached 25 percent of GNP. See Lewis 1987:285; Duruflé 1988:20–9. Consumption on the part of households and the government administration accounted for 99 percent of GNP in 1980 (idem 1988:27–8).

currents of social action, a trend manifest most strikingly in a dynamic Mouridism propelled forward by the youth, university students, and young intellectuals (M. Fall 1985; Copans 1988:239–51). This *reprise* was accompanied by growing demands of the Mouride leaders at the national political level and by ominous tensions between the confréries. On a wider scale, corporatist structures carefully constructed by the regime in the 1960s and early 1970s – most notably student organizations, teachers' associations, and the trade union confederation – began to splinter, giving rise to political protests on the part of groups that the regime could no longer "colonize" or control.

Senghor's electoral reforms of 1976 represented one attempt to canalize and contain challenges to the ruling party's claim to ideological and social hegemony. Two opposition parties were selected and licensed by the regime, one "Marxist–Leninist" and one rightist ("liberal"). These parties were to contest elections against "the moderate and centrist" ruling party, now renamed the Parti Socialiste (PS).[6] This arrangement was also short-lived. In the late 1970s it was impossible to mask the regime's monopoly on state power behind the façade of a narrow and controlled multiparty system. The "loyal opposition," compromised by its own inefficacy within the limits of this new electoral game, became more assertive. Illegal opposition parties regrouped and gathered momentum. Frustration with the regime mounted as the ruling party clung to power. The government was assaulted by accusations of electoral engineering, manipulation, and fraud. Voters abstained from elections orchestrated within the three-party system and Senghor's position weakened. "In this crisis-ridden context, it was reasonable to think that correction of the economic disequilibria would involve, at the political level, the adoption of authoritarian measures likely to aggravate the social crisis" (Diop and Diouf 1990:83). In December 1980 Senghor resigned.

Senghor handed power to his *dauphin,* Prime Minister Abdou Diouf, a member of the regime who was known for his administrative competence, who was untainted by the most blatant excesses of corruption of the Senghor era, and who maintained excellent relations with the Tidjane and Mouride confréries. Abdou Diouf would now preside over the factious government administration and ruling party constructed by his predecessor. His presidential project would be twofold: first, to consolidate his own power within a ruling coalition that was composed of elements that were politically and economically much stronger than Abdou Diouf himself; and second, to ward off total economic collapse by sustaining major inflows of external resources. The economic project would require the regime to move toward reforms conceived by the IMF and the World Bank: government austerity, deflating the state apparatus, and economic restructuring. The political project would require Abdou Diouf to sustain old clientelistic networks in order to hold the wolves at bay and to preserve the regime's ever-weakening political base. Simultaneously, he would have to construct clientelistic networks of his own, networks that would be more powerful than those of his rivals.

6. See D. Cruise O'Brien 1978; Fatton 1987:7–15.

What Momar Coumba Diop and Mamadou Diouf call the "grand crises of the regime of Abdou Diouf" would emerge out of the contradictory imperatives of this dual project. These crises would crystallize "around the difficulties of the ruling class in reconciling an economic logic [largely defined by international financial institutions] with a political logic captured by clientelistic networks of mercenary support" (1990:24). As the economic vise tightened, Abdou Diouf would turn, as Senghor had, to the commercial sector, where patronage resources could be generated on a large scale even in the absence of direct state expenditures. The size of the fortunes accumulated in trade and the clout of those vested most directly in state-mediated commerce would compromise Abdou Diouf on all fronts.

As institutions for organizing the use of state power, the regime and government bureaucracy were paralyzed by the contradictory pressures of salvaging the economy on one hand, and salvaging the regime on the other. The demise of the textile industry over the course of the 1975–85 years was one symptom of the deepening crisis. Efforts to sustain networks of political control and support crucial to the regime's survival dissipated the capacity of "the state" to maintain centralized administrative control over markets. Along with this control went the regime's capacity to extract resources via commercial circuits to fund the current expenditures of the state, as well as its capacity to structure from above the private distribution of commercial rents and profits. State power was fragmented and privatized by powerful elements that proceeded to reappropriate old monopolies in the import–export sector. This chapter traces these processes as they unfolded in the textile trade.

BREAKDOWN OF OLD STRUCTURES OF MARKET CONTROL

In the early 1970s import restrictions and taxes became more formidable to protect a textile industry in *plein essor*. The rapid expansion of local production and sales in the early 1970s attests to the efficacy of this system. There was an abrupt change in the mid-1970s, when vast parallel markets for textile goods and extensive circuits of fraudulent importation developed with stunning speed.

The spectacular rise of smuggling, fraudulent importation, and a quasilegal trade in *friperie* (imported used clothes) reflected and increased the political and economic weight of Senegalese businessmen who entered the textile trade through political channels in the 1970s. It also reflected the growing autonomy of state agents responsible for enforcing commercial regulations. Profits to be made in circumventing import taxes and restrictions were considerable. Cost differentials between inexpensive foreign goods (from the Far East, India, Eastern Europe, etc.) and made-in-Senegal goods were very wide, making smuggling and fraud lucrative. In 1980 import taxes and controls were designed to nearly double the cost of most foreign textile goods on the domestic market.

As long as import restrictions sustained the high cost structure of the local market, Senegalese textile importers could collect rents on less costly imported goods, just as the European maisons de commerce had in the earlier period. By avoiding taxes and customs duties, the importer appropriated rents formerly collected by the state treasury. The intensification of smuggling and fraud in the late 1970s and 1980s, however, introduced de facto competition in the textile trade. As a result, importers' rents fell along with effective rates of market protection. They responded by seeking out cheaper and cheaper goods on world markets. One large textile importer argued in 1985 that commercial margins for those escaping formal controls could exceed 100 percent.[7]

Commercial incentives for smuggling and fraud had always existed. In the 1950s and 1960s, however, the illegal textile trade was suppressed effectively and kept to what the government and the industry defined as tolerable proportions. Textile goods smuggled into Senegal by *pirogue* or on foot from the Gambia or Mauritania supplied a small faction of the local market in the early 1960s. The Senegalese government viewed this small-time trade as an irreducible margin of "structural smuggling" that did not threaten the local textile industry or the overall level of customs receipts.[8] Big-time smuggling and fraud developed with speed and ferocity in the mid- to late-1970s. Profits from this trade were often reinvested in the same activity, fueling the "incessant growth" of the unregulated and irregular textile market.[9] In 1981 one group of analysts in the ministry of industrial development estimated that 70 percent of all textile goods sold in Senegal were imported fraudulently or illegally.

The unregulated and irregular textile trading circuits that developed in the 1970s had deep roots in the political world. Some of Senegal's most powerful private interests were involved, including importers close to the Mouride confrérie and *hommes d'affaires sénégalais* linked to those in highest political office. "Importers of grand standing" used political investments, political position, and connections in *milieux politiques* to enter the textile trade and/or to protect their activities from both their competitors and state agents who were trying to enforce the law. *Magouille* (payoffs and kickbacks) helped to secure the complicity of strategic customs agents and bureaucrats. State agents who condemned the rise of smuggling and fraud, and there were many, did not command the power, authority, or resources to stop it.

Three currents of unregulated or irregular textile importation developed in the 1970s. Each was embedded in a different part of the *milieu politique*.

Contraband

The Senegalese-Gambian border has always been the major axis of the contraband circuit. Gambia's import taxation policy is liberal by Senegalese standards. Because the Gambia has no local industry to protect, the purpose of import taxation is to generate revenue for the government. Foreign goods are imported

---

7. From an interview in Dakar, April 1985.
8. "A certain element of 'structural smuggling' has existed for decades and is impossible to eliminate. . . . [T]his would be about 3–4 million meters a year out of a total market of 60–65 million meters" (SONED 1979:61).
9. *Liberté* (Dakar), "L'industrie textile: la mort en fraude," no. 1 (1 mars 1985): 20.

under freely granted, open licenses. This system allows Gambian importers to buy from the world's cheapest suppliers. Imports were taxed at an average rate of 20 percent in the 1960s and about 30 percent in the 1970s.[10]

Its role as an entrepôt for goods clandestinely reexported to Senegal has long been an element in Gambia's "modest prosperity": in the mid-1960, goods destined for final sale in Senegal represented about 10 percent of all Gambian imports and generated about 15 percent of the Gambian government's total revenues from import duties (Hazlewood 1967:119–20). United Nations analysts estimated that from 1960–3, 80 percent of all cigarettes imported to the Gambia were illegally reexported to Senegal. For shoes, the figure was 70 percent and for textiles, 50 percent.[11] Similar studies undertaken by the French government in the mid-1960s argued that the UN figures were inflated. Senegalese-Gambian contraband trade was "not negligible, although not a serious problem to the Senegalese textile industry."[12] In the early 1960s smuggled goods from the Gambia represented an estimated 1 percent of all Senegalese imports. About half of all contraband goods were textile products, amounting to an estimated 7 percent of all textiles consumed in Senegal.[13]

As sales of Senegalese groundnuts in the Gambia increased in the late 1960s, the reverse trade in consumer goods grew in scope and volume. In 1969 the smuggling of textiles, shoes, cigarettes, and radios from the Gambia into Senegal first emerged as a serious issue in the Dakar business press.[14] The two-way contraband trade assumed full-blown proportions in 1974 as the rural areas recovered from the Sahelian drought. By the mid-1970s, the risks involved in this trade had clearly diminished. The foot and *pirogue* traffic was left to small-frys and most goods smuggled across the border were transported by truck. Senegalese importers opened offices or employed full-time commercial agents in Banjul, the Gambian port and capital city. In the major cities of Senegal's interior, smuggled products replaced made-in-Senegal goods in merchants' stalls. One source estimated that in the 1980s, 80 percent of all goods on sale in Kaolack and MBour were contraband. For Touba, the figure cited was even higher.[15]

Around 1980 the contraband circuit was extended to the largest marketplaces

10. See Bonnardel 1978:634.
11. As reported in République Française, Ministère de la Coopération 1965:24.
12. Ibid.: 25–7. Knit good smuggled into Senegal from Gambia caused alarm among the owners of Dakar knitting firms in 1964. A crackdown on this trade in 1965 dealt with the problem effectively.
13. Most of the contraband textile trade in the 1960s was carried out by "petits commerçants sénégalais, . . . venant s'approvisionner personnellement en territoire Gambien" (ibid.: 23). One 1960 study cited in the French government's 1965 report estimated the value of the Senegal–Gambian trade at 370 million CFA francs (c.i.f. stage) and 500 million CFA francs (wholesale stage). Yaw Owusu Sekere, in a 1963 ISEA study, estimated that in 1961 contraband from the Gambia equalled about 10–15 percent of all legal textile imports to Senegal.
14. *Africa* (Dakar), "La Fraude: un fléau national," no. 47 (1969): 29–53.
15. *Promotion* (Dakar), "La Fraude: du scandale de Touba à l'incompétence des ministres," no. 21 (7 mars 1985).

in Dakar. Sandaga, a sprawling market in the heart of the city, became one of the capital's principal distribution centers for manufactured goods. Innumerable stalls in this flourishing marketplace specialized in the sale of contraband goods.[16] Sandaga's array of duty-free imports was complete, ranging from textiles, shoes, processed foods, and cosmetic products to cassette tapes, televisions, and stereo equipment. Other major marketplaces of Dakar (HLM, Colobane, Tilène) quickly followed suit. In part, these markets were organized, financed, and supplied through the parallel market centers in the interior.

Textile goods occupied an important place, probably the leading place, in the contraband import trade in the 1970s. Most contraband textile goods entering through the Gambia competed directly with the traditional staples of the Dakar textile industry. Japanese cotton prints (*imprimés* and wax prints) taxed at a rate of 30 percent in the Gambia poured into Senegal. On the Senegalese market, the same goods imported though legal channels were subjected to licensing and much heavier import taxes. Importers circumvented legal channels and consumers profited from the difference. The importation of *imprimés* via the Gambia became big business after 1975 (Diouf 1977; Fall 1984).

It is clear that the Mouride marabouts played an important role in the development of the Senegal–Gambia contraband circuit. Uncertainty revolves around how much the important marabouts profit directly from this trade. Marabouts became involved in the consumer goods trade in the rural areas in the 1970s and some invested in transport and commercial finance (lending). The Mouride confrérie also used its influence to protect the two-way contraband trade from government intervention. In Dakar, the role of the Mouride hierarchy in organizing and protecting parallel markets has been overt and conspicuous. Unregulated markets provide a source of employment and income for thousands of adherents. M.-C. Diop (1981:100) writes that the merchants of Sandaga and Tilène:

compete directly with some of the large French and Lebanese commercial firms of Dakar; they sell goods of the same quality at lower prices. It is among these commerçants that one finds most of the heads of the *dahiras* [Mouride "base communities" or associations], and the commerçants themselves have created one of the most representative *dahiras* of Dakar. Certain of these commerçants are members of federations of *dahiras* and [in this capacity] they play the role of [local] representatives of the Khalif Général. They occupy a very important niche in the organization of the confrérie; their function consists of organizing the urban Mouride clientele and acting as the liaison between this clientele and the central administration of the confrérie.

Dakar's taxi network and the *cars rapides* business, both also organized by the Mourides, served the same functions.

Urban trade and transport became an integral part of the social and economic structure of Mouridism in the late 1970s and early 1980s as drought and the collapse of the groundnut sector pushed waves of refugees into the cities. In Dakar, the confrérie emerged as a crucial intermediary between the government and the city's poorest social strata, the social strata able to pose the most direct threat to political order in the capital. The Mouride marabouts did not hesitate to play this card.

16. *Le Soleil*, "Un marché Dakarois: Sandaga," 1 and 2 octobre 1983: 12–13.

An ill-advised government attempt to descend on "the Mouride market," Sandaga, to confiscate contraband goods occurred in the early 1980s. Observers believed that the initiative was interrupted and called off abruptly "by authorities at the highest level of government," and that confiscated goods were returned to merchants at the demand of the Mouride leaders.[17] The government subsequently closed its eyes to this urban symbol of Mouride commercial power. According to one agent of the ministry of commerce, "powerful *intérêts en jeu*" and "political arrangements" ensured that the government would not interfere with the contraband circuit – either in the rural areas or in Dakar.[18] Sandaga market remained a bastion of political and electoral support for the ruling party.

Fraud

Fraud in the textile import trade was rooted in other networks and segments of the *milieu politique*. Fraudulent imports passed through legal channels (the ministry of commerce and customs control), but escaped or subverted import restrictions and the taxation process. This sort of importation took many forms in Senegal, some as complex as the system of import regulation itself. In the textile trade, common forms of fraud were under-invoicing of imports, deliberate misclassification of goods under the customs code, manipulation of the *admission temporaire, transitaire,* and *entrepôt fictif* regimes (intended for reexports), false documentation of the origin of products, falsification of quantities imported, the importation of banned goods, the manipulation or disregard of import quotas, and simple nonpayment of import taxes.[19] Fraud irritated local manufacturers in the 1960s, when it was a regular or sideline business for some importers dealing in nonstaple textile goods, such as garments and other specialty items. Fraud did not become a major threat to the local industry until the 1970s. For some firms, fraudulent importation came to represent a problem as serious as contraband.

In the 1970s and 1980s *hommes d'affaires sénégalais* – including politicians, their relatives (wives), and friends – found fraudulent importation to be a fast and low-cost way of generating cash. Fraud required access to the funds and contacts needed to purchase goods from foreign suppliers (commercial credit, suppliers' credit, or cash), knowledge of import regulations or connections to someone who knew how to manipulate the system, and access to the documents needed to shepherd goods through the bureaucratic maze – commercial licenses, *autorisations préalables*, etc. In the case of under-invoicing, the complicity of the foreign supplier was enough. In most cases, however, fraudulent importation required the help of the customs service, the ministry of commerce, and/or influentials in other parts of the administration.

Large-scale fraud assumed a blatant character in the 1980s. Cases cited most

17. From interviews with textile importers and retailers in Dakar, April and December 1985.
18. From an interview with a former high-ranking official of the ministry of commerce, Dakar, April 1958. He said, "How to normalize the situation? Legalize it."
19. SONED 1979:61; GOS, Ministère du Développement Industriel, "Rapport du Groupe du Travail Textile," 25 septembre 1981: 24; Fall 1984.

often in this regard involved the unloading of containers of banned textile goods at the Port of Dakar, at midday. The International Airport at Dakar-Yoff was another major point of disembarkation of fraudulently imported goods, especially in the 1980s. (It seems that the airport was the avenue of choice for the businesswomen who entered the textile trade in the 1980s.) Many argued that large kickbacks to customs controllers and ministry of commerce officials became standard operating procedure in the textile import trade. A middle-ranking bureaucrat in the ministry of commerce said, "Of course they have to pay; it happens all the time."[20] Rumors of the wealth of high-level customs officials did not surprise or impress anyone in Dakar. One analyst in the ministry of finance said jokingly that the system of import control had been reduced to a bribe-extracting mechanism.[21]

Friperie

The importation of *friperie* was a separate business that was entangled in complex social issues and monopolized by a small, politically powerful clique. Technically speaking, this category of imports includes both used clothes and rags. Senegal imported about 100 tons a year of rags in the 1960s, presumably for shredding and reweaving into blankets at SCT. Used clothes were effectively banned from the Senegalese market until 1973 for a number of reasons, a central one being the desire to protect the "normal" textile trade from "unfair" competition.

There was a complete turnaround in 1973 when 2,000 tons of used clothes arrived on the Senegalese market. These clothes were purchased in the U.S.A. or the Netherlands in bales of 200 kilos. At that time, *friperie* could be purchased abroad for 200 CFA francs per kilo, far below the cost of the raw materials contained in a kilo of clothing. Registered *friperie* imports reached 3,000 tons a year by the late 1970s. In the early 1980s registered *friperie* imports of 6,000 tons a year were supplying an estimated 40–60 percent of total domestic demand for clothing.[22] Competition from these goods transformed the Senegalese market for textiles and sent the local industry reeling.

For the price of one meter of the most basic locally produced cloth, a man could outfit himself completely in *friperie*. For the same price, three children could be dressed in imported used clothes. For the poor in Senegal's urban and

---

20. From an interview that took place at the Dakar Chamber of Commerce, commercial regulation office, January 1986.
21. From an interview with an analyst working on industrial protection in the forecasting division of the ministry of finance, April 1985. Exporters were also in on this business. One representative of a Korean Textile Trade Mission to Dakar was asked in a November 1985 interview why he was in Senegal, given that Korean textile goods were banned from the local market. He responded with "No problem! I have a politician."
22. On the 1960–72 period, see République Française, Ministère de la Coopération 1965:11; and the following issues of *Marchés Tropicaux*: 14 janvier 1967:189; 21 mars 1970:948; 8 mai 1971: 1,399; and 26 mai 1972:1,474. For the development of *friperie* imports between 1974 and 1978, see ibid. (17 février 1978) and SONED 1979:102.

rural areas, *friperie* provided some relief from inflation and the general erosion of purchasing power in the 1970s. For the importers, *friperie* could generate profits ranging up to 100 percent and running into the hundreds of millions of CFA francs a year.[23] A multitude of local wholesalers, retailers, and micro-retailers collected markups that generated an income mass that exceeded one billion CFA francs a year in 1978 (SONED 1979:102).

From 1973 to 1978 a single firm monopolized the *friperie* trade: Apollo-TM et Cie. This firm was created by a first cousin of then Prime Minister Abdou Diouf and a Senegalese businessman who became wealthy in Zaire. It was a perfect marriage of political influence and money. Serigne NDiaye and Tampsir MBoup created Apollo-TM with 100 million CFA francs and received authorization (over the objections of the ministries of finance and industry) to import unlimited quantities of *friperie*.[24] The two businessmen quickly built a *friperie* empire and accumulated personal fortunes.

The profits of Apollo-TM were reinvested in not only *friperie*, but also in other commercial activities. In 1976 Apollo-TM purchased a long-established French commercial company in Dakar, SPCA-Thubet, and began importing luxury goods, including Jaguar automobiles.[25] The government then granted SPCA-Thubet exclusive rights to import Japanese automobiles, hitherto banned from the Senegalese market. The value of this market was estimated at 5 billion CFA francs a year in 1978.[26] In 1980 another commercial firm owned by Serigne NDiaye and Tampsir MBoup (ICOPAL) was licensed (along with two other companies) to import rice. These *hommes d'affaires* epitomized the rapid rise of Senegalese businessmen in the late 1970s. They were renowned for their political connections and business acumen.

In 1978 a second firm, this one based in Kaolack (COSISAL), was authorized to import used clothes, again over the objections of the ministry of industry.[27] Government sources argue that Mouride businessmen close to the confrérie's central administration entered the *friperie* trade at that time, entrenching this business even more deeply in the most powerful quarters of Senegalese politics. The first *friperie* import quota was imposed in 1978, providing the framework within which Apollo-TM and COSISAL organized their oligopoly.

Friperie imports outraged local textile manufacturers and were a devastating

23. *Marchés Tropicaux* ([17 février 1978]:484) reported that total profits generated in the *friperie* business could exceed the cost of the imported goods by 300 percent. SONED (1979) reported that *friperie* profits at the import-wholesale stage were about 60–100 percent.
24. From an interview with a former employee of the Sotiba Group, October 1984. *Le Soleil* (7 novembre 1978:1) reported that the annual turnover of Apollo-TM in 1977 was 990 million CFA francs.
25. Appolo–TM acquired SPCA–Thubet for 150 million CFA francs (*Le Soleil*, 7 novembre 1978:1). For a detailed account of the activities of this firm, see Fayama 1977.
26. *Le Soleil*, 7 novembre 1978:1.
27. GOS, Ministère du Plan et de la Coopération, Comité Interministériel des Investissements, "Procès verbal concernant le cas de la Société Kaolackoise de Friperie," 15 octobre 1975; SONED 1979:102. Djilly MBaye reportedly represented the interests of the Mouride confrérie in the *friperie* trade (from an interview with an economic advisor in *la Présidence*, April 1985). See M.-C. Diop 1981.

blow to the local industry. Manufacturers and government sources argued that recorded imports of "used clothes" concealed rampant fraud in the *friperie* trade. Two issues were involved. The first was importation in excess of registered volumes and quotas. One government source reported that when legal *friperie* imports reached 2,000 tons, actual volumes exceeded that figure by 300 percent.[28] The second issue was *"fausse friperie"* – the use of the *friperie* customs code classification to import new, low-priced clothes. This maneuver allowed importers to circumvent the taxes and quantitative restrictions normally applied to imported garments. In spite of a maelstrom of protests from the industry and the ministries of industry and finance, the *friperie* trade grew steadily in the 1970s. The *friperie* quota was raised from 3,000 tons to 6,000 tons per year in 1980. Three or four new firms were licensed to enter the business in 1984. Dakar's textile manufacturers argued that *friperie* on this scale could clothe all of Senegal.

"Senegalization" of the textile trade

The fifty-year struggle for control over Senegal's market for textile goods entered a new and decisive phase in the 1970s. Contraband, fraud, and *friperie* transformed the domestic market for textile goods, introducing unprecedented levels of competition and steadily undermining the positions of both the French maisons de commerce and the Lebanese.

The first phase of this struggle ran from the 1930s to the early 1960s. During this period the maisons de commerce clearly dominated the market thanks to monopolies granted and enforced by the colonial state and its postcolonial successor. These French trading houses monopolized the importation of staple textile products that were destined primarily for the rural areas. In the 1950s, they became the exclusive wholesalers of locally manufactured goods, also targeted for the most part at the rural market. Local production and the importation of staple textile goods were integrated into a tight, oligopolistic circuit that ensured high profit margins for both the maisons de commerce and the local industry. Lebanese merchants acted as the retail distributors of these staple goods. After World War II, Lebanese firms and some private French businessmen began to import on their own account, concentrating on competitive, urban-centered niches in the textile market (i.e. the market for "nonstaple" goods). When it came to goods purchased all over Europe in small quantities, and to markets that were sensitive to rapidly changing fashions, the maisons de commerce were not interested. Importing vast quantities of standardized goods was their forte.

The second phase, from the mid-1960s through the mid-1970, was marked by the expansion of these nonstaple "niches" in the textile trade and by the growth of the Dakar textile industry. Independent Lebanese textile importers became more powerful as the market for ready-made garments, specialty textile goods,

---

28. GOS, Ministère du Plan et de la Coopération, Comité Interministériel des Investissements, "Procès verbal concernant le cas de la Société Kaolackoise de Friperie," 15 octobre 1975.

and household textile goods developed along with urbanization and the rise of a Senegalese salariat. Lebanese competition hastened the retreat of the maisons de commerce into domains of the textile import trade that they could control and monitor on an on-going basis through licensing. As the local industry grew, the European trading houses imported less, centering their operations around the distribution of locally manufactured textile goods. The maisons de commerce remained the exclusive buyers of made-in-Senegal cloth, fixing prices among themselves to keep margins high, and distributing to Lebanese semiwholesalers. Until the 1970s, aside from a few exceptional cases, Senegalese traders were excluded from all but the lowest echelons of the domestic textile market.

The third phase began between 1973 and 1975, when the irregular and unregulated textile trade introduced competitive pressures that neither the Lebanese nor the maisons de commerce could withstand. Restrictive systems of licensing and taxation that had protected and regulated the market in the earlier period now became mechanisms for marginalizing long-time importers. Lebanese businessmen were blocked at the administrative level by government officials actively promoting *hommes d'affaires sénégalais*.[29] Senegalese importers using privileged "bureaucratic facilities" or circumventing official circuits altogether introduced untaxed textile goods onto the market. These goods patently undersold textiles imported by Lebanese merchants who found themselves confined to legal (taxed) channels.

In the late 1970s Dakar's major Lebanese textile importers followed the path trod by the maisons de commerce a decade earlier. They began to retreat from the textile import trade, leaving the market to Senegalese importers who had access to the political facilities needed to make importation profitable.[30] One analyst of Senegal's Lebanese community said in 1985 that "the policy of promoting *hommes d'affaires sénégalais* has strangled Lebanese commerce. If not for the civil war in Lebanon, most would have left Senegal after 1975. It's very difficult for them to do business here now."[31] Some of the largest Lebanese textile dealers dealt with this problem by transferring the headquarters of their textile import operations to the Gambia. From there, they could supply the Senegalese contraband circuit from Banjul.

The maisons de commerce faced the same problem. Import licensing no longer guaranteed them control over the market for staple textile goods. The director of one of these firms complained that signed *autorisations préalables* to import *imprimés* and wax prints could be purchased easily in Dakar. By the late 1970s about 90 percent of all the textile goods sold in Senegal by the dominant French textile dealers – CFAO, CITEC, and CNF – were locally produced. In 1980 the

29. In an interview in Dakar in January 1986, one Lebanese importer said that the year 1975 ushered in the era of the *homme d'affaires sénégalais*. After 1975, he said, it became "impossible" for Lebanese traders to obtain import authorizations.
30. From interviews with textile dealers, commercial agents within the textile industry, and at the ministry of commerce, April and December 1985 and January 1986. See *Le Soleil*, 1 et 2 octobre 1983:12–13.
31. From a discussion with a fellow researcher in Dakar, November 1985.

CFAO stopped importing, explaining this with the comment that "we left the market to smugglers." The CNF's Senegal-based textile division, NOSOCO, stopped importing "because NOSOCO's minimum commercial margin is 10 percent. We cannot compete with small commerçants who escape import taxes and engage in more-or-less legal activities."[32]

For the maisons de commerce, purchases from the local factories were the last bastion of monopoly control in the 1970s. In 1980 this arrangement began to crumble. Manufacturers were instructed by the ministry of commerce that the textile industry would no longer be exempt from the government's policy of inserting *hommes d'affaires sénégalais* into the wholesale trade. The Dakar textile industries were now required to make 50 percent of all their factory-door sales to a list of Senegalese businessmen named by the government.[33] Sotiba–Simpafric added the names of 10–15 Senegalese businessmen to its list of exclusive clients. By 1984 about fifteen more names had been added. The number of buyers at Icotaf jumped from six to forty and within a few years, to sixty. According to the manufacturers and industry analysts, not all of the new clients had commercial installations or the funds needed to buy from the factories. Many of the new clients at Sotiba–Simpafric were politicos, bureaucrats, or their agents and relatives. Lebanese merchants (still excluded from Sotiba's list of distributors) advanced funds to these new intermediaries, paid the *prête-noms* (front men) a commission of 5–10 percent, and then distributed the goods themselves.[34]

Though Senegalese *prête-noms*, Lebanese merchants finally circumvented the wholesale distribution circuits controlled by the maisons de commerce.[35] Lebanese distributors did not play the game of price-fixing, and they promptly began to undersell the large French trading companies. In 1985 CITEC, CNF, and CFAO were preparing to withdraw from the textile trade in Senegal altogether. "Due to the political situation, for us, *les Français*, the textile trade in Senegal may be finished." CITEC's director said simply, "one must envision the

32. From interviews with employees of the CFAO, CITEC, and NOSOCO in Dakar, December 1985 and January 1986.
33. *Lien Economique* (Dakar), mars 1979; SCIMPEX, *Circulaire n. 43–80 du 1 octobre 1980;* GOS, Ministère du Commerce, Direction du Commerce Intérieur et des Prix, *Circulaire n. 02664 du octobre 1980;* GOS, Ministère du Commerce, Direction du Commerce Intérieur et des Prix, *Note sur les mesures à prendre pour l'amélioration des circuits commerciaux de distribution*, 5 avril 1982.
34. Information on the new lists of exclusive clients and the *prête-nom* system is from interviews at a Lebanese-owned textile distribution company in April 1985 and with commercial directors of Sotiba–Simpafric in April and December 1985, ministry of commerce agents in November 1985, and the commercial directors of NOSOCO, the CFAO, and CITEC in December 1985 and January 1986. Diouck (1986:16) also discusses the system.
35. The *prête-nom* system centered around sales by Sotiba–Simpafric. Icotaf began selling directly to Lebanese and Senegalese distributors around 1983. It seems that Icotaf's distribution policy changed for a number of reasons. First, a new director of marketing came in under the firm's new owners in 1982. Second, Icotaf products became very difficult to sell on the Senegalese market in the mid- to late-1970s, forcing Icotaf to take whatever clients it could get.

closing of CITEC in the near future."[36] Commercial advantages secured through the use of state power had enabled the French maisons de commerce to dominate Senegal's textile trade for decades. By 1980 Senegalese *hommes d'affaires* had gained near-complete control over this market in the same way. One former textile importer said "to deal in textile goods now, you need proper arrangements in the political world that the French and Lebanese just don't have."[37]

This shift was manifest in data registering legal imports of textile goods to Senegal. Registered imports of cotton fabric fell continuously in quantity and value over the course of the 1970s. From 1977 to 1980 legal imports of all cotton fabrics, including semifinished goods, fell from 2,902 tons to 1,828 tons. Registered imports of *imprimés* fell in current value from 1.1 billion CFA francs in 1972 to 20 million 1983. In 1985 and 1986, *écru* destined for printing at Sotiba represented 87 percent and 88 percent of registered imports of cotton goods. Over 80 percent of all registered imports of synthetic cloth in the same years were semifinished goods, processed by Icotaf.[38] In a textile market inundated with imported finished goods, official import statistics (and thus import tax receipts) in the mid-1980s were showing that Senegal imported almost nothing for direct sale on the consumer market.

CRISIS IN THE TEXTILE INDUSTRY

The government described the situation of the Dakar textile industry in the late 1970s as catastrophic and alarming. Its official view was that "reconquering the local market is indispensable for the survival of the textile industry." The ministry of industry zeroed in on the problem, arguing in 1981 that "rapid measures must be undertaken to stop illegal importation if the textile industry in Senegal is to survive."[39]

Contraband, fraud, and *friperie* undermined the commercial foundations of the Dakar textile industry. High profits, high costs, low productivity, failure to renew capital stock, and the domestic market monopolies of the 1960s and early 1970s left the industry extremely vulnerable to competition of any kind. The competition it faced in the mid-1970s and 1980s was devastating. Loss of captive markets was reflected in production cutbacks and falling, often negative rates of profit for all firms in the industry. Wage compressions, layoffs, recurrent strikes, stocking of unsold merchandise, bankruptcies, and firm closures were the result.

36. From interviews in Dakar, December 1985 and January 1986. By 1990 the CFAO and CITEC had closed down operations in Senegal. CNF (through NOSOCO) "maintained a small presence" on the market, with one store in downtown Dakar selling Sotiba's products and top-of-the-line wax prints imported from England and Holland.
37. From an interview with a leading Lebanese textile dealer in Dakar, April 1985.
38. GOS, Ministère des Finances et Affaires Economiques 1983b:470; Touré 1985; Julie Senghor, "La Filière textile au Sénégal" (a report prepared for the GOS, Ministère de l'Industrie et de l'Artisanat, Cellule de Restructuration Industrielle), n.d. (1990?):75–87.
39. GOS, Ministère du Développement Industriel, "Rapport du Groupe du Travail Textile," 25 septembre 1981:24.

Recovery of the rural areas from drought in 1975–7 did not interrupt the downward spiral. Nor did the rise in urban consumption that was fueled by state borrowing and spending between 1974 and 1977.[40] The demise of the Dakar textile industry was proclaimed a national crisis in 1978.

By the end of the 1970s the industry's total workforce had been reduced by 40 percent. Financial losses and arrears on payments in the industry accumulated into the billions of CFA francs. The secondary segment of the industry, comprised of knitting and garment-making firms, was the first to disappear. Major textile mills were on the brink of closure in the late 1970s. Massive state subsidies did not arrest the process of decline. From 1974 to 1988 a relentless series of firm bankruptcies and closures reduced the number of firms "conducting industrial activity" in Senegal's textile sector from about twenty to three.[41]

Deteriorating conditions: The basic textile industry

In the 1960s and 1970s the two largest firms in Senegal's textile industry were Sotiba–Simpafric and Icotaf. Sotiba–Simpafric was the most profitable firm in the sector and the largest private employer in Senegal. In the 1970s it was generally viewed as the strongest firm in the business. Its capital stock was fairly modern by the standards of the Dakar textile industry because its owners had invested a share of the profits of the late 1960s and early 1970s in increasing the factory's production capacity. Sotiba–Simpafric enjoyed a monopoly on producing printed cloth. As a base for printing, it used gray cloth produced by its local subsidiary, STS, as well as gray cloth imported from the Far East.

Icotaf ranked second in terms of turnover and employment. Its two factories – at Pikine and Rufisque on the Dakar periphery – were among the oldest and most obsolete in the textile sector. Unlike Sotiba–Simpafric, Icotaf was a fully integrated operation. It bought Senegalese cotton to spin, weave, and dye an array of textile products. Icotaf was the monopoly producer of all staple fabrics other than prints. In the 1960s and early 1970s it paid attractive dividends to its European stockholders but did not modernize its capital stock, tending to rely instead on ever higher rates of domestic market protection to ensure a market for its goods. Sotiba–Simpafric and Icotaf were protected by import licensing and by tariff barriers that were designed to raise the cost of competing imports by 40–210 percent (depending on product category).[42]

40. GOS, Ministère du Plan et de la Coopération 1985:4; Duruflé 1988:26.

41. The firms operating at the end of 1990 were Sotiba–Simpafric, CCV, and SOSEFIL. CCV, still owned and managed by the Groupe Dufour, was viewed throughout the 1980s as the best-run firm in the industry. A small and conservatively run spinning firm, it had avoided extensive diversification of production. As an intermediate goods supplier, it had never benefited from import protection to the degree that the finishing industries had. SOSEFIL also appeared to be a solid operation. Its goods enjoyed high rates of protection on the domestic market, but its product – sewing thread – was not interesting to *fraudeurs* and *contrebandiers*. Sotiba–Simpafric's (Sotiba's) survival was in question at the end of 1990.

42. GOS, Ministère des Finances et Affaires Economiques, Direction de la Prévision, "Rapport préliminaire sur l'Etude de la Structure des Incitations Industrielles au Sénégal," juillet 1985:57.

Sotiba–Simpafric lost its market to contraband. The years 1975–7 seem to have been the turning point. Printed fabrics made in the Far East entered through the Senegal–Gambia contraband circuit, undermining Sotiba-Simpafric's rural market for its major product line, *imprimés*. Some observers declared dramatically that prints made in Senegal "disappeared" from rural markets in the late 1970s and early 1980s. The firm was forced to cut back production of *imprimés*, close down one production department, and export at a loss.[43]

Sotiba–Simpafric's management became even more resistant to government efforts to collect data on its operations during this period, making it difficult to quantify the impact of imports on the firm's production, sales, and profits. Inside observers report "nefarious effects of uncontrollable, illegal competition" on the firm's returns and domestic-market sales after 1978. In spite of production cut backs, Sotiba–Simpafric stocked large quantities of *imprimés* from one year to the next.[44] Production vacillated erratically as the firm worked to liquidate stocks. Profits fell and wages were compressed. The length of the work week was reduced by 20 percent in 1978. Sotiba–Simpafric wanted to lay off almost half of its workforce in 1978; the government blocked this move and compensated the firm with ever larger subsidies.[45] This period of crisis was punctuated by a change in ownership in 1980–1 (discussed below), which did not reverse the downward trend. The firm's treasury dwindled. Wildcat strikes stopped production frequently in the 1980s. Arrears on payments to suppliers and local banks accumulated. Treasury difficulties in the 1980s led Sotiba–Simpafric to demand cash-on-delivery payments from major buyers, disrupting sales to industrial and commercial clients alike.

Sotiba–Simpafric fared well during the 1975–82 period compared to Icotaf. Contraband and fraud – what the firm's director in 1978 called *importations sauvages* – made Icotaf's products "virtually unsalable." Piece goods liquidated by European manufacturers at rock-bottom prices, imported fraudulently to Senegal, flooded the domestic market. Icotaf incurred losses on almost all sales from 1974 onward. No dividends were paid to stockholders after 1974. Icotaf's financial position deteriorated steadily.[46] Although good rains fueled rural demand for textiles in 1975, Icotaf cut back production, accumulated large stocks, and exported at a loss. One of the government's economic research agencies, SONED, reported that Icotaf's losses were 5 CFA francs per kilo in 1975. By 1977 Icotaf was reporting losses of 169 francs per kilo. In 1980, cumulative

---

43. Information on the contraband trade in *imprimés*, Sotiba–Simpafric's rural marketing problems, and Sotiba's responses is from J.-B. Diouf 1977; GOS, Ministère du Développement Industriel, "Rapport du Groupe du Travail Textile," 25 septembre 1981:24; Fall 1984; and from interviews with management-level personnel at Sotiba, Icotaf, and CCV in November 1984 and April 1985. See SONED 1979: annexe, p. 31; *Le Soleil*, 1 juin 1983:14–16.

44. Fall 1984; Ba 1985; and interviews with former and current employees of Sotiba in November 1984 and April 1985.

45. Sotiba–Simpafric compressed wages by reclassifying workers' job categories (*Le Soleil* [6 novembre 1978]:1). Subsidies are discussed later in this chapter.

46. GOS, Ministère du Développement Industriel, "Rapport sur l'industrie textile," juin 1976; interviews with former Icotaf representative in Mulhouse, April 1986.

losses on sales alone totaled 1.1 billion. The ministry of industry explained simply that "due to market competition and above all to fraud, Icotaf is forced to sell below its costs of production."[47]

The index of industrial production for spinning and weaving fell 22.6 percent between 1974–9 and 29 percent between 1977 and 1980. During this time total output at Icotaf fell by at least 35 percent.[48] The firm operated at less than 40 percent capacity in 1979 (SONED 1980). Compressions of personnel in 1977 were followed by work stoppages, employee walkouts, and the firing of 350 workers. In 1978 Icotaf–Rufisque was closed. Icotaf did not pay its cotton supplier, SODEFITEX, or the Dakar electric power company that year. To generate cash, Icotaf exported at a loss in 1976, 1977, and 1978. The firm's finances were described as "catastrophic" by government auditors in 1978 who determined that Icotaf's debts exceeded by far the returns that could be generated by liquidating the company.[49]

Massive government subsidies kept Icotaf hobbling along but did not redress the marketing problem. In 1978 Icotaf's owners informed the prime minister of their intention to close down completely because, they said, "no industry is viable in the face of *importations sauvages.*" Icotaf's director explained to the press in Senegal that "our firm has experienced losses over the last three years that are not tolerable. Orders from our clients have been reduced to zero. The problem lies in the abnormal importation of very low-priced goods which has become possible in the last few years."[50] Icotaf was kept open through most of the 1980s at great government expense.

The crisis that emerged in the basic textile industry was evidenced most dramatically in production cutbacks, layoffs, arrears in payments to suppliers and creditors, and ultimately in the closure of firms. Although records of total sales (*chiffre d'affaires*) reported by firms in the sector tended to be rather unreliable, they do show that important drops in sales revenues were registered throughout the basic textile industry after 1975 (see Table 6.1). Increases in exports (thanks to a new export subsidy program, discussed below) account for much of the growth observed in 1981–3. Sotiba's exports, which had totaled 25 percent of production in early 1980, had risen to 65 percent of production by 1983. Sotiba's

47. GOS, Ministère du Développement Industriel, "Rapport du Groupe du Travail Textile," 25 septembre 1981:9–10. Figure on losses per kilo in 1975 is from SONED 1980: annexe. In 1976 losses amounted to 15 percent of total sales. In 1981 losses on sales totaled 200 million CFA francs.

48. This index measures production at STS and Icotaf. STS's production remained constant over the course of the 1974–80 period (Ministère du Développement Industriel, "Rapport du Groupe du Travail Textile," 25 septembre 1981: 3).

49. On the crisis at Icotaf, see *Le Soleil* (6 novembre 1978): 1; *Taxaw* (Dakar), no. 10 (juin 1978): 8; and SONED 1980: annexe, pp. 11–13. Icotaf was in *cessation de paiement* to SODEFITEX and SENELEC in 1978 (GOS, Mission de Contrôle de l'Application du Contrat-Programme Icotaf, 6 janvier 1982). Information was also drawn from GOS, Ministère du Développement Industriel, "Rapport sur l'industrie textile," juin 1976, and a November 1984 interview with a former employee of the Sotiba Group.

50. *Africa* (Dakar), "Entretien avec M. Paul Warnier, Directeur de l'Icotaf," no. 103 (1978):25–7.

Table 6.1. *Change in sales revenues: Sotiba, Icotaf, STS, 1975–83*

Year	Sales, current value[a]			Growth, base 1975 (constant prices)[b]		
	Sotiba	Icotaf	STS	Sotiba	Icotaf	STS
1975	7,500	2,200	1,323			
1976	6,500	n.a.	1,200	−14	n.a.	−11
1977	6,700	n.a.	1,500	−20	n.a.	+1
1978	7,000	2,157	1,546	−20	−15	0
1979	8,000	2,400	1,300	−17	−14	−23
1980	9,300	2,429	1,431	−11	−20	−22
1981	15,630	2,495	1,643	+41	−23	−15
1982	18,880	3,206	2,300	+45	−15	0
1983	14,000	3,700	2,600	−3	−13	+1

[a] In million CFA francs.
[b] As deflated by the Consumer Price Index.
Sources: *Le Fichier Industriel*, 1975–83; *Le Sénégal en Chiffres*, 1982–3; *Afrique Industrie*, 1 nov. 1984; SONED 1979.

domestic sales also rose sharply in 1981–2. There is a particular explanation for this.

In 1981 Gambia's President Jawara, overthrown by a coup d'état while traveling abroad, called on Senegal to intervene militarily to restore order in the Gambian capital and reinstate his regime. Senegal obliged. Its military forces occupied the Gambia in late 1981 and 1982. During the period of occupation, the Senegalese army controlled the border and effectively suppressed the Senegal–Gambia contraband trade.[51] Although the occupation of the Gambia coincided with a catastrophic groundnut harvest which reduced rural spending power considerably, domestic market sales of made-in-Senegal fabrics increased by 45 percent in late 1981. For Sotiba–Simpafric 1981–2 was a boom year. Its export sales and domestic market sales totaled 19 billion CFA francs, breaking all past records for marketing revenues. The temporary respite from contraband also allowed Icotaf to liquidate stocks on the domestic market. The situation in Gambia normalized at the end of 1982, when Senegalese troops were withdrawn. Contraband circuits were reconstituted, and Sotiba–Simpafric's sales on the domestic market fell from 7 billion francs in 1980/81 to 4.9 billion in 1983 (in current values).[52]

Senegal's military occupation of Gambia gave birth to the Senegambia Con-

51. From interviews with management personnel and ESGE interns working in the Dakar textile industry, April 1985; and from GOS, Mission du contrôle de l'application du contrat-programme Icotaf, 6 janvier 1982. See *Promotion*, no. 21 (7 mars 1985); Ba 1985.
52. GOS, Ministère du Développement Industriel, "Etude sur le secteur textile au Sénégal dans la définition du prix de cession du coton," janvier 1985.

federation. The centerpiece of this project was a customs and monetary union that would bring Gambian import control and taxation policies more closely in line with Senegal's.[53] In spite of much diplomatic and technocratic activity, moves toward economic union – the "most delicate and sensitive" aspect of the federation project – never got past the planning stage. One Dakar journal wrote that all efforts toward economic union floundered on the resistance of Senegalese and Gambian *hommes d'affaires* who "constitute a united pressure group ferociously opposed to Senegambian economic integration . . . for motives of self-interest that are obvious to everyone."[54] No doubt the *hommes d'affaires* were supported on this issue by the majority of Senegal's rural population. In 1989 the confederation was dissolved. On the Senegalese side, political constraints once again ruled out moves to reconstitute the structures of market control that had, in an earlier period, provided both the textile industry and the state treasury with a revenue base.

Collapse of the secondary segment of the industry

Overall output and the number of firms in the secondary segment of the textile industry grew steadily between 1968 and 1973. In 1975 fifteen knitting and garment-making firms, employing a total workforce of about 600, existed in Senegal. Most of these were Lebanese- and French-owned knitting firms, protected by heavy taxes and quantitative restrictions on imported knitwear. Four or five artisanal-scale garment firms employing fifteen to twenty workers each were created by Senegalese entrepreneurs in the early 1970s. Some of them were implanted in SONEPI's *domaine industriel.* La SIV, the only industrial-scale firm producing garments of woven cloth, specialized in filling contract orders for the government. Together, all firms in this segment of the industry supplied about 50 percent of the officially estimated market for clothing in the early 1970s (SONED 1979:51, 104).

Friperie imports destroyed this segment of the textile industry. New and used clothes imported as *friperie* sold for retail prices ranging from 10 to 50 percent of the factory-door prices of locally made goods. In 1976 and 1977 the volume of registered *friperie* imports exceeded the volume of locally produced clothing by a ratio of more than ten to one.[55] Senegal's ministry of industry documented financial losses and massive stocking in this segment of the industry in 1976 and described the situation as critical. The ministry argued that "rapid and severe

53. Throughout the 1970s the Senegalese government had accused the Gambians of "economic aggression" in the form of smuggling. The Gambians were unmoved. Events of 1981–2 allowed the Senegalese government to "extract cooperation" from Gambian officials on the customs union project.

54. *Liberté,* "Sénégambie: L'union traine les pieds," no. 1 (1 mars 1985): 25.

55. Registered imports of *friperie* in 1976–7 totaled 2500 tons. The output of local knitting firms was 165 tons in 1976 and 1977. See SONED 1979:51, 104–5. Information on the market for used clothes is from interviews at the ministry of finance, textile manufacturing firms, and the Centre Sénégalais du Commerce Extérieur, November and December 1984.

restrictions must be placed on the importation of *friperie* to save the knitting and garment-making sector."[56]

On paper, the market was well-protected. In 1975 registered imports of clothing were below 1968 levels. Local knitting firms specialized in T-shirts, underwear, and baby clothes. Importation of these products was banned from 1977 onward. Yet *friperie* and fraud developed with impressive force. Production and sales in the secondary segment of the textile industry fell by more than half between 1977 and 1980 alone.[57] Nearly all of the knitting firms had declared bankruptcy and/or shut down by 1982.

MABOSE and TMS were the only knitting firms to survive into the 1980s, and after 1985 they too would close. Production at MABOSE fell by half between 1975 and 1976.[58] By the late 1970s the firm had laid off 60 percent of its workers, cut production drastically, and closed down its synthetic blends department. MABOSE was cut off from bank credit in 1985 when production fell below 30 percent of capacity. TMS also reduced its workforce by 60 percent between 1975 and 1980. Stocks at TMS tripled in the late 1970s and losses led the firm's European shareholders to pull out in 1978. By the early 1980s three-quarters of its knitting operation was closed. "We cannot compete with *friperie* and fraud."[59] In 1988 TMS no longer existed.

In garment-making, all the smaller firms closed while La SIV hung on by a thread, working at 30 percent capacity in 1979. Loans not repaid to the national development bank were converted to BNDS equity in La SIV in the mid-1970s, making the bank 85 percent owner of the firm by 1977. La SIV's losses and debts exceeded 2 billion CFA francs in 1983. Contract orders for government uniforms made occasional work for a skeleton crew, reduced from 350 in 1973 to about 70 in 1985.

One Dakar publication reported that "La SIV has been killed by *friperie* and Sandaga market."[60] Applying this argument to the case of La SIV, however, was an act of overgeneralization. La SIV's major problem in the mid-1980s was the government's inability to pay its bills, to contract new orders, and to offer new loans. Like the fortunes of many government-sponsored firms created to fill government contracts, the fortunes of La SIV were linked directly to the financial health of the government. One analyst summed up the problem this way: "One of the biggest problems facing local firms at this time [1984] is the bankruptcy of

56. GOS, Ministère du Développement Industriel, "Rapport sur l'industrie textile," juin 1976.
57. From interviews at MABOSE and the Centre Sénégalais du Commerce Extérieur in November 1984; and GOS, Ministère du Développement Industriel, "Rapport du Groupe du Travail Textile," 25 septembre 1981:3; and Diouf and Kanté 1984. See *Marchés Tropicaux* (30 mars 1968):877; ibid. (17 février 1978):483–4.
58. From interviews at MABOSE in November 1984 and April 1985.
59. From interviews with TMS management in November 1984.
60. *Liberté*, no. 1 (1 mars 1985):20. Information on La SIV is from *Le Fichier Industriel*, 15 janvier 1976; Bossard Consultants (for the Centre Sénégalais du Commerce Extérieur), "La SIV: Etude de préfaisabilité pour la réhabilitation de l'usine actuelle," n.d. (1981?); Tall 1982; and interviews at La SIV.

the government. The government can't pay its bills, forcing them to go under."[61] La SIV was an example.

Household textile goods: "concurrence déloyale"

The banning of imported, staple blankets from the local market in 1961 allowed SCT and Icotaf to cover domestic demand in this product category in the 1960s and early 1970s. In 1974 SCT assumed monopoly control over the local production of blankets. A second firm specializing in household textile goods opened in 1974. ISLIMA, a Belgian venture with Senegalese participation, was established with plans to supply 50 percent of domestic demand for terry-cloth products (mostly towels). It also hoped to export. It was granted generous concessions under the Senegalese Investment Code and a local monopoly on the production of terry cloth, along with substantial tariff protection against imports.[62] This investment, as it turned out, was singularly ill-timed. ISLIMA never functioned normally.

Official import statistics showed that the local industry covered one-half of Senegalese demand for blankets, towels, and other household textile goods (*linge de maison*) in 1976 and 1977. Meanwhile, large quantities of inexpensive Chinese goods passed illegally into Senegal via the Gambia. At the Port of Dakar, low-cost goods passed through customs untaxed and/or grossly undervalued.[63] Fraudulent and contraband imports swamped the local market for household textile goods in 1974. For SCT and ISLIMA, the results were disastrous.

Production at SCT fell by 50 percent after 1976. Production cutbacks did not keep pace with the constant regression of local sales. The firm manager reported that "well-organized and deeply entrenched parallel market circuits have disrupted production and forced us to carry large stocks from one year to the next." Personnel was compressed by 30 percent and temporary work stoppages (*chômages techniques*) became frequent and protracted. SCT suffered financial losses every year after 1975. Total losses reached 65 million CFA francs in 1981.[64]

ISLIMA lost money during its first year of existence and every year thereafter. What the owners called "unfair competition [*concurrence déloyale*] from smuggled Asian goods" forced ISLIMA to operate at 20 percent of capacity. In 1984 the factory closed down for a 14-month workers' strike precipitated by the elimination of nonwage benefits. After one year of *chômage technique*, stocks

61. From an interview at the IFC (World Bank Group) in Washington, D.C., October 1984.
62. GOS, Ministère du Plan et de la Coopération, Comité Interministériel des Investissements, *Dossier sur l'ISLIMA*, 1974.
63. According to one report, for example, blankets from the United States were imported fraudulently at a cost of $9–14 a dozen. They were sold to local retailers for 5,500 CFA francs each (about $20). The importer collected substantial returns (from interviews at the Foire Internationale de Dakar, Journée Textile, November 1984).
64. From interviews at SCT in April 1985; and GOS, Ministère du Plan et de la Coopération, Comité Interministériel des Investissements, *Dossier #34044*, 1982.

from three years back still sat in ISLIMA's warehouse. Cumulative losses over the 1975–83 period totalled nearly 200 million CFA francs.[65]

Vertical disintegration

The Senegalese government relied on an escalating structure of tariff protection to encourage vertical integration in the textile industry. Downstream (final stage) producers were "compensated" for the high cost of locally made intermediate goods by higher tariffs on imported finished products. As the overall structure of tariff protection eroded in the 1970s, final-stage producers sought to cut costs by using cheaper, imported inputs. The horizontally-segmented structure of the industry facilitated this process. Some finishing industries simply abandoned their domestic suppliers. Others were able to use monopoly buyer positions to force upstream producers to sell below production costs. Local value-added in the textile industry fell by 25 percent (in current prices) between 1974 and 1979.[66] The bulk of this drop can be attributed to the growing use of imported *écru* as a base for dyeing and printing at Icotaf and Sotiba–Simpafric.

Faced with unprecedented competition in the mid-1970s, Icotaf cut costs by importing inexpensive gray cloth from the Far East and the Côte d'Ivoire.[67] Its own *écru* became "surplus" production. Some of this surplus was sold in Europe: Icotaf exported over one million meters of cloth and 200 tons of thread, sold at a loss of 30 percent, in 1976. The following year Icotaf repeated this operation on a slightly larger scale.[68] Part of Icotaf's problem was solved when it shut down the Rufisque weaving factory in 1978, terminating employment for over 300 workers.

Sotiba–Simpafric was obliged by contract to purchase all of STS's output of gray cloth. In the mid-1970s Sotiba cut costs by importing more *écru* from the Far East and by using its monopoly buyer position to force down STS's asking price. Profit margins at STS fell from nearly 20 percent in 1972 to 0.4 percent in 1975.[69] A 1977–9 investment program was shelved because treasury reserves were depleted. Beginning in 1978 Sotiba–Simpafric forced STS to sell below its production costs. STS lost 127 million CFA francs in 1979 and generated losses

65. GOS, Ministère du Développement Industriel, "Rapport du Groupe du Travail Textile," 25 septembre 1981: annexe 3; FIDUSEN, Société d'Expertise Comptable, "Analyse de gestion sur les quatre derniers exercices [ISLIMA]," 1984; and interviews with ISLIMA directors in 1984.
66. Value-added in the textile industry fell from 6.4 billion CFA francs in 1974 to 4.9 billion in 1979 (GOS, Ministère du Développement Industriel, "Rapport du Groupe du Travail Textile," 25 septembre 1981:3).
67. Diouck 1986; *Taxaw*, no. 9 (mai 1978):6; and interviews with ESGE interns in December 1985.
68. Icotaf exported 1.4 million meters of cloth and 255 tons of thread in 1976. In 1977 Icotaf exported 2 million meters of cloth and 250 tons of thread. See SONED 1980: annexe 3, pp. 11–13. Senegal's external trade figures show a dramatic jump in exports of *écru* between 1972 and 1973. See Centre du Commerce International (UNCTAD/GATT) 1975:100.
69. World Bank, *The Economic Trends and Prospects of Senegal*, vol. 3: *The Industrial Sector*, unpub. ms., December 1979:63 (restricted circulation); GOS, Ministère du Développement Industriel, "Rapport sur l'industrie textile," juin 1976.

again in 1980 and 1981. Production began to fall and the workforce was reduced.
STS exported to Europe at a loss to liquidate stocks. The manager said "we were
strangled by Sotiba." In the early 1980s Sotiba–Simpafric's imports of Chinese
écru covered 75 percent of its demand for intermediate goods. Meanwhile, STS
fell into arrears with the electric company, the banks, and SODEFITEX, its
cotton supplier.[70] By 1988 STS had closed down completely.

Dakar's knitting firms were designed as partially integrated operations. They
used imported synthetic yarn as well as cotton yarn that was spun locally by
CCV. In the early 1970s the knitting firms consumed 40–50 percent of CCV's
output. With the demise of the knitting segment of the textile industry, CCV lost
its largest market. Like the other firms in the industry, CCV was forced to cut
production and carry stocks after 1975.[71] The two surviving knitting firms in
Senegal – MABOSE and TMS – began to substitute cheaper, imported knit
fabric for fabric they formerly produced themselves.[72] The integrated knitwear
factories were reduced to assembly operations, sewing garments made from
imported cloth.

Between 1977 and 1980 the index of industrial production for all Senegalese
manufacturing dropped by 10 percent. Senegal was hit by hard times, and this
certainly ruled out possibilities for real expansion of the Dakar textile industry in
the late 1970s and 1980s. The *dégradation de la conjoncture économique*, however, does not explain the near-total collapse of the textile industry during this
period. The market for made-in-Senegal textile goods began to disintegrate during the *conjoncture favorable* of 1974–7. Firms' profit margins were hit first,
and then they began to cut back production. One source reported that in 1981, the
production index for Senegal's textile industry was .79 of its 1969 level.[73] This
suggests that production and value-added had slumped to near 1965–6 levels.
Indices of production for textiles would continue to plunge in the early 1980s.
The Economist reported a 21 percent drop in production and value-added in the
basic textile industry between 1982 and early 1984. In 1985, production in the
secondary segment of the industry (plus leather industries, i.e. shoes) was 44
percent of its 1976 level.[74]

Production problems particular to the textile industry – antiquated capital
stock, inefficiency, etc. – are a necessary but insufficient explanation for the
nose-dive that textile manufacturing in Senegal took in the 1970s. These problems are constants in the history of the industry. They date back to the early

70. STS's workforce was reduced from 270 to 230 in 1979. The STS crisis was discussed in GOS,
    Ministère du Développement Industriel, "Rapport du Groupe du Travail Textile," 25 septembre
    1981; during interviews with a *conseiller technique* at *la Présidence* in April 1985; and in
    interviews with the director of STS in Thiès, January 1986.
71. From interviews at CCV in December 1985. See *Taxaw*, no. 10 (juin 1978):8.
72. From interviewees working for the ministries of industry and finance, November 1984.
73. GOS, Ministère du Développement Industriel, "Rapport du Groupe du Travail Textile," 25
    septembre 1981; UNIDO, "Country Brief: Senegal," 11 March 1982.
74. *The Economist, Quarterly Economic Review: Senegal, The Gambia, Guinea-Bissau, Cape Ver-
    de*, no. 1 (1986):22–3.

1960s and early 1970s, when the industry grew and was extremely profitable. The Dakar textile industry plunged into crisis in the mid-1970s because the system of import control that was designed to protect the industry from foreign competition was put to other ends. Through this process, the system of import control fell apart. Control over the textile trade shifted to domestic commercial interests formerly excluded from the textile trade, and to parts of the state apparatus that were most responsive to new demands for access to quick, low-risk, high-rent commercial opportunities. Politically mediated changes in the locus of control over the textile market undermined the privileged position of interests linked to local textile manufacturing.

THE STATE: CAPTURED BY CONTRADICTORY PRIVATE INTERESTS

The crisis in the textile industry was shaped by contradictory responses on the part of leaders of a regime who were torn between their interest in sustaining the process of light industrialization on the one hand and their need to sustain their own bases of political support on the other. At the level of economic planning, the growth of the textile industry was a high-priority goal in the 1970s. The government's commitment to light industrialization never wavered, and import controls remained the cornerstone of this project. Yet enforcing these import controls was difficult for institutional reasons, because state agents responsible for enforcing them were involved themselves in the unregulated and "irregular" textile trade, and for political reasons, because the stability of the regime became ever more dependent on its ability to make commercial rents available to strategic members of a spoils-oriented ruling alliance and political class. After the mid-1970s there was no effective action on the part of the regime to enforce restrictions on textile imports. Yet judging by government actions during this period, allowing the textile industry to collapse completely was unacceptable. Subsidizing the industry directly was the makeshift response to this dilemma. Net result: two powerful groups of private actors working at cross-purposes – industrialists and Senegalese importers – both collected rents and subsidies at the expense of a weakening and fragmented government that was on the verge of bankruptcy.

"State interests" versus the regime's political needs

Over the course of the 1970s the government's capacity to siphon resources out of the traditional circuit of merchant capital – the import–export trade – deteriorated dramatically, with catastrophic results for public finances. In effect, the state lost its prime internal source of revenue. Breakdown of the system of import control crippled the capacity of the government to tax what had long been, and what remained, its leading source of fiscal receipts. Taxes on imports generated about 40 percent of all government receipts in 1967/68. In 1980 this figure was still 40 percent, not because import tax receipts were maintained at 1968 levels, but because all internal sources of government revenue (most notably fiscal receipts from the groundnut trade) dwindled.[75]

One 1980 study estimated that contraband alone cost the government 38 billion CFA francs, or almost 30 percent of total fiscal receipts collected from all sources in that year. This estimate of the cost to the government of the contraband trade represents a ninefold increase (in current values) over a 1969 estimate of the fiscal drain created by the Senegal–Gambia contraband circuit.[76] The costs of fraud compounded the drain on the state treasury. Customs records indicate that by the mid-1980s, the government collected almost no taxes on textile imports. Private traders who were able to circumvent taxes profited at the government's expense.

The rise of unregulated textile markets not only contributed to the impoverishment of the state in the 1970s, but also made official goals for the development of textile production virtually impossible to realize. Yet government planners' commitment to the growth of this industry, and the regime's financial investment in this project, escalated considerably over the course of the decade. The industrial transformation of Senegalese cotton and further import substitution in textiles were "major axes" of the Fifth and Sixth (1977–86) Development Plans.

In 1976 the ministry of industry argued that "the size of the national market for textile goods opens possibilities for the extension of existing firms and the implantation of new ones at all stages of the textile manufacturing process."[77] Senghor's position was that "national markets for our import-substitution industries are far from exhausted."[78] The Fifth Plan, drawn up in 1975 and 1976, discusses the textile industry at length:

> Cotton production is growing rapidly. It is essential for the national collectivity that this cotton be transformed in Senegal into textile products. . . . Our goal is to triple the amount of cotton processed by the local industry and to cover 88 percent of domestic market demand for textile goods by 1981. . . . An integrated textile industry thus constitutes a major axis of national industrial development in the 1977–1981 period.[79]

Senegal adopted a "selective" policy of industrial development in 1976 which concentrated state efforts on *secteurs de choix dits prioritaires*. These "priority sectors" were based on the industrial transformation of domestic raw materials: the fishing industry, the chemical industry (processing phosphates), and the cotton textile industry.[80]

---

75. World Bank, "Sénégal: Memorandum Economique," unpub. ms., 5 novembre 1984 (restricted circulation).
76. *Africa* (no. 47 [1969]:25–53) estimated that smuggling across the Senegalese-Gambian border cost the state 4–5 billion CFA francs in import taxes in 1969. In 1979–80, the Government of Senegal collected about 53 billion CFA francs in import taxes and duties, out of total fiscal receipts of 130.6 billion (World Bank, "Sénégal: Memorandum Economique," unpub. ms., 5 novembre 1984 [restricted circulation]).
77. GOS, Ministère du Développement Industriel, "Rapport sur l'industrie textile," juin 1976.
78. President Senghor, address to the Conseil Economique et Social, 25 March 1977, Dakar (as reported by *Marchés Tropicaux* [1 avril 1977]:766).
79. GOS, Ministère du Plan et de la Coopération 1977a:91–9. Senegal produced 4,000 tons of cotton in 1970 and 15,000 tons in 1975.
80. The other priority sector was tourism.

Between 1977 and 1985 the government outlined ambitious goals for import substitution in the textile sector.[81] It planned to replace imported intermediate textile goods (*écru*) with locally made inputs, create 3,000 new jobs in the textile industry, and double production destined for the local market. Both the Fifth and Sixth Plans stated that success hinged on "reconquering the domestic market for textiles." The ministries of planning and industry argued consistently in the 1970s that government goals for the textile industry "will not be achieved unless fraudulent importation is suppressed. This requires rigorous measures at the level of import control and above all, a crackdown on those engaging in illegal trading activity (*répression vis-à-vis des fraudeurs*)."[82]

In 1969, the year smuggling first emerged as a national issue, a Dakar publication with links to the local French business community argued that "the government can easily attack fraud and reduce it to 'acceptable' proportions. This is a matter of political will, not means. It is obvious that severe sanctions must be enforced vis-à-vis state agents responsible for carrying out the law."[83] *Le Soleil*, the national daily, argued in 1978 that "it is time to choose between *friperie* and

---

81. The government also envisioned a new branch of textile manufacturing: one aimed at export markets. A *grand projet* in the style of others of the period – financed by loans contracted abroad and guaranteed by the state – slowly took shape. A planned investment of 8 billion CFA francs was to finance the building and equipment of an integrated spinning, knitting, and garment assembly complex: SOTEXKA (Société Textile de Kaolack). In addition to guaranteeing the loans, the government owned 28 percent of this project. Two factories were to be built: a cloth-making unit in Kaolack and a garment-making unit in Louga. The government paid a high economic premium in choosing these politically strategic sites, remote from the country's main industrial center and port. Kaolack was the economic and political capital of the groundnut basin. Djilly MBaye, a prominent Mouride businessman linked to the confrérie, would be invited into the project as a private shareholder, owning a 28 percent stake in the project. (Other private Senegalese shareholders owned 11 percent of SOTEXKA.) Louga, at the center of one of Senegal's oldest groundnut-growing regions, happened to be the hometown of then Prime Minister Abdou Diouf. The World Bank declined to participate in what it deemed to be an "uneconomic" project. Financing was found elsewhere, most notably from the Banque Islamique de Développement, which acquired a 20 percent share in the project. By the early 1980s huge sums of capital had been borrowed abroad and disbursed, but no factories existed. New loans were contracted. In the mid-1980s factories existed but had yet to begin operations. In the late 1980s the Kaolack factory opened, operated for a short time at 20 percent of capacity, and then shut down because the firm had no treasury to finance its operations. The total cost of the project had reached 24 billion CFA francs. Equipment purchased in the 1970s was now anti-quated by world standards; hopes for exporting had evaporated. Dakar's basic textile industry remained firmly opposed to the SOTEXKA project over the course of the entire period, antic-ipating (correctly) that whatever SOTEXKA produced would end up on the domestic market. For the state, the SOTEXKA project was a major fiasco. The beneficiaries were the project's equipment supplier (Maurer Textiles, which along with Europ Continents held 13 percent of SOTEXKA's shares) and the private parties who succeeded in absorbing a large share of the 24 billion francs that had been contracted over the course of fifteen yeas to finance this project. As one observer said, "SOTEXKA was a political thing." See *Marchés Tropicaux*, no. 2,143 (5 décembre 1986):3,106.

82. GOS, Ministère du Développement Industriel, "Rapport du Groupe du Travail Textile," 25 septembre 1981:21–2; GOS, Ministère du Plan et de la Coopération, Commission Nationale de Planification (n. B-6), *Rapport Provisoire*, 1982: 6.

83. *Africa*, "La Fraude: un fléau national," no. 47 (1969): 25–53.

the textile industry."[84] By the late 1970s the political contingencies of the situation dictated the outcome of this choice.

The political clout of what one Dakar journal called the smuggling lobby was enormous.[85] Powerful domestic commercial interests were not only located within the ruling coalition itself, but also in networks of rentiers ensconced in a sprawling bureaucracy of administrative and parastatal institutions. The Mouride confrérie and Mouride leaders had come to depend upon the import trade as a source of revenue. Rents generated in state-mediated commerce were playing an increasingly important role in fueling the system of political clientelism, generating mercenary support for the regime, and sustaining a weakening ruling coalition.

The regime's tendency to turn to commercial rents as a source of patronage was apparent in the 1960s, conspicuous in the 1970s, and all-consuming in the 1980s. Under the presidency of Abdou Diouf, the near-bankruptcy of the state and the external debt crisis eviscerated the regime's capacity to rely upon hiring and lending as sources of patronage. The commercial sector was a source of rents that could be transferred from French commercial and industrial interests to *hommes d'affaires senégalais*. By tolerating fraud and contraband, the regime could also engage in a roundabout operation that transferred (forfeited) state revenues into private hands. This is what happened.

The dilemmas that paralyzed the regime in the face of contraband and fraud transcended the need to buy the support of strategic segments of the ruling coalition and the political class. A population that was increasingly alienated from, and exasperated with, the regime and the ruling class amassed in the cities in the late 1970s and 1980s. The unregulated import circuits controlled by the Mourides had come to serve as economic infrastructure for drawing an important part of this population, albeit in indirect and tenuous ways, into the established political order. Mouride leaders organized followings within these commercial circuits and were thus able to extend (or maintain) their political influence even as part of their social base "exited" from the groundnut economy. As the threat of mass anger began to worry the regime as much as the problem of generating votes for the ruling party, maintaining the organizational structures of the confrérie and influence of the Mouride marabouts over their followers took on renewed urgency. Weakening the material base of the confrérie by cracking down on contraband was an option that ran directly counter to the regime's short-term political needs and interests.

Meanwhile, extensive parallel market circuits and *friperie* distribution networks generated income for innumerable middlemen and retailers both inside and outside the confrérie, offering employment that neither the state nor the "formal sector" could provide to an increasingly impoverished population. Contraband, fraud, and *friperie* also clothed the Senegalese who were hit the hardest by inflation, drought, and the government austerity programs that compressed

84. *Le Soleil*, "Crise de textile: la friperie mise en cause?," 6 novembre 1978:1.
85. *Liberté*, "Le Textile: la mort en fraude," no. 1 (1 mars 1985): 20.

standards of living in the late 1970s and 1980s. After the government raised the prices of bread, rice, oil, and urban transport repeatedly in the late 1970s and early 1980s, one official in the ministry of commerce considered the option of suppressing the irregular and unregulated textile trade. He remarked that "it is politically unwise to squeeze the people on all fronts simultaneously."

After decades of French monopolies over high-profit markets for textile goods, it was impossible to ignore the fact that unregulated and irregular markets were controlled by Senegalese businessmen, and that they provided consumers with something foreign-controlled markets did not supply: low-cost goods to meet basic needs. The local union publication cited at the beginning of this chapter summarized the core of this legitimation problem it asked in 1978, "[I]n whose name, and on the basis of what justification, should we sacrifice the *friperie* trade for the benefit of *les industriels français du textile?*"[86]

Le Soleil reported that "[b]ehind the textile war, enormous interests are at stake."[87] It is difficult to overstate this point. The crisis in the textile industry set "state interests" (i.e., needs of the treasury, development goals) against private interests, commercial interests against industrial interests, and Senegalese interests against foreign interests. Most fundamentally, the regime's need to sustain established patterns of economic growth and revenue extraction was pitted directly against its short-term interest in remaining in power. During the twilight years of Senghor's rule and the decade of his successor, these trade-offs paralyzed the regime's ability to mediate contradictory pressures in a way that would guarantee the interests of "the state" or the interests of capital operating in Senegal. This outcome reflected the weakening of the state as an instrument for organizing the use of power.

Concessions to manufacturers: Shifting financial losses onto the state

In the 1970s the owners of the Dakar textile industry pressured the government with demands for effective protection against competing imports and for state subsidies. The government responded by steadily increasing tariff rates and by instituting progressively more restrictive systems of import licensing. These measures did not stem the rise of smuggling and fraud, and the regime resisted all pressures to put an end to the *friperie* trade. Yet as losses mounted in the textile industry, the ability of the industrialists to extract financial concessions from the government was enhanced. Cost-of-production subsidies, commercial subsidies, and outright state grants kept the major firms in the industry afloat for at least a decade – from the late 1970s through the mid-1980s.

Faced with deepening crisis in the textile industry, the government met manufacturers' demands for new import quotas, *valeurs mercuriales*, and taxes on

---

86. *Taxaw*, "Textile: halte aux manoeuvres contre les hommes d'affaires sénégalais," no. 12 (août 1978): 4.
87. *Le Soleil*, "Les friperiers: Non! Nous ne sommes pas responsables de la crise du textile" (7 novembre 1978): 1.

imports. Import duties were reimposed on EEC products in 1977. Duties on all imports were raised in 1979 and twice again in 1980. A *valeur mercuriale* of 300 CFA francs per kilo for *friperie* was imposed in 1976 and quadrupled in the early 1980s. Manufacturers demanded more extreme measures.

In 1978 the government instituted the most restrictive licensing system for textile imports that Senegal had ever known. Now all textile imports – regardless of origin, nature, and value – were placed under a new, severely restrictive licensing (*autorisation préalable*) system.[88] Each and every import transaction, with the notable exception of *friperie*, would now require prior state authorization. Requests for authorization were subjected to the review and veto of a textile commission composed of representatives of each firm in the industry. The commission was mandated to veto requests to import anything likely to compete with locally made textile goods. The ministry of commerce, charged with the bureaucratic task of issuing licenses, was to follow the recommendations of the textile commission.

The licensing system introduced in 1978 was ineffective for two reasons. First, textile imports by-passed or skimmed through the official bureaucratic circuit in ever larger volumes. Second, the ministry of commerce did not respect the veto of the textile commission. The "abusive and anarchic" distribution of *autorisations préalables* remained characteristic of the licensing process.[89] By the early 1980s several commission members deemed participation to be a waste of time.

On paper, the textile industry was more protected from import competition after 1978 than it had ever been in the past. The ministry of industry reported a regular fall in registered textile imports, and a marked drop after 1978. The ministry added that this fall was accompanied by a surge in fraud and smuggling.[90] As it became overwhelmingly clear that formal import controls were no longer effective, manufacturers demanded that the government suppress illegal importation through the use of force. They supplied the customs service and police with names and addresses of known *fraudeurs* and demanded that search and seizure operations be conducted in merchants' shops and warehouses. The government declined to act, arguing such maneuvers were too costly. Manufacturers then offered to finance seizure operations. In the 1980s the Senegalese customs service was not provided with the vehicles, petrol, or personnel required to control the borders adequately or to circulate in Dakar. Textile manufacturers

---

88. *Le Journal Officiel du Sénégal, loi n. 78–200 du 11 mars 1978*, was intended "to limit textile imports strictly, so as to reserve a large part of the national market for the local industry. . . . The only imports that will be authorized are those that will not compete with locally produced goods." On the operation of this system, see *Marchés Tropicaux* (22 septembre 1978): 2,511; SONED 1979:33.

89. *Lien Economique*, mars 1979: *Le Soleil* (1 juin 1983): 14–16; GOS, Ministère du Développement Industriel, "Rapport de la commission chargée de l'étude sur le secteur textile," 9 janvier 1985; and interviews at MABOSE, SONEPI, SCT, and the ministry of finance, November 1984 through November 1985.

90. GOS, Ministère du Développement Industriel, "Rapport du Groupe du Travail Textile," 25 septembre 1981.

offered to provide the border control contingent with vehicles and petrol. The government resisted these pressures.[91] In 1981 Abdou Diouf issued a call for "the enforcement of legislation on the books" and the "normal and rigorous functioning of the customs control service."[92]

The industry was much more successful in obtaining large financial subsidies from the government. In the 1970s declining or negative rates of profit made industrialists' threats to simply close down the largest textile firms quite credible. Sunk costs had been amortized many times over. The value of capital stock was low because owners had avoided investments in modernization.[93] The largest manufacturers did not hesitate to remind the authorities that factory shutdowns would contribute to "revolutionary ferment" in Dakar. In the face of what was popularly perceived as blackmail, the regime responded with financial concessions to the industry.

Concessions were justified by the government on two grounds. First, subsidies would protect employment. The largest textile firms were among the leading private employers in Senegal, and the industry as a whole employed about 9–13 percent of the private sector wage labor force. The government was not interested in seeing these jobs disappear in the context of a deteriorating economic and political situation. It also feared workers' reactions to any attempts to close the major firms. In legal terms, workers in the textile industry had little power. They were subordinated to the government and to employers through the multilayered hierarchical structures, controlled from above, that made up the national-level trade union federation, the CNTS. Although organizing labor in this way weakened the workers' bargaining power, the CNTS structure as a whole had become an increasingly unreliable instrument of control. The government-created union hierarchy was not only the site of complex, internal power struggles (in which the ruling party played a direct role), but also the site of emergent union tendencies that challenged the hegemony of both the CNTS and the PS. Particularly worrisome from the government's perspective was the growing alienation and/or assertiveness (what the authorities called "anarchistic tendencies") of textile workers' syndicates at the firm level. Frequent illegal strikes reflected the more general deterioration of government control over politically strategic segments of the urban population. In the face of deepening crisis within the industry, the government sought to weaken and preempt the mobilization of "autonomous" union tendencies and to use existing union and party structures to ward off a major explosion of workers' frustration. "Protecting employment" in the textile

91. Ibid.; Lettre du Directeur Général de l'ICOTAF au Ministère du Développement Industriel, 16 octobre 1984; *Le Soleil*, 1 juin 1983: 14–16; Fall 1984.
92. GOS, Ministère du Développement Industriel, "Rapport du Groupe du Travail Textile," 25 septembre 1981: 24.
93. After 1973 new investment in the textile industry stagnated at less than one percent of value-added. The ministry of planning reported that of all manufacturing sectors in Senegal, the textile industry was among those investing the least during the period of the Fourth Plan (1974–8). See GOS, Ministère du Plan et de la Coopération 1977b.

industry meant that the government would subsidize firm-level losses to allow employers to compress wages, employment, and nonwage benefits *gradually*.[94]

Officials in the ministry of industry advanced a second rationale for subsidizing financial losses in the textile industry. These officials believed that they could encourage industrialists to invest in modernizing their plants. Modernization would lower costs of production, and thus make the industry more competitive – better equipped to compete with foreign imports. Injecting cash into the industry would provide the industry with the breathing space and resources needed to undertake productivity-enhancing investment. Manufacturers, for their part, accepted subsidies in exchange for explicit commitments to carry out modernization projects that were planned in cooperation with the ministries.

Concessions to the industry did protect some employment in the 1970s and 1980s. Continuous financial transfers from the government allowed the largest firms to remain open while chronic losses on operations accumulated. Manufacturers, however, failed to make good on their commitments to invest in the factories. Even under these conditions, financial transfers to the industry continued unabated in the 1970s and in fact became more substantial over the course of the decade. The pattern was repeated in the 1980s.

Special financial dispositions, ad-hoc cost-of-production and commercial subsidies, fiscal advantages, and outright grants to firms in the textile industry proliferated in the 1970s. In this way losses generated in this industry were transferred from private manufacturers to the state. It began in 1976, when the regime intervened to slow the dramatic deterioration of Icotaf. The government's handling of the Icotaf crisis opened the door to industry-wide demands for state relief and compensation for growing financial losses.

By the time Icotaf's condition had deteriorated to the critical point in 1976, the commitment of Ets. Schaeffer to this firm had already eroded.[95] The Senegalese government stepped in with a massive bailout plan elaborated in the context of a five-year *"contrat-programme."*[96] The program suspended the quasi-totality of

94. Workers were organized into shop-level workers' committees that were linked to textile unions (*syndicats*) in segments (i.e., branches) of the industry. These *syndicats* were subordinate to an umbrella organization, the Fédération des Syndicats Textiles. This federation was subordinate to its own umbrella organization, the CNTS. The government's interest in weakening the textile unions was manifest in its decision in the early 1980s to remove workers in the secondary segment of the industry from the Fédération des Syndicats Textiles. This was followed by a "renewal" of the leadership of the Fédération des Syndicats Textiles when the ruling party engineered a complete "renewal" of CNTS leadership. The result was a split in the textile federation. Tendencies loyal to the old leadership of Ibrihima Guèye (allied with Babacar NDiaye, the deposed leader of the CNTS) refused to recognize the new textile federation leader, Moctar Seye, who was "parachuted" into this position by the new head of the CNTS, Media Diop. At the same time, unions affiliated with opposition parties emerged in some firms in the basic textile industry, underscoring the growing fragmentation of union structures. On the CNTS, the PS, and the autonomous unions in the 1980s, see Diop and Diouf 1990:223–49. Information on the textile unions is also from interviews with agents of the Inspection du Travail in Dakar, and with representatives of factions of the CNTS in November and December 1985.
95. From interviews with former representatives of Ets. Schaeffer in Mulhouse, April 1986.
96. For a description of the Icotaf rehabilitation programs and their failures, see SONED 1980: annexe, pp. 11–13.

Icotaf's fiscal obligations to the state, provided new government subsidies on domestic inputs (cotton, water, and electricity), and exempted Icotaf from duties on imported capital goods and inputs. In return, Icotaf agreed not to reduce its workforce. It also agreed to undertake an extensive modernization program valued at over 4 billion CFA francs. These investments were to be financed by Icotaf revenues earned through the new tax breaks (valued at 1.3 billion francs for 1976–9), through loans to Icotaf from external public lenders (guaranteed by the state), and by the government of Senegal.[97]

During the first year of the *contrat-programme*, Icotaf accepted state subsidies but did not implement Phase One of the investment program. The 1976 arrangements were suspended in 1977 and replaced by a second five-year *contrat-programme*, this one even more generous to Icotaf. The firm collected millions in government subsidies over the next two years but declined to meet its commitments to invest in renovating its factories. By 1978 Icotaf had accumulated almost 2 billion CFA francs in new debts to the state. Over three hundred workers had been laid off, and the Rufisque weaving factory was closed. At that point, it was clear that the second *contrat-programme* had failed like the first.[98]

Icotaf signed a third *contrat-programme* with the government in 1979. This one wrote off 1.4 billion francs in debts to the state and increased subsidy rates for electricity and cotton. Icotaf's remaining debt was rescheduled over a ten-year period. Normal criteria for using the Investment Code to grant tax breaks to private firms were put aside and the firm was raised to the most favorable status under the Code. This exonerated the firm from a new series of fiscal obligations for the next fifteen years. Icotaf promised to "renew its capital stock completely."[99]

Icotaf, under new management after 1981 (see below), continued to avoid investment in renovation in the 1980s. Cut off from the banks in Dakar because of successive defaults on loans and "lack of creditworthiness," it continued to accumulate losses, incur new debts to the state, and collect large operating subsidies from the government. A new government-sponsored modernization program was accepted by Icotaf in 1985, but the planned investments were not made. The spinning and weaving units ceased functioning and Icotaf conducted a marginal business in dyeing imported bazin cloth for sale on the local market. State subsidies averted a complete shutdown of the factory from 1976 to 1987 but the government failed to accomplish its stated objective: the modernization of

97. From interviews with former representatives of Ets. Schaeffer in Mulhouse in April 1986; GOS, Mission du contrôle de l'application du contrat-programme Icotaf, 2 janvier 1982; Rocheteau 1982:116–7.
98. SONED 1980: annexe, pp. 11–13; GOS, Ministère du Développement Industriel, "Rapport du Groupe du Travail Textile," 25 septembre 1981: 3; GOS, Mission du contrôle de l'application du contrat-programme Icotaf, 2 janvier 1982.
99. Information on the 1979 contrat-programme is from GOS, Ministère du Plan et de la Coopération, Comité Interministériel des Investissements, *Dossier Icotaf #34015*, 1979–80; GOS, Ministère du Plan et de la Coopération, Commission Nationale de Planification n. B-6, *Rapport Provisoire*, 1982:4.

Icotaf. One observer commented: "Why should Icotaf bother to invest when it can get everything it wants from the government without doing so?"

Cost-of-production subsidies became the main focus of government dealings with the textile industry as a whole between 1976 and 1981. Water, electricity, and cotton subsidies granted to Icotaf were extended to the other firms. Utilities costs were subsidized for the entire basic textile industry after 1976.[100] The electricity subsidy, set at a rate of about 30 percent, cost the government almost 100 million CFA francs in payments to Icotaf alone in one year: 1980. As cotton prices on world markets climbed erratically after 1975, the government established a fixed local selling price for Senegalese cotton.[101] The fixed price arrangement was renewed by the government every year between 1976 and 1980. The subsidy ranged from 5–35 percent over this period, averaging 20 percent a year and costing the government a total of 2.5 billion francs. The cotton subsidy system was revised in 1981 when the government began to pay a set percentage (about 20 percent) of the local firms' cotton costs.[102] In July 1984 the government set the price of cotton sold to the local industry at 520 CFA francs per kilo. The world market price at that time was 700 francs per kilo; the set price held when world prices climbed to 820 francs in December 1984. A rough estimate of direct cost-of-production subsidies (water, electricity, and cotton only) paid by the government to the textile industry between 1975 and 1985 is 6–7 billion CFA francs.[103]

Icotaf bailouts also paved the way for industry-wide tax breaks. Exonerations from direct and indirect taxes proliferated in the late 1970s and 1980s as firms arranged ad hoc, sweeping tax relief plans with the authorities. New fiscal concessions normally reserved for companies undertaking major investments were granted to large, old firms in the textile industry. This was accomplished by

100. A *fonds de préférence* for electricity was set up for the textile industry in 1976.
101. The selling price of cotton to the local industries was set at 325 CFA francs per kilo. The average world-market price for cotton between 1976–7 and 1980–1 was 404 CFA francs per kilo. On the cotton subsidy from 1976–80, see SONED 1980: annexe no. 1.5.
102. The cotton subsidy was set in 1981 at 17 percent plus *frais non exposés* (export costs: shipping, insurance, etc.). In 1985 world market prices plunged to 350 CFA francs per kilo, relieving pressure on the industry and on the government.
103. The cotton subsidy probably totaled about 4 billion CFA francs over the 1975–85 period. We can estimate electricity and water subsidies to Icotaf during this period at 1 billion francs and double that figure to get an estimate for the entire textile industry. The cotton program was less effective as a tool for subsidizing the textile industry than it might have been because of endless delays, fights, and confusion over who, precisely, was to pay whom. In the 1970s the government paid SODEFITEX the difference between the subsidized local price and the world market price. After 1980 SODEFITEX refused to accept this arrangement, forcing the local industries to pay full price and to seek reimbursement themselves from the government's Caisse de Stabilisation et Péréquation des Prix (CPSP). Because the CPSP claimed to have no cash to pay the local firms, the manufacturers received I.O.U.s from the CPSP. In this way, the government went into debt vis-à-vis the local textile industry. By the mid-1980s Icotaf, STS, and Sotiba–Simpafric refused to pay the government for electricity, telling the electric company, SENELEC, to "go collect the money from the CPSP." In 1990 the CPSP owed SODEFITEX 6 billion CFA francs. The industries owed SODEFITEX 1 billion francs (GOS, Ministère de l'Industrie et de l'Artisanat, "Secteur textile: filature," 22 août 1990).

using the dispositions of the Investment Code.[104] The government saw these exceptional deals as a way of rehabilitating the textile industry.

The single most important – and controversial – tax break granted to the textile industry was the exoneration of all taxes on imported intermediate goods. This 1979 decision allowed the finishing industries to import *écru* from the world's cheapest suppliers in unlimited quantities, duty free.[105] Detaxation of imported *écru* swept away all prospects for increasing the local production of this critical intermediate good. It reversed fifteen years of official efforts to promote the vertical integration of the basic textile industry. The ministry of industry urged the administration to rescind the decision.[106] SONED argued that "the application of this law [detaxing *écrus*] will lead to the pure and simple shutdown of all industrial weaving activity in Senegal, and eventually, to the closure of the spinning firms."[107]

For Sotiba–Simpafric, the tax break on imported écru was worth more than 2 billion CFA francs in 1980. For STS, detaxation of imported *écru* was the beginning of the end. STS quickly lost the market that it had been created to supply – Sotiba's printing factory.[108] STS was left to drown in its losses and to seek financial redress directly from the government.

Removing taxes on unfinished gray cloth also neutralized any incentive Icotaf might have had to modernize its weaving plants. As soon as Icotaf could substitute cheaper imports for *écrus* that it produced itself, the firm began to restructure operations. Icotaf's own weaving plants plunged deeper into disrepair and neglect as the firm concentrated on dyeing bazin. Icotaf imported two million meters of untaxed *écru* every year in the early 1980s. Government loans that were earmarked for modernizing the firm's weaving operations were diverted into increasing the firm's dyeing capacity. In 1985 30 percent of Icotaf's business consisted of "*opérations de négoce*" – i.e., the resale of imported goods that were dyed by Icotaf. In 1988 the Icotaf factory was used for this purpose only.[109]

104. One official at the Ministère du Plan et de la Coopération said that the government's "primary means for rehabilitating the textile industry" during the Sixth Plan [1981–5] was granting the major firms in the industry the most favorable dispositions of Senegal's Investment Code (interview, April 1985).
105. *Le Journal Officiel du Sénégal, loi n. 79-18 du 24 janvier 1979*. This law exonerated all *écrus* and chemical products imported by the textile industry from import taxes. At the time import duties on *écru* were about 65 percent. Duties on imported chemical products were 49 percent. See SONED 1979:88–9 and idem 1979: annexe, pp. 6, 32. In 1980 Sotiba–Simpafric imported 25 million meters of *écru* at 125 CFA francs per meter.
106. GOS, Ministère du Développement Industriel et de l'Artisanat, "Rapport annuel de la Direction de l'Industrie," 1980:24.
107. SONED 1979:88–9 and idem 1979: annexe, p. 32. A detailed cost–benefit study intended to lay the groundwork for the installation of a new weaving factory is presented in SONED 1980.
108. In 1978–9 STS's *écru* sold for 191 CFA francs per meter, compared to 125 CFA francs per meter for Chinese *écru* (SONED 1979: annexe, p. 6).
109. Returns to Icotaf on these *opérations de négoce* averaged 7 percent (with returns of 15 percent in some product lines in the early 1980s) compared to negative rates of return on virtually all goods woven by Icotaf except those sold to the government (Diouck 1986; Julie Senghor, "La Filière Textile au Sénégal [a report prepared for the GOS, Ministère de l'Industrie et de l'Artisanat, Cellule de Restructuration Industrielle]," n.d. [1990?]).

The Dakar textile industry, which consumed about four thousand tons of Senegalese cotton at its peak, consumed only about seven hundred tons by the end of the 1980s.

The government also found a way to provide the industry with direct commercial subsidies. Sales of made-in-Senegal textiles on markets outside of the CEAO, the West African Economic Community, were first subsidized in 1980. The original subsidy of 10 percent of f.o.b. value was raised to 15 percent in 1983.[110] These export rebates allowed textile firms to collect a return on products sold at, or slightly below, costs of production. Exports of Senegalese textile goods, which had been marginal and declining for the industry as a whole in the 1970s,[111] rose as a result in the early 1980s.

Sotiba–Simpafric exports grew from 25 percent of production in 1980 to 65 percent of production in 1981–3. The spinning firm CCV exported 40 percent of its production to its parent firm in France after 1980, collected the export subsidy, and ended up with a 12 percent rate of return on these sales. STS, ISLIMA, and Icotaf did the same thing, clearing out stocks and generating cash.[112] The export subsidy programs were subject to schemes that allowed manufacturers to benefit in unintended ways. For example, Sotiba–Simpafric reportedly collected subsidies on exports to the Gambia. These goods simply reentered Senegal via parallel market circuits. Sotiba–Simpafric's products could be sold at, or just below, cost on the local market while the firm collected a return from the government.

Unwilling and unable to control illegal and fraudulent importation of textile goods, the government resorted to subsidies to stabilize the large firms in the textile industry. These subsidies transferred a growing share of the financial losses generated in this industry from private manufacturers to the state. As the World Bank noted dryly, "the proliferation of *dispositions exceptionnelles* [direct cost-of-production subsidies, fiscal advantages, etc.] has centralized all financial risk in this industry at the level of the government."[113] Meanwhile, the government failed to extract counterpart concessions from the industry in the form of investments in modernization. Analysts in the ministry of finance (1985) commented that the reduction of costs of production in the textile industry through a variety of exonerations from payment of taxes, etc. subsidized (*profité*) firms

---

110. After 1982 the base for calculating this subsidy was supposed to be local value-added, not the f.o.b. value. Textile manufacturers, however, report that they were paid the subsidy based on f.o.b. value. The ministry of finance reported that "the export subsidy is applied in ways that do not respect the law. The base, which should be local value-added, is sometimes f.o.b. value" (GOS, Ministère des Finances et Affaires Economiques, [Direction de la Prévision], juillet 1985). One 1985 ministry of industry report identifies the f.o.b. value a the basis for calculating the export subsidy paid to firms in the textile industry (GOS, Ministère du Développement Industriel, "Etude sur le secteur textile au Sénégal dans la définition du prix de cession du coton," janvier 1985). See also *Marchés Tropicaux* (18 juillet 1980): 1,794.

111. Senegal's total exports of manufactured textile goods fell from 2,300 tons in 1970, to 1,352 tons in 1976, to 643 tons in 1980.

112. From interviews with the industrialists, April and December 1985.

113. As cited in Diouck 1986.

continuing to use antiquated and inefficient technology. When placed in broader perspective, it becomes clear that an industry which had subsisted on rents extracted from consumers in the earlier period was now subsisting on rents drawn directly from the national treasury and the state's investment budget. These sums would be rolled into the national debt.

No serious effort to "reimpose discipline" on textile imports was ever undertaken. The ministry of finance reported in 1985 that tariffs designed to protect the local textile industry were ineffective. A finance ministry analyst charged with studying the textile industry in 1985–6 remarked casually that "textile import controls are a joke. No one respects or tries to enforce the laws." One ex-official of the ministry of commerce reported that according to the ministry's informal estimates, 80 percent of the domestic textile market was supplied with contraband or fraudulently imported goods in 1984.[114] *Friperie* was included in the latter category.

The new "community of interests"

The decline of the Dakar textile industry over the course of the 1975–85 period was punctuated by important changes in the structure control over the industry. These changes coincided with the Senghor–Diouf transition. The foreign industrialists who had controlled the basic textile industry since the early 1950s pulled out of Senegal when President Senghor did, leaving the state holding the bag and forcing the regime to come up with a new way of running the industry while accommodating the commercial interests of its own members, their clientele, and the Mourides.

In an earlier period nationalization of the basic textile industry might have been the government's solution to the problem of French divestment. In 1980 this was not an option. "Structural adjustment" demanded privatization of state-owned industries, not the creation of new ones. Another solution was found. In 1980 and 1981, at the highest levels of government, arrangements were made to have ownership of the core of Dakar's basic textile industry transferred to *hommes d'affaires sénégalais.*

Loans from three state-owned banks and transfers from the national treasury financed the acquisition of Sotiba–Simpafric, STS, and Icotaf by the owners of Apollo-TM: Senegal's *friperie* magnates.[115] The Sotiba Group was born. In the

---

114. From interviews in April and November 1985.
115. One source reported that Sotiba–Simpafric's assets were valued at 1.25 billion CFA francs in November 1979. In 1980 STS became full subsidiary of Sotiba–Simpafric, shortly before the foreign owners of the basic textile industry began to withdraw from Senegal. With loans from the BNDS, the USB (a bank that was 80 percent government-owned), and the BSK (a bank that was 51 percent government-owned), the *friperie* enterprise Apollo–TM acquired 61 percent of Sotiba–Simpafric in 1980. Sotiba–Simpafric owed 400 million CFA francs in debts to the state treasury at the time. In lieu of paying the government, Sotiba–Simpafric used the 400 million to buy 60 percent of Icotaf in February 1982. At the same time, Serigne NDiaye acquired 25 percent of Sotiba–Simpafric in his own name. Sotiba–Simpafric purchased the remaining 40

early 1980s the Sotiba Group accounted for 72 percent of total production in the textile industry and 80 percent of total sales. The largest private firms in Senegal were now in the hands of two *hommes d'affaires* whose meteoric rise in the Dakar business world had been fueled by the potent combination of political influence on one hand and access to lucrative opportunities in the textile import trade on the other. Meanwhile, the buyout of Sotiba–Simpafric, Icotaf, and STS was generous to the long-time owners of these firms. One declared that "ultimately, we got out of Senegal without losing a cent."[116]

The regime justified the expense of this extraordinary deal by arguing that it would contribute to the suppression of fraud. Financing the acquisition of the basic textile industry by Apollo-TM would help to eliminate the conflict of interest between textile producers and Senegalese textile importers, the conflict of interest that was driving the industry into the ground. In exchange, Apollo-TM was to practice "self-restraint" in the import trade. As the ministry of planning explained, "the repression of fraud in the textile trade presupposes that the movement to associate importers and industrialists in one community of interests should be undertaken and pursued under the active sponsorship of the state."[117]

The transfer of ownership was accompanied by a government decision to end all *friperie* imports by the end of 1980. Within months, however, this decision was reversed. The *friperie* quota was increased from three thousand tons to six thousand tons in December 1980. Only two firms were licensed to import this quota at the time: Apollo-TM and COSISAL, a Kaolack-based firm linked to powerful Mouride businessmen. In the early 1980s, the owners of the basic textile industry were also Senegal's largest importers of *friperie*. The Sotiba Group embraced a community of interests that appeared to be most contradictory.

At the time of the buyout, all of the outstanding debt to the state of Icotaf, STS, and Sotiba–Simpafric was wiped off the books. The new owners would start with a clean slate. They pledged to undertake the factory modernization projects that the government had pushed since the mid-1970s, and contracted additional loans from the state-owned banks in Dakar for this purpose. Yet for all the public money pumped into the industry in the 1980s, the government's success in realizing the goal of factory modernization was no greater than it had been in the 1970s. Sotiba–Simpafric continued to produce high-quality *imprimés* on the base of imported *écru*, and its design department continued to create attractive prints. In 1986, however, the investment program at Sotiba–Simpafric was still in the planning stage. Between 1980–5 only 30 percent of agreed-upon sums were invested in Icotaf, and this money was spent to convert Icotaf into a bazin dyeing operation, not to modernize the weaving plant.[118] STS, the weav-

percent of Icotaf before the end of 1982 (from interviews with former and current executives of the Sotiba Group in November 1984 and April 1985). Figures on the weight of the Sotiba Group in the Dakar textile industry's total production and sales are from Aly Diop NDiaye 1985.

116. From an interview with a former owner, April 1986.
117. GOS, Ministére du Plan et de la Coopération, Commission Nationale de Planification (n. B-6), Sous-Commission: Textiles, *Rapport Provisoire*, 1982.
118. From interviews with managers and interns at Icotaf and Sotiba, November 1984 through December 1985, and with a ministry of finance analyst in April 1985.

ing factory owned by the Sotiba Group, languished because Sotiba–Simpafric would neither purchase its écrus, invest in its factory, nor pay its bills to the banks and the government.

The owners of the Sotiba Group amassed resources in the form and measure needed for investment in industry. They acquired through a stroke of fortune the core of a basic textile industry badly in need of renewal. But like the former owners, they were not interested in making investments that would enhance or even maintain the productive capacity of the industry.

The financial positions of Icotaf and Sotiba–Simpafric deteriorated considerably after 1981. In spite of a continuing inflow of loan capital from the government banks, neither firm was able to maintain treasury resources adequate to cover routine operating costs. Icotaf began factory-door sales to retailers to earn cash.[119] Sotiba–Simpafric and Icotaf sometimes came up short on cash when payday came around, and wildcat strikes at the factories were frequent in the mid-1980s as a result. Bank loans that financed the buyout in 1980 and 1981 were not repaid, and by 1985 both Icotaf and Sotiba–Simpafric were in arrears with virtually all of their creditors. According to one BNDS agent, "the banks cannot press the Sotiba Group for repayment due to their political ties."[120] Eventually the Dakar banks refused to extend new loans to cover day-to-day operations. Insiders at Icotaf and Sotiba–Simpafric believed that occasionally, funds from the president's office paid workers' wages. Arrears to SODEFITEX and SENELEC, the cotton and electricity suppliers, accumulated.

The internal accounts of Sotiba–Simpafric and Icotaf fell into disarray. One industry analyst claimed that Sotiba's own financial controller had never seen the books. Ministry of industry representatives were not allowed access to the factories. In the late 1980s the Sotiba Group was rocked by its biggest scandal of all when one of the principal partners tried (unsuccessfully) to sue the other for embezzling 9 billion CFA francs from the Sotiba Group. Eventually, STS and then Icotaf were closed down. Sotiba–Simpafric was near bankruptcy at the end of the decade. Sales had dwindled to 10 billion CFA francs in 1988. Operating losses reported that year totaled 2.3 billion CFA.[121]

It seems that after 1981, revenues generated in the basic textile industry (the inflow of loans, sales revenues, and government subsidies) were transferred out of manufacturing and into the commercial sector or abroad. When they acquired the basic textile industry, Serigne NDiaye and Tampsir MBoup created a holding company for their Dakar operations called SOMICO S.A. and registered it not in Dakar, but in Monaco. SOMICO owned an import–export company which handled all business of the Sotiba Group, most notably the importation of *écrus* from the Far East. The commercial empire of these two *hommes d'affaires* grew and diversified in the 1980s. SPCA–Thubet, acquired in 1976, imported Japanese

---

119. From interviews with textile dealers in Dakar, January 1986.
120. From an interview in April 1985. Employees and clients of the Sotiba Group made the same point in interviews, November 1984 through January 1986.
121. As reported by Caisse Centrale de Coopération Economique (CCCE), Direction de Dakar, "Version provisoire du rapport [sur le] secteur textile," 29 mai 1990.

automobiles, chemical products, luxury goods, and was granted a duty-free concession at the Dakar-Yoff airport. ICOPAL, another part of this commercial empire, was a big importer of staple alimentary products, a product category governed by quotas and licensing. And Apollo-TM conducted the lucrative *friperie* trade under a state-granted oligopoly. Around 1983 the Sotiba Group bought a controlling share in the short-lived Banque du Commerce Sénégalais (BCS). The BCS, the first commercial bank in Dakar owned completely by private Senegalese businessmen, was paralyzed in 1986 by an embezzlement scandal.[122] It collapsed soon thereafter, along with most of the state-owned banks in Dakar. One official in the ministry of finance commented that "the *hommes d'affaires sénégalais* in the textile industry are not manufacturers, they are rentiers, collecting revenues from sales and state subsidies to finance speculative operations in other domains."[123]

This was government-supported local private capital in Senegal in the 1980s. An observer pointed to a fundamental constraint on its development as a productive force in the national economy when he remarked that "Sotiba has done the only rational thing. Why should entrepreneurs take risks when they can have assured profits in other ways?"[124]

In other segments of the Dakar textile industry foreign owners also pulled out after 1980, reflecting a pervasive pessimism about prospects for recapturing the local market and a consensus that the political and economic changes of 1979–81 did not bode well for import-substitution industry. It is clear that the Sotiba Group operated on this same premise. A prominent and politically influential Senegalese businessman, Cheikh Fall, took majority ownership of TMS, the knitting firm.[125] TMS limped along filling contract orders for Senegal's Club Méditerranée beach resort until it closed in the late 1980s. The French Société Cotonnière Transocéanique divested from SCT and a local Lebanese business group, the Groupe Choucair, took over the firm.[126] By the end of the decade, SCT was also closed. In 1984 CCV and SOSEFIL, a spinning firm and a thread-dyeing firm, were the only French-owned firms left in the industry. And in 1989 the Dollfus Mieg Corporation divested from SOSEFIL "because of the general economic and political climate."[127]

122. The Sotiba Group owned at least 33 percent of the BCS. On the scandal, see *Le Soleil* (9 janvier 1986): 9.
123. From an interview in Dakar, April 1985.
124. From an interview at the ESGE, December 1985.
125. Cheikh Fall was the director of Air Afrique, the airline that was jointly owned by the government of France and the governments of the CFA monetary zone until 1980. In the early 1970s he was viewed as one possible successor to President Senghor.
126. The Choucair family was firmly established in large-scale importation and had extensive real-estate holdings in Dakar. Some leading members of the Choucair family were Senegalese citizens. See *Sénégal Industrie*, Numéro Spécial, janvier 1985: 40.
127. Caisse Centrale de Coopération Economique (CCCE), Direction de Dakar, "Version provisoire du rapport [sur le] secteur textile," 29 mai 1990: 29. SOSEFIL was sold to Redda Attieh, an important Lebanese businessman in the Dakar textile trade.

The trend of disinvestment that was manifest in the pullout of foreign capital and the running-down of the textile industry was mirrored in other sectors of light industry swamped by irregular imports, most dramatically in shoe, soap, and cosmetic-product manufacturing. The net result was the reversal of a process of industrialization that had been based on import substitution in the domain of consumer goods. On a wider scale, it is also impossible to miss the parallel between this process of disinvestment and the one that was underway in the groundnut basin, where producers were disinvesting from groundnut production over the course of the same period. The link between these two processes lies in state-regulated and state-controlled markets.

Commercial circuits created by colonial merchant capital and managed by the state after independence drained resources from the rural sector – the productive base of the economy – and into clientelistic networks and the coffers of the state, into the treasuries of import-substitution industries, and into the hands of the old commercial houses still vested in the textile trade. These commercial networks became the site of intense struggles among those positioned to appropriate these resources, as well as the site of struggle between the rural producers of this wealth and those who wanted to claim it. Rent-seeking in state-controlled commercial circuits reduced the capacity of producers in agriculture, and the willingness of producers in industry, to expand production.

For the textile industry, this was almost as true during the 1960–75 period as it was for the post-1975 period. Investment during the period of the industry's growth was shallow and limited for the most part to efforts to cover the domestic market more broadly. By investing in producing a diversified array of finished goods, the industry cast a wider net over rents to be had on the local market. What changed after 1975 was not this rent-seeking logic, but rather the identity of the group collecting rents. The source of this change was the regime's interest in generating and channeling commercial rents (and cash) to an expanding class of rentiers, and the ability of politically powerful and strategically placed individuals to seize opportunities to propel this process forward on their own account.

The strategic use of state power cultivated the rise of an indigenous rentier class in Senegal, anchoring it in the regime and in state-mediated commercial circuits. This process drained the state of the resources and of the coherence it needed to sustain the Dakar textile industry, one of the most imposing manifestations of private capital's (limited) interest in engaging directly in production in the Senegalese economy.

THE COMPROMISES OF ABDOU DIOUF

Abdou Diouf presided over a state on the brink of bankruptcy, a state apparatus commandeered by its own agents and their political allies, and a ruling coalition stretched to a near-breaking point by competition for power within the post-Senghor order and by increasingly violent struggles over the shrinking national pie. In trying to establish his own political preeminence within a regime that had

been built by Senghor, Abdou Diouf relied on the support of the Islamic confréries, Senegal's external creditors, and Jean Collin. The Mouride confrérie
remained the regime's most reliable network of support in an electoral arena
dominated by an unstable ruling party, the Parti Socialiste (PS). External creditors sustained the inflow of external resources, and thus provided the state with
cash as its own resource base withered away at the grassroots. External resources
were funneled into an ever more centralized set of institutions linked directly to
the offices of executive power in the presidency. The World Bank was interested
in strengthening executive power in order to regulate and monitor more closely
state finances and the disbursement of its funds. At the institutional level, then,
external creditors' interest in "institution building" complemented Abdou
Diouf's efforts to reconcentrate spending authority (and political power) at the
top, in the hands of a loyal set of ministers and top administrators. Within the
cabinet, ministries, and institutions of the presidency, Jean Collin played a leading role in efforts aimed at consolidating Abdou Diouf's political control over the
ruling party and strategic parts of the state apparatus.

Collin, often viewed as the *éminence grise* of the Senghor years (he had served
as minister of finance and then, minister of the interior), emerged as the *éminence grise* of the Diouf regime.[128] The post of Sécretaire Général du Gouvernement made Jean Collin a de facto prime minister. He masterminded the manipulation of factions within the ruling party and the opposition, the game that
allowed Diouf to survive in face of challenge and resistance within the PS.[129]
Allies and clients of Abdou Diouf and Jean Collin moved up the administrative
hierarchy and inward, closer to the center of power. Gradually many of the party
barons of the Senghor years were eclipsed by Abdou Diouf's own administrative
barons. Some of these new barons were co-opted in from the opposition parties.
Echoing the deepening popular disillusionment and cynicism of the Abdou Diouf
years, one Senegalese said, "The old corrupt Ministers were replaced with new
corrupt Ministers – the so-called technocrats."[130]

The ruling party weakened. Abdou Diouf "parachuted" his own allies into top
positions, progressively alienating entrenched powerbrokers at middle ranks of
the PS. At the same time, the reservoirs of patronage resources that helped to
sustain the party in the past – government hiring, lending, the groundnut circuit,
spending on social services – dried up. The regime bought time for the PS and
threw the opposition off-balance by lifting the ban on opposition parties in
1981.[131] Opposition parties proliferated; the old clandestine left resurfaced. Over
fifteen parties registered to contest the 1983 elections. Abdou Diouf had no bread
to offer the masses in the voting season of 1983; he offered this new electoral
game instead. The PS won amid cries of electoral fraud and manipulation. The
social crisis deepened.

128. On Jean Collin's career in Senegal, see *Africa Confidential* 30, no. 7 (31 March 1989): 4; and
     Diop and Diouf 1990:104–8.
129. See Diop and Diouf 1990.
130. From an interview at Dakar's Marché HLM, January 1986.
131. See Fatton 1987:15–19 inter alia.

There was a sentiment in Dakar in 1985 that Abdou Diouf was weaker than his predecessor and even less able to master the powerful political networks ensconced in the administration. Diouf was dependent for an electoral mandate upon a compromised and divided ruling party, one that he could neither strengthen nor destroy. Although the president succeeded in increasing his own personal authority, in building his own power base within the state apparatus, and in outmaneuvering the opposition both within and outside of the ruling party, he did so by destabilizing established political structures and networks rather than by subordinating them to his authority. Those at the top of the regime failed to assert control over a fragmented administrative apparatus and parastatal institutions on the periphery of presidential power. Their willingness to do so was compromised by their continuing dependence upon clientelistic networks rooted in the state apparatus and by their fears of political collapse. Donal Cruise O'Brien and Christian Coulon wrote in 1989 (pp. 153–4) that "Diouf has still not gained control. . . . The [ruling party] has never been in such a state of confusion and division."

Old and new patronage networks coexisted in an increasingly unstable, anarchic political and economic environment. The new barons and *hommes d'affaires* of the Diouf regime competed with those of the *ancien régime* for a share of the resources to be had. External creditors' designs were frustrated by continuing resistance to policies aimed at diminishing "intermediary costs" in agricultural trading circuits, especially in the groundnut sector (Duruflé 1988: 77; Diop and Diouf 1990:22). The rice trade and the state's petrol monopoly remained major plums, as did subsidies to the parastatals and new loans aimed at restructuring, modernizing, and enhancing the efficiency of government-owned enterprises. State-controlled banks in Dakar continued to loan to big borrowers long after the credit squeeze of the early 1980s cut off most of the *hommes d'affaires* of the 1970s.[132] Fraud and contraband were "uncontrollable"; one observer commented that "corruption at the level of the customs service is one of the few sources of direct government patronage left in Senegal."[133] What the World Bank called the *grands dossiers* – the sugar monopoly of the Companie Sucrière Sénégalaise (CSS) and the flour-milling monopoly of the Grands Moulins de Dakar – were impervious to external pressures for reform, as was the Dakar textile industry. And in defiance of the IMF's zealous campaign to resuscitate the state treasury, the government made no serious moves to tax the economic base of the rentier class: urban real estate and commerce. As the economic and

132. Rising interest rates and the credit squeeze led the GES to demand a debt moratorium for *hommes d'affaires sénégalais* in 1982. The government (via the state banks) complied by writing off 40 percent of all interest due on loans granted to Senegalese businessmen. Remaining debt was rescheduled over a ten-year period. All legal action against *hommes d'affaires* in arrears with the banks was suspended, as were moves to repossess debtors' assets. See *Marchés Tropicaux* (8 octobre 1982): 2,712; ibid. (1 avril 1983): 856; *Le Soleil*, "Rencontre des membres des GES," 16 and 17 avril 1983; and ibid., "Les GES: mécontents des banques," 8 août 1984.

133. From an interview in Dakar, January 1991.

political situation deteriorated, *hommes d'affaires sénégalais* based their calculations on ever-shorter time horizons. Large sums were transferred abroad.

Abdou Diouf remained in power, but "structural adjustment" was not producing the results desired by its architects. The old industrial base was shrinking, but new investment was not forthcoming. Private buyers did not rush forward to purchase state-owned enterprises put up for sale under new privatization programs. Meanwhile, the rural crisis deepened. Total agricultural production (including food crops) fell below 1979 levels in 1983–4 and 1984–5. The good rains of 1985–6 produced a mediocre groundnut crop of 600,000 tons and total agricultural output which barely reached 1979 levels. No strategy to deal with the problem of the exhaustion of the land (what Bernard Founou calls the *surexploitation de la nature*) had emerged. The World Bank had sounded the alarm in 1970 when rural producers purchased only 13,000 tons of fertilizer, their main defense against this critical problem. In 1983–4, only 3,000 tons of fertilizer were used in the groundnut basin.[134] There was a general consensus that real rural incomes were lower in the 1980s than they had been in the 1970s. Duruflé (1988:44–5) reports that indices of real growth, including overall production and employment, stagnated or regressed after 1979.[135]

In the mid-1980s the World Bank pressed for more radical measures to shrink the state, make deeper cuts in government spending, and free markets. Between 1986 and 1988, quantitative import restrictions designed to protect most subsectors of light industry were suppressed. The textile import regime was the last to go. In 1988, quotas, *autorisations préalables, valeurs mercuriales,* and licensing regimes governing the importation of textile products were dismantled. Taxes and duties were standardized across product categories. The standard rate of import taxation on "products similar to those manufactured in Senegal" was gradually reduced from 96 percent in 1983 to 68 percent in 1988. "Because of the magnitude of fraud," the fixed tax rate for "imports similar to locally manufactured goods" was raised to 74 percent in 1989. Again "because of fraud," *valeurs mercuriales* were quickly reimposed on textile imports.[136]

These reforms had three major effects. First, the suppression of quantitative restrictions dealt the final blow to the Dakar-based operations of the traditional maisons de commerce. Second, it guaranteed the irreversibility of the process of deindustrialization that was already underway. Third, it concentrated all pres-

134. The figure of 13,000 tons can be compared to fertilizer use of 62,000 tons in 1967 (World Bank 1974:63). On 1983–4, see Elliot Berg Associates 1990:83. On 1985–6, see Duruflé 1988:30.
135. Duruflé (1988:31) argues that World Bank data showing growth of Senegal's GNP in the 1980s are based on wishful thinking. His conclusions are supported in the main by the Elliot Berg Associates study that was commissioned by the Bank: "It is not surprising that the output data do not indicate that Senegal has moved to a sustainable growth path, or that the economy has been made significantly more productive and flexible than it was a decade ago. . . . Senegal's economy . . . is probably less competitive [than it was in 1980]" (Elliot Berg Associates 1990:iii inter alia).
136. Charbel Zarour, "Etude sur l'impact de la NPI [Nouvelle Politique Industrielle] sur les secteurs industriel et commercial," a report prepared for the World Bank, Dakar, août 1990 (restricted circulation).

sures for rent-seeking in the import trade at the level of the customs service, *la douane*. The World Bank tried to plug this huge leak in the state treasury by computerizing the customs service "to enhance its efficiency." For its part, the government shadowed customs officers with troops from the Senegalese army, presumably to enhance their reliability. These measures did not produce the hoped-for results. Exasperated external creditors began to consider sending French customs agents to staff *la douane*. This shift in thinking seemed to epitomize Gilles Duruflé's (1988:84) assessment of the entire process of "structural adjustment" in Senegal: "Conscious of their failure, the external creditors proceeded to a rampant recolonization."

Conclusion: States, capital, and capitalist states

It would be incorrect to see in the replacement of the colonial state by the postcolonial state merely a distinction without a difference. The colonial state provided imperialism with a quite direct and unmediated instrument for control in the interests of [capital] within the colonial social formation. The postcolonial state . . . is something more of an unpredictable quantity in this regard. . . . Under African conditions, [there has sometimes been an] ironic kind of 'threat' to imperial interests: the crystallization in many African settings of a state too weak and too internally compromised . . . to effectively guarantee the ongoing generation of surplus and accumulation of capital.

John Saul 1979:350–1

Where . . . is the social agent to champion capitalist transformation?

Richard Sandbrook 1985:39

Analysts of comparative politics have turned their attention to explaining differences in state capacities and in degrees of state autonomy that are observed across contexts.[1] These differences are registered in the relative success (or failure) of states in promoting social transformation or, in more precise formulations, capitalist development. State ideologies and the development of coherent state institutions that can overpower societally based opposition to state goals are often put forward as "independent" or causal variables to account for the successes of some states in promoting capitalist development. African cases make an important contribution to this line of research. If the Newly Industrializing Countries (NICs) of Southeast Asia represent the archetypal strong, entrepreneurial states, then many of the sub-Saharan African cases represent the archetypical counterfactuals. Many African states apparently lack the autonomy, institutional coherence, and capacity required to promote sustained capitalist development. Senegal is an example.

The analysis cannot stop there, however, for it is necessary to explain why strong and coherent states have emerged to promote capitalist development in some contexts but not in others. Are state ideologies and strong, coherent state institutions "independent variables"? When this question is asked, the concerns

---

1. See, for example, Evans et al. 1985:350–60; Anderson 1986; Haggard 1987; Migdal 1988.

of comparative political analysts begin to intersect with another current of debate, one that revolves around the extent to which capitalist states are, or can be, "truly autonomous" from capitalist social classes.[2] Can capitalist development be attributed to ideologies and institutions that are brought forth by the autonomous will of state managers, as suggested by those who seem to want to advance a theory of "true" state autonomy? Or does sustained capitalist development, and the ideologies and state-building processes that accompany and promote it, reflect the power already achieved of capitalist social classes?

Here again, when one is standing Africa, far away from the world centers of capital accumulation, one gains a wider view of the range of historical possibility and of the issues at stake. It becomes possible to reject the notion of true state autonomy. The social origins and class character of the state are decisive variables in accounting for the institutional capacity and political will (as manifest in ideology and coherence of purpose) of the state to promote and sustain capitalist development. This is as true for the industrial capitalist states as it is for the so-called late developing countries. States have social bases, and the study of comparative politics is cast adrift when it loses its moorings in this basic fact.

STATES AND CAPITAL

In the *Eighteenth Brumaire of Louis Bonaparte*, Karl Marx distinguished between a class "in itself" and a class "for itself."[3] When its existence as a class was not challenged directly, Marx pointed out that France's nineteenth-century bourgeoisie had great difficulty using state power to promote shared class interests. The bourgeoisie constituted a class in itself based on a common position in the social relations of production, but could not always act for itself to advance shared class interests. As the Second Republic fell into disarray, the Bonapartist state emerged to mediate intraclass conflict and to sustain the overall process of private capital accumulation. Although Bonaparte did not represent the bourgeoisie in a direct sense, the existence of the regime and of the state itself depended on the maintenance a capitalist social order. The regime's need to sustain and accelerate the process of capitalist economic development – that is, the process of private capital accumulation – constituted the critical nexus between its actions and the interests of members of the dominant class. Nicos Poulantzas elaborated these ideas in a theoretically generalizable way, arguing that if the conditions that sustain modern capitalism are to be perpetuated, the state must mediate conflicts between factions of the capitalist class in a way that promotes the interests of capital as a whole. To complicate matters, the successful capitalist state must mediate and contain interclass conflict as well.[4]

Marx and Poulantzas propose a model that views the state in capitalist society as functioning with "relative autonomy" to reproduce the conditions that sustain

2. Skocpol 1985:6; Evans et al. 1985:347, 356. See also Krasner 1978.
3. Marx 1968:171.
4. Poulantzas 1973; 1978.

the expansion of capital and to safeguard existing class relations. Many analysts of peripheral capitalism adopted this formulation. The peripheral capitalist state would function to sustain and promote the expansion of capital. In African studies the model that emerged defined the function of the state as promoting either "the development of underdevelopment" or "dependent development."[5] Conceptualizations of existing class relations grappled with the difficulty of defining the class character of ruling strata when local capital was weak. The terms state bourgeoisie, auxiliary bourgeoisie, and bureaucratic bourgeoisie resolved this conceptual difficulty in a way that was consistent with the model Marx and Poulantzas proposed for understanding the relationship between state and class power in capitalist society. By using terms like "state bourgeoisie," analysts posited a structural and necessary connection between the interests and position of holders of state power on one hand and the expansion of capitalism in particular national contexts on the other. As Mouzelis (1989: 452) argued, "the expression 'state bourgeoisie' implies either an a priori linkage or class affinity between state bureaucrats and various bourgeois elements . . . ; [or] that state bureaucrats play a role that in 'normal circumstances' the bourgeoisie is or should be playing; [or] . . . that those in control of the state apparatus are part and parcel of the bourgeois class." Ascribing some sort of bourgeois character to African ruling classes was a theoretical construct based on assumptions or expectations about how state power would be used and/or assumptions about how the process of class formation would unfold.

Africa's current crisis is marked by negative rates of economic growth, stagnant or falling productivity in agriculture, and disinvestment on the part of capital. In this context, it becomes clear that the "function" of sustaining conditions which promote the expansion of capital is not common to all states. Africa's crisis is a reminder of the historical specificity of the capitalist state. As Brenner (1977) has argued, the existence of a world capitalist economy does not guarantee that all states within it will operate in accordance with the logic and needs of capital.

What, then, gives the capitalist state its particular character – its capacity, its structural need, and its impetus to promote capitalist development? Why are capitalist states inclined, even driven, to mediate conflicts within the dominant class, as well as intraclass conflicts, in accordance with the interests of capital? The answer cannot be found at the level of the state itself, in the character of state institutions and state ideologies. The answer lies in the character, dynamics, and reproduction requirements of the social formation as a whole. The case of Senegal supports this argument by way of counterfactual, for within this social formation the structural hegemony of capital was not assured.

In Senegal the role of state power in safeguarding existing class relations stymied, undercut, and neutralized the capacity and the willingness of those in control of the state to deepen and expand the process of capital accumulation. The political and economic hegemony of the postcolonial ruling class rested

5. See Leys 1975; Beckman 1980.

upon control over monopolistic commercial circuits, not production. Through these commercial circuits, the dominant social stratum appropriated a share of the social surplus from peasant producers of export crops. By regulating access to exchange networks, those in control of the state were also able to regulate access to the prime locus of capital accumulation within the national economy.

Those who gained control over the postcolonial state relied, for their internal source of political power, upon a rural "aristocracy" and rural notables rooted in precapitalist forms of agricultural production. State control over commercial circuits that channeled resource flows into and out of the rural economy helped to cement this alliance of elites and, at the same time, to sustain and reinforce the social relations of production that allowed rural notables to exercise power over their clients, followers, and dependents. Senegal's postcolonial ruling coalition was built upon this deeply rooted social base. It came to embrace a professional stratum that was deeply divided in its visions and ambitions. It also included the most dynamic elements of a nascent business stratum, a social group that was torn between its interest in appropriating agricultural surpluses on its own account and its interest in gaining access to rents and wealth mobilized by the state. The consolidation and reconsolidation of the regime over time expanded and sustained a ruling coalition composed of these disparate and in some ways fundamentally antagonistic elements. Through this process, a critical nexus was forged between the use of state power on one hand and the interests of various elements within this ruling coalition on the other. The nexus lay in the particularistic distribution of rural surpluses, rents, and other resources mobilized by the state.

A Senegalese ruling class exists in itself. It shares a common, material base in the appropriation of resources and rents mobilized in state-controlled commercial circuits. But this material base and the ad hoc and mercenary rent-seeking activities which countered centrifugal tendencies pulling at the ruling coalition did not provide a common ground for the emergence of a coherent, class-based project. Anchored in a precapitalist rural elite and in commercial monopolies, the ruling stratum was politically incapable of attacking the problem of economic stagnation at its roots by transforming existing structures of control over rural production and surplus appropriation. Likewise, this ruling class, confronted with the erosion of its own material base, was not able to reorganize and deploy state power in the effort to reinvigorate and shore up the decaying neocolonial economy. In this sense, the ruling class does not act for itself. Yet there is no "Bonapartist state" to step in on its behalf.[6] Senegal's ruling elite presided over and accelerated the deterioration and collapse of its own material base.

The dynamics of this process were manifest clearly in the import trade and the textile sector, just as they were in the rural economy. The development of the Dakar textile industry was predicated on the use of state power to capture domestic markets. Protection from competing imports and production monopolies gave

6. Callaghy (1984:186) makes a similar point, arguing that the notion of a "Bonapartist state" does not fit in the Zairian case.

foreign interests linked to textile manufacturing an extraorunary amount of control over the local market for textile goods. State-mediated and -enforced control over markets, rather than the drive to generate surplus value through the exploitation of wage labor, promoted the growth of this subsector of industry. This structure of control over markets freed the owners of industry from the need to continually reinvest in order to deepen the process of industrial production, to intensify the exploitation of labor by enhancing productivity, or to offset depreciation of capital stock by replacing productive capacity that was used up in the manufacturing process. State-enforced commercial monopolies enjoyed by these firms also constrained possibilities for investment in new industries on the part of local capital. Tight control over importation allowed the state to extract, in the form of taxes, its share of the rents generated in this part of the commercial circuit. These facts were constants in the industry's history. So was the fundamental uncompetitiveness of the industry in the face of international competition. What changed over time was the locus of control over state power in Senegal, and the constellation of private and political ambitions that influenced its use.

The process of gathering and sustaining a postcolonial ruling coalition was marked by the regime's reliance on the distribution of patronage resources to an ever expanding clientele, and by the concomitant strengthening of spoils-oriented political factions linked directly or indirectly to the regime. Patron–client relations structured around differential access to state resources enforced political cohesion within the dominant social stratum and worked to preclude or preempt organized challenges to the political and economic status quo. The logic and dynamics of this patronage-based "mode of domination" worked over time to redefine the internal locus of state power. The dispersion of power and prerogative within the state apparatus facilitated the political co-optation of restive elements like the nascent business class because the state became more responsive to particularistic demands. As factions grew within the bureaucracy and the ruling party, they were able to capture subunits of the state apparatus – some of the parastatals, ONCAD, the ministry of commerce, the customs service, etc. Factional conflict within the regime took on the character of intraclass conflict which, at the end of the day, betrayed a common interest in extracting wealth from the state itself and from state-structured commercial circuits.

Expanding the reservoir of patronage resources mobilized and privatized in these ways was what Mouzelis (1989) would call a reproduction requirement of the regime. The process of sustaining and expanding the regime, however, worked over time to subvert the capacity of the state to reproduce existing economic structures.

Three processes worked together to produce this outcome. First, the ability of "the state" to accumulate resources on its own account (in the national treasury, for example) eroded as these resources were privatized by members of the political elite. Fraud in the import circuit, corruption in the groundnut marketing board, and the *détournement* of resources flowing through the parastatals, state banks, and state-owned enterprises were prime examples.

Second, the ability of "the state" to expand the pie, and thus its relative share, was both constrained and compromised. In the rural sector, the state was constrained because, like merchant capital, it relied on control over exchange circuits to gain access to the agricultural surplus. The accumulating class had no direct means of reorganizing and intensifying production to increase the total surplus. Control over labor, the use of inputs, farm size, crop choice, production techniques, investment, etc., all lay in the hands of producers and rural authorities (from household heads to rural notables). Rural producers were tied to commodity production, but would expand their total output of groundnuts only within the constraints imposed by their interest in protecting the "subsistence floor" of the household and the community. The ability of the state to expand commodity production, even within these social relations of rural production, was compromised by the regime's overriding interest in draining wealth out of the rural sector. The tendency to intensify the exploitation of an impoverished groundnut-producing peasantry succeeded only in driving producers away from state-controlled groundnut purchasing circuits and markets for inputs (fertilizer). The groundnut economy decayed and the state's monopolies over rural trade disintegrated.

Third, these pressures drove the regime to open new domains of the economy – commercial circuits previously untapped for patronage resources – to politically mediated rent-seeking. Commercial monopolies that sustained Dakar's textile industry broke down as the political class and its allies moved into state-created rentier activities in the import trade. The long-protected domestic market was swamped with low cost goods imported via contraband circuits, through fraud, and under the regime's special dispensation to a clique of powerful *friperie* dealers. Dakar's textile industry lost its market, foreign capital pulled out, and the industry collapsed. The same story could be told of the shoe industry, the cosmetic industry, and the plastic-goods industries. Net result: As the political need of the regime to mobilize and distribute patronage resources grew, the productive bases of the neocolonial economy eroded away.

There has been a certain coherence or logic to the process of economic decline in Senegal which cannot be uncovered by focusing on clientelism, the privatization of state resources, or bureaucratic inefficiency in isolation from the broader political and economic forces that gave rise to these patterns of political behavior. Disintegration of neocolonial trading monopolies and the forms of production that they sustained is one reflection of the privatization and parcellation of state power that accompanied the reappropriation of the ex-colonial state apparatus by powerful elements in postcolonial society. The state apparatus that had been used to underpin the hegemony of French merchant capital became the instrument of a ruling class that, like merchant capital, was not sited in the production process. This ruling class could not serve as "the social agent to champion capitalist transformation" because such a process threatened the social, economic, and political bases of its own power.[7]

The ex-colonial state became an instrument for reproducing established forms

---

7. This is Sandbrook's (1985:39) phrase.

and social relations of production, and the internal configurations of power that corresponded to them. This instrument was used to accommodate the mercenary and short-term interests of disparate elements contained within the ruling coalition, and thus, to counter or neutralize centrifugal forces that threatened the political status quo. The fragmentation and privatization of state power that resulted diminished the usefulness of the state as an instrument for implementing broad-gauged, long-term projects and strategies – such as stabilizing the rural economy or sustaining Senegal's established industrial base.

The compromised character of the state as an agent or vehicle for gathering and deploying power was also manifest in failures and short-circuiting of "transformative" impulses that originated over time from within the state itself. What others[8] have defined as impulses to construct a developmentalist state,[8] an entrepreneurial state,[9] a bourgeoisie tied to foreign capital,[10] and an integral, hegemonic state[11] were all dissipated in the effort to preserve and expand a ruling coalition held together by clientelistic networks of mercenary support. Those in control of the state apparatus were unable to forge an alternative, composite solution to the political needs and economic interests of the ruling coalition as a whole.

These same forces make the current crisis most difficult to transcend. Just as regime consolidation did not give rise to a ruling class able to guarantee the reproduction of the neocolonial order, it preempted or deflected the emergence of an indigenous social stratum with the political power and economic need to successfully push a "nurture capitalism" project. Perhaps more importantly, state power does not exist in the form or measure necessary for such an undertaking. The particularistic and ad hoc use of the economic prerogatives of the state to create and sustain this ruling coalition weakened the state as an instrument for structuring economic activity, deploying economic resources, and mediating the conflicts of economic interest inherent in postcolonial society. Structural economic crisis is the result.

The weakness of capital as a force structuring relations of production within this social formation is a critical variable in explaining this outcome. And capital was weak. The fact that the state and regime were dependent upon forces that tied Senegal into the world capitalist economy does not contradict this observation. Nor does the fact that reproducing this social formation required resources from abroad (resources provided at the discretion of France and the multilateral creditors) and the existence of an export-oriented agricultural sector. As John Saul's statement cited at the head of this chapter suggests, "dependence" in itself cannot – and does not – guarantee the hegemony of "the interests of capital" within the state or the social formation at large.

Imperialism and colonialism did not transform Senegal into a capitalist soci-

8. See, for example, Schumacher 1975.
9. As described by Rocheteau 1982.
10. As described, for example, by Anson-Meyer 1974:92–5.
11. As described by Fatton 1987. For commentary, see Diop and Diouf 1990:25–9 inter alia.

ety. The dominant role of merchant capital in the colonial economy reflected the limits of capital's role in structuring the social forces and relations of production. And even merchant capital was weak, for the colonial state was forced to intervene in markets directly, on a widespread and on-going basis, in efforts to both sustain groundnut production (through the SIP, French colonialism's agricultural "cooperatives," for example) and in efforts to preserve the predominant position of French trading conglomerates (through the active enforcement of commercial monopolies). The weakness of capital within the social formation was reflected in the postcolonial political dominance of social groups that were not the "bearers" of capitalist interests – the rural religious elite and the professional stratum that lived off the state (the political class). We can accept the argument that the long-run interests of this ruling strata lay in sinking roots into the production process to expand the productive bases of the economy, increase the absolute size of the social surplus, and increase its relative share of this surplus. As the case suggests, however, we cannot assume that these interests will be acted upon and realized. Political contingencies particular to the postcolonial situation are important in explaining why not.

Paul Baran (1952) identified the essence of the problem some forty years ago in an analysis of ruling alliances in "backward societies." In these situations, agricultural production is organized around precapitalist modes of production and bourgeois elements are too weak, and too afraid of the threat of radicalism from below, to constitute an independent force in either the economic or the political sphere. Baran argued that the alliance between landed interests ("parasitic feudal overlords") and business interests rests upon political, social and institutional structures "set up to guard and abet . . . existing property rights and privileges" (ibid: 95). These arrangements stem the rise of capitalist forces which would split the ruling coalition and jeopardize the existing structure of domination. This situation finds an analog in Senegal, where the nature of the ruling alliance and political efforts undertaken to preserve it constrained possibilities for reform and economic development.

In Senegal the rise of an independent accumulating class represented a threat to the cohesion of the ruling coalition, to the economic bases of the regime, and to the prevailing mode of domination. This threat presented itself concretely in 1960 in the form of a stratum of Senegalese merchants who were prepared and eager to commercialize the groundnut crop on their own account – that is, a business stratum interested in decentralized private control over rural commercial circuits. Why was this so threatening? The development of private and more competitive groundnut trading circuits would deprive the regime of direct access to the export crop. In principle, this arrangement would not be fatal for the regime, for groundnuts could still be taxed at the point of export. What was more important from the perspective of the regime was the fact that state-controlled commercial circuits were the critical institutional mechanism for incorporating rural notables, the rural elite, and their dependents (the producers) into an economic-political hierarchy linked directly to the state. At the same time, direct state control over the groundnut crop preempted the emergence of a powerful class of rural traders whose ambitions could prove difficult to contain. The business stratum, for its part, did not withdraw its support for Senghor in order to oppose state control over groundnut marketing because the alternative – Mamadou Dia's grassroots vision of the socialist project – threatened to cut them out completely. Senegalese rural traders, too weak economically and politically to act decisively on their own account, staked their hopes on cashing in the political support that they provided for the Senghoriste political parties of the 1950s and 1960s.

A political solution to the problem of the nascent business stratum was found in using state power to promote the rise of a rentier class, linked to and dependent upon the regime. This solution, moreover, met composite needs. The rural religious leaders and strategic members of the Dakar-based political elite could be easily incorporated into the emergent rentier class. Rentierism was an economic corollary of a mode of domination that was rooted in commerce and brought to life through clientelism. Using state power to satisfy the short-term, particularistic interests of disparate elements within the ruling coalition retarded and deflected processes that threatened to produce intractable conflicts of interest within the ruling class. Rentierism also served as a mechanism for enforcing a degree of political discipline on members of the ruling coalition, for one could always be excluded from the spoils of the system. And state-mediated rent-seeking could be pursued within the existing structures of control over production and surplus appropriation. It was the obvious route to accumulation for the politically powerful in a situation where exchange circuits constituted the prime locus of accumulation, and where these exchange circuits lay under state control.

In Senegal the strengthening of a bourgeoisie was a threat to the existing political and economic order. Nothing could be farther removed from the situation that confronted Louis Bonaparte, who was forced to strengthen a weak and internally divided bourgeoisie in order to stabilize the regime, its economic base, and the social order.

Political dynamics that gave rise to rentierism as a dominant mode of wealth accumulation in Senegal were not unique to this case. Others have observed similar processes in richer and more complex African economies. John Iliffe, for example, has argued that there are three "models" of capitalist–politician relations in postcolonial Africa.[12] In one of these, the regime seeks to:

prevent the emergence of private African capitalism in any form. One example of this approach was Nkrumah's Ghana . . . [Nkrumah] feared, according to a senior advisor, 'that if he permitted African business to grow, it will grow to the extent of becoming a rival power to his and the party's prestige.' Moreover, within the Convention People's Party were many men anxious to use state power to channel the economy's surplus in their own direction. . . [Nkrumah] deliberately confined local capitalism to small-scale operations . . . (1983:77).[13]

12. These models are the ones wherein the regime seeks to prevent the emergence of private African capitalism; the "parasitic capitalism" model (state agents expropriate private property and thus acquire business interests of their own) exemplified by Zaire; and the "nurture capitalism" model à la Kenya and Nigeria (which remain in any case rather qualified examples of such a process). See Iliffe 1983:77–87.
13. See also Beckman 1976.

C. de Miras (1982:228–9), after reviewing the Ivoirian government's efforts to promote a local capitalist class via *"ivoirisation"* in the 1970s, writes that:

[T]he state does not appear to be the motor force [*structure-relais*] pushing the development of an indigenous private sector. The state appears to be more of a regulator which, through a moderate and controlled Ivoirianization, has been able to maintain within its orbit a *milieu aux ambitions économiques* which only the State could satisfy, without permitting a social class independent from the State to emerge . . . It seems that the State seeks to ensure that . . . no social faction is able to detach itself to constitute a counter-power [to the state itself].

Thomas Callaghy (1987:116) argued that "Mobutu does not want an autonomous bourgeoisie and has worked to stunt the growth of one." Another observer of Zairian politics said, "[T]he intention of the President [is] to prevent the development of a bourgeoisie with an economic base which could escape his control" (ibid:101). These arguments have been echoed in some analyses of Senegalese politics. Rita Cruise O'Brien (1979:108) maintained that the Senghor regime feared a true national bourgeoisie which could constitute a serious alternative force in politics, likely to ally with the ever problematic intelligentsia.[14]

Rentierism in postcolonial sub-Saharan Africa can be seen as a political strategy aimed at smothering and deflecting forces that would promote the emergence of an independent, capital-accumulating class. Yet regimes are not omnipotent; the best laid designs can clearly backfire or unravel. The failure of clientelism and machine politics in Senegal to fully subordinate and disorganize subordinate social strata (as manifest in the social crises of the 1980s, for example) is proof of this fact. Can rentierism thus be seen as a mode of "primitive accumulation" – a form of plunder that serves, either by default or by design, to amass resources in the form and measure necessary for productive investment? Will rentierism strengthen social strata that are interested in reproducing their wealth through productive investments? Variation observed even in the African context suggests a compelling answer to this question: It depends. It depends upon the extent to which rentierism occurs in a context which both allows and obliges accumulators to protect their gains via productive investment.

"Historically, the build-up of wealth in the hands of specific 'potential' investors has occurred time and time again without discernable effect" (Brenner 1977:67). Brenner specifies conditions under which productive investment (i.e., innovation in the production process) occurs: "It is only a system which is organized so that the accumulation of capital via innovation is enforced by the very structure of the social productive relations that can turn an accrual of potentially productive resources from outside to the service of economic development" (ibid). The capitalist variant of social productive relations not only "forces" holders of wealth to invest in order to maintain and reproduce their

14. Anson-Meyer (1974), Rocheteau (1982), and Fatton (1987) are among those who argue that the Senegalese regime has tried to promote an indigenous bourgeoisie. The analysis presented here suggests that the regime's efforts in this direction were so compromised, and so marginal when compared to countervailing efforts to obstruct and deflect the indigenous business class into state-mediated rentier activities, that the thesis of Anson-Meyer et al. is virtually impossible to sustain.

gains over time, but also implies the existence of a social, legal, and economic context that makes investment a rational strategy for individuals who are interested in expanding and reproducing their wealth. In Senegal neither condition pertained.

State power in Senegal was used not only to create opportunities for the accumulation of wealth in Senegalese private hands, but also to structure opportunities for the deployment of that wealth. State power was used to promote foreign (not local) private investment in monopolies in the light industrial sector. The *loi sur le domaine national* of 1964 protected peasants' rights over land. For indigenous holders of private wealth, the regime created very lucrative and low-risk opportunities for deployment of wealth in state-mediated commercial activities. The repayment of capital contracted through bank loans was not enforced, thereby reducing pressures to invest that money in profit-making activities of any kind. And wealth accumulated in these ways could be freely sent abroad, at fixed exchange rates, where it was insulated from whatever disasters might befall the Senegalese economy and ruling class. To use Brenner's formulation, there was no social or economic mechanism to force holders of wealth to undertake inherently risky investments in productive assets and activities in Senegal. Microeconomic rationality worked to sustain rentierism as a dominant mode of wealth accumulation.

Rentierism itself created an economic and political context that was most unpropitious for economic projects that immobilized otherwise liquid assets (fixed investments) and subjected these assets to political and economic risk. Arbitrary and unpredictable patterns of taxation, contract enforcement, government subsidization, and state intervention in markets made it difficult to calculate basic parameters that would affect the profitability of investments. Entrepreneurial success was highly sensitive to the political maneuverings of individuals who exercised the economic prerogatives of the state. The need to make extensive political investments to ensure the profitable functioning of enterprises inflated "transactions costs" and made them unpredictable. And the state was unable to provide some of the basic economic and legal infrastructure ("public goods" such as an expeditious bureaucracy, reliable public utilities, and a coherently functioning judicial system) that capital requires in order to expand. These problems were aggravated by the bankruptcy of the state in the 1980s. As Sandbrook argues in *The Politics of Africa's Economic Stagnation:*

Capitalism flourishes only within the context of the political, legal, and economic conditions [that are conducive to market relationships and investment]. As patrimonial states decay, they become less and less capable of providing this fertile climate. Capitalism cannot but remain stunted in this environment. Indeed, in extreme cases, a parasitical and chaotic state push[es] the modern economy close to collapse.[15]

The *hommes d'affaires sénégalais* (and their female counterparts) of the 1970s and 1980s responded rationally to the structure of incentives and risks that they faced in the local business environment. Their preference for rentier activities

---

15. Sandbrook 1985:121, 33–5. For the example of Zaire, see Callaghy 1984; and MacGaffey 1987.

cannot be explained in behavioral terms ("Senegalese" values, attitudes, inherent dispositions); it must be explained in structural terms. Foreign capital displayed the same disinclination to make fixed, productive investments in Senegal. Foreign owners of established industries amortized their investments quickly and then avoided reinvestment, relying instead on the ability of the state to protect their commercial monopolies. The textile industry is a prime example. The structure of incentive and risk produced only marginal and hesitant efforts on the part of private capital to expand the productive bases of the neocolonial economy. In the recent period, this structure of incentive and risk led to economic decay.

"If it really was the simple 'instrument' of the 'ruling class,' [the state] would be fatally inhibited in the performance of its role. Its agents absolutely need a measure of freedom in deciding how best to serve the existing social order."[16] Senegal is a case that demonstrates the power of Ralph Miliband's point. The state in Senegal lacked the autonomy required to curb the destructive tendencies inherent in an economic system organized around the "parasitical" or non-productive process of extracting wealth via commercial circuits. It also lacked the autonomy required to create conditions that would facilitate and enforce the need for productive investment on the part of those who appropriated the social surplus. Why did it lack this autonomy? Because there was no social class with the interest, the collective need, or the power to forge a state that was autonomous in these ways. Reproducing existing social relations, the existing mode of domination, and the existing mode of production did not require the state to promote capitalist development – on the contrary, the "reproductive logic" of the social formation and the political order "required" that the state assume a quite different form. Where capital did not enjoy structural hegemony, instrumental control over state power lay in the hands of a ruling stratum driven by other political needs and economic interests.

The sustained and self-expanding accumulation of capital requires a relatively autonomous state. Capital's needs, however, are not always served. States that can function in the interests of capital are the historical product of social struggles that emerge as societies are progressively organized around capitalist social relations, forms of production, and modes of accumulation. Lonsdale (1981: 167) sums up the point: "The relative autonomy of the state is a consequence of capitalist hegemony as much as its guarantee."

The apparent autonomy of the capitalist state – the political need of governments to foster job creation and profit-making in the private sector, to mediate class and other social conflicts in order to reproduce a capitalist social order, and to expand capitalist accumulation in order to generate the state's revenue base – reflects the hegemony of capital. The capitalist state will appear to be more autonomous (i.e., the state will be "stronger") in situations where labor is strong and politically well-organized (more so in France, then, than in the United States); when capital faces a deep crisis of accumulation (as during the Great

---

16. Miliband 1977:87–8, as cited by Fatton 1987:6.

Depression); and/or when capitalist classes succeed in placing herculean demands for pump priming on the state (as in cases of late industrialization in Europe). State agents if they are to be successful will have to innovate at the level of ideas (ideology) to come up with solutions to problems faced by capital, to regulate the tensions in capitalist society, and to mobilize support and consent. They will also have to create tools (institutions) to implement these ideas and to construct social coalitions that support state initiatives. Analyses showing that capitalist states have the capacity to innovate in order to regulate social, economic, and international problems do not contradict the argument that these states are structurally dependent upon capital. On the contrary, they reinforce and elaborate this argument, giving it real substance and political meaning through concrete analyses of how capitalist states have actually worked in particular, historically defined contexts.

The argument that the capitalist state operates with *relative* autonomy from capital is difficult to "test" if we confine analysis to the universe of capitalist states. At the most abstract level, whatever the capitalist state does can be seen as part of the effort to maintain the basic conditions that capital requires in order to expand in the long run. State agents operating with relative autonomy to regulate extraordinarily complex political and economic problems may come up with misguided or contradictory initiatives. If this is systematically the case, however, then it will become difficult to reproduce the state and existing class relations. The economy and state will plunge into crisis. In the effort to avoid this outcome, governments may undertake to regulate and contain both class conflict and international conflict in ways that impose certain costs and constraints on capital, or on particular factions thereof. But the theory of relative autonomy of the capitalist state holds when the state imposes costs and constraints on capital, either by mistake or by design. Is it possible to test and thus reaffirm the analytic power of a theory of *relative* state autonomy which holds even under these conditions?

It is possible to do so by looking at cases where, as Sandbrook (1985) says, "capitalism fails." States that are not embedded in a capitalist social formation, that have reproduction requirements that contradict the logic of capital, and that are the instruments of dominant classes that are profoundly threatened by the expansion and deepening of capital cannot be effective agents of capitalist development. For those who argue that the state's overriding impulse to promote and sustain capitalist development is a universal phenomenon, explainable without reference to the hegemony of capital (i.e., for those who argue that capitalist states are "truly autonomous"), African case studies such as the one presented here are useful correctives.

STATES AND SOCIETIES

It is difficult to understand the state in sub-Saharan Africa without taking into account economic and social structures that make these states different from those found in capitalist political economies. Goran Hyden (1980) and Joel

Migdal (1988) are among those who have directed attention toward rural Africa in order to explain the weakness of the African state. Hyden focuses on the noncapitalist ("precapitalist") bases of agriculture, describing how Tanzanian peasants sought to preserve the semiautonomy and coherence of their communities in the face of the intrusive ambitions of the state and the corrosive acid of the market. To a large extent, they succeed. Because they control their own labor, land, and means of subsistence, they have been able to constrain the state's attempts to "capture the peasantry." Political leaders who are bent on harnessing rural land and labor to the production of commodities are frustrated. Hyden argues that at the same time, peasant society nurtures and sustains "an 'invisible' economy of affection," structured around the mutual reciprocities of kinship, interdependence, and friendship rather than market relationships. This invisible economy "provides opportunities for social action outside the framework of state control" (Hyden 1980:28). Hyden describes how the economy of affection ultimately "infiltrated" the Tanzanian state, disorganizing its internal workings and sapping its organizational coherence. These processes waylaid the task of building Tanzanian socialism.

Joel Migdal (1988) has generalized this theme, arguing that many Third World states are weak because the societies over which they govern are strong enough to resist (to survive in the face of) the demands and transformative impulses of state managers. For Migdal, social organizations that are fragmented, localized, and semiautonomous (such as peasant communities) compete with the state for authority and power. Often, these social organizations win, circumscribing the scope of state authority and control. Hyden's and Migdal's detailed and broadly comparative analyses are representative of a growing literature on state–society relations that takes conflict and competition between the state and society as its analytic focus. The dynamic that they have uncovered is one of state "versus" society.[17]

One strength of this work is its capacity to demonstrate in very graphic ways that states differ across national contexts in their institutional structures and modes of functioning. Writers like Hyden and Migdal argue convincingly that this happens because societies are not all alike. The limitation of the state–society model is that all social forces, a priori, are viewed as lying outside of the state.

To put Migdal's model to use, for example, we must assume that all states have the same basic objectives. With this common yardstick, one can measure differences in state capacity or strength. Midgal defines the common objective as "the drive for state predominance" (1988:15). For the new states of the Third World, the drive to transform society so that the state can be predominant is universal. Migdal's purpose is to show that such states may prove to be weak in the face of societies that are able to ignore, thwart, or subvert the state's attempts

---

17. Migdal proposes a model of stark conflict. States that "overpower their own societies" are "strong," whereas states that fail in their quest to "make all the rules" and to restructure society in accordance with their modernizing designs are weak.

to rule by its own laws.[18] The ability of social forces to break down the state's organizational defenses, penetrate its inner workings, and eventually capture the state is the ultimate sign of state weakness. Midgal's and Hyden's depictions of the weak state illuminate many of the social forces and processes at work in Senegal.

As in Skocpol's notion of a "truly autonomous" state, however, in the "state versus society" model there is no social agent or source to explain the roots, character, or purposes of state power. The assumption that all states seek to transform and overpower society dispenses with the need to inquire into the purposes of state power in any particular setting. The model, then, frees analysts from the need to seek within society (or anywhere else for that matter – the forces of imperialism would be one ready alternative) an explanation for the driving impulses of the postcolonial state. The state appears to be "suspended in mid-air" (Hyden 1980:19). We are left in the difficult position of having a model of state-society relations that strips the state of its social content. From this starting point, it is impossible to identify the social origins and social character (e.g. class character) of the state and state power.

States are rooted in particular, historically configured social relations of power, production, and surplus extraction. Recognizing this at the outset makes it possible to specify and explain the driving impulses of the state in a context-specific way. The purposes of state power are shaped and constrained by the spectrum of possibilities open to a given ruling stratum that is interested in reproducing its own power.

Very basic constraints lie at the level of the "mode of production," as Hyden's work suggests.[19] Society-centered theorists underscore the fact that subordinate social strata have the capacity to resist subordination and exploitation. Forms of resistance take shape within the social relations that organize production and control over economic resources. These constraints, however, are not external to the state – they are inherent in the material and social bases of ruling strata. They shape the mechanisms of exploitation and modes of domination that create and underpin ruling strata. Within these contexts, the purposes of state power are defined by the ways in which powerful elements within society seek to gather, organize, and reproduce their power at the level of the state.

In postcolonial Africa, regime consolidation was a process of gathering, organizing, and reproducing power. It happened within and through the use of state apparatuses forged under colonialism. The ruling classes that emerged were, as Murray (1967) said, composite formations. They embraced powerful elements in society that based their claims to power and wealth on their ability to mobilize ethnic and regional solidarities, on religious authority, on old legitimacy (pre-

---

18. Hyden's (1980) portrayal of how the Tanzanian state became enmired and entangled in the kinship-based "economy of affection" conveys the same image.

19. Semiautonomous peasant communities are better equipped to resist the exploitation of other classes than are wage-laborers who need to be "exploited" via the labor–capital nexus in order to survive. The forms of resistance that workers are capable of mounting, however, can be more direct and more immediately devastating to the ruling class.

colonial aristocracies), on forms of authority created by the colonial state (many chieftaincies; positions within the colonial state), and also on wealth and capital already accumulated. These sources of political and economic power were often overlapping, and sometimes contradictory.[20] What Bayart (1989:230–40) called the coalescing of elites within the matrices of the state crystallized political arrangements which through their own logic and contradictions played a role in shaping the purposes of state power.

A model which juxtaposes the state and society makes it difficult to perceive the contradictory social character and compromised purposes of these regimes, and thus their ambivalence in the face of the "transformative project." Separation and juxtaposition of state and society also makes it difficult to perceive and to account for the political need of these ruling strata to use state power to maintain and reinforce societally based forms of power. An approach that aims at deciphering the social bases of these states, by contrast, opens possibilities for understanding these apparent paradoxes. Societally based forms of power underpinned the political dominance of postcolonial ruling strata. This helps to explain why their need to appropriate a share of the social surplus was realized through existing mechanisms of extraction, rather than through efforts to transform rural society. Exploiting agriculture in this way led regimes to shore up the very social relations of production that constrained their power. Political and economic needs inherent in the nature of these ruling strata are critical in explaining why the conservative impulse – the drive to preserve the existing social order – has been just as striking as the transformative impulse identified by Migdal and Hyden. Herein lies the source of contradictions that compromised and weakened the postcolonial state.

Lonsdale writes that the "fusion of elites" produced ruling strata that "may not have had any joint interest other than the maintenance of a social order, . . . but quite what social order . . . was itself a question. Its answer depended very much upon the way in which the fused elites had themselves been formed and the type of power they now exercised" (1981: 153). The task at hand involves understanding these coalitions in terms of the political and economic needs – and interests – that they contained. To do this it is necessary to transcend a fixation on ethnic identities that, in itself, conveys little information about how power is acquired and reproduced. It is also necessary to go beyond formalistic and economistic definitions of class interests, for in the course of pursuing their economic interests, ruling strata must also attend to the problem of holding onto power.

This path of comparative analysis was cleared by the exemplary work of writers like Barrington Moore, Jr. (1966) and Cardoso and Faletto (1979). They show how processes of economic change that are set in motion by the rise of capitalism and by imperialism are not only reflected in, but also shaped by, struggles for power that are played out within ruling classes. Economic change

---

20. These contradictions could be contained in the power bases of one person, as in the case of merchant-chiefs or chiefly presidents.

produced shifts in the locus, balance, and character of power within states. Old ruling classes seeking to protect their power confronted new contenders, rooted in new forms of trade and production. In Latin America and in Europe, old landed classes, merchant strata, agricultural capitalists, financiers, and eventually nascent industrial bourgeoisies warred and allied as they sought both to organize their collective power at the level of the state and to establish or maintain dominance within heterogeneous ruling coalitions.

In the histories written by Barrington Moore and Cardoso and Faletto, the ongoing processes of state formation and capitalist development do not appear to be driven or controlled by elites striving to promote "development" (or social transformation) for its own sake. Rather, history is driven forward in large part by competing and often contradictory efforts on the part of internally differentiated ruling classes to maintain power in the face of social and economic changes that they can neither control completely nor reverse. Old ruling strata, if they are politically or economically incapable of taking advantage of new openings, seek to hold back the tide of "the great transformation." Change is propelled forward by those who will be strengthened by it and who are best placed to reap its rewards. As Cardoso and Faletto (1979:80) write, the social groups contained within these dominant classes "were not just the mechanical result of an 'economic structure'; they tried to develop or modify that structure as a means of imposing or maintaining their particular form of domination."

Dominant and ascendent social strata in Latin America and Europe built, rebuilt, and reorganized power within the state apparatus in order to both maintain old forms of social control and to stabilize and guarantee new ones. Processes of institution-building and state formation that emerged were not always cumulative and linear. Reorganizations of state power that were driven by conflicting political needs and interests often failed to contain struggles for dominance; often political bargains that were enshrined in institutions reproduced and intensified underlying tensions that produced instability at the bottom and conflict at the top. Attempts to channel and structure forces producing social and economic change often grew out of the need to *reconcile* conflicting political needs contained within dominant strata. The impulse to reconcile reflected a shared interest in preserving and expanding established modes of domination. Political contingencies thus shaped the particular forms of state and the various forms of capitalist development that appeared over time and across contexts.

Economic policies that promoted industrialization in Brazil from the 1930s to the 1950s, for example, were not technocratic solutions to economic problems or the net result of the triumph of an urban bourgeoisie. Rather, industrialization policies and attendant strategies aimed at controlling popular forces were forged in attempts to accommodate and reconcile the economic interests and political needs of a ruling coalition that embraced both a growing urban bourgeoisie and the most "backward" elements of the old ruling class, the owners of nonexporting, low-productivity latifundia (Cardoso and Faletto 1979:129, 139–41). In eighteenth-century France, the sale of offices to bourgeois elements helped to reconcile two competing forms of social power by channeling "the commercial impulse" into the exploitation of feudal privilege (Moore 1964:59). The marriage of iron and rye in Prussia was yet another of these composite solutions that crystallized political arrangements aimed at reconciling the divergent political and economic needs of a heterogeneous dominant class. Through their own logic and contradictions, these arrangements produced the economic constraints and political forces that gave capitalist development its particular character, and its own violent history, in each setting.

Initiatives of ascendent social strata and old factions seeking to preserve their position are shaped by the ways in which these groups perceive the implications of change for their own futures. Their initiatives are shaped by assessments of possibilities for action that are open to them, given their existing economic bases and the extent to which they believe that established modes of political domination can withstand, be reinforced, or be expanded under changing conditions. Under these constraints, even the most "revolutionary" and apparently autonomous of states – the "bureaucratic-authoritarian" colonial state in sub-Saharan Africa being a good example – is likely to shrink away from social transformation and to fall back on conservative options (Phillips 1989).

"Revolutions from above" that destroy the political power of the most conservative elements within ruling coalitions, and thus clear the way for ascendent capitalist classes, happen in societies that have passed the point of no return. Ellen Kay Trimberger argues that "the institutionalization of a modern bureaucratic polity" – itself an artifact of economic and political changes that weakened the old patrimonial order – was the precondition for revolutions from above in Egypt in 1952 and in Peru in 1968 (1978:151). In these cases, coups d'état led by progressive military modernizers destroyed crisis-ridden ruling alliances that contained at their core both old landed elements and rising bourgeoisies. In doing so, these regimes were able to "destroy internal blocks to capitalist development" (ibid:148). Like Louis Bonaparte, the modernizing bureaucrats of Egypt and Peru were forced to ally with and strengthen the rising capitalist class, depoliticize the masses, and promote capitalist industrialization in order "[t]o consolidate a status quo in which their own power and status was no longer in danger" (ibid:10). The "organized power" of rising capitalist classes and the fact that the military was forced to coalesce with them "to save the state" suggests that these military modernizers were not as autonomous vis-à-vis capital as Trimberger maintains. The process of breakdown and reconstitution of the ruling alliance demonstrated the power already achieved by capital. These cases support Trimberger's argument that state power can play a decisive, even necessary role in facilitating and accelerating the process of capitalist transformation. They also support the argument advanced here: This requires a social agent – powerful and ascendent capitalist classes that provide the economic base and political guarantee for such a project, and that array behind the transformative project because they see it as the way to reproduce and enhance their own power.

The entrepreneurial role of capitalist states rests on the same foundations. By definition, the "triple alliances" that deepened the process of capitalist development in Latin America and Southeast Asia rested in part on already-existing, indigenous capitalist classes. These alliances also worked to strengthen local capital. From the perspective of this discussion, what distinguishes the East Asian NICs from other cases is not only the total and abrupt defeat of the colonial power in World War II and the nationalization of Japanese assets, but also the defeat of landlord classes. In Taiwan, Japanese colonial rulers expropriated the great landlords. Guomindang land reforms of 1949–53 crushed the "second tier of tenant landlords" (Amsden 1985:84–7). What the Nationalists had envisioned but failed to do in China in the 1930s and 1940s because "would-be expropriated landlords were stalwarts of the Nationalists," the Mainlander government was able to achieve in Taiwan "because it was under no obligation to the rural Taiwanese elite" (ibid). Just as significant were the methods subsequently employed by the Guomindang state in extracting the rural surpluses that financed further militarism and industrialization. Mechanisms of state extraction worked to shore up a rural society organized along a "bourgeois model of individual family farming" and to increase not only output, but productivity as well (ibid: 85). In southern Korea, war, occupation, and land reforms in the early 1950s ended the dominance of a conservative landlord class that had used state power in the immediate post-World War II years "in traditional fashion to protect social privilege rather than to foster growth" (Cumings 1987:66). Rural class relations may be as important as inflows of American aid in explaining the relative autonomy of the East Asian states and their political capacity to organize and deepen the process of capitalist development.[21] At this level, the contrast with Senegal is striking.

In Africa, where political independence brought heterogeneous and fissiparous coalitions to power, the fusion or coalescing of elites at the level of the state brought together elements constituted within very different precapitalist modes of production, merchant strata, bourgeois elements, professional strata, and complex hybrids thereof (Bayart 1989). The weakness of local capital in general was compounded by its political weakness within these alignments. Possibilities for the expansion of capital were constrained by the nature of state power as it is constituted at the moment, and by level and forms of capitalist development already achieved.

Bourgeois elements and the political class (so-called petty bourgeois elements) were forced to share power with elites rooted directly in precapitalist agrarian societies. In some cases this alliance was manifest starkly at the level of the ruling coalition itself, as in Senegal or in the Northern Nigeria/Southern Nigeria alliance. In others it was not obvious at the level of the ruling coalition per se but was nonetheless embedded in the structures of political control (varied forms of "indirect rule") that allowed regimes to govern rural society while extracting a share of the agricultural surplus. The collective power that these ruling strata now exercised rested on the marriage of state power, existing methods of extracting the surplus, and a mode of domination that shored up authority-based (as distinct from market-based) forms of social control in the countryside. These arrange-

21. See Peter B. Evans 1987:221.

ments narrowed the political and economic possibilities that were actually open to would-be capitalist strata, and hence, shaped the ways in which indigenous capitalists defined and sought to pursue their interests. As Baran's analysis suggests, they were likely to seek to preserve the power that they had already accumulated by working within prevailing arrangements, even if these arrangements constrained possibilities for the expansion of capital. Where would they have found the collective interest in risking all by pushing a transformative project?

Debates over the existence or nonexistence of African bourgeoisies have highlighted variations across cases, showing that in places like Kenya local capital had both more weight within ruling coalitions and more room to maneuver on the ground. Most notably, lucrative possibilities for local private investment in commercial agriculture existed in Kenya. This fact itself implied both the existence of a rural wage labor force and of well-developed institutional structures, inherited from colonialism, for subsidizing investment and supporting commercial production in this critical sector of the economy. Political and economic factors such as these are critical indicators of variation in the strength of capital within African social formations and hence, of conditions that affect the strength and character of local capitalist classes. They help to account for the extent to which a universal phenomenon – the accumulation of resources in the political sphere – fuels the specific practice of productive investment in any given setting.[22]

Generalizing across cases, it is fair to say that the postcolonial political order has had contradictory effects on possibilities for local capital accumulation. Perhaps the ultimate expression of the dialectical qualities of this process is the emergence of new space for private capital accumulation in the context of the decay or collapse of the state. Janet MacGaffey's (1987) analyses of Zaire document this process in detail. In Zaire the crumbling of the state's administrative capacity under the weight of pillage and corruption on the part of its "parasitic aristocracy" – what some see as the virtual collapse and withdrawal of the state from much of Zaire's interior – has been accompanied by the rise of a small but growing class of capitalist entrepreneurs in Zaire's "second economy." In Northeast Zaire, including the regional center of Kisangani, men and women without connections to the state have accumulated resources and invested in coffee plantations, sawmills, furniture factories, ranches, gold and diamond mining, and in an array of commercial activities as well. Looking at the second economy as a whole, MacGaffey writes that "the scale and intensiveness of these activities have profound implications for . . . understanding the processes of class formation" (ibid:111). Rather than developing with state support and through ruling classes, capitalist processes of production and accumulation may begin to develop "against" them.

22. For example, Leys (1978:253) reports that "modern forms of plunder" (e.g., smuggling, theft) financed the acquisition of productive land on the part of some Kenyans in the 1970s. Resources accumulated through politics in the form of patronage, kickbacks, etc. financed some of the private investment in Kenyan industry that is documented by Swainson (1980).

In Senegal as in Zaire, state-sponsored rentierism in the context of an increasingly anarchic political-administrative environment has contributed to a decline in productive investment in the "official economy" while giving rise to a parallel economy that operates beyond the scope of state control. In Senegal's second economy of entrepreneurs without connections to the state, however, possibilities for the accumulation of resources on the scale and the form necessary for productive investment are more concentrated and circumscribed than they are in Zaire. For Senegalese businesspeople who do accumulate wealth on a significant scale, access to foreign bank accounts and to state-mediated commercial activities remains open, creating options for deployment of wealth that are apparently more lucrative and certainly less risky than options for productive investment that exist in the Senegalese economy.

In Senegal the productive bases of the economy are narrowing under the pressure of disinvestment and exhaustion of the productive potential of rain-fed land. As rentiers cluster around and within the weakening state, the unproductive extraction of wealth continues. That this is the case is, in large part, the result of how state power was consolidated and used in postcolonial Senegal. Relations of power and social control that underpinned and structured the postcolonial state ended up "determining" a form of economy that "turned in upon itself" and collapsed.[23]

---

23. These are Brenner's phrases, used in the context of an argument about the feudal order of European serf lords and the stagnation-prone and regressive economic tendencies inherent in it (1977:46).

Appendix: Exchange rates

Table A.1. *Approximate averages of exchange rates. One U.S. dollar in CFA francs 1958–90*

Years	CFA francs
1958–68	247
1969–71	278
1971–2	256
1973–4	230
1975	225
1976	239
1977	245
1979	213
1980	211
1982	272
1983	381
1984 (November)	451
1985 (February)	502
1990 (December)	236

Note: As of January 1992 the value of the CFA franc remains fixed at 50 CFA to one French franc.

References

Adamolekun, 'Lapido. 1971. "Bureaucrats and the Senegalese Political Process." *Journal of Modern African Studies* 9, no. 4: 543–59.

Ahounou, Jacqueline, et al. 1983. "Gestion des Petites et Moyennes Entreprises (PMEs): Un exemple Sénégalais – La SIFAEMA." Dakar, ENSUT, Université de Dakar, mars.

Ajayi, JFA, and Michael Crowder (eds.). 1973. *History of West Africa*, vol. 2. New York: Columbia University Press.

Alavi, Hamza. 1972. "The State in Post-Colonial Societies – Pakistan and Bangladesh." *New Left Review*, no. 74 (July–August): 59–81.

Amin, Samir. 1969. *Le Monde des Affaires Sénégalais*. Paris: Editions de Minuit.

1971. "La politique coloniale française à l'égard de la bourgeoisie commerçante sénégalaise (1820–1960)." In *The Development of Indigenous Trade and Markets in West Africa*. Edited by Claude Meillassoux, pp. 361–76. London: Oxford University Press.

1973. *Neo-colonialism in West Africa*. New York: Monthly Review Press.

1981. "Preface." In Bernard Founou-Tchuigoua, *Fondements de l'économie de traite au Sénégal*, pp. 9–14. Paris: Editions Silex.

Amsden, Alice H. 1985. "The State and Taiwan's Economic Development." In *Bringing the State Back In*. Edited by Peter Evans, Dietrich Reuschemeyer, and Theda Skocpol, pp. 78–106. Cambridge University Press.

Anderson, Lisa. 1986. *The State and Social Transformation in Tunisia and Libya, 1830–1980*. Princeton, N.J.: Princeton University Press.

Angliviel de la Beaumelle, R. 1947. *L'Industrie cotonnière et la France d'Outre-Mer*. Paris: Syndicat Général de l'Industrie Cotonnière Française.

Anson-Meyer, Monique. 1974. *Mécanismes de l'exploitation en Afrique: l'exemple du Sénégal*. Paris: Editions Cujas.

Arrighi, Giovanni. 1973. "Labor Supplies in Historical Perspective: A Study of the Proletarianization of the African Peasantry in Rhodesia." In *Essays on the Political Economy of Africa*. Edited by Giovanni Arrighi and John S. Saul, pp. 180–234. New York: Monthly Review Press.

Ba, C[heikh] K[oureyssi]. 1984. "Rapport de Premier Séjour en Entreprise: SOTIBA–SIMPAFRIC." Dakar: Ecole Supérieure de Gestion des Entreprises, 31 juillet.

1985. "Mémoire de stage de longue durée à SOTIBA–SIMPAFRIC: Gestion des ressources humaines." Dakar: Centre Africain des Etudes Supérieures en Gestion (CESAG), décembre.

Banque Mondiale. *See* World Bank.

Baran, Paul. 1952. "On the Political Economy of Backwardness." *The Manchester School*, January: 66–84. (Reprinted in *The Political Economy of Development and Underdevelopment*, Edited by Charles K. Wilber, pp. 87–98. New York: Random House, 1984.)

Barker, Jonathan. 1973. "Political Factionalism in Senegal." *Canadian Journal of African Studies* 7, no. 2: 287–303.
    1985. "Gaps in the Debates about Agriculture in Senegal, Tanzania, and Mozambique." *World Development* 13, no. 1: 59–76.
Barry, Boubacar. 1985. "Le Sénégal 1960–1980: L'Arachide, bourgeoisie bureaucratique, et sécheresse." Paper presented at the Colloque sur les Indépendances Africaines: Origines et Conséquences du Transfert du Pouvoir, 1956–1980; University of Zimbabwe, 8–11 janvier.
    1988. "Neocolonialism and Dependence in Senegal." In *Decolonization and African Independence.* Edited by Prosser Gifford and W[illia]m Roger Louis, pp. 271–294. New Haven, Conn.: Yale University Press.
Bates, Robert. 1981. *Markets and States in Tropical Africa.* Berkeley and Los Angeles: University of California Press.
Bauer, P. T. 1954. *West African Trade: A Study of Competition, Oligopoly, and Monopoly.* Cambridge University Press.
Bayart, Jean François. 1989. *L'Etat en Afrique.* Paris: Fayard.
Beckman, Bjorn. 1976. *Organising the Farmers: Cocoa Politics and National Development in Ghana.* Uppsala: Scandinavian Institute of African Studies.
    1980. "Imperialism and Capitalist Transformation: Critique of the Kenyan Debate." *Review of African Political Economy,* no. 19: 48–62.
    1981. "Ghana, 1951–78: The Agrarian Bases of the Post-Colonial State." In *Rural Development in Tropical Africa.* Edited by Judith Heyer, Pepe Roberts, and Gavin Williams, pp. 143–67. New York: St. Martin's.
    1982. "Whose State? State and Capitalist Development in Nigeria." *Review of African Political Economy,* no. 23: 37–51.
Behrman, Lucy C. 1970. *Muslim Brotherhoods and Politics in Senegal.* Cambridge: Harvard University Press.
Bellot, Jean-Marc. 1985. "Sénégal: crise du développement rural." *Le Mois en Afrique,* nos. 233–4 (juin–juillet): 43–51.
Berg, Elliot J. 1960. "The Economic Basis of Political Choice in French West Africa." *American Political Science Review,* no. 54: 391–405.
Berman, Bruce. 1984. "Structure and Process in the Bureaucratic States of Colonial Africa." *Development and Change* 15:161–202.
Berrier, Robert Jim. 1978. "The Politics of Industrial Survival: The French Textile Industry." Ph.D. Thesis, Department of Political Science, Massachusetts Institute of Technology, Cambridge, Mass.
Berry, Sara. 1983. "Agrarian Crisis in Africa? A Review and an Interpretation." Paper prepared for the Joint African Studies Committee of the SSRC and ACLS, September 1983, for presentation at the Annual Meetings of the African Studies Association, Boston, December.
Berry, Sara. 1984. "The Food Crisis and Agrarian Change in Africa: A Review Essay." *African Studies Review* 27, no. 2: 59–112.
Bienen, Henry. 1974. *Kenya: The Politics of Participation and Control.* Princeton, N.J.: Princeton University Press.
Biersteker, Thomas. 1987a. "Indigenization and the Nigerian Bouregoisie." In *The African Bourgeoisie.* Edited by Paul Lubeck, pp. 249–80. Boulder, Colo.: Lynne Rienner.
    1987b. *Multinationals, the State, and Control of the Nigerian Economy.* Princeton, N.J.: Princeton University Press.
Bonnardel, Régine Nguyen Van Chi. 1978. *Vie de relations au Sénégal: la circulation des biens.* Dakar: IFAN.
Bonnefonds, Asté Léon. 1968. "La transformation du commerce de traite en Côte d'Ivoire depuis la dernière guerre mondiale et l'indépendance." *Les Cahiers d'Outre-Mer, Revue de Géographie,* no. 84 (octobre–décembre): 395–413.

Brenner, Robert. 1977. "The Origins of Capitalist Development: A Critique of Neo-Smithian Marxism." *New Left Review*, no. 104 (July–August): 25–92.

Brett, E. A. 1973. *Colonialism and Underdevelopment in East Africa: The Politics of Economic Change 1919–1939*. New York: NOK Publishers.

Bye, Pascal, and Yvon Le Moal. 1965. "Commercialisation et diffusion des produits alimentaires importés." Dakar: Institut de Science Economique Appliquée (ISEA).

Callaghy, Thomas M. 1979. "The Difficulties of Implementing Socialist Strategies of Development in Africa: The 'First Wave.' " In *Socialism in Sub-Saharan Africa*. Edited by Carl G. Rosberg and Thomas M. Callaghy, pp. 112–29. Berkeley and Los Angeles: University of California, Berkeley Institute of International Studies.

———. 1984. *The State-Society Struggle: Zaire in Comparative Perspective*. New York: Columbia University Press.

———. 1987. "Absolutism, Bonapartism, and the Formation of Ruling Classes: Zaire in Comparative Perspective." In *Studies in Power and Class in Africa*. Edited by I. L. Markovitz, pp. 95–117. Oxford: Oxford University Press.

Campbell, Bonnie. 1973. "The Social, Political, and Economic Consequences of French Private Investment in the Ivory Coast, 1960–1970: A Case Study of Cotton Textile Production." Ph.D. Thesis, University of Sussex.

———. 1974. "Social Change and Class Formation in a French West African State." *Canadian Journal of African Studies* 8, no. 2: 285–306.

———. 1975. "Neocolonialism, Economic Dependence, and Political Change: A Case Study of Cotton and Textile Production in the Ivory Coast, 1960–1970." *Review of African Political Economy*, no. 2: 36–53.

Cardoso, Fernando Henrique, and Enzo Faletto. 1979. *Dependency and Development in Latin America*. Berkeley and Los Angeles: University of California Press.

Carponnier, François. 1959. *La Crise de l'industrie cotonnière française*. Paris: Editions Génin.

Casswell, N. 1984. "Autopsie de l'ONCAD: La politique arachidière du Sénégal, 1966–1980." *Politique Africaine*, no. 14, (juin): 39–73.

Centre du Commerce International (UNCTAD/GATT). 1975. "Programme intègre de promotion des exportations sénégalaises (rapport sur la mission effectuée à Dakar par André R. Navet, Conseiller en Développement des Exportations)," décembre.

Chambre de Commerce de Marseille. 1950. *XXVème Conférence des Chambres de Commerce de la Méditerranée et de l'Afrique Française*, 12–13 octobre 1950. Marseille.

———. 1953. *XXVIIIème Conférence des Chambres de Commerce de la Méditerranée et de l'Afrique Française*, 24–5 septembre 1953. Marseille.

Charbonneau, René. 1961. *Marchés et marchands d'Afrique Noire*. Paris: Editions de la Colombe.

Chardonnet, Jean. 1956. *L'Industrialisation de l'Afrique*. Paris: Publications de l'Institute Universitaire de Hautes Etudes Internationales, no. 26.

Chazan, Naomi. 1983. *An Anatomy of Ghanaian Politics: Managing Political Recession, 1969–1982*. Boulder, Colo.: Westview.

CINAM (Compagnie d'Etudes Industrielles et d'Aménagement du Territorie). 1961. *Notes sur l'industrialisation du Sénégal, étude réalisée à la demande du Gouvernement du Sénégal*. Dakar, mars.

CINAM et SERESA (La Compagnie d'Etudes Industrielles et d'Aménagement du Territoire et La Société d'Etudes et de Réalisations Economiques et Sociales dans l'Agriculture). 1960. *Rapport général sur les perspectives de développement du Sénégal, réalisé à la demande du Gouvernement du Sénégal en 1959*, vols. 1–5. Dakar.

Cissé, Daniel. 1969. *Problèmes de la formation de l'epargne interne en Afrique Occidentale*. Paris: Editions Présence Africaine.

Cohen, Michael A. 1974. *Urban Policy and Political Conflict in Africa: A Study of the Ivory Coast.* Chicago: University of Chicago Press.

Coleman, James S., and Carl G. Rosberg, Jr., eds. 1964. *Political Parties and National Integration in Tropical Africa.* Berkeley and Los Angeles: University of California Press.

Collier, Ruth Berins. 1982. *Regimes in Tropical Africa: Changing Forms of Supremacy 1945–1975.* Berkeley and Los Angeles: University of California Press.

Coly, Omar. 1971. "SONEPI et la promotion industrielle des Sénégalais." Exposé soumis à l'Institut de Coopération Internationale de l'Université d'Ottawa, 15 juin.

"Le Commerce franco–coloniale en 1937." 1938. *Bulletin Quotidien de la Société d'Etudes et d'Informations Economiques,* no. 165 (25 juillet).

Commission des Communautés Européennes. 1974. *Les conditions d'installation d'entreprises industrielles dans les états Africains et Malagache associés.* Vol. 18: *République du Sénégal.* Bruxelles, juillet.

Copans, Jean. 1988. *Les Marabouts de l'Arachide: La confrérie mouride et les paysans du Sénégal.* Paris: L'Harmattan. First published in 1980 (Paris: Le Sycomore).

Cottingham, Clement. 1970. "Political Consolidation and Centre-Local Relations in Senegal." *Canadian Journal of African Studies* 4, no. 1 (Winter): 101–20.

Coquery-Vidrovitch, Catherine. 1979. "Vichy et l'industrialisation aux colonies." *Revue de l'Histoire de la Deuxième Guerre Mondiale,* no. 114 (avril): 69–94.

Coulon, Christian. 1981. *Le Marabout et le Prince: Islam et pouvoir au Sénégal.* Paris: Editions A. Pedone.

Courtois, Guy. 1971. "Le Rôle des capitaux privés étrangers dans le développement economique: l'exemple du Sénégal." Thèse de doctorat (3ème cycle), Université de Paris.

Crowder, Michael. 1968. *West Africa under Colonial Rule.* Evanston, Ill.: Northwestern University Press.

——— 1978. *Colonial West Africa: Collected Essays.* London: Frank Class and Co. Ltd.

Cruise O'Brien, Donal B. 1967. "Political Opposition in Senegal: 1960–1967." *Government and Opposition* 2, no. 4 (July–October): 557–66.

——— 1971a. *The Mourides of Senegal: Political and Economic Organisation of an Islamic Brotherhood.* Oxford: Oxford University Press (Clarendon Press).

——— 1971b. "Co-operators and Bureaucrats: Class Formation in a Senegalese Peasant Society." *Africa, Journal of the International African Institute* 41, no. 4 (October): 263–77.

——— 1975. *Saints and Politicians: Essays in the Organisation of a Senegalese Peasant Society.* Cambridge University Press.

——— 1978. "Senegal." In *West African States: Failure and Promise.* Edited by John Dunn, pp. 173–88; 245–7. Cambridge University Press.

——— 1979. "Ruling Class and Peasantry in Senegal: 1960–1976." In *The Political Economy of Underdevelopment: Dependence in Senegal.* Edited by Rita Cruise O'Brien, pp. 209–27. London: Sage Publications.

——— 1984. "Des Bienfaits de l'inégalité: l'état et l'économie rurale au Sénégal." *Politique Africaine,* no. 14.

Cruise O'Brien, Donal B., and Christian Coulon. 1989. "Senegal." *Contemporary West African States,* Edited by Donal B. Cruise O'Brien, John Dunn, and Richard Rathbone, pp. 145–164. Cambridge University Press.

Cruise O'Brien, Rita. 1972. *White Society in Black Africa: The French of Senegal.* London: Faber & Faber Ltd.

——— 1975. "Lebanese Entrepreneurs in Senegal: Economic Integration and the Politics of Protection." *Cahiers d'Etudes Africaines* 15, no. 57: 95–115.

——— 1979. "Introduction." In *The Political Economy of Underdevelopment: Dependence in Senegal.* Edited by Rita Cruise O'Brien, pp. 13–37. London: Sage Publications.

Cumings, Bruce. 1987. "The Origins and Development of the Northeast Asian Political Economy: Industrial Sectors, Product Cycles, and Political Consequences," in *The Political Economy of the New Asian Industrialism*, edited by Frederic C. Deyo, pp. 44–83. Ithaca, N.Y.: Cornell University Press.

Diarra, Mamadou. 1972. *Les Etats africains et la garantie monétaire de la France.* Dakar: Les Nouvelles Editions Africaines.

Diedhiou, Joachim. 1978. "Entreprise textile STS: étude géographique." Université de Dakar, Faculté de Lettres et des Sciences Humaines, Département de Géographie, novembre.

Diop, Majhemout. 1972. *Histoire des classes sociales dans l'Afrique de l'ouest.* Vol. 2: *Le Sénégal.* Paris, François Maspero.

Diop, M[omar] C[oumba]. 1981. "Les Affaires mourides à Dakar." *Politique Africaine* 1, no. 4 (novembre): 90–100.

Diop, Momar Coumba, and Mamadou Diouf. 1990. *Le Sénégal sous Abdou Diouf.* Paris: Editions Karthala.

Diop, Salif, and Yoro Kanté. 1983. "Politique générale d'entreprise – étude diagnostic de la Manufacture de Tricotages Mécaniques du Sénégal." Dakar: Ecole Supérieure de Gestion des Entreprises.

——— 1984. "Politique générale d'entreprise – cas de la 'SBS.' " Dakar: Ecole Supérieure de Gestion des Entreprises, 31 juillet.

Diouck, Ibrihima. 1986. "Diagnostic de la situation commerciale d'Icotaf: rapport de stage du 1 août au 31 décembre 1985." Dakar: Centre Africain des Etudes Supérieures en Gestion (CESAG), janvier.

Diouf, J[ean]-B[aptiste]. 1977. "Le service commercial de la SOTIBA–SIMPAFRIC et la circulation des tissus fancies, waxes, et guinée – mémoire de stage." Université de Dakar (CREA).

Documentation et Analyses Financiers des Sociétés Anonymes (DAFSA-KOMPASS). 1985. *Les Liaisons financières.* Vol. 2: *Analyses des secteurs – filatures/tissages. Paris: DAFSA.*

Duruflé, Gilles. 1988. L'Ajustement structurel en Afrique: Sénégal, Côte d'Ivoire, Madagascar. Paris: Editions Karthala.

Ediafric, La Documentation Africaine. 1965. *Memento de l'economie africaine au sud du Sahara, 1965.* Paris: Ediafric.

——— 1969. *Sociétés et fournisseurs d'Afrique Noire et de Madagascar.* Paris: La Documentation Africaine.

——— 1970a. *La Politique africaine en 1969.* Paris: La Documentation Africaine.

——— 1970b. *L'Industrie africaine en 1969.* Paris: La Documentation Africaine.

——— 1976. *L'Industrie africaine en 1975.* Paris: La Documentation Africaine.

Ediafric, La Documentation Française. 1976. *L'Economie sénégalaise en 1975.* Paris: La Documentation Française.

Eisenstadt, S. N., and René Lemarchand. 1981. *Political Clientelism, Patronage, and Development.* Beverly Hills, Calif.: Sage Publications.

Elliot Berg Associates. 1990. "Adjustment Postponed: Economic Policy Reform in Senegal in the 1980s (a report prepared under USAID/Dakar contract)." Dakar, October.

Engberg, Holger L. 1973. "The Operations Account in French-Speaking Africa." *Journal of Modern African Studies* 11, no. 4: 537–45.

Ergas, Zaki. 1982. "The State and Economic Deterioration: The Tanzanian Case." *Journal of Commonwealth and Comparative Politics* 20, no. 3: 286–308.

Europa Yearbook. 1983. *Africa South of the Sahara, 1982–1983.* London: Europa Publications.

Evans, Peter [B.]. 1979. *Dependent Development: The Alliance of Multinational, State, and Local Capital in Brazil.* Princeton, Princeton University Press.

Evans, Peter [B.]. 1987. "Class, State, and Dependence in East Asia: Lessons for Latin Americanists." In *The Political Economy of the New Asian Industrialism*, Edited by Frederic C. Deyo, pp. 203–26. Ithaca, N.Y.: Cornell University Press.

Evans, Peter B., Dietrich Reuschemeyer, and Theda Skocpol. 1985. "On the Road to a More Adequate Understanding of the State." In Evans et al., *Bringing the State Back In*, pp. 347–66. Cambridge University Press.

Ewing, A. F. 1968. *Industry in Africa*. London: Oxford University Press.

Fall, A[madou] M[anel]. 1984. "Rapport de fin de stage: la fraude dans le domaine textile, le cas de la SOTIBA–SIMPAFRIC." Dakar: Université de Dakar, Faculté des Sciences Juridiques et Economiques.

Fall, Mar. 1985. "La question islamique au Sénégal: la religion contre l'Etat?" *Le Mois en Afrique*, no. 229–230 (février-mars 1985):37–46.

Fanon, Franz. 1965. *The Wretched of the Earth*. London: MacGibbon & Kee.

Fatton, Jr., Robert. 1987. *The Making of a Liberal Democracy: Senegal's Passive Revolution, 1975–1985*. Boulder, Colo.: Lynne Rienner.

Fauré, Y.-A., and J. F. Médard. 1982. *Etat et bourgeoisie en Côte d'Ivoire*. Paris, Karthala.

Fayama, André Soungalo. 1977. "Rapport de Stage Effectué à SPCA-Thubet." Dakar: Université de Dakar, Faculté des Sciences Juridiques et Economiques.

Ferrandi, Jacques. 1962. "L'Industrialisation du Sénégal." *La Revue de l'industrie belge*, no. 5 (mai): 279–93.

First, Ruth. 1970. *Power in Africa*. New York: Pantheon.

Flynn, Peter. 1974. "Class, Clientelism, and Coercion: Some Mechanisms of Internal Dependency and Control." *Journal of Commonwealth and Comparative Politics* 12, no. 2: 133–56.

Foltz, William J. 1964. "Senegal." In *Political Parties and National Integration in Tropical Africa*. Edited by James S. Coleman and Carl G. Rosberg, pp. 16–64. Berkeley and Los Angeles: University of California Press.

——— 1965. *From French West Africa to the Mali Federation*. New Haven, Conn.: Yale University Press.

——— 1969. "Social Structure and Political Behavior of Senegalese Elites." *Behavior Science Notes* 4, no. 2: 145–63.

——— 1977. "Social Structure and Political Behavior of Senegalese Elites." In *Friends, Followers and Factions: A Reader in Political Clientelism*. Edited by Steffen W. Schmidt, James C. Scott, Carl Landé, and Laura Guasti, pp. 242–50. Berkeley and Los Angeles: University of California Press.

Forrest, Tom. 1987. "State Capital, Capitalist Development, and Class Formation in Nigeria." In *The African Bourgeoisie*. Edited by Paul Lubeck, pp. 307–42. Boulder, Colo.: Lynne Rienner.

Founou-Tchuigoua, Bernard. 1981. *Fondements de l'economie de traite au Sénégal: la surexploitation d'une colonie de 1880 à 1960*. Paris: Editions Silex.

Gellar, Sheldon. 1976. *Structural Changes and Colonial Dependency: Senegal 1885–1945*. London: Sage Publications.

——— 1982. *Senegal: An African Nation between East and West*. Boulder, Colo.: Westview.

Gellar, Sheldon, Robert B. Charlick, and Yvonne Jones. 1980. *Animation Rurale and Rural Development: The Experience of Senegal*. Ithaca, N.Y.: Cornell University Rural Development Committee, Special Series on Animation Rural.

Gerschenkron, Alexander. 1952. "Economic Backwardness in Historical Perspective." In *The Progress of Underdeveloped Countries*. Edited by Bert Hoselitz, Chicago: University of Chicago Press.

Gouvernement du Sénégal (GOS), Centre Sénégalais du Commerce Extérieur. 1980. "Diagnostic d'entreprises sénégalaises. Chap. 1: Secteur textile et confection. Etude réalisée par MM. Jean-Luc Gonfard et Michel Lefebvre." Dakar, 30 juin.

——— 1982. *Répertoire des exportateurs du Sénégal*. 2ème edition. Dakar.

1985. *Programme de la Journée Nationale du Textile*, 6ème FIDAK, 30 novembre 1984. Dakar, 15 septembre.

Gouvernement du Sénégal (GOS), Chambre de Commerce et de l'Industrie, Région du Cap Vert (CCI-RCV). 1966. *Guide de l'investisseur au Sénégal*. Dakar, juillet.

1980. Dakar, février.

Gouvernement du Sénégal (GOS), Ministère des Finances et Affaires Economiques, Direction de la Statistique. 1980. *Situation économique du Sénégal, 1959–1979*. Numéro Special. Dakar.

1981. *Analyse du commerce extérieur du Sénégal, 1981*. Dakar.

1983a. *Evolution conjoncturelle, 1983*. Dakar.

1983b. *La Situation économique du Sénégal, 1982*. Dakar.

Gouvernement du Sénégal (GOS), Ministère du Plan et du Développement (avec le Ministère de la Coopération de la France). 1965. *Le Secteur textile au Sénégal*, vols. 1 and 2. Dakar, juillet-août.

Gouvernement du Sénégal (GOS), Ministère du Plan et de la Coopération. 1977a. *Bulletin Semestriel d'Information sur l'Exécution du Plan*, no. 4. Dakar, février.

1977b. *Bulletin Semestriel d'Information sur l'Exécution du Plan*. Dakar, août.

1985. *Projet du VII Plan de Développement Economique et Social, 1985–1989*. Dakar, mars.

Gouvernement du Sénégal (GOS), SONED (Société Nationale d'Etudes). 1974. *Recensement Industriel, 1974*. Dakar.

1976. SONED (Société Nationale d'Etudes), Ministère des Finances et Affaires Economiques, Direction de la Statistique, et Ministère du Plan et de la Coopération. *Les Activités du secteur économique moderne au Sénégal d'après les résultats du recensement général des entreprises*, vols. 1–3. Dakar, juin.

1977a. *Eléments d'intégration industrielle*. Vol. 1: *Bilan du processus d'industrialisation*. Dakar, avril.

1977b. *Eléments d'intégration industrielle*. Vol. 7: *Résumé et conclusions*. Dakar, avril.

1979. SONED, Ministère du Développement Industriel et de l'Artisanat. *Le Textile au Sénégal, le marché intérieur et l'industrie locale*. Vol. 1: *Rapport principal*. Dakar: SONED, juin.

1980. SONED, Ministère du Plan et de la Coopération. *Le Textile au Sénégal*. Vol. 2: *Projet de filature–tissage d'écrus support d'impression. Etude préliminaire*. Dakar: SONED, juin.

Gouvernement du Sénégal (GOS), SONEPI (Société Nationale d'Etudes et Promotion Industrielle). 1971. *Coût des facteurs industriels au Sénégal*. Dakar.

1973. *Guide de l'investisseur: coût des facteurs industriels au Sénégal*. Dakar, mars.

1975. *Guide de l'investisseur: coût des facteurs industriels au Sénégal*. Dakar.

Guernier, Eugène (ed.). 1949. *Afrique Occidentale Française*, vols. 1 and 2. Paris: Encyclopédie Coloniale et Maritime.

Gutkind, Peter C. W., and Immanuel Wallerstein. 1976. "Introduction." In *The Political Economy of Contemporary Africa*. Edited by Peter C. W. Gutkind and Immanuel Wallerstein, pp. 7–29. Beverly Hills, Calif.: Sage Publications.

Halpern, Jan. 1972. "La Confrérie des mourides et le développement au Sénégal." *Cultures et Développement* 3, no. 1: 99–125.

Hazlewood, Arthur. 1967. *African Integration and Disintegration: Case Studies in Economic and Political Union*. London: Oxford University Press.

Hirschman, Albert O. 1979. "The Turn to Authoritarianism in Latin America and the Search for Its Economic Determinants," in *The New Authoritarianism in Latin America*, Edited by David Collier, pp. 61–98. Princeton, N.J.: Princeton University Press.

Hopkins, A. G. 1973. *An Economic History of West Africa*. New York: Columbia University Press.

Humblot, Paul. 1951. "La Libération des échanges et l'Union Française d'Outre-Mer." *Recueil Penant* (janvier–mars).

Hyden, Goran. 1980. *Beyond Ujamaa in Tanzania*. Berkeley and Los Angeles: University of California Press.

IDET-CEGOS. 1974. *Etude des circuits de distribution au Sénégal*. Dakar, mai.

Iliffe, John. 1983. *The Emergence of African Capitalism*. Minneapolis: University of Minnesota Press.

IMF. *See* International Monetary Fund.

Industries et Travaux d'Outre-Mer. 1956. "La structure des prix en AOF: structures et pratiques commerciales," no. 27 (février): 61–73.

Institut de Science Economique Appliquée (ISEA). 1964. "Les Industries du Cap-Vert: analyse d'un ensemble d'industries légères de l'Afrique Occidentale." Dakar: ISEA, janvier.

International Monetary Fund (IMF). 1970. *Surveys of African Economies*. Vol. 3: *Dahomey, Ivory Coast, Mauritania, Niger, Senegal, Togo, and Upper Volta*. Washington D.C.: International Monetary Fund.

1977. *World Debt Tables*. Washington D.C.: International Monetary Fund.

ISEA. *See under* Institut de Science Economique Appliquée.

Jackson, Robert H., and Carl G. Rosberg. 1982. *Personal Rule in Black Africa: Prince, Autocrat, Prophet, Tyrant*. Berkeley and Los Angeles: University of California Press.

Jacquemot, Pierre. 1983. "Le FMI et l'Afrique Sub-Saharienne." *Le Mois en Afrique*, no. 211–12 (août–septembre): 107–119.

Jacquot, Michel-Jean. 1963. "La Politique douanière et la coopération franco-africaine." *Penant: Revue de Droit des Pays d'Afrique*, décembre.

Jodoin, Michèle. 1963. "Les Industries manufacturières de la région Dakaroise." Université de Montreal, Département de Géographie, Montreal.

Johnson, Jr., G. Wesley. 1971. *The Emergence of Black Politics in Senegal: The Struggle for Power in the Four Communes, 1900–1921*. Stanford, Calif.: Stanford University Press.

Joseph, Richard. 1976. "The Gaullist Legacy: Patterns of French Neo-Colonialism." *Review of African Political Economy*, no. 6: 4–13.

1987. *Democracy and Prebendal Politics in Nigeria: The Rise and Fall of the Second Republic*. Cambridge University Press.

Kaplinsky, Raphael. 1980. "Capitalist Accumulation in the Periphery: The Kenyan Case Re-examined." *Review of African Political Economy*, no. 17: 85–105.

Kasfir, Nelson. 1987. "Class, Political Domination and the African State." In *The African State in Transition*. Edited by Zaki Ergas, pp. 45–61. New York: St. Martin's.

Kay, G[eoffrey] B. 1975. *Development and Underdevelopment: A Marxist Analysis*. London: The Macmillian Press Ltd.

Kennedy, Paul. 1988. *African Capitalism*. Cambridge University Press.

Kitching, Gavan. 1980. *Class and Economic Change in Kenya*. New Haven, Conn.: Yale University Press.

Klein, Martin A. 1968. *Islam and Imperialism in Senegal: Sine-Saloum, 1847–1914*. Stanford, Calif.: Stanford University Press.

Krasner, Stephen D. 1978. *Defending the National Interest*. Princeton, N.J.: Princeton University Press.

Krueger, Anne. 1974. "The Political Economy of the Rent-Seeking Society." *American Economic Review* 64: 291–303.

Langdon, Steven. 1977. "The State and Capitalism in Kenya." *Review of African Political Economy*, no. 8: 90–8.

1980. *Multinational Corporations and the Political Economy of Kenya*. London: Macmillian.

LeDuc, Gaston. 1953. "Les Hauts Prix en Afrique Noire." *Industries et Travaux d'Outre-Mer*, décembre.
1954. "Les Hauts Prix en Afrique Noire." *Industries et Travaux d'Outre-Mer*, janvier and février.
Lele, Uma, Nicolas Van de Walle, and Mathurin Gbetibouo. 1989. *Cotton in Africa: An Analysis of Differences in Performance.* Washington, D.C.: The World Bank.
Lemarchand, René. 1977. "Political Clientelism and Ethnicity in Tropical Africa: Competing Solidarities in Nation-Building." In *Friends, Followers and Factions: A Reader in Political Clientelism.* Edited by Steffen W. Schmidt et al., pp. 100–23. Berkeley and Los Angeles: University of California Press.
Lemarchand, René and Keith Legg. 1972. "Political Clientelism and Development: A Preliminary Analysis." *Comparative Politics* 4: 149–78.
Lewis, John P. 1987. "Aid, Structural Adjustment, and Senegalese Agriculture." In *The Political Economy of Risk and Choice in Senegal.* Edited by John Waterbury and Mark Gersovitz, pp. 283–325. London: Frank Cass.
Leys, Colin. 1975. *Underdevelopment in Kenya: The Political Economy of Neo-Colonialism.* Berkeley and Los Angeles: University of California Press.
1978. "Capital Accumulation, Class Formation, and Dependency: The Significance of the Kenyan Case." *Socialist Register*, pp. 241–66.
1982. "African Economic Development in Theory and Practice." *Daedalus*, Spring: pp. 99–124.
Lonsdale, John. 1981. "States and Social Processes in Africa: A Historiographical Survey." *African Studies Review* 24, nos. 2–3 (June–September): 139–225.
Ly, Abdoulaye. 1981. *L'Emergence du néocolonialisme au Sénégal.* Dakar: Editions Xamle.
MacGaffey, Janet. 1987. *Entrepreneurs and Parasites: The Struggle for Indigenous Capitalism in Zaire.* Cambridge University Press.
Mackintosh, Maureen. 1975. "The Late Development Hypothesis versus the Evidence from Senegal." *Human Resources Research* 3, no. 6 (February): 5–16.
1989. *Gender, Class, and Rural Transition: Agribusiness and the Food Crisis in Senegal.* London: Zed Press.
Mahmoud, F. M. 1983. "Indigenous Sudanese Capital – A National Bourgeoisie?" *Review of African Political Economy*, no. 26: 103–23.
Mamdani, Mahmood. 1976. *Politics and Class Formation in Uganda.* New York: Monthly Review Press.
Mansour, Fawzy. 1978. "Some Notes on Social Stratification and Social Change in Africa: Some Theoretical Considerations." *Africa Development* 3, no. 3 (July–September).
Markovitz, Irving Leonard. 1970. "Traditional Social Structure, the Islamic Brotherhoods, and Political Development in Senegal." *Journal of Modern African Studies* 8, no. 1 (April): 73–96.
Power and Class in Africa: An Introduction to Change and Conflict in African Politics. Englewood Cliffs, N.J.: Prentice Hall.
1987. "Introduction: Continuities in the Study of Power and Class in Africa." In *Studies in Power and Class in Africa*, Edited by I. L. Markovitz, pp. 3–19. Oxford: Oxford University Press.
Marseille, Jacques. 1974. "L'Investissement français dans l'empire colonial: l'enquête du gouvernement de Vichy, 1943." *Revue Historique*, no. 512 (octobre–décembre): 409–32.
1982. "L'Industrialisation des colonies: affaiblissement ou renforcement de la puissance française?" *Revue Française d'Histoire d'Outre Mer* 69, no. 234: 24–34.
1984. *L'empire colonial et capitalisme français: histoire d'un divorce.* Paris: Albin Michel.
Martens, George. 1983a. "Révolution ou participation: syndicats et partis politiques au

Sénégal: première partie." *Le Mois en Afrique*, nos. 205–6 (février–mars): 72–9, 97–113.

1983b. "Révolution ou participation: syndicats et partis politiques au Sénégal: deuxième partie." *Le Mois en Afrique*, nos. 209–10 (juin–juillet): 78–109.

1983c. "Révolution ou participation: syndicats et partis politiques au Sénégal: troisième partie." *Le Mois en Afrique*, nos. 211–12 (août–septembre): 54–68.

1983d. "Révolution ou participation: syndicats et partis politiques au Sénégal: quatrième partie." *Le Mois en Afrique*, nos. 213–14 (octobre–novembre): 63–80, 97–109.

Marx, Karl. 1968. "Eighteenth Brumaire of Louis Bonaparte." In *Selected Works in One Volume*. pp. 94–179, 704–9. Moscow: Progress Publishers.

Meillasoux, Claude. 1971. *The Development of Indigenous Trade and Markets in West Africa*. London: Oxford University Press.

Mérat, Louis. 1937. "La Loi douanière coloniale de 1928 et l'évolution économique des colonies." *Revue Politique et Parlementaire* (Paris), 10 (septembre).

Migdal, Joel. 1988. *Strong Societies and Weak States: State-Society Relations and State Capabilities in the Third World*. Princeton, N.J.: Princeton University Press.

Miliband, Ralph. 1977. *Marxism and Politics*. New York: Oxford University Press.

De Miras, C. 1982. "L'entrepreneur ivoirien ou une bourgeoisie privée de son état." In *Etat et bourgeoisie en Côte d'Ivoire*. Edited by Y.-A. Fauré et J.-F. Médard, pp. 228–9. Paris: Karthala.

Monguillot, M. 1944. "L'Evolution du régime douanier colonial, en particulier depuis le 1 septembre 1939." *Conférences de l'Ecole Supérieure Coloniale*, Paris.

Moore, Jr., Barrington. 1966. *Social Origins of Dictatorship and Democracy: Lord and Peasant in the Making of the Modern World*: Boston: Beacon.

Morgan, W. B., and J. C. Pugh. 1969. *West Africa*. London: Methuen and Co. Ltd.

Morgenthau, Ruth Schachter. 1964. *Political Parties in French West Africa*. London: Oxford University Press.

Moussa, Pierre. 1957. *Les Chances économiques de la communauté franco-africaine*. Paris: Librarie Armand Colin.

Mouzelis, Nicos. 1989. "Political Transitions in Greece and Argentina: Toward a Reorientation of Marxist Political Theory." *Comparative Political Studies* 21, no. 4 (January): 443–66.

Murray, Roger. 1967. "Second Thoughts on Ghana." *New Left Review*, no. 42 (March–April): 25–39.

Mytelka, Lynn Krieger. 1983. "The Limits of Export-Led Development: The Ivory Coast's experience with manufactures." In *The Antinomies of Interdependence*. Edited by J. G. Ruggie, pp. 239–70. New York: Columbia University Press.

Nascimento, Jean Claude, and Marc Raffinot. 1985. "Politique de prix agricoles et comportement des producteurs: le cas de l'arachide au Sénégal." *Revue Economique* 36, no. 4 (juillet): 779–96.

NDiaye, Aly Diop. 1985. "Analyse sectorielle: les industries textiles au Sénégal." Dakar: Ecole Supérieure de Gestion des Entreprises, juillet.

Nelson, Harold, et al. 1974. *Area Handbook for Senegal*. Washington D.C.: American University Foreign Area Studies (FAS).

Newbury, C. W. 1968. "The Protectionist Revival in French Colonial Trade: The Case of Senegal." *The Economic History Review* 21 no. 2: 337–48.

Person, Yves. 1982. "French West Africa and Decolonization." In *The Transfer of Power in Africa: Decolonization, 1940–1960*. Edited by Prosser Gifford and W[illia]m Roger Louis, pp. 141–172. New Haven, Conn.: Yale University Press.

Pedler, Frank. 1974. *The Lion and the Unicorn in Africa: The United Africa Company, 1787–1931*. London: Heineman Press.

Peter, J. 1970. "Bilan et perspectives de l'industrie sénégalaise en 1969." *Revue Juridique et Politique*, no. 3 (juillet–septembre): 419–90.

Pfefferman, Guy. 1968. *Industrial Labor in the Republic of Senegal*. New York: Praeger.

Phillips, Anne. 1977. "The Concept of 'Development.'" *Review of African Political Economy*, no. 8: 7–21.

——— 1989. *The Enigma of Colonialism: British Policy in West Africa*. London: James Currey.

Portères, Roland. 1952. *Aménagement de l'économie agricole et rurale au Sénégal: rapport de la Mission Roland Portères*. Dakar: Gouvernement Général de l'AOF, Territoire du Sénégal, mars–avril.

Poulantzas, Nicos. 1973. *Political Power and Social Class*. London: New Left Books.

——— 1978. *State, Power, Socialism*. London: New Left Books.

Rabeil, Jacques. 1955. *L'Industrie cotonnière française*. Paris: Génin.

René-Leclerc, M. C. 1933. *Débouchés et méthodes de vente aux colonies*. Paris: Conférence du Commerce Colonial (18–20 mai 1933), Comité National des Conseillers du Commerce Extérieur de la France.

République Française, Ministère de la Coopération (avec le Ministère du Plan et du Développement du Sénégal). 1965. *Le Secteur textile au Sénégal*, vols. 1 and 2. Dakar: juillet–août.

Richard-Molard, Jacques. 1952. *Afrique Occidentale française*. Paris: Berger-Levrault.

Rimmer, Douglas. 1984. *The Economies of West Africa*. New York: St. Martin's.

Robinson, K. E., and W. J. M. Mackenzie. 1960. *Five Elections in Africa*. Oxford: Oxford University Press (Clarendon Press).

Robson, Peter. 1983. *Integration, Development, and Equity: Economic Integration in West Africa*. Boston: George Allen & Unwin.

Rocheteau, Guy. 1982. *Pouvoir financier et indépendence économique: le cas du Sénégal*. Paris: Karthala-ORSTOM.

Roire, C. 1971. "Les Grandes compagnies commerciales et le marché africain." *Le Mois en Afrique*, no. 64 (avril): 66–78.

Rothchild, Donald, and Naomi Chazan, eds. 1987. *The Precarious Balance*. Boulder, Colo.: Westview.

Sandbrook, Richard. 1972. "Patrons, Clients, and Factions: New Dimensions of Conflict Analysis in Africa." *Canadian Journal of Political Science* 5,1: 104–119.

——— 1985. *The Politics of Africa's Economic Stagnation*. Cambridge University Press.

Saul, John S. 1979. "The Unsteady State: Uganda, Obote, and General Amin." *The State and Revolution in East Africa*, pp. 350–90. New York: Monthly Review Press.

Schatz, Sayre P. 1984. "Pirate Capitalism and the Inert Economy of Nigeria." *Journal of Modern African Studies* 22, no. 1: 45–57.

Schumacher, Edward J. 1975. *Politics, Bureaucracy, and Rural Development in Senegal*. Berkeley and Los Angeles: University of California Press.

Sekyere, Yaw Owusu. 1963. "Notes sur le commerce de contrebande Gambie-Sénégal, 1956–1961." Dakar: Institut de Science Economique Appliquée (ISEA), janvier.

Shaw, Timothy. 1982. "Beyond Neo-Colonialism: Varieties of Corporatism in Africa." *Journal of Modern African Studies* 20, no. 2: 239–62.

Shenton, Robert W. 1986. *The Development of Capitalism in Northern Nigeria*. Toronto: University of Toronto Press.

Shivji, Issa. 1976. *Class Struggles in Tanzania*. London: Monthly Review Press.

Sklar, Richard. 1979. "The Nature of Class Domination in Africa." *Journal of Modern African Studies* 17, no. 4: 531–52.

Skocpol, Theda. 1985. "Bringing the State Back In: Strategies of Analysis in Current Research." In *Bringing the State Back In*. Edited by Peter B. Evans et al., pp. 3–43. Cambridge University Press.

Société Africaine d'Edition. 1975. *Guide du commerce au Sénégal, 1974–1975*. Dakar.

——— 1976. *Le Sénégal en chiffres, 1975*. Dakar.

——— 1979. *Le Sénégal en chiffres, 1978*. Dakar.

——— 1984. *Le Sénégal en chiffres, 1982–1983*. Dakar.

SONED. *See* Gouvernement du Sénégal (GOS), SONED.

SONEPI. *See* Gouvernement du Sénégal (GOS), SONEPI.

Suret-Canale, Jean. 1950. "L'Industrie des Oléagineux en AOF." *Cahiers d'Outre-Mer*, no. 11: 280–8.

———. 1964. *Afrique Noire: l'ère coloniale 1900–1945*. Paris: Editions Sociales.

———. 1968. "L'Industrie en AOF au lendemain de la deuxième guerre mondiale." *Revue Economique de Madagascar* 3:27–53.

———. 1974. "Difficultés du néocolonialisme français en Afrique tropicale." *Canadian Journal of African Studies* 8, no. 2: 211–33.

Swainson, Nicola. 1980. *The Development of Corporate Capitalism in Kenya: 1918–1977*. Berkeley and Los Angeles: University of California Press.

Syndicat Général de l'Industrie Cotonnière Français (SGICF). 1957. *Tarifs douaniers et fiscaux et régimes d'importation des filés et tissus de coton et de fibranne dans les pays d'Outre-Mer*. Paris: SGICF.

———. 1967. "Numéro spécial sur l'Outre-Mer." *Revue Mensuel de l'Industrie Cotonnière Française*, no. 6 (juin).

Tall, Cheikh Omar Tidiane. 1982. "Société Nouvelle pour l'Industrie du Vêtement, SONIV–Etude de faisabilité." Dakar: Centre Sénégalais du Commerce Extérieur, septembre.

Thompson, Virginia, and Richard Adloff. 1958. *French West Africa*. London: George Allen & Unwin.

Touré, Amadou. 1984. "Structures économiques et intégration africaine: les principaux freins et blocages à l'intégration de la CEAO." *Le Mois en Afrique*, no. 215–16 (décembre 1983–janvier): 75–100.

Touré, Seila. 1985. "Rapport sur l'industrie textile sénégalaise." Dakar: Ecole Supérieure de Gestion des Entreprises.

Traoré, Boubacar. 1978. "Rapport de stage effectué à SCIMPEX." Dakar: Université de Dakar, Faculté des Sciences Juridiques et Economiques, avril.

United Kingdom (UK), Government of the, Naval Intelligence Division. n.d. (1942?). *French West Africa*. Vol. 1: *The Federation*. London.

United Nations Development Project (UNDP). 1984. *Assistance à la révision de la stratégie industrielle – mission de M. Lionel Zinsou: 24 octobre–6 novembre*. Dakar.

United Nations Industrial Development Organization (UNIDO). 1972. *Country Paper on the Actual Situation of Senegalese Industrialization and the Project of the Zone Franche Industrielle de Dakar*. New York: UNIDO, 28 March.

———. 1982. *Country Industrial Development Brief: Senegal*. New York: UNIDO, Division for Industrial Studies, Regional and Country Studies Branch, 11 March.

Verdier, R. 1971. "Evolution et réformes foncières de l'Afrique noire francophone." *Journal of African Law* 15, n. 1: 85–101.

"La Vie de l'AOF." *Bulletin du Comité de l'Afrique Française*, 2ème série, no. 18 (janvier–février 1956): 27–8.

Wade, Abdoulaye. 1959. *Economie de l'ouest africain (Zone Franc): Unité et croissance*. Paris: Présence Africaine.

Waterbury, John. 1987. "The Senegalese Peasant: How Good Is Our Conventional Wisdom?" In *The Political Economy of Risk and Choice in Senegal*. Edited by John Waterbury and Mark Gersovitz, pp. 47–73. London: Frank Cass.

Warren, Bill. 1973. "Imperialism and Capitalist Industrialization." *New Left Review* 81 (September–October): 3–44.

Webster, J. B., and A. A. Boahen. 1967. *History of West Africa: The Revolutionary Years – 1815 to Independence*. New York: Praeger.

Williams, Gavin. 1981. "The World Bank and the Peasant Problem." In *Rural Development in Tropical Africa*. Edited by Judith Heyer, Pepe Roberts, and Gavin Williams, pp. 16–51. New York: St. Martin's.

Winder, R. Bayly. 1962. "The Lebanese in West Africa." *Comparative Studies in Society and History* 4, no. 3 (April): 296–333.

World Bank (Banque Mondiale). 1970. *Situation et perspectives économiques du Sénégal* Vol. 5: *L'Industrie*. Washington D.C.: The World Bank, 1970.
1974. *Senegal: Tradition, Diversification, and Economic Development*. Washington D.C.: The World Bank.
(Banque Mondiale). 1981a. *Rapport sur le développement dans le monde*. Août.
1981b. *Adjustment in Low-Income Africa: 1974–1978*. Washington D.C.: World Bank staff working paper no. 486, August 1981.
1981c. *Accelerated Development in Sub-Saharan Africa*. Washington, D.C.: The World Bank.
Zeitlin, Maurice, and Richard Earl Ratcliff. 1988. *Landlords and Capitalists: The Dominant Class of Chile*. Princeton, N.J.: Princeton University Press.
Zuccarelli, François. 1970. *Un Parti politique africain: l'Union Progressiste Sénégalaise*. Paris: R. Pichon et R. Durand-Auzias.

PERIODICALS

Africa (Dakar).
Africa Confidential.
Africa Research Bulletin, Economic Series.
Afrique-Asie.
Afrique Expansion.
Afrique Industrie.
Afrique Industrie – Infrastructures.
Le Bulletin de l'Afrique Noire.
Le Bulletin de la Chambre de Commerce et de l'Industrie – Région Cap Vert (Dakar).
Le Bulletin Quotidien de la Société d'Etudes et d'Informations Economiques.
Les Chroniques d'Outre-Mer.
The Economist, Quarterly Economic Review: Senegal, The Gambia, Guinea-Bissau, Cape Verde.
Europe France Outre-Mer.
Le Fichier Industriel (du Sénégal).
Hommes et Organisations d'Afrique Noire.
Industries et Travaux d'Outre-Mer.
Jeune Afrique.
Le Journal Officiel du Sénégal (Gouvernement du Sénégal).
Le Journal Officiel de l'Afrique Occidentale Française.
Le Journal des Textiles (Paris: Syndicat Général de l'Industrie Cotonnière Française).
Liberté (Dakar).
Lien Economique (Dakar).
Marchés Coloniaux.
Marchés Tropicaux et Méditerranéens.
Le Monde (Paris).
Le Moniteur Africain du Commerce et de l'Industrie (Dakar and Abidjan).
New African (London).
Notes Documentaires et Etudes (La Documentation Française).
Le Point Economique (Chambre de Commerce de Dakar).
Promotion (Dakar).
Sénégal d'Aujourd'hui (Dakar).
Sénégal Industrie.
Le Soleil (Dakar).
Taxaw (Dakar).
West Africa (London).

Index

groundnut producers, 205; in textile trade, 218–21, 231, 235

Melia Ruling of 1950, 66n89

merchant capital, 10–11; and balkanization of AOF, 134; collapse of market structures forged by/for, 208; colonial political counterparts of, 43, 259; in colonial Senegal, 10–11, 31, 38, 46–7, 259; and Dakar textile industry, 32, 75–6, 131–2, 136, 256; and fiscal receipts of government, 130, 231; inability to enhance productivity, 46–7, 205, 257; relations with French groundnut industries, 47; and Senegal's postcolonial state/regime, 11, 24, 32, 78, 130, 165–6, 205, 256, 257; *see also* maisons de commerce

Migdal, Joel, 6, 264–6, 267

migrant labor, *see navetanes*

millet, *see* food crop production

ministry(ies): Government of Senegal, 178–9; of commerce, 181, 192, 194, 195; of finance, 180–1, 193, 195

Mouride confrérie: and Abdou Diouf, 248; and dispersion of power within regime, 204; and groundnut economy, 40–7; groundnut pioneering, 41, 86–7, 106; growing autonomy of, 201–4; and import trade, 212, 214–15, 234; marabouts as groundnut producers, 41, 87, 106, 108; marabout-disciple relations, 41, 87, 107–8; and parallel groundnut trade, 202; and Touba, 43, 202–3, 213; and urban parallel market/ Sandaga market, 214–15; urbanization of economic bases of, 203–4, 214, 234; *see also* groundnut production; Islamic confréries; Islamic leaders; ruling coalition in Senegal

Mouridism, 41; urban "revival" of 1980s, 209–10

navetanes (migrant agricultural laborers), 41n30, 55

neocolonialism: in Africa, 1–2, 4, 15, 21; and interests of capital, 20–4, 132–6, 252; Senegal's transition to, 4, 12; term, 15n5

Newly Industrializing Countries (NICs), 252, 270

OCA (Office de Commercialisation Agricole), 91, 123, 126, 129, 183

Office de Commercialisation Agricole, *see* OCA

Office National de Coopération et d'Assistance au Développement; see ONCAD

ONCAD (Office National de Coopération et d'Assistance au Développement), 123n76, 129, 171, 180, 181, 199, 203, 208, 256; collapse of, 204–5; evasions of, 202; replaced by SONAR, 205

pacte colonial, 32–4, 37, 38, 39, 44, 47; denounced by Senghor, 66n89, 84; updated after World War II, 49–58

parallel markets, 6; cost to government, 232; government response to, 203, 234; for groundnuts, 202–3, 205; link between groundnut and textile circuits, 213; Sandaga market, 214–15; Senegal-Gambia contraband circuit (textiles), 212–13; supplying low-cost goods, 235; and textile export subsidy, 242; in textile trade (contraband), 211–13, 221, 223, 228, 257

Parti Africain de l'Indépendance (PAI), 88, 89, 94n25

Parti du Regroupement Africain-Sénégal (PRA-Sénégal), 89, 94

Parti Socialiste (PS), 210, 237, 248–9

patron-client networks: in commercial circuits, 27–9; issue of "reciprocity," 18n13; as political institutions, 17–18; and regime consolidation, 17–19; within ruling coalitions, 19; and state formation, 19–20; *see also* patronage politics

patron-client networks in Senegal: in commercial sector, 79, 126, 195, 234; built within ruling party/state apparatus, 95–7, 172–3; cooperatives and *communes* as building blocs, 80, 97; and rural "brokered constituencies," 98; and Diouf regime, 210–11, 248–9; *see also* patronage politics in Senegal; political machine

patronage politics: and commercial rents, 27–9, 79, 257; material conditions for, 18, 26; as mechanism of co-optation/control, 19; as "mode of domination," 18; narrowing scope of politics, 99; and politicized accumulation, 19; and regime consolidation, 17–9; rentierism as economic corollary, 260; in the United States, 18

patronage politics in Senegal, 99; and the customs service, 249, 250–1; embedded in rural social relations, 43, 92, 98, 108; and foreign borrowing, 173, 177, 208–9; and fragmentation of state, 182, 208, 256; and groundnut marketing board, 123, 180, 181; and market controls, 79, 126; within ministries of commerce and finance, 180–1, 192, 193, 194, 195; political machine of 1950s, 80–6, 89; in *Quatre Communes*, 81; in reappropriation of state, 256; and regime consolidation (1960s), 79, 80, 83, 89, 95–9; and rentier class, 187, 208, 231, 247; and rural cooperatives, 43, 87, 108; and structural adjustment, 248–50; in textile trade, 212, 231, 234; and urban *communes*, 97, 180; *see also* Senghor regime

peanuts, *see* groundnut production

peasants/peasantry, 6, 10; debt trap, 45–6, 107; exploitation by merchant capital, 43,

For EU product safety concerns, contact us at Calle de José Abascal, 56–1°,
28003 Madrid, Spain or eugpsr@cambridge.org.

www.ingramcontent.com/pod-product-compliance
Ingram Content Group UK Ltd.
Pitfield, Milton Keynes, MK11 3LW, UK
UKHW042151130625

459647UK00011B/1287